OFF THE RAILS

The Privatisation of
Freight Railways in Australia
and New Zealand,
and the Consequences

Spencer Naith

BA, BCA

Off the Rails:
The Privatisation of Freight Railways in Australia and
New Zealand, and the Consequences

© 2024, Spencer Naith

ISBN: 978-0-473-70176-5

A catalogue record for this book is available from the National Library of New Zealand.

The author asserts the moral right to be identified as the author of this work in accordance with the New Zealand Copyright Act 1994, and the Australian Copyright Act 1968.

Cover design and typesetting by DIY Publishing, Wellington, New Zealand

Set in Museo Sans

Printed and bound by IngramSpark

The author is responsible for any errors and omissions.

Cover photo: an interstate train in South Australia.
Reproduced with permission of the Licensor through PLSclear
Photographer not identified.
© Road Transport Media Ltd, Britain
Photo published by Railway Gazette International, 17 Sept 2015

Contents

Part A: Prologue   1

   1. Introduction   2

   2. A Brief History of Australian and New Zealand Railways up to 1990   11

   3. An Overview of the Rail Freight Industry Today   43

Part B: The Commonwealth and Australian Rail Reform   64

   4. The Roles of the Commonwealth Government in Australian Land Transport   65

   5. Commonwealth Initiatives on Rail Development in the 1990s   86

   6. Procrastination and Evasion   119

   7. Transport Sector Reform by Commissions and Councils   144

   8. Australian Road Reform   163

Part C: Outcomes   178

   9. How and Why the Rail Freight Industry Changed   179

   10. Privatisation – Hopes and Outcomes   212

   11. The Privatisation of Four Vertically-Integrated Railways   231

   12. Competition Outcomes   260

Part D: Analyses — 291

- 13. The Application of Economic Concepts to Rail Reform — 292
- 14. Vertical Integration versus Vertical Separation — 332
- 15. The Profitability of Rail Networks — 349

Part E: Epilogue — 382

- 16. Some Observations — 383
- 17. Summing-up — 411

Part F: Appendices — 435

- Appendix 1. Case study – the privatisation and renationalisation of New Zealand's railways — 436
- Appendix 2. The History of Efficiency as Applied to New Zealand's North Island Main Trunk Line — 487
- Appendix 3. A Chronology: Significant Events in the Last 50 years of Australasian Commercial Freight Railways — 493
- Appendix 4. Differences between railways in Australasia & North America — 501
- Appendix 5. Managing Access to Rail Networks — 510
- Endnotes — 527
- Acknowledgements — 558
- Image Credits — 560
- Glossary — 561
- References — 574
- Contents in Detail — 597
- Index — 608

Part A

Prologue

1. Introduction

2. A brief history of Australian and New Zealand railways up to 1990

3. An overview of the freight rail industry today

1. Introduction

Railways and highways – different expectations

If railway lines were roads, there would be nothing of much consequence to write about, because governments fund and maintain roads and highways without much fuss about justification. Over the last forty years, governments in Australia and New Zealand have invested much less in railways compared to highways, on a per route-kilometre basis. Both roads and railways are used to convey vehicles which carry people and freight. So, what is the key difference? Roads in Australasia have never been expected to make a profit, with a few exceptions of toll roads in or close to major population centres. By contrast, since the 1980s, commercial freight railways have been expected to be profitable, whether government-owned or in the private sector.

Up to the 1950s, railways had been the dominant land transport mode for freight, with sidings connecting the majority of industrial sites to the rail network. In Australasia, such sidings have mostly disappeared with changes in land use, particularly in the cities. Railways are now much less important for land transport, having become subordinate to highways, except in the transport of mineral ores and coal. Originally, governments provided railways as a social service; now they provide roads and highways in the same way, and the role for existing freight railways is unclear. As both cause and consequence, governments' investments in highways and road infrastructure have left freight railways in a poorer position to compete for traffic. This begs the question: what is now the appropriate role for freight railways, in addition to hauling millions of tonnes of bulk commodities such as coal, mineral ores and grains?

By 1990, none of the six government-owned railways in Australasia could show profits, or at least break even. Governments had to subsidise them just to keep them going, and so they did not fund much asset renewal and development as well. Hence, the railways' asset condition continued to decline. The extent of the cost to public funds in Australia was estimated then to be $4 billion per year.[1] All the rail systems had been trimmed in size in previous decades, and most had reduced their staff numbers substantially by this time. But still the deficits continued. Governments never considered closing down these loss-making enterprises, presuming there had to be some benefit in retaining them in some form. Indeed, around the world, most government-owned railways operate in deficit, and are supported to continue to operate. The formal closing down of a national public railway system is a rare event.[2] Most countries that have ever had a railway network built still use it.

The background to the transformation of freight railways

In the 1980s, governments in Australia and New Zealand followed the USA and the UK in adopting a macroeconomic theory of capitalism different from the one that had prevailed from the 1930s to the 1970s (known as Keynesianism). Neoliberalism was based on the notions that free markets and competition were superior bases for human interactions compared with cooperation. Tenets of neoliberalism include the following: free market mechanisms should prevail in the economy, competition will produce maximum efficiency, and there is an ideal of 'small government'. This means that state intervention in the economy is seen as detrimental, and therefore public sector activities should be privatised wherever possible, because otherwise they cannot compete on the same basis with the private sector for profits or market share.

Neoliberalism has become so dominant in many countries that its doctrine has been described as a state religion, with economists fulfilling the role of the priesthood.[3] Both Australia and New Zealand have experienced at least three decades of neoliberal economics in their governments' policies. Although the unintended consequences of neoliberalism are now evident, such as increased inequality in society, Treasuries and big business still pressure governments to hold to neoliberal orthodoxy.

In the 1980s and 1990s, the neoliberal ideals prompted the sale of many types of government assets and services in both countries, including electricity generation and distribution, ports, airports and railways. Sales of government assets are known euphemistically as privatisation, putting the emphasis on the process rather than the initiator. Privatisation distances governments from the reality that in most cases the assets were ultimately paid for by taxation. Therefore it is moot whether governments are actually the owners, or should they act as agents for the general public, providing stewardship of the assets.

In some industries, privatisation worked well to achieve efficiencies, but prices have risen noticeably, and there is now doubt about whether in the longer term the outcomes have been beneficial for society and the environment. For the rail industry, the evidence for success of privatisation is less obvious.

'Rail Reform' became the generic term to describe, in Australia but not in New Zealand, all aspects of government-initiated change to the rail industry, both proposed and actual. The use of this term dates back at least to 1991.[4] The companion term 'Road Reform' is a contraction of 'Road Transport Reform', which has been in use since the 1990s; it means the reform and harmonisation of regulations covering vehicle registration, road user charges and road safety issues, all of which were originally State regulated. It also covers the issue of trucks not having to pay for the damage they cause to roads, due to much heavier axle-loads than cars.

The common solution developed in the 1990s for the problem of railway deficits was to separate the passenger rail operations (which required continuing financial support) from the freight, then sell the latter for whatever they could get. It was an article of faith that the private sector, unlike governments, knew how to run businesses profitably. This was wishful thinking – expecting all privatised rail companies to be profitable over the long term. Some are profitable, and some not. The significant difference now appears to be whether or not the companies control the rail networks they use, and maintain them to a consistent standard in the long term. In some cases, profits were made in the short term only by cutting back on network maintenance, a recipe for ultimate failure of the business.

The disposal of government railways was a series of separate events, unsystematic and incremental, each prompted by limited objectives. Because of neoliberal faith in the outcomes of privatisation, little thought was given by governments to any longer timeframe and bigger picture, or what might result beyond the achievement of those limited objectives. But with hindsight, there are identifiable themes and an interconnectedness among these events. This book explains what happened, and why, when governments in Australia and New Zealand sold their freight railways.

Government bias

It is apparent that the majority of Australian federal governments have been biased in their support for the haulage of freight by road. To what extent this bias is intentional, it is hard to say, but it has historical origins and has been consistent for at least five decades. It appears to be independent of political parties, and of economic theories and beliefs, but it distorts the competition in land transport between the rail and road modes. Such support has undesirable consequences for government spending, the environment, railway networks, road users and the general population.

Looking at the big picture for freight transport by land, it is evident that railways now are under-utilised for intercity general freight, particularly in the eastern states of Australia, despite rail being many times safer and more fuel-efficient compared to haulage by road.[5] There are many reasons for this situation that I will tease out and bring to light in this book. The road mode has a greater market share in comparison with other developed economies, with adverse effects on the environment, the public, and government spending. I assert that this is a 'market failure' brought about by the Commonwealth Government's bias toward road transport, which remains largely unresolved. To quote industry observer Dr Philip Laird: [6]

> "Australia also has the highest road freight activity per capita in the world, and road transport uses much more fuel than rail or sea for a given long distance or bulk freight task. Clearly, there is ongoing need for improvement in energy use, and we cannot be 'relaxed and comfortable' about market forces delivering, on their own, the necessary gains."

Commercial and other freight railways

This book includes only commercial freight railway organisations, be they government or business entities. The essential criterion is that they are selling their services, competing for business against other modes of transport, and sometimes against one another.

Commercial freight railway organisations almost always have multiple clients with differing requirements. Consequently, they have the management problem of allocating the organisation's resources to provide different services all at the same time to meet their various clients' needs, while operating in a competitive business environment. Optimising the use of rail resources (including line capacity, maintenance capability, locomotives, wagons and staff) is therefore an on-going and necessary challenge to stay both cost-competitive and profitable.

By contrast, the miners' railways that operate in the Pilbara region of Western Australia are not expected to make a profit and are therefore excluded from this story. Their use of railway engineering and technologies is similar to that of commercial railways, but miners' railways do not operate and compete as individual business entities. They are purpose-built and an integral part of the miners' supply chain operations, known in the industry as 'pit to port'. The miners' railways are operated to optimise the flow of iron ore right through this supply chain. Hence, although the Pilbara ore trains are very long and heavy, and extremely energy efficient, other aspects of miners' railways are often less than optimal. This happens because the profitability of these railways as separate entities is irrelevant to the iron ore mining companies.

For similar reasons, Queensland's privately-owned sugar cane railways are also excluded.

Outline of this book

The book is structured to tell the stories of rail privatisation, and also to provide some analyses and comparisons. For this reason, I have often cross-referenced within the book.

In Part A, chapter 2 looks at the historical situations and trends that led up to the period of transformation (approximately 1990 to 2020) that is the focus of this book, to provide the reader with a backgrounder.

Chapter 3 provides an overview of the freight railway industry as it is today – the fundamentals and main concepts, the two principal ways in which the industry has been changed, the constraints that remain, a who's who in the industry today, and the current competitive position between rail and road in the interstate freight market (i.e., not including the intrastate bulk flows of grains, export coal and minerals.)

Part B, *The Commonwealth and Australian Rail Reform*, chapters 4 to 8, deals with the significant influence the federal government of Australia and its agencies (collectively, 'The Commonwealth') have had on the Australian rail industry. The Commonwealth has at various times been inactive, reactive, obstructive, and latterly more proactive towards the freight rail industry.

Part C, *Outcomes*, looks at what happened during the transformation:

- Chapter 9 describes the various ways by which railways changed owners and structures, the advent of the Australian Rail Track Corporation (ARTC), and the underlying reasons that motivated governments to make changes.
- Chapter 10 investigates why privatisation was the method favoured by governments for what was called in Australia "Rail Reform".
- Chapter 11 explains what happened, including the similarities and differences, when four formerly government-owned vertically-integrated railways were privatised as-is.
- The Commonwealth Government believed that introducing competition to the railway industry would bring about efficiencies. Chapter 12 assesses how competition evolved in each network, and also how the railways in New Zealand adapted to its long-standing competition with road.

Part D, *Analyses*, provides various analyses of expectations versus reality:

- Chapter 13 examines how concepts in the theory of economics were applied to rail reform in Australia, and whether they were helpful in guiding successful

outcomes. These concepts include Efficiency, Monopoly, Competition, Competitive Neutrality, and Barriers to Entry.
- Chapter 14 considers Vertical Integration versus Vertical Separation, and what the consequences were for the railway industry.
- Chapter 15 discusses the unprofitability of most railway networks and why this is so.

Part E, *Epilogue*, covers some general observations from the three decades of change:
- Chapter 16 explores some unforeseen consequences, and how the elements of the national discussion on land transport have made planned and coordinated change such an impossibility in Australia.
- In Chapter 17, I draw together the various elements, interpret and sum up.

Part F, *Appendices*, is a collection of topics that did not fit into the main structure of the book as that evolved over seven years of research and writing:
- Appendix 1 is a case study that details what happened to New Zealand's railway over three decades from the 1990s onward: from privatisation by trade sale, a resale to avoid bankruptcy with the government resuming ownership of the rail network, then renationalisation by the government to resolve a dispute with the owner over network access charges and a threat to withdraw services. Finally, it looks at how KiwiRail has fared under successive governments, which have different perceptions of the value of railways to New Zealand, and consequently different inclinations to invest for improvement and development.
- Appendix 2 is a story that illustrates that efficiency in railways depends very much on where the focus is, i.e., what resource is to be used efficiently, and the

inevitability of contradictions and trade-offs. What is considered efficient today will change in the future.
- Appendix 3 is a chronology of significant commercial events in the last forty years of Australasian railways.
- Appendix 4 discusses the reasons for the major differences between Australasian and North American railways, because North American railways have sometimes been offered as a model for Australia and New Zealand to emulate. Their different histories and cultures make these comparisons unhelpful.
- Appendix 5 analyses a policy conflict between the Australian Productivity Commission and the railway industry, that shows why, for multiple reasons, auctioning cannot be used for allocating train paths in the interstate market.

An extensive glossary is provided to explain acronyms and other rail industry and political terms, unusual words, and to identify the major players in the story.

2. A Brief History of Australian and New Zealand Railways up to 1990

The purpose of this chapter is to provide a background to the main topics discussed in this book, to enable readers to understand why governments chose to change their involvements with freight railways after 1990. The histories of the development of individual railways in Australia and New Zealand have been amply covered by many books and journal articles, and it is not my intention to compete with these.[7] However, there are similarities in the development of railways in Australasia, so what follows can be taken generally, unless otherwise stated.

The development of railways in the colonies

The railway systems of the Australian colonies were mostly the instruments of their governments, although there were a few private sector investments. Railways in each colony were built to link the capital cities and main ports to their hinterlands, the inland regions. Hence the state networks that evolved tend to be radial in character, and were not built with any plan of eventually linking to form a nationwide network. Before the six colonies became a federation of six states, long distance trade among the colonies depended on coastal shipping around the Australian continent. It was not until the negotiations leading up to Federation in 1901 that any thought was given to the possibility of forming a nationwide railway network. By then, more than 20,000 km of track had been laid, using three different gauges (track widths).[8]

In New Zealand, there were several separate coastal colonial settlements under one government from the 1870s onward. Coastal shipping was the way people and goods were transported around the country, so the trend was for single rail lines to be built to open up each port's hinterland for pastoral farming, timber extraction or coal mining. Initially there were broad, standard and narrow gauges, but the government in 1870 decided that narrow gauge was to be built everywhere to minimise construction costs. The short sections of other gauges were soon converted, and their locomotives shipped off to Australia. As lines reached further inland, branches were built particularly in the hinterlands of Invercargill, Dunedin, Christchurch, Wellington and Auckland. The South Island Main Trunk line from Christchurch to Dunedin to Invercargill was completed by 1879.

The networks that extended south from Auckland and north from Wellington were finally joined on the volcanic plateau in the centre of the North Island in 1908 after 23 years of construction. The formal opening, with the last spike being driven in by the Prime Minister on 6 November 1908, was an event of national significance. Yet even after the completion of this, the North Island Main Trunk Line, there were still nine separate sections of railway administered by the New Zealand Government Railways[9] (NZGR), plus one private rail line that was taken over by NZGR at the end of 1908. The rail networks in each island were not joined up until the 1940s, and the realisation of one national network did not eventuate until the government rail ferry service started operating between Wellington and Picton in 1962.

Australia: a nation-wide standard-gauge network?

Decisions at Federation

In 1897, a National Convention on Federation considered what responsibilities the future federal government should have. Railways were included, specifically that the federal government should lead and finance any national gauge unification program. Accordingly, the Constitution has several sections giving powers to the federal government to build railways, to acquire state railways, and to ensure uniformity in railway rating structures so as to reinforce the common market objective of the federation.[10] However, a majority decision made by the States in the lead-up to founding the federation was that ownership and operation of state railways would not become a federal responsibility, in contrast to the post and telegraph systems which did become a federal enterprise. Hence the Commonwealth accepted a responsibility for building railways only for nation-building.

When the Commonwealth of Australia was created in 1901, the railway networks of four colonies had already met at their borders in the 1880s. Queensland's narrow-gauge met the New South Wales standard-gauge network at Wallangarra[11], and Victoria's broad-gauge met the New South Wales line at Albury. In both places, both passengers and freight were transferred between trains across a common platform. Both Victoria and South Australia had broad-gauge networks, but still their trains changed locomotives at the border. The Western Australian rail network and the North Australian Railway remained separate, isolated from the other networks by thousands of kilometres of mainly desert country.

In 1910, a national conference of Railway Commissioners chose the international standard gauge, 4 feet $8\frac{1}{2}$ inches (1,435 mm), to be the *standard gauge* for Australia in the future. Thus, standard-gauge was used when construction started in

1911 on the new Trans-Australia Railway across the Nullarbor Plain connecting the states of Western Australia and South Australia. When it opened in 1917, there were breaks-of-gauge at each end – at Kalgoorlie (WA) there was a narrow-gauge network, and at Port Augusta (SA) there was broad-gauge. This line had been built to deliver on a commitment made to Western Australia in order to secure that colony into the federation, and Commonwealth Railways was formed to operate this railway. Thereafter, as one commentator wrote, [12]

> "the passage of the years has shown the Commonwealth to be somewhat of a 'reluctant leader' on railway standardisation."

The Commonwealth Government's approach was, for over 80 years, to make progress through co-operative and joint initiatives with the States. In 1920, a Royal Commission was established to report comprehensively on gauge standardisation, but its proposals for large scale gauge conversions were never acted on. Only two modest standard-gauge projects were undertaken – the extension of a NSW northern branch line from Kyogle to Brisbane in 1932, and an extension of the Commonwealth Railways' transcontinental standard-gauge line from Port Augusta to Port Pirie (SA) in 1937.

Studies and reports

The Second World War period highlighted the difficulties and delays in using railways for moving troops and their munitions and supplies, there being twelve breaks-of-gauge across the country at that time.[13] In March 1945, Sir Harold Clapp[14] produced a major report, *Standardisation of Australia's Railway Gauges,* which included extensive and expensive changes:
- The Perth/Fremantle line to Kalgoorlie be standardised and built on a new route to avoid the steep grades and tight curves of the narrow-gauge formation;
- The conversion of South Australian narrow-gauge, and acquisition and conversion of the Silverton Tramway,

to create a standard-gauge line to Broken Hill, which would (together with West Australian conversion above) create a transcontinental standard-gauge route linking Brisbane and Sydney to Perth;
- The conversion of the entire South Australian and Victorian broad-gauge networks, so that the whole of south-east Australia could be linked into the national standard-gauge network.

Despite this report calling for railway systems to be viewed from a national standpoint, rather than continuing with what Clapp called "a State outlook", no progress was made at the time due to the intransigence of State governments, each of which found reasons not to support the report's proposals. However, the Clapp Report was influential a decade or more later, after the death of its author.

In 1956 a committee of Federal Members of Parliament, chaired by William Wentworth, produced a report on rail standardisation, with the main recommendation that: [15]

> "While there may be considerable doubts as to the justification for undertaking large-scale standardisation of Australian railways under present circumstances, there can be no reasonable doubt that the standardisation of certain main trunk lines is not only justified, but long overdue."

Progress at last

The Wentworth Scheme, as it came to be known, put forward the proposal that only the capital cities should be linked by standard gauge, with little change to the networks of other gauges. Thus, its focus was on removing the break-of-gauge handicaps on the long-distance inter-capital routes. The three major rail standardisation projects supported were:
- In Victoria, from Wodonga to Melbourne
- In Western Australia, from Perth and Fremantle to Kalgoorlie
- From Broken Hill (in NSW) to Adelaide via Port Pirie.

In January 1962, a new standard-gauge line to Melbourne was opened, built parallel to the existing broad-gauge line, thus still keeping the two different gauge networks physically separate. It was not till decades later that any intrastate trains in Victoria would travel on standard-gauge lines.

In Western Australia, the standardisation of the interstate line was combined with deviations as proposed in the Clapp Report, and achieved in two stages. A new dual-gauge route from Midland in the eastern suburbs of Perth to Northam was built with a ruling grade of 1:200, replacing the original line that had a ruling grade of 1:40. It was opened in February 1966. Narrow-gauge networks still diverge from Northam to the north and to the south, while the interstate line eastward towards Southern Cross was converted to standard gauge. A second deviation was built from Southern Cross to Kalgoorlie, to the north of the old line and passing through Koolyanobbing, the site of a new iron ore mine. This section was opened in August 1968. The Leonora to Esperance narrow-gauge line was then isolated, passing through Kalgoorlie, so it was standardised in 1974 by WestRail. The freight-only dual-gauge line in Perth, southwest of Midland, was built to the bulk port of Kwinana, as well as to the container port at Fremantle, as originally proposed.

In South Australia, the standardisation of the interstate line from Port Pirie to Broken Hill in NSW was opened in 1970, eliminating the breaks-of-gauge and thus creating one continuous standard gauge line linking Perth with Sydney and Brisbane. The only mainland State capital city not connected at this time was Adelaide. Broad-gauge track still existed south of Port Pirie through Adelaide and connecting with the Victorian network. However, Adelaide was notionally included into the standard-gauge inter-capital network by means of two wagon bogie exchange centres that operated at Dynon Yard in Melbourne, and at Port Pirie. These centres enabled loaded wagons to be transitioned across the breaks-of-gauge within hours, this process being much more efficient than the transference of the freight itself between differently-gauged wagons.

When Australian National Railways converted its line from Crystal Brook (near Port Pirie) to Adelaide from broad to standard gauge in 1982, a new automated bogie exchange centre was opened at Dry Creek Yard in Adelaide, replacing the one at Port Pirie. It was necessary because the line connecting Adelaide to Melbourne still remained as broad gauge. The conversion of this line to standard gauge was not completed till 1995, only as a result of the Commonwealth's 'One Nation' initiative of 1992.

Thus, 98 years after politicians first thought about creating one Australian railway network with one gauge, something approximating it had been achieved. By 1995, it was a network that linked all the main population centres, but excluded the container ports and all the regional and rural areas of Queensland, Victoria and Western Australia. It was not a national railway system, just a physical network of varying quality. The Victorian Government commented in 1998 about the standardisation of the Melbourne to Adelaide line:[16]

> "The *One Nation* program achieved a standard gauge line but failed to deliver a quality network appropriate for interstate trains. If rail speed over this section [between Geelong and Ararat] could be raised to 100 kph this would reduce the journey from Melbourne to Adelaide by nearly two hours."

In 1995, this standard-gauge network was still being managed by five separate government-owned railway authorities, each focused on their own state-based networks, three of which had a majority of track that was not standard gauge. The original notion of one Australian nation-wide one-gauge railway network was not achieved, and now it never will be. It isn't needed.

The advent of trucking: regulation of railways' competition

The First World War provided a major impetus for the development of motorised vehicles able to carry freight by road, and after this war, thousands of soldiers returned from Europe having learnt how to drive. Trucks and lorries were used increasingly for local freight transport, replacing horse-drawn vehicles. Their numbers and capacities grew quickly through the 1920s, and Railways began to sense the loss of business. With the coming of the Great Depression (1929 to 1936), politicians were concerned to protect their government's investment in their railways, and to avoid a costly duplication of transport infrastructure at a time when cutting government expenditure was the only acceptable response to falling revenues from taxation. (This was prior to the world-wide adoption of an alternative macro-economic philosophy where governments would borrow and spend during a depression – known now as Keynesian economics.)

In Australia, all states protected their railways from road competition by legislation, mostly introduced around 1930. In New Zealand the Transport Licensing Act (1931) was extended in 1936 to provide protection of railways, covering all freight conveyed on land. It gave the railways an effective monopoly on long-distance freight transport.

However, in the regional and rural areas, local transport companies were able to do business because they were local, entrepreneurial and had contacts within their communities. In these areas, there was, and often still is, an attitude of not wanting to have lifestyles and activities dictated by the big city. Hence there would have been some resentment at the imposition of restrictions on the use of road transport. In the Depression years of the 1930s when money was scarce, local trucking companies were able to participate in localised bartering of goods and services, whereas the railways, with their centralised accounting systems, were not. Thus, because of the growth of trucking, and the reaction to regulation of road transport in competition with rail, that traffic **from** the rural branch lines began to decline ahead of the reduction of traffic **to** the rural areas. This was to be significant later on when branch line closures were being considered.

New Zealand: the place of railways in society

When I was a young man working in New Zealand Railways (NZR) in the 1970s, I heard older men around me tell of how their fathers had encouraged them to join the railways, because it was the best career available to a young man then. Their fathers had experienced the heyday of rail, when it was the normal way that people travelled around the country. Trains were also the normal way to deliver much that they used in everyday life.

Much of the population lived on the farm or in country towns prior to the Second World War. Their needs came to their town or village typically in four-wheeled wagons which were left in the station yard to be unloaded by the recipients. The diversity of supplies included bulk fertiliser and lime for the farms, bagged cement, sawn timber. Station staff unloaded 'small lots' onto the deck of the goods shed – crated beer, sacks of potatoes and carrots, bags of sugar and flour, and boxes of fruit. Occasional outgoing consignments in highside wagons would be of scrap iron, barrels of cullet, or crates of empty beer bottles going back to city breweries for washing and re-use.

Deliveries by rail to the provincial cities would include wagon-loads of coal for the local industries[17], and tank wagons of petrol for local distribution by road from the rail-served bulk installation. All the produce of the region left by rail, whether it was frozen meat, butter and cheese from the dairy factory, bales of wool, bagged root crops, or boxes of fruit. Typically, the local freezing works (export abattoir), the dairy factory, the sawmill and/or the woolstore were all connected to the railway yard by private sidings, which might each be several hundred yards long and cross local streets. It was the norm for NZR to shunt wagons to and from the yards and sheds of the local industries.

In the 1920s and 1930s the railway was the 'glamour industry' of the times. The local station master had prestige in the town, attended the Chamber of Commerce and always wore a smart uniform. The railways were an integral part of the life of town and of the nation. The design and technology of steam locomotives had improved over the decades such that they became much the fastest of transport machines. Because the rail industry was 'vertically integrated' (to use a phrase from economics that few had heard of till the 1980s) the variety of trades and jobs available in the Railways was as wide as anywhere. If a man could get a job in the Railways, he was set for life.

In the 1970s, the older men around me were now approaching retirement and had an awareness that things had changed. They had not encouraged their children to join the Railways. The glamour industry of the fifties, sixties and early seventies was clearly the airlines. The romance of travel had gone from national to international. Their sons aspired to be pilots and their daughters to be airline hostesses. Then in the eighties the glamour industry had become finance, and in the nineties it was computers – anything to do with making and using them.

Railways in decline

During the Second World War, the railways in both Australia and New Zealand were used intensively because of the war effort, but due to shortage of money and manpower, they were not maintained well. Road carriers had been taking freight off the railways since the 1920s, with an interruption during the war years when petroleum-based fuels were scarce because they were imported. By contrast, the railways in both countries had access to adequate supplies of good quality coal to power their steam locomotives, and indeed coal was a significant commodity to haul because all major industries[18] were powered by coal.

After the war and into the 1950s, the railways in both countries focused on locomotive replacements. The last steam locomotives were built in the early 1950s and were technically superior because they burnt fuel oil, now more available. However, at the same time, from the 1950s and into the 1960s, railways invested in the replacement of old and worn-out steam locomotives with new diesel-powered ones. But government money was never enough to keep up with the need for other types of asset renewal. Wagon fleets and signalling systems were aging and becoming unreliable, leading to operational problems. They were also expensive to maintain.

Commercially and operationally, State Railways carried on in much the same way as they had done for decades. The internal structures were still based on the military model from the earliest days of establishment – staff were considered like 'officers and other ranks', and it was rare[19] that anyone from the 'other ranks' was promoted to the 'officers'. The low-level supervisors identified with the workers that they supervised and from whom they were drawn, and were mostly still union members. The unions were strong and staff numbers remained much the same, although financial losses were mounting.

Railways remained as government departments, providing government services, so government policies and budgets were the focus for railway managers.[20] In Australian states, the scope of railway operations was intertwined with government policies right through to the 1990s, particularly for rural areas. In New South Wales, freight traffic incurred heavy losses, except for bulk grain and coal. In mid-1975, the railways had staff at some 435 freight handling stations, and for many of these stations, the staff costs exceeded the gross revenue of the freight handled. It was estimated that operating losses on freight traffic were accumulating at a million dollars a week.[21] The cost of railways, both freight and passenger, was a major item of State Governments' spending.

The NZR network at its peak in 1953 included forty short rural branch lines[22] that were not attracting much traffic after the advent of rural trucking services. NZR saw them as a maintenance liability. The lack of traffic justified cutting back on maintenance of the tracks, stockyards and buildings. In due course, the lack of traffic and the cost of restoration of each line would be used to justify its closure. The proposed closure of many of these branch lines created protests from local residents who valued the presence of their railway line as a means to hold down prices of trucking services. This was a no-win situation for the local members of parliament, to whom the protesters went for help. Politicians from rural electorates learned to distance themselves from railway matters. Typically, their response was that the closure of branch lines and rural stations were decisions for NZR to make, not the government.

Shrinking networks

All the government-owned railways in Australasia had a period of closing branch lines, due to various factors:
- Reduced line capability as a result of wartime and subsequent under-spending on track and structures maintenance
- Competition for freight from road carriers
- The need to replace old steam locomotives with diesel-electric ones – closing branch lines reduced the numbers of new locos needed
- Post-war prosperity led to increased car ownership and reduced demand for rural passenger train services.

For these reasons, branch lines had ceased to have an economic development role and were no longer of much relevance to their local communities.

2. A Brief History up to 1990

The shrinking of networks was not implemented anywhere as one policy; rather, each line was considered on its merits, and the whole process extended from the 1950s to the 1980s. Where the remaining traffic on the branch line travelled only on that line, the decision was straightforward, and these were the first lines to be closed.[23] However, in most cases, traffic from and to a branch line also travelled on other lines in the network, so the profit/loss calculation was much more difficult. Often it was just a comparison of branch line operating and maintenance expenses versus the revenue directly attributable to the branch line. Because revenues were attributed only to the station of origin, the value of the traffic terminating on the branch line was ignored.[24] Thus, when the branch line was closed, it was almost certain that all its traffic at that time was lost to road from the rest of the network as well.

The table below shows the extent of reduction in size, measured in route-kilometres, of each of the formerly government-owned networks, from their maximum extent to their current extent. Line closures all happened before 1990 and therefore were not as a result of privatisation.

State Networks	Maximum Route-kms	Year of max. extent	Current size operational	Comments
Queensland	10500 kms	1932	7734 kms	Current includes both the QR and Aurizon networks
New South Wales	10000 kms	1942?	7071 kms	Current includes the ARTC, RailCorp & CRN networks
Victoria	7668 kms	1942	4223 kms	Both include branch lines which extend into NSW[25]
Western Australia	7005 kms	1948	5500+ kms	Current includes both ARTC and Arc Infrastructure lines
South Australia	7039 kms	not known	3950 kms	Current includes both ARTC and Aurizon lines
Northern Territory	1690 kms	current	1690 kms	
Tasmania	851 kms	not known	667 kms	Both include Emu Bay Railway
New Zealand	5689 kms	1953	3898 kms	Includes mothballed lines

Railways as government departments

Because railways everywhere were government departments, directly responsible to their ministers in Cabinet, governments felt themselves at liberty to use their railways as a means to deliver some policies quite unrelated to freight or passenger transport.

Maintaining full employment

For example, in New Zealand, NZR was used up to the early 1980s as a way of maintaining full employment.[26] Any men without work and without reasonable work prospects or qualifications were sent by the Labour Department to the Railways. In rural areas they joined the local track maintenance gang. In the towns and cities, they were hired at the goods shed to load and unload freight into and out of box or highside wagons. This was manual labour, mostly unassisted by machines, until the 1980s. The unintended consequence was that NZR had thousands of under-employed front-line service workers who were unsuitable for and untrained in customer service. Railways became known for high levels of damage and loss of goods, through carelessness and theft. Another source of employment for the Labour Department to exploit was the railway workshops in the four major urban areas. The workshops, which in the heyday of steam were regarded as fine examples of industrial production, became notorious for slack productivity and wastage.

However, the workshops acquired over time a training role which the government came to recognise and value. Because they were the only sites of heavy engineering in New Zealand,[27] NZR became the main provider of hands-on experience for apprentices in the heavy engineering trades. There was demand elsewhere for these trade skills and many tradesmen left the NZR workshops after gaining their 'ticket'. NZR also provided summer holiday employment for many engineering students, who had a requirement to show practical experience as a component of their engineering degrees. Thus, NZR contributed to the NZ economy in ways that went unaccounted for.

Resisting inflation

Another way in which some governments used their railways as a policy instrument occurred during the 1970s, when the economies were experiencing increasing rates of inflation. All governments were slow to raise railway rates and fares, with the result that revenues fell well behind the rates of growth in operating costs.

In Western Australia, the State government decided to hold gazetted rates at the July 1975 level for another year, despite cost increases over two years of 30%. WestRail estimated that this decision caused a loss of about 8% of its gross annual income.[28]

In New Zealand, given that much freight was still required by regulation to be moved by rail, the government tried to combat inflation by freezing railway freight charges in 1971. Because the railways were integral to the majority of economic activity, it was believed that stabilised freight charges would act as a drag on inflation. This policy did not stop the inflation rate climbing to 18% by 1976,[29] but it did result in freight that was previously being carried by road, both legally and illegally, being diverted increasingly to rail. NZR's annual tonnage hauled went from 11.3 million tonnes in 1972 to a peak of 13.6 million tonnes in 1977. However, deficits in NZR's accounts increased significantly, making the railways look like more of a loss-making operation than it was. There was never any thought of compensation for the effects on NZR of the government's inflation policy, because NZR was an arm of government, not a separate organisation. These deficits accumulated and were eventually written off when NZ Rail Ltd was separated from the Railways Corporation in 1990.[30]

As a result of the rates freeze, the railway system became clogged. By 1973, the supply of empty wagons for reloading was frequently insufficient to meet the demand. Freight increasingly became lost in the system for weeks at a time, when delivery within a few days was previously the norm. (This was at a time well before computing systems became available to keep track of wagons and freight consignments.)

Wellington's marshalling yard became so full of loaded wagons that the shunters had not enough vacant track space on which to shunt wagons for trains to their onward destinations.[31] NZR had a policy of appointing marshalling yard supervisors from somewhere other than where the vacancy was, so that they would be supervising relative strangers rather than former workmates. Consequently, when congestion hit Wellington yard, the supervisors did not know the detail of how the yard was operated, and were unable to oversee any solution to the congestion problem. This operational knowledge was solely in the heads of the senior shunters who had worked there for many years. But in a time of crisis there was no way for them to put their heads together to find a workable solution because they all worked on different shifts around the clock. Two temporary solutions were instigated: storing loaded wagons at an adjacent station yard (Ngauranga) to create shunting space in Wellington yard, and stopping some wagons from arriving into Wellington from the north, which then created congestion at Palmerston North marshalling yard. It took some months for this situation to be sorted out.

Part of the medium-term solution to the congestion on the rail system was ironically to shift some of the additional freight by road. NZR and the Road Transport Association co-operated, in a program called Operation Freightroll,[32] to charter some road transport operators to move freight in the regions on behalf of NZR. Nevertheless, the problems of delayed and lost freight continued and NZR's reputation suffered badly among the business community.

2. A Brief History up to 1990

Deregulation in New Zealand

Livestock traffic

The rigidity of the regulations to protect the NZR began to soften in the 1960s. The first commodities to be allowed to go by road were household removals and livestock. Both were types of traffic that benefited greatly from being loaded just once, because trucks could go directly from house to house and farmyard to farmyard.

NZR experienced a major decline in livestock haulage over the 1960s, from a majority market share to almost nothing. Many consignments of sheep and cattle up till 1960 originated at small town saleyards, all of which had a siding from the local station yard. The holding pens and loading races were part of the infrastructure provided by NZR. The last flows of livestock retained to rail were the movements of hundreds or thousands of animals at a time from the major saleyards to the abattoirs, all of which had private sidings. That there were whole trainloads of livestock was partly due to economics, and partly due to the fact that livestock going for slaughter were less bruised when they travelled by rail compared with travel by road.[33]

The loss of livestock traffic had benefits for NZR in reducing maintenance costs – for washing wagons after each load, and for frequent repairs to wooden wagons and wooden stockyards, needed to prevent stock from escaping. Livestock traffic was also operationally inefficient – a full load of sheep or cattle was 3 tonnes in a four-wheeled wagon of 8 tonnes tare. Given that most wagons were repositioned empty, this meant hauling 16 tonnes of tare weight for every 3 tonnes of payload. Livestock traffic was seasonal. In summer, it could be hard to meet the demand for wagons, and NZR's reputation suffered amongst farmers. However, in the winter, demand was low and siding space had to be found for wagons to be stored.

The seasonality, the diversity of livestock traffic flows, the complications to do with wagon cleaning and repairs, the need to unload and feed the stock on long trips, all combined to make the fleet of livestock wagons the most difficult to manage on a daily basis. Computers did not exist, so managing the fleet was all done with paper and pencil, and many phone calls. Many railway staff were not sorry to lose this business to road carriers.

The increasing competition with NZR

During the 1960s and 1970s, New Zealand Railways' response to the threat of competition from road carriers was to have experienced commercial officers appointed as Transport Licensing Officers. These men defended the Railways' rights, under the Transport Licensing Act, to carry all freight beyond a prescribed distance. Freight shippers had to show, in semi-judicial situations, why their freight should be exempted from the regulations protecting rail. Sometimes improvements in facilities or service resulted from these transport licensing appeals, and the traffic stayed on rail. Often, exemptions were granted, and consequently the road carriers gained more business and the roading industry was strengthened.

The Transport Licensing Act had protected NZR from competition since 1936 where freight was to be transported over 30 miles (48 kilometres) and there was a rail service available. This restriction influenced how companies with a national presence supplied their markets – typically they would have manufacturing plants or warehousing in each of a number of cities such as Auckland, Hamilton, Palmerston North, Wellington, Christchurch, Dunedin and Invercargill. Distribution among these centres would be by rail, and from these centres to provincial towns would be by rail or road. In 1962, the distance limit was increased to 40 miles (64 kms), and in 1977 to 150 kilometres (93 miles).

This last increase had an unintended effect of opening up many more opportunities for some companies to transport their products wholly by road. They developed the ruse of breaching

2. A Brief History up to 1990

the distance restriction by observing it, using their network of warehouses. They could, for example, waybill products and direct a truck from Auckland to their warehouse in Hamilton, then within minutes the same truck with the same load would emerge from the Hamilton warehouse with a fresh waybill and continue to some other destination.

Recognising the political unacceptability of continuing to protect the under-performing railway system, the government repealed the Transport Licensing Act in 1983, effectively deregulating land transport completely and exposing NZR to unrestricted competition. Its annual tonnage hauled went from 11.5 million tonnes in 1982 to 8.9 million tonnes in 1988. A new government with a reforming zeal came to power in 1984, and in 1990 a representative of the Ministry of Transport was able to justify deregulation: [34]

> "the fundamental aim of achieving reductions in transport costs is being achieved. Rail freight rates on main trunk routes fell up to 50% between 1983 and 1990. Long distance rail and road services have been improved and accelerated, particularly in the inter-island market."

Protection from competition by road carriers had created an organisational culture in NZR that expected freight shippers to come to the railway to do business, and that attitude persisted for some years after deregulation. There was no entrepreneurial culture of going out and winning new business. It was not until the early 1990s that a freight marketing division was set up, branded later as TranzLink. Until then, NZR was unable to meet the challenge of competition in the market place.

Instead, the response in the 1980s was on stemming the financial losses. Staff numbers were cut drastically by various means (see below), and ways to improve productivity were pursued. An operational policy was adopted that would result in running fewer bigger trains, using stronger drawgear, and more powerful combinations of locomotives. A new operating plan to put this policy into effect was designed, replacing over a three-year period the previous production-oriented freight train timetables.[35] This new operating plan also provided for better customer service by the planned linking of train services, including rail-ferry sailings, to provide more reliable wagon transit times right across the network.[36] Selected tunnels on main routes were 'daylighted',[37] or had their floors lowered to enable international 8-foot 6-inch containers to be carried on standard wagons instead of on a limited number of well wagons.[38]

Deregulation of Australian road & rail competition – the effects on railways

All States had had legislation to restrict competition from road carriers with their railway systems since 1930. This applied to both intrastate and interstate traffic, because initially there was no distinction. Freight on rail that was to be moved interstate was transhipped from one railway system to another where they met,[39] and was reconsigned there. In Victoria and New South Wales there were some road haulers licensed to provide services on designated routes, and if traffic was hauled distances greater than 20 miles, mileage and weight-based levies would apply.[40] In New South Wales at least, these levies were passed on to the railway as compensation for loss of traffic.

In the decade following the end of World War Two, interstate road transport expanded due to two situations. The Bureau of Transport Economics summarised these circumstances:[41]

> "Accelerated economic growth increased trade between the States. Rail and sea transport were unable to cope with the increased trade due to a run-down of railway equipment and losses of shipping during the War. The appeal of long-distance road transport to customers was boosted in 1949 by a nationwide railway strike. All forms of state road regulations imposed to protect the railways were lifted for the duration of the strike, so that

the road transport industry could accommodate the displaced demand for transport services caused by the railway strike. Thus, many new customers were exposed to door-to-door service offered by the hauliers. After the strike, the States reimposed higher taxes on road haulage to protect the rail operations and even refused to grant permits, for interstate movements. Despite these moves, the long-distance road haulage industry continued to expand."

In 1954 a road haulage company (Hughes and Vale Pty Ltd) challenged the legality of the States' imposition of taxes on interstate trade, asserting that they contravened section 92 of the Commonwealth of Australia Constitution Act. This Act stipulated that trade and commerce between the States should be absolutely free. The Australian High Court upheld the State Transport Act, but Hughes and Vale appealed to the Privy Council in London, which declared it invalid in respect of interstate traffic. Following that precedent, the Australian High Court subsequently declared similar legislation in other States invalid. Although the state of the roads was not suitable, interstate freight by road grew rapidly, and has grown year by year ever since. Because road haulers were not common carriers, they were free to cherry-pick the most profitable freight flows, leaving the less profitable freight on rail.

The State Government levies on freight transport by road still applied to all traffic within state borders, but in Victoria, a practice developed called locally 'border hopping'. Intrastate freight would be carried by truck across the state border in the north into New South Wales or west into South Australia, before being delivered to destinations within Victoria. This applied particularly to the towns along the border defined by the Murray and Murrumbidgee Rivers. By this means, the levies could be evaded, because the trip was ostensibly 'interstate'.

The levies were very unpopular, and political pressure built up for their removal. South Australia was the first State to repeal its 1930s legislation in 1963. Other States followed, and New South Wales abolished the levy on road services competing with the railways in 1973.[42]

With the loss of traffic to road competition, and the effects of rising inflation rate which led to frequent wage increases, railway deficits increased constantly during the 1970s and 1980s. Because of the deficits, governments were reluctant to provide capital for asset renewals or upgrades, and so the railways became more run down. The problems seemed intractable. To a large extent, railways were unmanageable by today's standards. There was no management information available, hence no analysis and planning of options for the future. There was a

> "general acceptance at all levels of the status quo in management methods, service levels operated, operating procedures, staff relations and many other vital aspects".[43]

State Rail even lost traffic to road in hauling Hunter Valley bulk coal to Newcastle:

> "...in the Hunter Valley during the 1985 rail strike, road transport of coal was used and thereafter the road transport industry sought and received a guaranteed share of coal transport for road as a permanent buffer against any future difficulties in the rail system." [44]

As government organisations, railways in Australia were greatly involved in moving the annual grain harvests from rural trackside silos to the cities and to export ports. Close relationships between the railways and the grain storage authority in each State had existed since the rural rail networks were built. States regulated all export grain transport to be by rail to ensure the lowest cost for the State's harvest as a whole, as part of a system of pooling storage, handling and transport costs across all grain-growing areas in the State. When the harvests were larger than average and the railways struggled to cope, the State governments were blamed. When there were droughts and small harvests, maintenance was cut back to save money. By the 1980s, all aspects of railways' grain operations needed renewal and modernisation, and most of these continued into the 1990s:

- specialised 4-wheeled wagons were old and needed replacement,
- most branch lines in the grain-growing areas were old, with light-weight rail, requiring the continued use of old under-powered light axle-load locomotives past the end of their economic lives, and therefore restricting the gross weight and size of trains,
- rail sidings at grain storage silos were too short to accommodate whole trains, therefore requiring that trains be broken up for loading and re-assembled after loading,
- most silos could load rail wagons only in daylight hours, restricting the efficient cycling of wagons between silos and port,
- the movement of wagons to position them for loading was accident-prone and unsafe by modern standards – on sloped rail sidings wagons were positioned to the loading chutes using gravity with men riding the wagons to activate the hand-brakes, or on flat sidings both empty and loaded wagons were moved by men levering crowbars under the wheels.

In 1988, a Royal Commission into the storage, handling and transport of grains produced a report that recommended deregulation of many aspects of grain handling and marketing in the grain industry, including removal of the restriction on using only rail. Only the New South Wales government responded in subsequent years by commercialising its grain storage and freight rail agencies, and building road receival facilities at the grain export ports at Newcastle and Port Kembla. The other States maintained the status quo, including retention of grain harvests by rail.[45]

By 1991, the situation for regulated commodities was as follows:[46]

State	Traffics
New South Wales	Under the NSW Environmental Protection Act, coal was usually required to be transported by rail, if available. The use of road transport for export grain was constrained by limited road receival facilities at export ports.
Victoria	Domestic grains, cement, briquettes, limestone and petroleum were regulated to be transported by rail, with carriage by road allowed under permit in certain circumstances.
Queensland	Coal, coke, domestic grains (except seed grains)[47], limestone, liquefied petroleum gas, minerals and ores and raw sugar were regulated to be transported by rail. With the exception of grains, road permits were issued when "road transport was more competitive for the carriage of these restricted goods".
South Australia	No restrictions.
Western Australia	Truck licences were not granted for domestic grains, fertilisers, bulk petroleum, bulk ores and minerals, or some timber. Partial regulation of bulk petroleum and fertilisers.
Tasmania	Permit fees applied to the road haulage of bulk cement, bulk fertiliser, limestone, timber, logs, coal and sulphuric acid.

In submissions to the Industry Commission (see in Chapter 5, under *The Industry Commission's 1991 Report*) in support of continued regulation, the Western Australian Government wrote: [48]

> "... there are three key principles governing current thinking on regulation in WA:
> - the market-place must be free of significant distorting influences which might result in misallocation of resources or inflated rail deficits if deregulation occurred;
> - if regulation is maintained, rail rates should be set at least as high as those which road transport would charge if it were permitted to operate assuming charges covered road track costs (ie, "competitive" rating);

- a public interest argument exists in favour of regulation where it can be established that it does not impose significant efficiency losses and promotes other policies such as minimisation of the undesirable social and environmental externalities associated with road transport."

The Victorian Government said:

"Deregulation of the regulated commodities is not proposed. The Government believes that imperfections in the market, whereby not all social costs of alternative modes of transport would be taken into account in the modal choice decision, dictate that the final outcome of deregulation would be undesirable for the community. (Submission 58, p.25)"

The Tasmanian Government stated in relation to its Rail Protection Fees scheme:

"Whereas the original aim was to limit modal competition and ensure a base level of freight and revenue for rail, the emphasis has changed to social objectives. These include limiting road damage by heavy vehicles, reducing the social and environmental impacts associated with heavy vehicle traffic in sensitive areas, and most importantly, discouraging an increase in heavy vehicle traffic on Tasmanian roads."

Staff reductions, but accumulating deficits

New Zealand

The number of staff in NZR was approximately 23,000 in 1982. This was reduced to less than 10,000 by 1989[49] as a consequence of corporatisation, the intent of which was to make Railways more focused on operating profitably. The labour-intensive parcels business was sold to the Post Office, which promptly closed it down. The Road Services branch, which operated passenger and parcels coaches between cities and from the cities to most rural towns and communities, was sold.

The downsizing of NZR preceded privatisation by some years. During this time, many staff were withdrawn from country stations, and the automation of track maintenance and reconstruction led to a restructuring and reduction of track staff numbers. Both of these programs impacted rural communities in particular. Because of the previous government policy of using the railways to disguise unemployment, it was inevitable that some older men, particularly rural Maori, who were laid off in the 1980s never found paid work again. Although they would have acquired skills, these skills were specific to railway work, so being made redundant made these men unskilled again in the general job market.

Freight train crews were cut from three to two in 1987 by ceasing to have guards (and guards vans) at the rear of freight trains. They were replaced by Flashing Rear End Devices, attached to the coupler of the last wagon, which signalled the brake-pipe pressure continuously to the driver. This replaced one of the Guard's functions, providing him[50] with continuous assurance that his train was intact. Later, after modification of some locomotives to improve drivers' visibility and communications capability, crewing of freight trains was reduced from two to one.

Prior to the sale and privatisation of New Zealand Rail Ltd in 1993, three out of the five workshops were closed mainly to reduce staff numbers, as part of an on-going drive to cut costs. The East Town (Wanganui) workshop had had a focus on manufacture and repair of tarpaulins for covering loaded highside and flat wagons, and construction and repair of wagons with wooden bodies. Because such wagons were among the first to be scrapped as traffic volumes declined for livestock, parcels and LCL traffic, this workshop was becoming obsolete by the time of its closure in 1986. However, because Railways was Wanganui's largest employer at the time, the loss of 450 jobs was keenly felt. The workshop site is now a yard for accumulating and loading logs to send by rail to export ports.

The Addington (Christchurch) workshops closed in 1990, occupied land that was wanted for building a realignment of the Main North Line to enable freight trains to arrive at and depart from Middleton Yard in the west of the city. The Otahuhu (Auckland) workshops were closed in 1992.

By the 1993 privatisation of New Zealand Railways Ltd, the number of railways staff had reduced to approximately 5000 people, and by 1997 had stabilised at around 4000. During the period from 1983 to 1997, the cost of staff (excluding severance costs) as a percentage of total operating costs fell from 60% to 42%.[51]

Australia

The ARRDO '*1981 Report on Rail*' (see below) was the first to identify and publicly advise the need for a reduction in staff numbers in Australian railways, providing the Railway Commissioners with a reason to start tackling what would have been a difficult task in a strongly unionised industry. The aggregated government railway staff numbers, including engineering activities, freight and passenger operations, were

- about 110,500 in 1979-80,
- about 83,300 in 1988-89,
- at 30 June 1993 nearly 61,800,[52] and
- about 36,000 by the late 1990s.[53]

This was a 67% reduction over some twenty years. However, with growth in freight traffic, the improvement in labour productivity across all government railways rose from 1.2 to 2.2 million net-tonne-kilometres per freight employee between 1991 and 1995,[54] a gain of 83%, before any privatisation. The means to reduce staff numbers were similar to the reductions that had happened in New Zealand, including ceasing to haul livestock (except in Queensland), removal of staff from rural locations, and removing guards and guards' vans from freight trains.

Yet despite these gains, Australian government railways continued to accumulate deficits. As the table[55] below shows, they looked to be getting worse year by year when reported in inflating dollars. However, when adjusted for inflation, the deficits after 1983-84 were steady but still serious – very concerning for the governments involved (New South Wales and Victoria)[56] in terms of debt servicing, and apparently evidence of problems not being tackled with enough vigour, or perhaps a need for fresh thinking about funding of railway operations.

Combined Australian Railway Deficits 1980-81 to 1989-90

Financial Year (a)	Current Prices $ million	Constant 1989-90 Prices $ million (b)
1980-81	768	1533
1981-82	955	1711
1982-83	1213	1960
1983-84	1548	2338
1984-85	1618	2311
1985-86	1708	2277
1986-87	1742	2164
1987-88	1655	1916
1988-89	2223	2357
1989-90	2100	2100

Notes: (a) Deficits estimated as operating expenditure including interest payments and depreciation, less operating revenue excluding subsidies. (b) Conversion of current price estimates to constant prices was based on national accounts implicit price deflators for non-farm GDP.

It was estimated and reported by the Industry Commission[57] that
- a little over half of the total deficit was attributable to urban rail systems, mainly in Sydney and Melbourne
- about one quarter of the total rail deficit was attributable to passenger services outside urban areas, and
- the remaining quarter was attributable to freight

services, which had suffered substantial real declines in freight rates over the 1970s, combined with a failure to adjust adequately for large rises in real wages.

Nevertheless, the Industry Commission, reviewing these deficits in its 1991 report, noted [58]

> "Large deficits persist despite substantial reductions in rail workforces with allied increases in productivity and, in some systems, a wide range of other reform measures; rising interest costs worked against any improvement in financial performance. The failure in recent years by railways to reduce more substantially their demands on public funds raises doubts about the adequacy of those reforms."

Australia: joint industry initiatives – ARA, ARRDO, RIC, NFI

Prior to any of the Commonwealth initiatives for change, various industry bodies were created to assist the rail industry.

The Australasian Railway Association

Historically, there was never any national co-ordinating railway authority in Australia, but the government-owned railways had long been loosely associated through the annual meetings of the Railway Commissioners. The purpose of these meetings was to discuss problems in common and to make inter-system working arrangements. This grouping re-established itself more formally in 1994 as the Australasian Railway Association (ARA). Its website[59] states:

> "It was intended that the new body would bring together all sections of a very large and diverse industry, to assist the future development of rail in Australia and New Zealand.... Ten years on the ARA has formed itself into an organisation with a mandate to unite the rail industry to work together and to influence government policy, particularly at the Federal level."

Twenty years on, it continues as a strong advocate for all aspects of the rail industry, contributing to the Productivity Commission's inquiries and to Parliamentary Committees. In addition, it sponsors an annual conference and special-topic working groups to bring industry leaders together for exchange of information and the formulation of a whole-of-industry approach to transport issues. Working groups of relevance to freight railways are diverse – they include Safety Policy, Asset Management, Inland Rail, Road Pricing Policy, Radio Spectrum Allocation, and Workforce Development.

The Australian Railway Research and Development Organisation

The 1980s has been described as a "decade of research and transport policy development".[60] The first research body was the Australian Railway Research and Development Organisation (ARRDO), created in 1978 as a company jointly owned by the five government railways of the time. Its board comprised the CEOs of those railways plus the Commonwealth Department of Transport. Its purpose was to conduct research on a range of topics that would enable the participants to improve their policies and procedures. Its first major report was *Rail in the 1980s: 1981 Report on Rail*. This report had many recommendations, aimed at increasing labour productivity, improving financial performance, and with a comprehensive investment program for main-line infrastructure to be funded by the Commonwealth in a similar way to the funding of national highways. However, in the words of one transport consultancy[61] – "The ARRDO Report on Rail foundered on politics, both inside and outside the railway systems." Nevertheless, its recommendations were acted on many years later. In its seven years of existence, ARRDO produced over 100 reports, with titles such as:

- *Public Service Obligations*
- *The Use of Demand Elasticities in Rail Planning*
- *Cost Evaluation System for Alternative Rail Strategies*

- *A Contribution Analysis of VicRail*
- *National Rail Investment Study*
- *Costing and Accounting Practices in Australian Railways*
- *Rail Pricing Guidelines*
- *Priorities for Further Research on Railway Track Maintenance*
- *Locomotive Replacement in Queensland Railways and WestRail*

These were worthy topics to enable evidence-based policy-making, but ARRDO reports may not have been helpful in assisting the board members in the management of their issues in what were highly political environments. Created under the Fraser Coalition Government, ARRDO was closed in 1986 after the Hawke Labor Government came to power, and after the State Railway Authority of New South Wales withdrew its support.[62]

The Railway Industry Council

The Railway Industry Council (RIC) was established in 1986 by the Federal and State Transport Ministers. Its membership was broader than that of ARRDO, comprising:

- Six representatives of the federal and state governments,
- The five chief executives of the railway organisations of that time,
- Thirteen representatives of various trade unions active in the railway sector, and
- An independent chairman.

The RIC's main objective was to develop and recommend a strategy to improve the viability and competitiveness of the rail industry. It produced a discussion paper in May 1990 – *"Rail into the 21st Century"*. However, by that time, the intent of the Hawke Labor government was strongly in favour of the development of the National Highway System, and so nothing resulted from the RIC paper.

The National Freight Initiative

The National Freight Initiative (NFI) was established in 1989 by the State railways, the federal government and freight forwarders who were rail users, to determine the feasibility of a national rail freight organisation to undertake interstate rail transport. This group commissioned consultants who produced a report in April 1990. Up till then, although the inter-capital standard-gauge network had been available since 1970, the service being delivered by the various rail organisations was poor, due to lack of priority for this traffic and lack of operational continuity at the system boundaries, causing delays. The report found that a new organisation specifically responsible for interstate freight was feasible.[63] As a result, the National Rail Corporation was created in February 1992.

3. An Overview of the Rail Freight Industry Today

Timetables are fundamental to Australasian railway culture

Culture is a word with a variety of meanings. Here I use it in its anthropological sense — as 'ways of thinking and doing, generally accepted within a group'. In this sense, there is a cultural similarity between the railways of Australasia and of Great Britain, because the railways built in British colonies were modelled on British railways designs and practice. Indeed, this culture is common to Europe, and to most of Asia and Africa because of former European colonisation and influence. Significantly, this culture is not shared with North American railroads, which have their own culture for historical reasons. The differences between these two major rail cultures are described fully in Appendix 4. Both Australia and New Zealand, as countries, are now greatly influenced by American common culture and business practices. However, because their rail cultures are so different, American railroad operational practices are generally not applicable to Australasian railways.

The first country in the world where railways were built was England. There, trains travelled at unprecedented speeds compared to horse-drawn vehicles, and were considered to be dangerous. They were good at moving along their purpose-built tracks but were not easily stopped. Therefore, keeping them apart from one another was essential. In an era well before the existence of any form of telecommunications, the railway timetable was developed as a basis for operations. Thus, railway timetables were first developed for safety reasons, and then came to be used later for convenience and commerce.

A fundamental of the Australasian railway culture is that each whole network and every train on it must operate to a planned timetable or schedule. Each train has a planned 'path' that takes account of its expected attributes (the assigned locomotive power and gross trailing weight) and therefore how fast it can go along each section of railway line, taking into account the grades and curvature. It does not matter whether the planning of the path has been done hours or months ahead of the train's actual trip on the day – a path must exist before each train departs.

The compilation and interaction of schedules planned for individual trains creates the timetable planned for each railway line. This enables and documents the sharing of the line's capacity among many trains, day by day and week by week. Sharing line capacity among different train operating companies is enabled by 'vertical separation', which in turn enables competition between operators.

Integration and separation

Australasian railway systems, under government ownership, were originally all both 'horizontally-integrated' and 'vertically-integrated'.

Horizontal integration meant that each railway system was owned and managed as one organisation which provided urban passenger, long-distance passenger, and all types of freight services. All the Australasian railway systems are now horizontally separated, at least to the extent of managing passenger and freight operations separately, and some to a greater extent of separation.

Vertical integration meant that each railway organisation provided all the rail functions and met all its own needs. The functions would include train operations, building and maintaining of tracks and structures (civil engineering), building and maintaining locomotives, wagons and carriages (mechanical engineering), property management, accounting and sales. Vertical integration was originally a matter of necessity because the development of railways preceded the industrialisation of the Australasian colonies – there were rarely any other organisations capable of supplying what the railways needed. Once established, the specialised railway workshops and facilities, and the specialised skills they trained and used, continued for generations as part of one government organisation.

The principle of universal timetabled train operations is not mandatory for a vertically-integrated railway system – North American railways are vertically-integrated but generally not timetabled. However, in Australasia this principle of universal timetabled train operations was a necessary pre-requisite for the separation of

- the control (and ownership) of railway lines, from
- the responsibility for operating trains and their services they provide to customers.

This is vertical separation – the separation of the management of railway infrastructure from the use of that infrastructure. The train operating companies became the customers of the railway track providers.

Open Access and competition

Vertical separation has enabled an operational concept known as 'open access', which has been applied by governments to railway networks in both Australia and Europe in the last three decades.

The purpose of Open Access is to permit different train operating companies to run their trains over the same routes, making it possible for these companies to compete with one another if they wish. Governments have usually created open access regimes in the hope that such competition would happen, which would then force the companies to become more efficient and thus lower the costs of transport to users. But such competition depends on there being surplus line capacity in the railway network when open access is instituted – capacity which the network provider can offer to the operating companies. Without this surplus capacity, and in the context of vertical separation of a working railway where there are already many train paths allocated, effective competition cannot happen.[64]

On the Australian mainland, such competition was possible and has evolved, but train operating companies have also carved up the freight market in ways that were not foreseen and which avoid direct competition in the market, even though they may share the same tracks. Vertical separation has also produced some unintended consequences. These and the outcomes from competition are explored later in this book.

From vertical integration and unified ownership to separation and fragmentation

Like almost all railway organisations around the world, the Australasian railway systems used to be vertically integrated. Many railways around the world have undergone some type of structural reform in recent decades. Like some European railways, the old Australasian state-based railway systems have been subject to horizontal separation and complete vertical separation of their freight businesses and networks. The outcomes have been both positive and negative, depending on one's framework for analysis, expectations and concerns.

Increasing complexity

Among the Australasian commercial railways, almost all had histories of government ownership for many decades, particularly during their periods of network expansion in the late nineteenth and early twentieth centuries.[65] They had the obligations of being 'common carriers'. Thus, they were expected to provide service to anyone or any company that sought to use them. Railways could not refuse consignments, unless for example they were physically too large to fit through tunnels or under bridges. Government railways were obliged to be 'all things to all people'. Consequently, they became increasingly complex operations as they grew in size and as the economies they served became more diverse.

However, the means to manage such operational complexity effectively never evolved until the 1990s, with the advent of computer-based information systems. Previously, organisations were unable to grasp the complexity and interconnectedness of their operations. Government railways managed their various functions separately, with matching organisation structures.

Resistance to change

By the 1980s, when the changes which are a focus of this book began, all the Australasian rail networks had been government-owned for generations. With organisational structures and processes typical of government bureaucracies, they had become somewhat inflexible operationally and commercially. They were unable to adapt to changes in their business environments, and had increasingly aged assets in need of renewal. Their deficits were growing larger, partly because they had very specialised staff roles and too many staff. Government railways were closed organisations, in the sense that they rarely sought talented people from outside. They recruited only into the lowest levels. Promotion was typically done by seniority, not merit. There was a strong sense among the staff of brotherhood, loyalty to one another, and operational coordination and cooperation. These attitudes supported their 'safety first' ethos, and were demonstrated when there were emergencies to respond to, but they provided added resistance to change lest some staff were disadvantaged by it.

Australasian railways today

Much has changed for all Australasian freight railways. (See chapter 9 for detailed descriptions of these changes.) All the government-owned freight operations and mobile railway assets (therefore not the rail networks) were sold into private ownership.[66] However, State governments are still the owners and operators of urban and regional passenger services.

The railway industry on the continent has become very fragmented. Vertical separation has spawned many train-operating companies and track providers. Many other companies provide support services to these train operators and track providers — services such as rolling-stock hire and lease, track and rolling-stock construction and maintenance. Only two companies now operate freight trains east-west across the continent, with a number of other smaller companies operating mostly regionally or intrastate.

In contrast to the former government-owned railways which ran trains that carried any and all traffic that was offering, today's freight trains are each operated usually for just one, or a small number of customers, on a pre-arranged and contracted basis. This greatly reduces both the requirement for shunting and marshalling of wagons, and the number of commercial relationships and transactions to process. Consequently, many fewer railway staff are now required both on the ground and in the office, and operating costs are less than they were under government ownership. There are even some contracts where the train operators' customers own their own rolling-stock, and the train operator just provides crews and accreditation for interacting with the track provider, i.e., as the notional owner of the trains.[67]

A multitude of track providers

Because vertical separation and changes in control of rail infrastructure were done by State governments over two decades, there are now a number of organisations providing Australia's rail networks. All the land under the rail networks remains in government ownership, but the responsibility for track management and maintenance has been devolved and fragmented, and in some cases this responsibility has been sold on.

The position in 2022 is:
- In Queensland, the majority of the network is still managed by government-owned Queensland Rail (QR), but Aurizon (formerly QR National) leases, manages and maintains the Central Queensland Coal Network (CQCN), 2670 kilometres[68] of heavy haul lines dedicated to bulk export coal traffic.
- In New South Wales, the network is now managed and maintained by three different organisations:
    — RailCorp / Sydney Trains (the urban passenger train operator owned by the NSW State Government) in the Sydney metropolitan area and extending as far as Newcastle in the north, Lithgow beyond the Blue Mountains in the west, to Macarthur in the south-west, and the whole Illawarra region south of Sydney;
    — The Australian Rail Track Corporation (ARTC) (owned by the Commonwealth) for the interstate lines, north to Brisbane, west through Broken Hill into South Australia, and south into Victoria; plus the Hunter Valley, strategic secondary lines, and the Metropolitan Freight Network within the Sydney urban area, and
    — The United Group for the remaining regional and rural branch lines.

- In Victoria, the Victorian Rail Track Corporation (VicTrack) owns the state network, and leases all but the freight yards, intermodal terminals and locomotive depots to Public Transport Victoria (PTV) which in turn subleases
    — To the ARTC the interstate lines (Melbourne to the NSW and SA borders), the line to Portland (a major grain export port in Western Victoria) and the Benalla to Oaklands (in NSW) branch,
    — The Melbourne metropolitan lines to Metro Trains, and
    — The remainder of the state network (known as the country network) to V/Line, the government-owned regional passenger train operator, which manages and maintains this network to passenger train standards.
- In South Australia, the ARTC manages the interstate freight lines, including across the Western Australian border to Kalgoorlie, while Genesee & Wyoming Australia Pty Ltd (GWA) leases the Tarcoola to Alice Springs line, owns the Alice Springs to Darwin line and operates from Adelaide to Darwin. It also controls three branch lines in the east of the state and an isolated network in the west of the state.[69]
- In Western Australia, the whole of the government-owned freight network is leased to and managed by the North American owned company Brookfield Rail. With one small exception (the Swan River bridge at Fremantle), freight trains do not normally operate on any part of the urban passenger network which is managed by Transperth.
- In Tasmania, the network is part of the government-owned vertically-reintegrated TasRail.

As will be explained in chapter 13 (under *Obtaining train paths across multiple access regimes*), the fragmented management of rail networks, especially in New South Wales and Victoria, does not make it easy for freight train operators to set up new services on behalf of their clients.

The track gauge issue

Despite the common cultural heritage of Australasian railways, there are different track gauges among the States. For reasons that have to do with the separate development of the Australian colonies and the parochialism of colonial governments, three gauges were used and are still in use:

- Broad Gauge, (5ft 3in = 1600mm) in Victoria and part of South Australia
- Standard Gauge (4ft 8½in = 1435mm) in New South Wales and part of South Australia
- Narrow Gauge (3ft 6in = 1067mm) in Queensland, Western Australia, parts of South Australia, and in the whole ofz Tasmania and New Zealand.

An oddity – triple gauge track in the rail-yard at Gladstone South Australia

Before the federation of the Australian colonies in 1901, there was little importance attached to the possibility of a national network being created. After federation, there were several initiatives to create a national network, but the expansion of the standard gauge network was spasmodic. A fuller description of this history is in Chapter 2.

By the 1990s, the standard gauge interstate network had grown finally to link all the state capital cities on the continent. This enabled the growth of interstate freight on rail, particularly on the long-haul east-west route connecting the eastern state capitals to Perth, where rail's market share of freight on land is about 80%, or 55% of the total when coastal shipping is taken into account. However, rail's market share of intermodal freight moving on each of the sectors between Adelaide, Melbourne, Sydney, and Brisbane is still less than 20%, for a number of reasons that will be explained in subsequent chapters. In all these sectors, road freight has the majority share, with sea freight now negligible. Between Brisbane and Melbourne, rail's market share is just over 30%.[70]

There has been a partial conversion of broad gauge to standard gauge in Victoria. The first interstate line was built parallel to the broad-gauge line from Wodonga to Melbourne, opening in 1962. The whole line from Melbourne to Adelaide via Geelong was converted from broad gauge in 1995,[71] along with three branch lines to Portland, Yaapeet and Hopetoun. In 2009 the broad-gauge line from Melbourne to Wodonga and the branch line from Benalla to Oaklands were converted to standard gauge. In 2015 the State government announced[72] a plan to standardise, and rebuild for heavier axle-loadings, over 1000 kilometres of broad-gauge track on the Murray Basin lines, so that minerals and grains could better access the export port of Portland in Western Victoria. The rest of Victoria's broad-gauge network remains, with a short section of dual gauge between Maryborough and Dunolly.

3. Overview

In Western Australia, the interstate line was rebuilt to standard gauge, including a 120 km section of dual gauge track on the main line from Northam through Perth suburbs to the bulk materials export port at Kwinana and the container port at Fremantle. The extensive narrow-gauge network remains, although there was a conversion to standard gauge for the Leonora to Esperance branch line that connects with the standard gauge main line at Kalgoorlie. All the interstate traffic goes to and from Perth, while the narrow-gauge network carries mainly bulk minerals and grains to the export ports at Geraldton, Kwinana and Albany. Hence there is no advantage converting any more of the narrow-gauge network to standard gauge, because the existing and potential traffic on the narrow gauge is all intrastate.

In Queensland, the narrow-gauge network remains. The standard-gauge line from New South Wales terminates at Acacia Ridge at the Brisbane Multi-User Terminal, where freight can be transferred between the two networks. However, there is a dual-gauge freight line from Acacia Ridge to the Port of Brisbane, shown on the next page.

Dual gauge track

A summary below of the current (2021) extent of railways in Australia shows route-kilometres of open lines, by gauge and state/territory. It includes commercial freight, passenger, heritage and miners' private supply chain railways:[73]

State:	ACT	NT	NSW	Qld	SA	Tas	Vic	WA	Total
Kms/gauge									
Broad			73		254		2358		2685
Narrow		3		8146	184	611		2970	11914
Standard	6	1690	7132	117	2561		1800	4701	18007
Other				4		7			11
Dual				36	22		47	207	312
Total	6	1693	7205	8303	3021	618	4205	7878	32929

A legacy of physical constraints

Physical constraints on modern freight train operations in the eastern states include
- track alignments from the 19th century that limit train speeds,
- bridge and tunnel clearances that are tight for 8'6" containers on conventional flat wagons, and
- shared lines in the cities where the electrification for suburban passenger trains prohibits the double stacking of containers – a practice that is now routine on the route from Perth to Melbourne and to Parkes (NSW).

Infrastructure constraints in New South Wales

All freight trains are constrained from achieving the average speeds considered normal elsewhere by
- sections of slow, winding single track lines to the north of the Hunter Valley, west of the Blue Mountains and south of Goulburn,
- 1880s winding route alignments (albeit of double track) immediately north, west and south of Sydney, and
- the bottleneck of Sydney's suburban network,

where freight trains have to share line capacity with Australasia's largest metropolitan passenger train service.

The construction of the Southern Sydney Freight Line, under ARTC control, has achieved the separation of most freight trains from passenger trains through the southern suburbs, but the bottleneck of shared tracks under RailCorp control remains through the northern and western suburbs.

Since 1985, RailCorp and its predecessors have operated a twice-daily weekday curfew for freight trains, during the peak hours of commuter passenger trains. This eliminates any potential operational conflicts between freight and passenger trains, enhancing the reliability of the commuter trains. Consequently, freight trains are denied access to the shared urban network for some 8 hours out of the 24-hour day on weekdays. This curfew is a real constraint for freight train operators, and a significant impediment to the growth of rail freight into and out of Sydney, and also between Port Botany and the intermodal terminals in the western suburbs. On the Northern Sydney corridor, an additional track has been built at great expense between Epping and Thornleigh to enable the segregation of north-bound freight trains, which are faced with an uphill climb from West Ryde to Hornsby. However, this new track was electrified, so that the intercity and regional passenger trains can overtake the all-stops suburban services during the curfew periods.

A new inland route for trains between Melbourne and Brisbane, bypassing Sydney, is currently being built. Designed and built by the ARTC, Inland Rail will use a majority of existing regional routes but also require some new standard gauge routes within NSW and a connection from an existing line in northern NSW into Queensland as far as Brisbane. An alternative route, dubbed the Great Australian Trunk Railway (GATR), was also proposed, to follow the most direct route possible between Brisbane and Melbourne.[74] It was reported to be shorter, with less hill-climbing and less curvature, and therefore faster than the ARTC route. However, as the inland route is being funded by the Commonwealth government, the ARTC route was chosen.

The curfews and the sharing of the Sydney network may also be an impediment to future growth of freight by rail within the Sydney metropolis. Because of on-going congestion on the roads that access Port Botany, transport planners have for some years called for many more (up to 40% of the total) import/export containers to be moved by rail between the port and intermodal terminals in the southern and western suburbs. But the statistics indicate that, up to mid-2014, the numbers are static and the percentage of container movements by rail is reducing below 14%.[75] However, with the Enfield terminal starting operations in August 2016, and Qube's Moorebank inland intermodal terminal and Pacific National's terminal at St Marys both due to open, this percentage will increase. But the capacity of the Sydney rail network to enable a significant increase in containers on rail has still to be tested.

In summary, the main line capacity issues in the Sydney area have been recognised and are being partially addressed, which is a necessary but not sufficient prerequisite for growth of freight on rail in the eastern states.

By contrast, in Brisbane, Melbourne, Adelaide and Perth the urban passenger networks use a different track gauge to the interstate network. Therefore, there are limited operational interactions between freight and commuter trains. Shared trackage remains where intrastate freight services operate. Examples include:
- in Brisbane, the north coast intermodal freighters, and freight trains from the Toowoomba region going into the Port of Brisbane;
- in Melbourne, the movement of steel products between Melbourne and Long Island, and containerised paper from Maryvale into Melbourne.

3. Overview

Other impediments to freight trains

Other impediments to the growth of railed freight are many and varied. In Brisbane, Sydney and Melbourne, the urban rail networks still used by freight trains are owned and controlled by State government bodies that are primarily concerned with facilitating passenger trains servicing the States' capital cities. Some other impediments include those arising from the ways in which state governments disposed of their rail freight businesses, from political influences, and from the fragmentation of the industry. These impediments will be discussed in chapter 16.

Train operators are showing caution about gaining new business (except for trainload bulk hauls of coal and iron ore) while they struggle to maintain profitability with the business they already have. There is a pervasive, if understated, attitude that growth of non-bulk freight on rail is difficult to achieve and may not actually be profitable. The difficulties are real and not comprehensively understood.

A who's who of freight train operators in Australasia

The train operators and their areas of operations, extant in 2022, are:

Freight Train Operating Companies	QLD	NSW	VIC	SA	WA	NT	TAS	NZ
Pacific National (PN)	Y	Y	Y	Y	Y			
Aurizon (formerly QR National)	Y	Y	Y	Y	Y	Y		
Qube Logistics		Y	Y		Y			
Southern Shorthaul Railroad (SSR)		Y	Y					
Specialised Container Transport (SCT)	Y	Y	Y	Y	Y			
GrainCorp		Y	Y					
Crawfords Freightlines as Sydney Rail Services (SRS)		Y						
Bowmans Rail				Y				
Watco	Y				Y			
TasRail							Y	
KiwiRail								Y

In 2010, this list above would have included at least another ten freight train operators which are now no longer in business as separate companies. Most have been bought out by the bigger operators that remain in the industry.

In March 2000, a parliamentary researcher writing about the issues remaining in rail reform, at the end of a decade of reform, summarised the situation for rail in Australia thus:[76]

> "The combination of circumstances the rail freight industry faces is unique to Australia. It includes low population density, long distances, the Federal structure of government, and the fragmentation of administration between rail and competing transport modes (notably road) and within the rail industry. In particular, State responsibility for the ownership and operation of railways has been a key influence on rail policy since colonial times including track gauges and operating standards. As a consequence, it has at times been difficult to advance reform even though Commonwealth and State governments have long recognised the need to improve rail efficiency."

The competitive position – rail versus road

One of the unintended consequences of the privatisation of the rail industry has been that data about freight volumes are no longer available to the government or anyone else, because they are commercially sensitive. When railways were government-owned, such data were published, or least available for research. Because the road freight industry is very fragmented, aggregate data about the scale of road carriers' operations must also be derived. Thus, it is extremely difficult to quantify what the competitive position between rail and road really is.

The Commonwealth Bureau of Infrastructure, Transport and Regional Economics (BITRE) in 2010 produced the most

authoritative report available on the movement of interstate freight in Australia, using estimated data for the period 1972 to 2007 and forecasted data for 2008 to 2030. The graphs that follow are copied from this report.[77] The interstate transport network in Australia can be seen as two distinct corridors:
- The North-South corridor is in the eastern states, from Queensland through New South Wales to Victoria, Tasmania and South Australia, and
- The East-West corridor is from the eastern states to Perth in Western Australia.

The graphs below show the actual and forecast growth in interstate freight, and the modal shares. The forecasts show that the freight task on the North-South corridor is expected to grow faster than on the East-West corridor. Road freight is the dominant mode on the North–South corridor, while interstate rail freight has mostly been the main mode on the East–West corridor.

The forecasts were based on past trends, therefore assuming that there would be no intervention to change these trends. In particular, in the North-South corridor, although the railed volume of freight has more than doubled, the rail mode has steadily lost market share to road transport over the last forty years, for reasons which will be explained in chapter 4. The forecasted growth of freight on the North-South corridor coupled with road freight's continuing dominance in this corridor is very disturbing for anyone concerned about road safety, air pollution and Australia's contribution to the global growth and consequences of greenhouse gases. There is a pressing need for the rail mode to increase its share of this transport task.

F6.2 Interstate freight estimates and forecasts on the North–South corridor by transport mode, 1972–2030

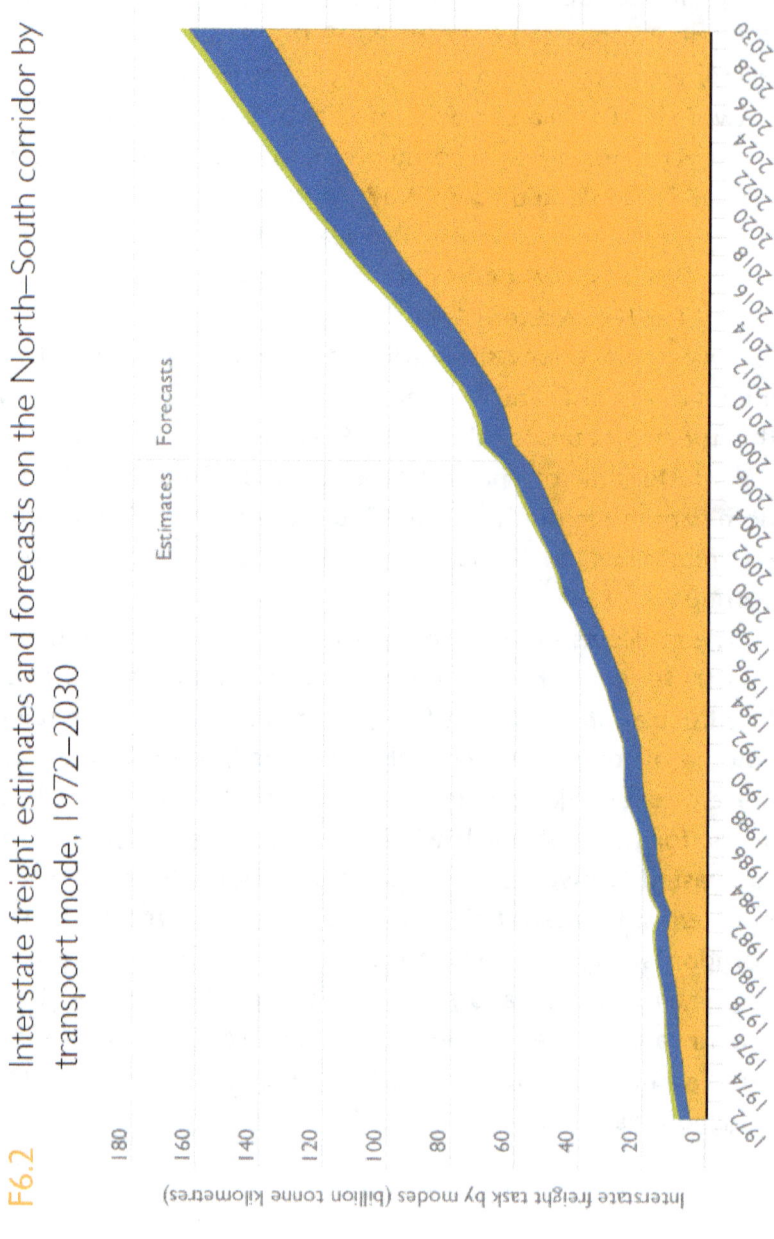

3. Overview

F6.3 Transport mode shares of interstate freight estimates and forecasts on the North–South corridor, 1972–2030

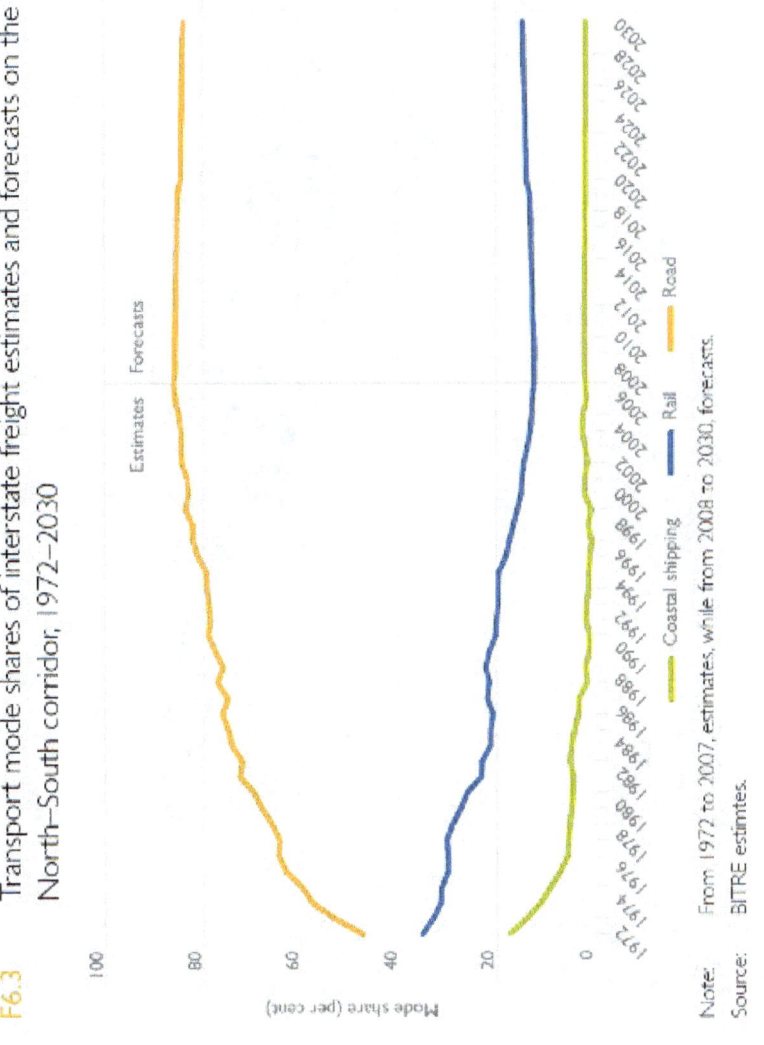

Note: From 1972 to 2007, estimates, while from 2008 to 2030, forecasts.
Source: BITRE estimates.

Off the Rails

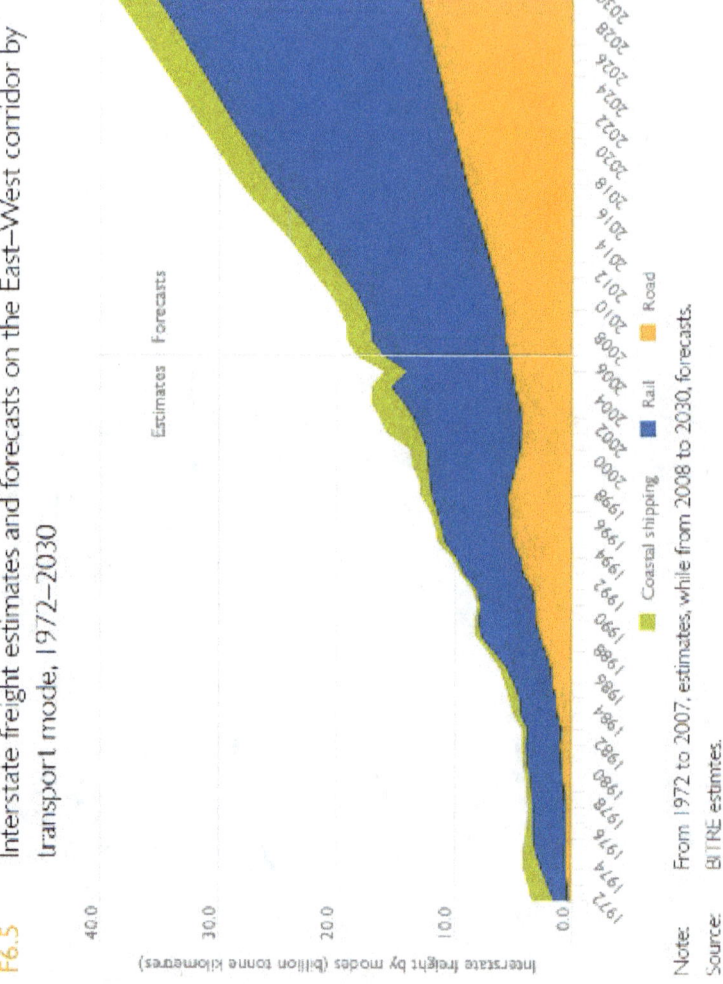

F6.5 Interstate freight estimates and forecasts on the East–West corridor by transport mode, 1972–2030

Note: From 1972 to 2007, estimates, while from 2008 to 2030, forecasts.
Source: BITRE estimates.

3. Overview

F6.6 Transport mode shares of interstate freight estimates and forecasts on the East–West corridor, 1972–2030

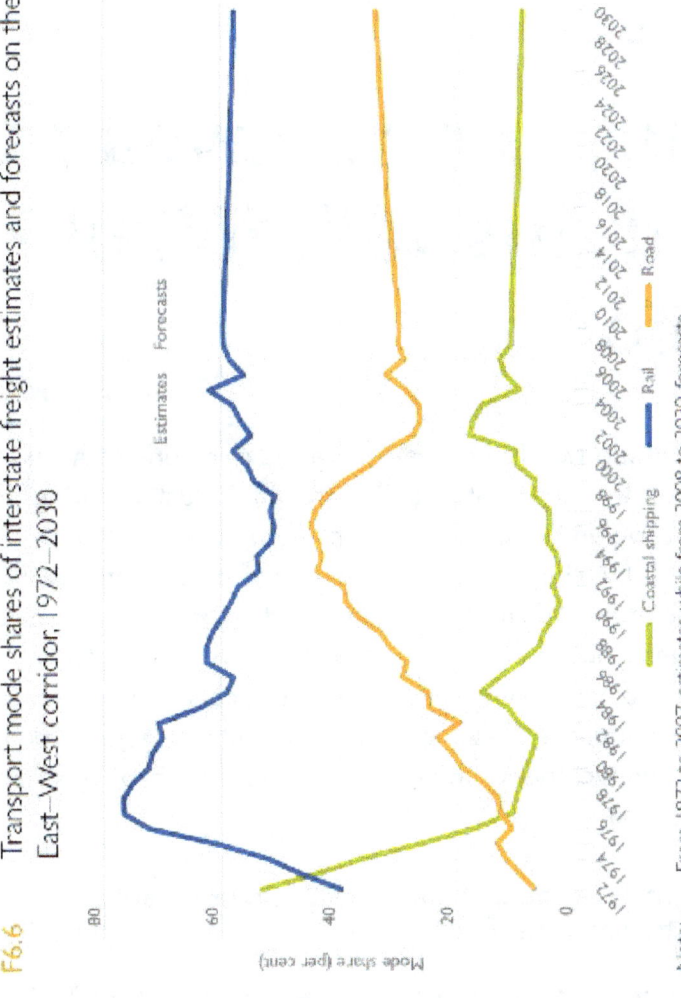

Note: From 1972 to 2007, estimates, while from 2008 to 2030, forecasts.
Source: BITRE estimates.

Part B

The Commonwealth and Australian Rail Reform

'The Commonwealth' is the federal government of Australia. Much of the story of the rail freight industry during the period covered by this book has been influenced, directly and indirectly, by what the Commonwealth has done, and by what it has not done. I include under the heading of Commonwealth: the federal politicians, the institutions of Parliament and the various federal government departments and other agencies that have published research and commentary on public policy and economic theory as applied to the reform of Australian land transport.

4. The roles of the Commonwealth Government in Australian land transport

5. Commonwealth initiatives on rail development in the 1990s

6. Procrastination and evasion

7. Transport sector reform by commissions and councils

8. Australian Road Reform

4. The Roles of the Commonwealth Government in Australian Land Transport

The Commonwealth Government's historic position on railways

The policies and actions of any government are shaped largely by the beliefs of political parties and their individual leaders. Hence, with a succession of governments over time, it is normal to have a mix of policy continuation, and radical policy changes that may be continued or suffer policy reversals. Yet, looking at the Commonwealth governments of Australia since Federation, there has been consistency in its approach to railways. It was described in 1995 thus: [78]

> "In practice, the Commonwealth's performance since Federation has been at best, one of wavering support and reluctant leadership, with individual state concerns, Federal/State financial haggling and rail system rivalries invariably being allowed to dominate the agenda."

Perhaps because railways were historically the responsibility of the States, the Commonwealth has usually been and still is indifferent to and uninvolved in railways, except where interstate trade is the issue. Hence, the Commonwealth funded the standard-gauge Trans-Australia Railway connecting the States of Western Australia and South Australia, and in 1917 formed the Commonwealth Railways to operate it.

Subsequently, the Commonwealth provided funds for some extensions to the standard-gauge network where these would yield benefits that were national in scope.

- In 1930 the extension of the NSW North Coast branch line from its terminus at Kyogle across the border to South Brisbane;
- In 1937 the extension of the Transcontinental line from Port Augusta to Port Pirie (SA);
- In 1962 a standard-gauge line was built from Wodonga to Melbourne that shared the rail corridor of Victoria's existing broad-gauge lines, but separate from and parallel to it;
- The interstate line between Kalgoorlie (WA) and Perth was converted between 1966 and 1968 from narrow to standard gauge, with two major deviations to avoid the steep grades and excessive curvature of the old route;
- In 1970 the previously narrow-gauge line from Port Pirie (SA) to Broken Hill (NSW) was re-opened as the last link in the standard-gauge network connecting Sydney to Perth;
- In 1980 a new standard-gauge line from Tarcoola (SA) to Alice Springs (NT) replaced the old narrow-gauge route to Alice via Oodnadatta and Marree.

In all these instances, the funds provided by the Commonwealth were not grants, but interest-bearing loans to the States, and for the last two above, to Commonwealth Railways or Australian National (AN). In 1983 AN converted the line from Adelaide to Crystal Brook (SA) to standard gauge, using its own loan-raising capability.

In 1980, the Fraser Coalition Government offered, at a time of high oil prices, to upgrade and electrify the Sydney-Melbourne line. However, this offer was withdrawn in 1981 after New South Wales and Victoria failed to make a positive response.[79]

It appears that governments at both the federal and state levels were reluctant[80] throughout the 1980s to invest significant amounts of money in what was seen as a loss-making industry. However, there was one exception to this trend – the Queensland Government had faith in its railways after downsizing in the 1980s, and QR had growing traffic in export coal. During the later 1980s, there were extensive grade and curve easements, track upgrading for heavier axle-loads, replacement of timber bridges by steel bridges, introduction of Centralised Train Control (CTC) systems to maximise line capacity, and electrification of over 2000 kilometres of track, and a new fleet of electric locomotives. This program was completed in 1989 at a total cost of $1.09 billion.[81]

When the last major interstate railway line (between Melbourne and Adelaide) was converted from broad- to standard-gauge in 1995, funded by the Commonwealth for the first time by grants under the *One Nation* program (see in chapter 5), the finalisation of one railway network connecting the State capital cities was seen by the Commonwealth as a major achievement. The fact that this main-line standardisation left the broad-gauge branch lines stranded, was a matter for the States of Victoria and South Australia to deal with if they saw fit. That there was no funding for the upgrading of track alignment on the main line also showed the limitations of Commonwealth involvement. This line was and still is of limited capacity because it is a single track with crossing loops[82], on alignments built in the 1880s. These alignments have some steep ruling grades and tight radius curves, which restrict the maximum and average speeds of long heavy freight trains.

Creation and funding of the National Highway System

Although the Commonwealth has the possibility in the Australian Constitution for involvement in railways for 'nation-building', there is no specific mention of roads in the Constitution. Nevertheless, a Commonwealth Bureau of Roads was established in 1964, which produced reports that proposed the formation of a National Highway System (NHS). The Whitlam Labor Government passed the National Roads Act 1974 that defined the NHS: a network of existing roads connecting all mainland capital cities, plus certain Tasmanian roads, with a combined length of about 16,000 kilometres. In 1992, two other highways were added to the NHS: the roads directly connecting Melbourne with Brisbane, and Adelaide with Sydney, bringing the total length to 18,500 kilometres.[83] This compares with about 8,270 kilometres[84] for the total length of the Interstate Rail Network.

One reason given for the creation of the NHS was that the main roads between the capitals were in poor condition, and were likely to remain that way without full Federal funding. The objectives for the NHS first stated in 1974 and revised in 1993 included:[85]

- "facilitating overseas and interstate trade and commerce;
- minimising the cost of the National Highway to the Australian community;
- contributing to ecologically sustainable development."

The first of these objectives is consistent with the long-standing position of the Commonwealth regarding land transport. The other two are revealing, and help explain how Australia remains one of the highest emitters per capita of greenhouse gas emissions[86] due to burning fossil fuels, at a time when minimising these ought to be a major priority for

4. The Roles of the Commonwealth

Commonwealth governments. There will be more about the effects of these objectives in following chapters.

Up until 1991, it was unclear which level of government had responsibility for any category of road. But at a Special Premiers' Conference in that year, the Commonwealth accepted sole funding responsibility for the NHS.[87] In reality, it had already been funding and continued to fund many more roads beyond those declared part of the NHS, by way of grants to the States.

Commonwealth spending on roads and highways during the 1980s and 1990s greatly exceeded its spending on railways. Comparable data on Commonwealth capital and maintenance spending on roads and railways, for the period F.Y. 1975 to F.Y. 1999, expressed in constant 1998-99 dollars, shows: [88]

- Total Commonwealth spending on roads and highways was $60.7 billion, of which
  — $42.8 billion was grants to States for non-NHS roads, and
  — $17.9 billion was spent on the NHS, of which $3.7 billion was spent on rebuilding the Hume Highway[89] alone.
- Total capital spending on railways was $1.2 billion, which was used
  — for the *One Nation* projects (see in chapter 5), and
  — for equity in the National Rail Corporation (see below) which was subsequently sold.

The spending by the Commonwealth on straightening and widening the Hume Highway had the effect of shortening the route to 870 kilometres, compared to the rail route of 960 kilometres. This cumulative investment, together with increases in heavy vehicle speed limits, has reduced Sydney-Melbourne heavy vehicle travel times from 15 hours to 11 hours since 1971.[90] A typical freight train transit time on the 1910-vintage rail alignment is 14 hours, which is still some hours more than is competitive to capture the overnight market for freight forwarders' traffic. This is one reason for the low market-share for rail in this sector.

During the same period that the Commonwealth spent $1.2 billion on rail projects, more than $0.6 billion was received back from the States and AN, repaying with interest previous loans for rail projects.[91] This further exacerbated the disparity of spending between the modes. Based on the figures above, Commonwealth investment in the NHS was about 30 times greater over the period than its investment in railways.

Commonwealth spending on the NHS and the Pacific Highway[92] has continued at similar levels, with much of the spending on augmenting highways from 2 to 4 lanes, and 4 to 6 lanes, and building by-passes around towns. The perceived need for such spending is the increasing numbers of heavy trucks now using these highways.

No comprehensive strategic planning for land transport

Despite the large amounts of money spent by the Commonwealth over two decades on highways, it has never played a role in leading any sort of strategic transport plan for the whole of Australia.

The Commonwealth government was continually advised in the 1990s, in several reports, of the need for it to be more pro-active in this way. In 1994 The National Transport Planning Taskforce was established by the federal Minister for Transport to undertake a wide-ranging review of transport planning, infrastructure investment and related transport matters. In its report, the first recommendation was:[93]

> "Commonwealth, state and territory governments negotiate (and seek endorsement of the Council of Australian Governments) to establish a framework for national strategic transport planning in Australia — a National Transport Infrastructure Network. Primary attention should be given to investments of national economic significance."

4. The Roles of the Commonwealth

This, and the majority of the Taskforce's recommendations, were not implemented.[94]

In 1997, the parliamentary committee who were authors of the *Planning not Patching* report took a broad view, commenting:[95]

> "It is essential that planning and the implementation of plans by the Commonwealth supports a strategic national perspective which integrates all forms of transport." [Para 2.39]
>
> "In Australia, the break-in-gauge development of rail is an example of how detrimental isolated planning can be to achieving an efficient and effective transport service for the nation." [Para 2.40]
>
> "For such a large expenditure item as transport to be potentially crisis driven is folly. The call for a national strategic approach to transport and the opportunity for the Commonwealth to take a leadership role in developing such a strategic approach is not new but it is overdue." [Para 2.42]
>
> "A strategic approach to planning and managing Australia's transport network is essential if the nation is to maximise efficiency and effectiveness. Infrastructure planning and investment cannot be narrow and limited through operating in isolation without consideration of competition between and within all forms of transport, and without coordination of decisions at all levels of government." [Para 2.60]
>
> "The committee recommends that the Commonwealth consult widely, develop and publish an integrated strategic plan for the national transport network by 1 July 1999." [Recommendation 4]

In 1998, the report of the House of Representatives Standing Committee, *Tracking Australia*, otherwise known as the Neville Report, had as its first recommendation:[96]

> "The committee recommends that the Commonwealth assume the leadership role and consult widely in developing an integrated national transport strategic plan to be published by 1 July 1999."

In May 1999, the Rail Projects Task Force report, *Revitalising Rail: The Private Sector Solution,* otherwise known as the Smorgon Report, had as its first recommendation:[97]

> "The Commonwealth Government takes the lead in developing an economically-driven National Transport Strategy that will secure a seamless domestic transport system embracing road, rail, sea and air transport"

In August 1999, the *Progress in Rail Reform* report stated in the Overview:[98]

> "The Commonwealth Government has a significant role in leading the reform process ... where a national approach is required. Priorities include developing an overarching national transport policy framework."

This is how the Commonwealth responded formally to these recommendations:[99]

> "The Neville reports recommend that the Commonwealth develop and publish an integrated strategic plan for the national transport network. The current structure of asset ownership and division of transport responsibilities does not permit the Commonwealth – on its own – to produce a 'national plan' that would commit other government and industry parties to deliver desired performance outcomes to users and the travelling public. Commercial operation, asset investment, management and regulation responsibilities for the land transport system reside with many parties, not just the Federal Government."

This response was, at face value, both deft and daft. The fragmentation of transport responsibilities was largely due to the historically derived split in responsibilities between the States and the Commonwealth. This was the most significant issue that each of the studies (referred to above) identified as the reason for needing changes in land transport planning. However, for a Commonwealth government not wanting to upset the sometimes-uneasy relationships between itself and State governments, the existence of the split in responsibilities was reason enough not to take the lead on strategic planning for transport. The Minister of Transport said around this time that the Government did not want to be seen "dictating national transport development".[100] Instead, it opted to involve all governments through the ATC: [101]

> "The Commonwealth will work with the Australian Transport Council (ATC) – the consultative forum of Australian transport ministers – to develop a coherent national planning process for strategic land transport infrastructure."

Significantly, the Minister talked only about "strategic land transport infrastructure" and not about any overarching land transport policy. Perhaps this omission was due to the position of a laissez-faire federal government not to have an explicit policy for activities in which the private sector played an increasing role, or perhaps it was recognition of the impossibility of reaching and maintaining a consensus where the Council of Australian Governments (COAG) was the decision-making body. Whatever, Australia continued without an integrated strategic plan for land transport until 2012 (see chapter 8 under *Infrastructure Australia and the National Land Freight Strategy*). This absence, and the absence of leadership in the development of Australia's transport policy, resulted in a *de facto* land transport policy which was unacknowledged, ad hoc, confused and incoherent. The consequences that have flowed from this are part of the story of this book.

There is more discussion on all the reports referred to above in chapters 5 and 6.

The creation of the Australian National Railways Commission

One significant change to Commonwealth policy on railways occurred in the early 1970s when the reformist Whitlam Labor Government offered for the Commonwealth to take over the State-owned railways, in a bid to create one national railway. Perhaps it was seeking to do for Australian railways what it had started doing for the National Highway System – funding upgrading programs. This national railway would have been all-inclusive, because vertically integrated railways were then the norm, and there was a need to improve both the networks and train operations and services. In Gough Whitlam's words, in 1975:[102]

> "In no area of Government responsibility is there a greater need for modernisation and reform than the railways. In no area have there been greater Constitutional and administrative obstacles to reform ... In Australia, far from uniting our country, the railway systems have been organised to disrupt the unification of the nation. They have been used to centralize our settlement, our commerce, in State capitals."

The response from four of the six State governments was, in effect, "not interested". It seems they saw the offer in the context of the perpetual tussle between the States and Commonwealth for control of functions. It therefore looked like a move to take away from the States one of their major responsibilities. Fifteen years later, the National Farmers Federation confirmed this belief in its submission to the Industry Commission Inquiry:[103]

> "... the refusal of most State politicians not to sell their railways to the Federal Government in the late 1970s has led to a decade of lost opportunity. Whatever possessed the State politicians to block the purchase of rail systems, it was certainly not the welfare of their constituents.

Even then the NSW and Victorian systems, especially, were making large losses, and the purchase terms were very generous. Evidently State politicians refused the Federal Government's purchase offer because inability to manipulate transport systems entails a loss of political convenience and power. (Submission 77, p.8)"

Only South Australia and Tasmania took up the offer because their rail systems were run-down and seen to be a perpetual drain on State finances. The Australian National Railways Commission (AN) was formed in July 1975 from the Commonwealth Railways, and the two State railways were transferred to AN from March 1978. AN went from having 2,000 kms of track and a staff of 4000, to a total of 7,890 kms, comprising three track gauges across initially six different networks and sections, and 12,000 staff. In 1980, a new standard-gauge line from Tarcoola to Alice Springs replaced the flood-prone route to Alice Springs from Marree.

The demise of Australian National Railways (AN)

Unlike other government-controlled railways of the time, AN was not subject to external control of its rates and fares. It was also freed from common-carrier obligations so that it could act more commercially, and exit from unprofitable traffics and lines. The federal government expected AN to reach financial break-even within ten years. However, the unfulfilled vision for one national railway left AN reliant on Commonwealth financial support to meet its annual losses for some thirty years. Even though the Commonwealth owned AN, it did not invest in its own rail business during the 1980s, consistent with its stance on not putting money into railways. In its 1990-91 Annual Report, AN commented that [104]

"no equity has been put into the business since its formation, with the result that there has been an excessive reliance on borrowed money to finance asset replacement and expansion."

In 1994, AN's majority traffic of interstate freight was transferred to the newly formed National Rail Corporation (NRC), for reasons explained below. This transfer or takeover of the interstate traffic gutted Australian National's business, leaving AN as a vertically-integrated rail operator servicing only intrastate freight within the economically small states of South Australia and Tasmania. It also retained its long-distance and rural passenger trains. However, AN also became an Open Access track manager, because it remained for another four years the interstate track provider from Broken Hill in NSW west to Kalgoorlie in WA. NRC became its first and major customer.

The loss of the interstate traffic left AN financially crippled; it had incurred debt to upgrade and modernise its part of the interstate network but had lost the revenue to service that debt. In April 1996, the Coalition Federal Government commissioned a report on how to deal with AN's losses. The Brew Report's recommendations were, in essence, to set up a national track access authority to manage the whole interstate network, and to sell all parts of AN except the interstate lines, or if there were no buyers, to close "unprofitable lines".[105] (The imprecise nature of this phrase is discussed in chapter 15.)

In November 1996, the Commonwealth Government announced a decision to sell off the remaining above-rail freight and passenger businesses of AN, and all lines other than those that formed part of the interstate network. Expertise in rail operations was taken into account in accepting bidders.[106] A year later, AN's above-rail business was privatised in three parcels:

- TasRail remained an integrated rail system, sold to Australian Transport Network (ATN) for $22 million, while the land under the network was transferred to the Tasmanian Government, with ATN granted a 50-year lease for its use;[107]

- the South Australian intrastate freight and maintenance business went to Australian Southern Railroad (ASR)[108] together with branch lines and the isolated lines on the Eyre Peninsula, for $57 million;
- the long-distance passenger operations were sold to Great Southern Rail for $16.4 million.[109]

AN continued to manage its interstate tracks and infrastructure till this was passed to the newly formed Australian Rail Track Corporation (ARTC) in July 1998. After this, AN was formally closed. Nevertheless, the federal government spent $50 million through to 2003 on environmental remediation of more than 600 former AN sites.[110]

The establishment of the National Rail Corporation (NRC)

As a result of the National Freight Initiative 1989 report (described at the end of chapter 2), and a parliamentary committee's recommendations in November 1989,[111] the National Rail Corporation (NRC) was founded in 1991. The Heads of Agreement drafted at the October 1990 Special Premiers' Conference set out eight broad conditions for the new corporation, including:[112]
- the requirement of commercial viability
- a 'clean-sheet' industrial agreement
- rights of access to state assets
- a 'no-disadvantage' provision to safeguard state rail systems during a transition period.

Thus, a new organisation was wanted to manage the interstate rail business, rather than asking AN to expand its operations, specifically because this would be an opportunity to start without any entrenched (and inefficient) work practices.[113]

NRC was not intended to be the kind of all-inclusive national railway organisation that the Whitlam Government had tried to set up in the 1970s by the creation of Australian National. Jointly owned by the Commonwealth, New South Wales and Victorian governments, NRC's purpose was only to achieve a significant improvement in rail's involvement in interstate trade. The combined loss on moving nine million tonnes[114] of interstate freight on the five existing rail systems was estimated to be $377 million in 1989-90.[115] NRC was expected to break even within three years and to be fully self-sufficient by the end of a five-year 'establishment period'. A new enterprise agreement with railway employees was a key element in this intended financial recovery, along with operating efficiencies derived from capital investments, and integrated train operations (such as not needing to change crews at the state borders).

The Commonwealth Government's intent in establishing NRC was to see interstate rail become effective and more efficient, whereas the New South Wales and Victorian governments [116]

> "saw the chance to use this commitment to extract a more favourable deal. ... Effectively, they were offered the chance to off-load a loss-making [business] on very favourable terms."

The deal that resulted was that the agreed proportions of ownership and equity funding were: [117]

- Commonwealth – 54% ownership and 72% of equity funds [118]
- New South Wales – 28% ownership and 18% of equity funds
- Victoria – 13% ownership and 8% of equity funds
- Western Australia – 5% ownership and 2% of equity funds.

The Western Australian government later pulled out of the deal. Queensland agreed to it but chose not to participate, and South Australia agreed but had no freight railway of its own because that had become part of AN some twenty years earlier.

One other aspect of the agreement was that the shares that each government held in the Corporation could be disposed of as governments saw fit after the first five years, something that could and did enable the privatisation of NRC after eleven years of government ownership.

Originally conceived as a vertically integrated railway, NRC never assumed control of the interstate network due to a change of federal government and consequent policy changes, and the advent of the National Competition Policy in particular (see in chapter 5). Instead, for five years after NRC started operating its own trains, it had to get access to track on commercial terms from five different government railways. However, the change of government policy was to NRC's advantage, because it could use all its equity funds to invest in new wagons and locomotives, terminal upgrades, and new communications and information technology. The *One Nation* rail infrastructure program (see in chapter 5), announced in 1992, funded $430 million[119] of various track upgrading projects, concluding in 1995 with the conversion of the Melbourne to Adelaide line from broad to standard gauge. With hindsight, NRC would have been very stretched to fund any track upgrading, although that appears to have been the governments' initial expectation back in 1990.

The performance of National Rail

Although founded in 1991, NRC did not commence its operations until February 1993.[120] Reasons included:
- Delays in getting the Shareholders Agreement ratified by State parliaments,
- Delays in establishing the initial management team, and
- Negotiating a new Enterprise Agreement with just two unions, which had replaced up to twenty-five unions previously covering State railways.

Over the next five years, its planned establishment period, NRC gradually assumed control of more and more functions from AN and the State railways. To achieve these functions, NRC had to:

- Transfer some staff from AN and the State railways to the NRC payroll
- Arrange training for transferred train crews to get route knowledge in adjacent States, so that crews would no longer have to change over at State borders
- Negotiate with each of the five existing railways that it took the interstate traffic from to get:
  — Access for its trains to their freight terminals to load and unload, and access for its locomotives and crews to their depots for fuelling and servicing
  — Interconnecting train paths within AN's and State networks. (The complexity of this task is described in chapter 13, under *Obtaining train paths across multiple access regimes*.)

NRC initially acquired a mixed collection of locomotives and wagons from Australian National, State Rail Authority of New South Wales, and V/Line Freight, in order to take over all their interstate freight contracts. These acquisitions had to include both standard- and broad-gauge rolling-stock. Their maintenance continued to be done by the railways that originally owned them. Therefore, NRC's control of much of its fleet through to the end of the establishment period (31 January 1998) was tenuous. Consequently, aspects of its customer service were haphazard.

NRC was expected by its owners to be able to break even after three years of operation. To achieve this, the plan[121] was to gain a large increase in revenue through the provision of reliable freight services that would increase market share; the alternative of simply raising rates would have deterred new business and driven existing traffic to road. However, NRC did not significantly improve its services for some years because of transitional issues with train pathing, access to freight terminals, and quality and availability of its rolling-stock. Also, the quality (curvature and grades) of the railway lines it had to use had remained unchanged.

The interstate traffics that NRC took over from AN, FreightCorp and V/Line Freight included intermodal containers, steel, and minerals from Broken Hill (NSW) to Port Pirie (SA). By 1997, NRC trains were connecting Brisbane, Sydney, Port Kembla (NSW), Melbourne, Long Island (Vic), Adelaide, Alice Springs (NT) and Perth.

After the conversion of the Melbourne to Adelaide line from broad- to standard-gauge was completed in June 1995, and with the advent of open access, NRC first encountered competition for interstate traffic from a private sector train operator. In July, Specialised Container Transport (SCT) started providing a competing service between Melbourne, Adelaide and Perth. A year later, TNT (later Toll), which had been a party to the National Freight Initiative that had led to the creation of the NRC, began its own services in the same sector. Both companies diverted revenue from NRC, with an estimated impact on NRC's revenues of $60 million per year.[122]

A former NRC General Manager wrote about its position at that time: [123]

> "It is perhaps surprising that the long-term damage to National Rail 'brand' ... was not greater. It occurred at a time when National Rail was totally reliant for its vital operating assets – locomotives and wagons – and for the quality of its service to customers, on the 'legacy' rail systems. The average age of locomotives was over 20 years, and consequently they suffered from a very high rate of failures, the network-wide effects of which disrupted operations in terminals as well as on track. Terminals were also generally congested, and paper-based management systems were not able to provide acceptable levels of reliability. National Rail's inherited customers attacked the company's continual service failures (not unreasonably), having expected (unrealistically) a rapid improvement in service when National Rail took over the business."

With the loss of revenue due to competition, and the need for on-going external payments to secure track access due to the interstate network not coming under NRC control, the financial outlook for NRC in 1995 was somewhat different from when it started in business two years earlier. Consequently, reaching the stage of operating profitably was delayed by about four years. However, by the last full financial year (2001-02) before NRC was sold, it was reaping the benefits of new and reliable locomotives – fuel savings, reliability, and fewer longer trains – as well as benefits from several other change initiatives.

In 1997, before the end of NRC's five-year establishment period, the three government shareholders announced their intentions to sell. However, according to NRC's 1998-99 Annual Report, "the shareholders are yet to agree ... on how the sale process is to be conducted".[124] In 2002, five years after this announcement, the NRC was sold jointly with FreightCorp for a combined sum of $1.17 billion[125] to become Pacific National, a joint venture between Patrick Corporation and Toll Holdings.

Perceptions of the railways problem in the early 1990s

Both the Federal and the State Governments had been heavily involved in facilitating land transport. As was described in chapter 2, the costs of providing services by the State-owned railway systems throughout the 1970s and 1980s had always exceeded the revenues received, for a variety of reasons. By the late 1980s, "approximately one third of public sector borrowings was being spent on rail deficits".[126] Therefore, railways were seen as a problem for which something had to be done.

By contrast, during the same decades and ever since, State and Federal Governments have also spent billions of dollars on building and maintaining roads and highways. However, no direct revenue has ever been expected from the provision of these government services of road building, maintenance and traffic management. The fact that governments levy fuel taxes and vehicle registration charges, and all this money disappears into a general account, indicates that highway provision and services have not been expected to be self-funding. Hence, there has never been a need to create trading organisations to sell access to roads and highways. If they existed, they would have financial accounts, and could be held accountable for their profits or deficits. In their absence, roads and highways are not seen to create debt problems for governments.

For both road and rail, Governments have for a long time paid for the 'way', be it the railway or the roadway/highway. The difference between the two modes was that on the roads the public were free to make their own way in their own vehicles, whereas on the railways there was always a need for specialised vehicles and traffic control. Hence the colonial/state governments also provided these transport services to the public, but collected fares and freight charges to compensate.

For convenience, and probably following the example of railway organisations in Europe, colonial governments created Railways Departments that spanned all railway activities, as one of several public services. In order to defray costs, they charged for the use of railway services. Because, in accounting terms, so many railway costs are 'fixed' and 'shared', there was never any way to link directly the charges to the costs incurred. These charges came to be set at 'what the market will bear' for each type of traffic or commodity. The resulting cross-subsidisation was accepted as normal, and indeed it was invisible, and of unknown extent. It was also unknowable because the estimation of actual costs per service was too difficult. Furthermore, this was not seen to be of any importance for about 100 years, until railways were corporatised from the 1980s onward. Also, railway fares and freight charges could and did become used by governments as instruments of social and economic policy, to achieve non-transport social policy objectives.

The point needs to be made that colonial governments in Australia and New Zealand built their railways to promote economic development, which would then provide them revenue through the taxation of individuals and businesses. Hence government-owned railways were not perceived by governments as businesses operating primarily for profit. Had that been the case, it is likely that they would all have been closed in the 1970s in the face of persistent 'losses'. Instead, they were kept operating, despite the deficits, because they served the state economies. As we saw in chapter 2, State governments regulated heavy traffics to rail in order to protect lightly-built regional and rural roads, and thus avoid significant road maintenance and reconstruction costs.

However, because railways departments used the accounting methods of trading organisations, they produced annual financial reports, and hence they looked like businesses to the media and the public. Expectations of business-like performance grew amongst customers and in the business community. Problems were readily identifiable: low productivity of assets and labour (partly due to railways having common carrier obligations), and poor service (resulting from railways' culture being production-oriented rather than customer-oriented). There came to be a pervasive expectation that railways should be operated commercially, and not be 'subsidised' by having their deficits funded by their governments, and ultimately from the public purse. Since reality did not meet expectations, and there were large and measurable deficits, railways came to be perceived as a major problem.

Common ownership and management of both the rail 'way', and the services provided on it, had made any distinction between these two types of government service indistinguishable, both to the public and to governments. It was only during the 1990s and beyond, with the ideological push for microeconomic reform pointing to privatisation and vertical separation of railways, that perceptions emerged and evolved about 'above-rail' and 'below-rail', and what might be privatised successfully. As will be seen in chapters 10 and 11, mistakes have been made along the way, and there was never a 'one size fits all' solution.

The decade of the 1990s was a time of development of thinking about freight railways in Australia. Particularly at the federal level, there were multiple initiatives that overlapped in their time frames, which stemmed from Parliament and various groups within the federal bureaucracy. These are described in the next two chapters.

5. Commonwealth Initiatives on Rail Development in the 1990s

We saw in the last chapter how government railways in both Australia and New Zealand came to be viewed by 1990 as the major financial problem in land transport. In Australia, the 1990s was a decade of Commonwealth Government policy initiatives on land transport, and investigations into railways initiated by the Government or by Parliament. In this chapter, each of these is looked at in mostly chronological order.

The Industry Commission's 1991 Report – 'Rail Transport'

In the context of the railways (and only the railways) being seen as the major problem in land transport, in May 1990 the Commonwealth's Industry Commission was asked[127]

> "to inquire into and report on factors leading to inefficient resource use in Australian railways, and to recommend action to reduce or remove such inefficiencies. Freight, urban and non-urban passenger rail services were to be covered. Specific issues set down in the terms of reference included management and work practices, pricing

policies, structural impediments to efficient operations, the funding of capital expenditure, regulations requiring some commodities to be transported by rail, and the effect that rail charges and regulations have on competing modes of transport."

The Industry Commission consulted widely and received some 170 submissions from governments and railway users. This was in the year before the National Rail Corporation was founded, so it uncovered user dissatisfaction with State Railways' performance in both the interstate and intrastate sectors. Its report summarised five major problems:[128]

"The ability of railways to meet the expectations of their customers is hampered by mistakes made in the past, and a continued reluctance of State governments to implement reforms which, although difficult, are essential to ensure the future viability of railways. In particular:
- the operating methods of railways have been changed only slowly, even though technological advances should have allowed large reductions in operating costs;
- many lines and services which are no longer viable have not been closed or discontinued, thereby reducing the ability of the remainder of the rail system to operate efficiently;
- fares and freight rates have not been flexible enough to obtain optimal use of the railway rolling stock and infrastructure;
- capital has been mis-invested; and
- governments have presented rail administrators with conflicting social and financial objectives, making it difficult for them to set and achieve efficiency goals."

BHP Transport, part of a major Australian steel producer, and a major interstate rail user, said in its submission,[129] that in addition to the inefficiency of transferring its freight between different gauges:

> "Rail efficiency has been of a low standard when compared to its main competitor, road. From a user's viewpoint, the problem seems to be traced to several institutionalised factors in the structure of railroads in Australia.
> 1. Five Government systems operating to a large extent independently of each other.
> 2. Government ownership introducing a mix of commercial and social demands.
> 3. Traditionally structured and highly unionised workforces with a large number of unions often with individual agendas.
> 4. Organisation structures which have not provided adequate linkages to market requirements.
> 5. The relatively low priority traditionally afforded research and development in the industry, a trend which is fortunately changing."
>
> "The management structure has allowed inefficiencies to manifest themselves in:
> - Inadequate and poorly maintained infrastructure causing capacity and speed restrictions.
> - Lower running priorities on interstate freight behind intrastate freight or passenger trains.
> - Inefficient and inadequate rolling stock.
> - The inability to monitor wagon movements effectively across state borders.
> - Little apparent management accountability for performance.
> - Poor management information systems and responsiveness. (Submission 32, pp.10, 11)"

The Industry Commission saw extensive reform of government railways as essential:[130]

> "Governments and railways are aware of many of these shortcomings and are attempting to address them through commercialisation, better management, improved work practices, reduced staff levels, and the replacement and upgrading of obsolete equipment.
>
> However, the Commission is of the view that such changes on their own will not be sufficient to achieve the substantial and sustained reform needed to ensure a viable railway system for the next century. In addition, the vigour with which such changes are being implemented varies considerably between different Australian rail systems.
>
> In the past railways have been used frequently as instruments of government social policy. To achieve reform there must be fundamental changes for each system in the relationships between the government and the rail authority, the government and the rail unions, and the government and rail customers. Rail authorities, unions and customers all have to be convinced that the rail system will be run as a commercial business and that the government will not override the actions of railway managers, even if changes in services do not suit its political agenda. Fundamental changes will be necessary."

In the Overview section of the report the Industry Commission said:[131]

> "There is no easy solution to railways' problems. The recommendations put forward in this report do not offer a painless way of overcoming the substantial problems that Australian railways face today and which have been allowed to accumulate over many decades. The Commission's recommendations imply hard decisions and difficult change for governments, railway management, rail employees and rail passengers.

> The recommendations involve major rationalisation of Australian railways. But ... substantial benefits are available to the community by implementing them."

The Commission made 27 recommendations, including these relating to freight transport:

> "3.1   The Commission recommends that railways be fully commercialised through their being corporatised, including incorporation under the corporations law. These processes of corporatisation and incorporation should be completed within three years."

> "5.1   The Commission recommends the introduction of road user charges which reflect more accurately the amount of road use and pavement damage caused by all classes of vehicles. A national vehicle registration scheme is a key element in achieving these changes."

> "5.2   The Commission recommends that State and Territory laws be amended to provide local governments, for all roads under their control, with effective capacity to impose specific pavement damage and externality charges on heavy vehicles. Such changes should be levied on the principals for whom the road haulage is provided. A process of appeal should be set up to settle disputes between the local authority and the principals responsible for the pavement damage or externalities."

> "10.1   The Commission recommends that State governments eliminate all regulation of traffics to rail, with the possible exception of dangerous goods, at the same time as appropriate road user charging mechanisms for pavement damage and externalities are introduced."

> "10.3   The Commission recommends that governments eliminate all their subsidies to bulk rail freight, in the first instance by not restraining their rail authorities

from reducing costs to international best practice. This reduction should be achieved within three years. During the transition period, authorities should refrain from increasing average bulk freight rates (in dollar terms)."

"11.2   The Commission recommends that there should be no restrictions on private ownership and operation of freight terminals, including common-user loading/unloading facilities."

"12.1   The Commission recommends that owners of railway tracks (whether they be governments, rail authorities or private owners) be required to allow access by other organisations (whether public or private) to operate on their tracks, subject only to capacity being available   and negotiation of a commercial agreement which sets the prices and conditions for access. The Commonwealth Government should require open access on lines controlled by AN and the NRC and, if necessary, should contemplate using its powers (over interstate trade and   international trade) to achieve open access elsewhere."

"12.2   The Commission recommends that each rail authority be required to operate its infrastructure network as a separate business centre, and to publish separate accounts concerning it."

"12.3   The Commission recommends that Commonwealth and State legislation be changed so that the coverage of the Trade Practices Act extends to railway authorities, whether incorporated under the corporations law or not. The Act should also provide the power to facilitate the settlement of disputes concerning monopoly pricing and anti-competitive behaviour (including access to track)."

Notwithstanding that issues to do with roads and highways were outside its brief, the Industry Commission recognised that subsidies provided to one mode do influence the business levels on the other. Some submissions said rail was more subsidised than road, others said the opposite. Rather than see subsidies persist, the Commission favoured their complete removal:[132]

> "Both the subsidisation of rail services and inadequate charges for heavy road vehicles must be eliminated to allow more equitable competition between modes."

> "Removing all subsidies is a far simpler policy option which increases economic efficiency compared to providing subsidies to both road and rail transport."

This was the reason for recommendation 5.1, because instituting Road User Charges, based on distance travelled and laden axle-weights, would be the best way to have road carriers pay appropriately. It is the system that has been in use in New Zealand since 1978. However, in the Australian context, it was aspirational, rather than practical, given the outcomes of the 1979 and 1988 truckies' blockades of the Hume and other highways. (See in chapter 8, under *The Need for Road Reform*).

The Commission noted also that freight transport users:[133]

> "... do not meet the opportunity cost of the capital embedded in the rail and road networks. The failure of either mode to meet these opportunity costs discourages the private sector from providing road and rail infrastructure; that function is left to the government sector."

This was an unusual perspective, ignorant of an historic market failure. The private sector had failed financially over a century ago in the provision of rail and road networks. Hence governments had taken on this role in the public interest. This is the norm in most areas of the world other than North America. Who would have known that the private sector was still "discouraged" in this matter?

It is noteworthy that although the Commission saw the desirability of open access on railways, it did not recommend vertical separation to achieve it. Given that there was no effective open access railway regime anywhere in the world at that time,[134] because it was just a concept, this was an understandable omission.

The Commission appeared to assume the continued existence of the State Railways plus the NRC, and there was no recommendation for privatisation.

The Industry Commission was directed to look into only regulatory, structural and economic issues affecting the railway industry. Others in the transport research community had looked at the physical aspects of the Interstate Rail Network in particular, and compared it to the National Highway System. They saw the effects of capital investment in highways, and the lack of it in railways – effects which the Commonwealth government and its advisors apparently could not see. Dr Philip Laird, a prolific analyst and writer about the situation of land transport in Australia, summed up the situation in the early 1990s thus:[135]

> "Rail's relative productivity and competitiveness has suffered as its infrastructure has become progressively more outmoded compared with the ever-improving National Highway System. In these circumstances, it is hardly surprising that rail has lost substantial market share to road notwithstanding significant reforms to rail operating practices and major labour-shedding in the rail work force over the past decade. By way of example, rail's modal share of Sydney-Melbourne land freight has fallen from about 43% in 1973-74 to just 21% in 1991-92." [136]

The One Nation Program

Paul Keating became the Labor Prime Minister of Australia on 20 December 1991. Only two months later, on 26 February 1992, he released *One Nation,* an economic program for the creation of 800,000 jobs by 1996. This was intended to be a fiscal stimulus at a time when Australia was in a prolonged economic recession, having had eight quarters of declining economic growth. In the past year, the numbers of unemployed had doubled, reaching 10%.

The *One Nation* document also had another agenda. Under the heading of Microeconomic Reform, it announced some significant changes:[137]

> "When this Government came into office the problem of inefficient performance was endemic in areas shielded from competition - including domestic aviation, electricity supply, shipping, railways, and telecommunications...As in all developed economies, these industries provide vital inputs to all our major export and import competing sectors. Australia was placed at a substantial disadvantage in competing against imports at home and in export markets.
>
> The Government has established a program of disposal of those businesses for which there is no compelling reason for Commonwealth ownership. For those enterprises retained in the public sector it has defined clearly the social goals to be pursued and reformed their accountability framework."

The *One Nation* document outlined Commonwealth spending proposals in several areas, including land transport, where the spending was to be entirely for infrastructure development. This included $430 million for a three-year rail upgrading program covering the Melbourne to Adelaide conversion from broad- to standard-gauge, standard-gauge access to Brisbane's main port, and various smaller upgrading

5. Commonwealth Initiatives

projects on the Melbourne-Sydney-Brisbane rail lines.

The National Rail Corporation had been founded the year before and was in the process of getting established. The *One Nation* funding was notable for being an equity injection into NRC, which project-managed the upgrades, rather than being in the usual form of interest-bearing loans. It looked as though the Commonwealth Government had responded to the call for leadership in funding the Interstate Rail Network, the *One Nation* program being the first ever Commonwealth rail investment initiative of nation-wide scope. To quote from a Parliamentary Research Paper:[138]

> "It has been portrayed as a new era of Commonwealth involvement in Australian rail – one of Government confidence in the industry and in its potential and an implicit acknowledgement that the time had come for it to assist intercapital rail infrastructure catch up with the now high design standards prevailing on the National Highways System."

The reality was different. During the years that $430 million was spent on rail projects, funded by *One Nation*, much more was spent from the same program on road projects:[139]

> "$602 million was allocated to road spending over the period 1991-92 to 1993-94, mainly to the national highway system, while an additional $255 million was allocated to road maintenance over this period."

Thus, the *One Nation* spending on rail was comparatively modest, thinly spread, and not enough to make much of a difference, except to enable competition on the Melbourne to Perth route by removing the break-of-gauge. From the Government's perspective, the *One Nation* program had achieved the objective of restimulating the economy, and did not need to be continued. Thus, after the *One Nation* rail spending was completed in 1995, the Commonwealth did not invest any more in rail until 1999.[140] That pause in investment in rail was not by chance. Advice on the condition of railway networks was by then available from the Bureau of Transport and Communications Economics, but this advice was ignored.

The adequacy of the interstate rail network

In 1994, the Commonwealth's Bureau of Transport and Communications Economics (BTCE) was asked by the National Transport Planning Taskforce "to undertake an assessment of the adequacy of transport infrastructure in Australia for the next 20 years." [141] The assessment covered four modes of transport – road, rail, sea and air – with the focus on freight. The BTCE was not asked how to consider any interdependencies between the modes to advise on how best meet the total future demand for freight transport, so it assessed the adequacy of each mode separately against their separate growth forecasts. It published its reports in 1995 including one titled *Adequacy of transport infrastructure – Rail*.

In order to reduce the size of the task, the BTCE selected only the rail lines connecting the State Capitals, plus Brisbane to Cairns. It assumed that the *One Nation* program of investments for 1992 to 1995 would be completed, and also the Queensland Government's $580 million mainline upgrading program 1992 to 1997.

It looked at two concepts of technical adequacy:
- that relating to the physical infrastructure characteristics which drive track and structure maintenance requirements, and
- that of the performance (output) of the infrastructure, meaning how the quality of the infrastructure constrains average train speeds and point-to-point times, and the potential economies of scale from increasing train lengths.

5. Commonwealth Initiatives

In its Summary of Findings, the BTCE wrote:[142]

> "Physical deficiency indicators show that most of the deficiencies in track infrastructure occur along corridors east of Adelaide. ... [but] All corridors have sufficient capacity to cope with the expected demand over the coming 20 years."

> "About $3.2B of investment [with benefits exceeding costs] in rail infrastructure is estimated to be warranted over the next 20 years. Sydney-Melbourne ($1.0B) and Sydney-Brisbane ($1.0B) are each estimated to warrant some 30 per cent of this. Melbourne-Adelaide ($0.5B), Brisbane-Cairns ($0.4B) and Adelaide-Perth ($0.3B) require lesser amounts. This proposed investment program is on about the same scale as One Nation funds for rail, requiring on average $150M annual expenditure over the planning period of 20 years. The One Nation rail investment program amounted to $429M over a 3 year period, representing on average of $142M expenditure per year."

> "Maintenance costs are estimated to amount to around $3.5B over the 20 year study period if the infrastructure projects suggested as warranted in this study are implemented. If no investments in infrastructure are undertaken, maintenance costs are forecast to be some $1B higher over the period."

This looked like a clear and reasonable course of action for the Commonwealth government to commit to and undertake, if it wanted to bring the Interstate Rail Network up to a standard that would enable railways to compete on a more equal basis with the National Highway System. However, in 1995, there was no clear direction on the future of the Interstate Rail Network. Agreement between the Commonwealth and States to create the ARTC did not come till September 1997, when the Australian Transport Council (ATC) met for the 'National Rail Summit' (see below).

Perhaps the deciding factor was this statement also in the BTCE report on rail adequacy, under the heading of Key Findings:[143]

> "As with sea ports, the major factor which underlies the need for new infrastructure investments is the necessity to maintain and improve rails' level of service. Technical capacity of the rail infrastructure should handle the projected demand. This contrasts with intercity roads, urban roads, and air ports where it is the growth in projected demand which drives the need for infrastructure expansion."

Given this statement, it would have been silly, from the Commonwealth's perspective, to invest in improving the railway network when the immediate need was apparently to invest in roads to meet the projected demand. Investing in rail capacity instead, to enable better service, would have taken years to make a difference to modal shares. The fundamental flaw in the BTCE's comment on rail adequacy was in its reliance on the freight projections. The lack of Commonwealth leadership and integrated planning for land transport infrastructure would have ensured that there was an inherent assumption in the projections that there would be no change to these trends. Hence, these projections for the next two decades would have been based on the growth trends over the previous two decades. Thus, the lack of 'thinking outside the square' created a self-fulfilling prophecy in which the roads would continue to carry more and more interstate freight compared to railways.

The National Competition Policy (NCP)

In Australia, the impetus for the various changes to government railways has been attributed[144] to the National Competition Policy. In 1992, (Labor) Prime Minister Keating established the National Competition Policy Review, which delivered its report in August 1993. Known as the Hilmer Report (taking the name of the committee chairman), it advocated, of particular relevance to railways:[145]

- "Application of competitive neutrality principles so government businesses do not enjoy a competitive advantage over their private sector competitors simply as a result of public sector ownership,
- Restructuring of public monopoly businesses to increase competition,
- Provision for third party access to nationally significant infrastructure."

These reforms were included in the Commonwealth Competition Policy Reform Act 1995, which, with supplementary agreements, obliged the State governments to enact legislation to give effect to these reforms. How this was to be achieved was for the States to decide. Those States that were assessed as having met the requirements were eligible to receive indexed funding from the Commonwealth.

Inherent in the thinking behind the National Competition Policy in relation to government businesses was an assumption that there must be more efficient ownership structures available than government ownership. It became a widely held view that government businesses could be managed more productively as companies, using the economies of scope, risk management and industrial relations practices of the private sector.

The Competition Policy Reform Act was passed in July 1995, the same month in which the very first private freight train operator (SCT) started services that competed with NRC. Until that time, all freight railway systems in Australia were still government-owned, and most were still vertically integrated. The Act obliged them all to provide third party access to rail infrastructure for commercial purposes (as opposed to just allowing heritage operators to operate trains for enthusiasts). Up to that time, the only train operator granted access to State networks was the NRC, which was charged essentially at prices that were whatever the market would bear. The Act required the State railways to develop commercial methods to manage track access, including pricing regimes that would be acceptable to the then recently-formed Australian Competition and Consumer Commission (ACCC).

Australian National established its Track Access Unit in 1995 to manage track access independently of its residual train operation activities after it lost its interstate business to NRC. A year later, New South Wales and Victoria each restructured their rail organisations to separate the above-rail from the below-rail. WestRail and Queensland Rail did not separate vertically until quite some years later.

The National Rail Summit of 1997

The Australian Transport Council's meeting of Commonwealth and State Transport Ministers on 10 September 1997 was dubbed the 'National Rail Summit'. Rail Reform objectives that were agreed upon included:[146]

- a national interstate network would be designated the Defined Interstate Rail Network (DIRN) which runs from Perth to Brisbane
- investment would focus on this network
- the most urgent need was for the DIRN to be operated as a single network with respect to investment, access and pricing, to replace the discrete state-based systems
- safety, and operational practices and standards on the DIRN would be made more uniform
- operators would be able to access the network through a single point of entry, the so-called one-stop-shop, to provide seamless access and operations across the network, and
- new infrastructure and access arrangements would include commercial principles, mechanisms and incentives in the relationship between track management and operators.

There were two major outcomes from the National Rail Summit: the creation of the ARTC (described in chapter 9), and the start of a study to review safety, technical and operational standards and procedures, focusing on impediments to efficiency in the interstate rail network. The outcome, seven years later, was the acceptance of a National Code on Rail Safety Regulation.

Research into the quality of rail freight service

In 1997, the Commonwealth's Bureau of Transport and Communications Economics (BTCE) published a report *Quality of Rail Service: The Customer's Perspective.* It was not something that had been sought by the rail freight industry or its customers, but instead it was one of series of BTCE research project reports on service quality in the transport and communications sectors, focussing particularly on government trading enterprises.[147] Nevertheless, it identified and filled a gap in the body of knowledge about potential reporting on railway performance, that of the customer's viewpoint.

Governments, as owners of railways at the time, were interested only in financial results. In addition to these, railway management produced data about only operational aspects, to assess efficiency levels in operations. For example, two commonly used measures were:
- punctuality of trains, because late trains incurred additional costs for crewing, as well as causing inefficiencies in the re-allocation of locos and wagons;
- availability of wagons – a measure of how well the function of repairing the wagon fleet was keeping up with demand, i.e., the rate at which operational wagons were being withdrawn temporarily from the active fleet for minor repairs and routine mechanical servicing.

The BTCE commented,[148] quite reasonably from the customer perspective on these measures, that

> "punctuality indicators do not show the percentage of freight made available to customers on time, [and] wagon availability figures do not show whether available cargo space is adequate."

Thus, the complete lack of data about rail freight customer service obscured the reality of a connection between service performance and financial results. This served to perpetuate governments' blindness in the 1990s to the need for investment in improving railway networks just to enable railways to compete more effectively against road carriers.

The BTCE wanted to identify the needs and priorities of users of rail freight services. It focussed on non-bulk freight (therefore excluding coal, grains and petroleum) because non-bulk was where there were modal options. It surveyed freight-forwarding companies, as both the major and the most discerning rail freight customers, about what features of rail freight service ranked in their decisions on modal choice for their customers' freight. Punctuality, meaning the on-time availability of freight at destination terminals, was the most critical. Late-arriving trains could cause problems for freight forwarding companies in scheduling their own equipment and staff, problems that could snowball during the day, impacting the quality of service to their customers. The survey found three other features were wanted, of equal importance:

- the care taken of freight and containers
- rail terminal efficiency, in terms of truck turnaround times, and
- supply of wagons for loading, when and where they were ordered.

The Neville Report – *Tracking Australia*

Two reports are mentioned in chapter 4 in the context of advising the federal government to take the lead in developing an integrated strategic planning capability for land transport. One of these reports was titled *Tracking Australia,* published in July 1998 by a House of Representatives Standing Committee, and tabled in Parliament in August 1998.[149] Because it was chaired by National[150] MP Paul Neville, it became known also as the Neville Report.

Sub-titled *"An Inquiry into the Role of Rail in the National Transport Network"*, its focus was on national interstate rail services, and what was required to ensure their on-going viability. Paul Neville, when discussing the report in Parliament on 8 February 1999, expressed his concern thus:[151]

> "If we are serious about rail being able to compete with modern road transport, if we are serious about the efficient distribution of bulk commodities, if we are serious about our commitments to the environment, if we are serious about road safety and if we are serious about the economic efficiency of Australia, the Australian rail system must be addressed."

The Neville Report was strongly critical of the implicit federal government policy on land transport, which was heavily weighted toward investment in highways. It warned:[152]

> "Without urgent and substantial investment in this infrastructure, major sections of the national rail network are likely to become irretrievable within ten years. In this context, the rationale for increased investment in rail infrastructure has to be about averting the potentially enormous costs of diminished or defunct rail services between major cities on the eastern seaboard, including increased road construction and maintenance, and the negative externalities associated with large and growing volumes of road traffic."

"There is no question that governments could and should be doing more, in terms of effective investment in and utilisation of Australia's public use rail infrastructure. For the Commonwealth, this means in the first instance the development of a national, strategic approach to transport planning which clearly defines and supports a role for rail in the national transport system, and in the second instance, the recognition of and commitment to fulfilling its responsibilities in that regard."

"The Commonwealth then has to develop a strategy to address the nation's considerable rail infrastructure needs."

"The Commonwealth needs to substantially increase the amount of funding allocated for investment in, and the longer term maintenance of, public use rail infrastructure."

Recommendation 14 of the Neville Report specified the scale of investment required:

"The committee recommends that the Commonwealth:
- undertake responsibility for investment in the declared national track;
- allocate, in addition to the $250 million committed to the Australian Rail Track Corporation in 1997–98, a further $750 million over three years for investment in the national track to be expended according to priorities developed by the Commonwealth and States/Territories; and
- allocate, on an agreed basis, an additional $2 billion over ten years from 2001 for investment in rail infrastructure of national strategic importance, to be directed primarily to the national track, and with provision for designated tracks of national importance (TONIs)."

5. Commonwealth Initiatives

Reforms in the 1990s had transformed the structure and operations of Australia's railways. The Productivity Commission found that there were significant improvements in the productivity of government-owned railways providing freight and passenger services over the period 1989-1990 to 1997-1998.[153] It found that the average annual growth in productivity was around 8%. Efficiencies in railway operating performance had included the replacement of manned signal boxes at stations with area signal boxes. These used modern technologies to remotely control colour-light signals and turnouts powered by electric motors, which created much efficiency in the use of labour.

However, in 1998, there was still a strong reluctance by the Coalition federal government to invest in any aspect of the railway industry while it continued to run up deficits, even if such investments could reduce those deficits by improving productivity. Although it owned the newly created Australian Rail Track Corporation (ARTC), its expectation was that the ARTC should be able to attract private sector investment for developing its network. Furthermore, the Coalition government's over-riding concern, with an election due in October 1998, was to constrain federal government spending to maintain surpluses. Investing $3 billion in rail networks would have been incompatible with its neoliberal ideology.

There was no formal response from the Coalition government to the Neville Report until April 2000. (See *'The Response from the Commonwealth Government'* in the next chapter.) However, two months before the Neville Report was tabled in Parliament, Prime Minister John Howard announced a private sector taskforce "to evaluate how governments can better facilitate viable major rail investment proposals developed by the private sector."[154] Also, within a month after the release of the Neville Report, the Federal Treasurer Peter Costello commissioned another study, this time from the Productivity Commission, into Progress in Rail Reform. (The report from this study is discussed in some detail below.)

The Smorgon Report – *Revitalising Rail: The Private Sector Solution*

The Rail Projects Task Force produced the Smorgon Report in May 1999 with 30 recommendations. It had been asked to advise on:

- The scope for private sector investment, and
- Unwanted barriers to private sector investment and what governments could do to remove these barriers.

The Task Force found barriers and structured its recommendations under headings describing these barriers. These are quoted below, but only recommendations relevant to the rail freight industry are included here:[155]

> "BARRIER 1: The lack of an integrated, national transport strategy
>
> *Recommendation 1: National Transport Strategy*
>
> The Commonwealth Government takes the lead in developing an economically-driven National Transport Strategy that will secure a seamless domestic transport system embracing road, rail, sea and air transport, and provide for the entry and exit of people and goods by sea and air at world competitive standards.
>
> *Recommendation 2: Balance road/rail funding*
>
> The Commonwealth Government develops a framework for assessing the allocation of its funding of road and rail projects on the basis of their relative efficiencies, using agreed and published 'level playing field' criteria.
>
> *Recommendation 3: A national rail authority*
>
> The Commonwealth, after appropriate negotiations with the other Governments, establishes and funds a national authority to:
>
> - administer the rail elements of the National Transport Strategy
> - acquire all national rail corridors and associated infrastructure

- ensure the efficient use of the existing system and its safety of operation, and recommend proposals for enhancement
- ensure that the infrastructure is used to the fullest advantage.

Recommendation 4: Framework for investment
Governments develop an appropriate framework for private and public sector investment that includes efficient taxing and charging regimes and competitive neutrality between government agencies and the private sector.

Recommendation 5: External benefits and costs
External benefits and costs of transport options be evaluated from a national perspective and in a transparent and consistent manner. These external benefits and costs to include those associated with accidents, congestion, pollution, greenhouse gas emissions, noise, reductions in the need for other infrastructure, and impacts on industrial development, employment and regional development.

Recommendation 6: Government support for major projects
The extent and nature of Commonwealth Government support for private sector proposals to develop major new interstate rail links be assessed against their economic, financial and social merit and conformity with the National Transport Strategy.

If the proposal is of strategic or national significance and warrants Commonwealth Government support, there should be greater flexibility to provide that support in the form best suited to project requirements, including direct financial support tailored to cash flow.

Recommendation 7: Inland Rail Bridge
If the feasibility studies being undertaken for the current two 'inland rail bridge' proposals establish that this concept has commercial merit, the Commonwealth should undertake an assessment of the case for government support in line with Recommendation 6.

Recommendation 8: Darwin to Alice Springs rail link
If the current level of government support offered to the private sector is found to be not sufficient for the Darwin to Alice Springs rail link to proceed, the Commonwealth should not commit any significant additional support without first undertaking an assessment in line with Recommendation 6."

"**BARRIER 2: Substandard national track**
Recommendation 14: Accelerate existing capital program
The $250 million already committed by the Commonwealth Government to upgrade the national track be brought forward for completion by December 2000 rather than by June 2002.

Recommendation 15: A major additional capital injection
The Commonwealth commits to spending an additional $470 million by June 2002 to bring the national track to a standard where it can provide a competitive and sustainable alternative to road transport.

- funding should be conditional on State Governments cooperating to achieve a number of other vital rail reforms-see Recommendations 16, 17, 27-30.

Recommendation 16: Strengthen ARTC
Commonwealth, State and Territory Governments confirm their commitment to the Australian Rail Track Corporation (ARTC) as a 'one-stop shop' to control the national track.

5. Commonwealth Initiatives

The corporation's main features being:
- Commonwealth Government ownership, with Ministers as shareholders and an independent board
- to control, manage and maintain the national track and associated corridors, taking account of the characteristics of the metropolitan systems with which the national network must interface
- a charter to make commercial decisions within a market environment influenced by government policies and support
- prohibited, by its charter, from owning or providing 'above' rail operations
- an access regime conforming with Competition Policy guidelines
- a long term outlook and expectation of continued operation, particularly the ability to negotiate long term agreements
- required to provide a 3-year business plan to the Commonwealth Government outlining the major features of its operations including its investment plans and resultant commercial implications.

Recommendation 17: The integrity of the national network

To maintain a genuine national network consisting initially of the track joining the mainland State capital cities and their ports, with connecting lines to Whyalla, Port Kembla, Newcastle, Alice Springs, Westernport and Kwinana:
- the New South Wales, Queensland and Western Australian Governments immediately transfer control of their components of the national track to the ARTC
- the Commonwealth should not transfer control of the Tarcoola-Alice Springs component of the national track from the ARTC to a successful bidder

for the development of the Alice Springs to Darwin rail link but rather permit access on commercial terms
- the Western Australian Government should not transfer control of the Kalgoorlie-Perth component of the national track to a successful bidder for WestRail
- the ARTC should be consulted if any Government proposes to sell track or land corridors, which may be suitable as components of the national track, particularly in urban areas."

"**BARRIER 3: A distorted investment environment**"
Under this heading were six recommendations covering details of business taxation law and administration, and of competition policy, that are of little importance for this story.

"**BARRIER 4: Unhelpful government project development processes**"
Under this heading were three recommendations seeking changes to bureaucratic processes.

"**BARRIER 5: Unfair competitive advantages for government operators**
Recommendation 27: Privatisation
All Commonwealth and State Government rail freight operators should be privatised.

Bidders for government rail freight operators should have no government ownership or control.

Until privatisation is achieved, rail operators in public ownership must be subject to competition from private operators on a level playing field including equal access to government-assisted transport services."

5. Commonwealth Initiatives

"**BARRIER 6: Inconsistent regulations and standards**

Recommendation 28: National approach to regulation and standards

Intervention by governments in the rail industry in pursuit of more efficient operations should be assessed on a case-by-case basis. Where a case can be clearly made, a national approach should be adopted in line with the objectives of the National Transport Strategy.

To avoid unnecessary differences and inconsistencies between jurisdictions, there must be a national mechanism for creating and maintaining regulations and standards.

Recommendation 29: National safety regulator

As a useful first step towards a single national rail safety regulator, the Commonwealth take a leadership role in establishing a national rail safety regulator to hold appropriate regulatory control, including accreditation, over ARTC and operators on the national network by December 1999. Specifically, the regulator will:

- enhance safe operations on the national rail network
- investigate, by a transparent process, any rail accident or incident on the national network
- establish effective interface safety management with relevant State safety regulators
- be prepared to transfer its investigation function to an independent, and possibly multi-modal, agency.

Recommendation 30: Transfer of State safety regulatory functions

The State Governments immediately establish timetables and mechanisms for transferring their rail safety regulatory functions to the national safety regulator."

The Coalition Commonwealth Government delayed its response to the Smorgon Report, as it had done with the

Neville Report, and would do so again with the Productivity Commission's report.

The Productivity Commission's 1999 Report – *Progress in Rail Reform*

Soon after the ARTC started operations in July 1998 on the former AN network, but still while the state-owned railways were in existence, the Federal Coalition Treasurer Peter Costello asked the Productivity Commission (PC) to inquire and report within a year on progress in rail reform. A copy of the Terms of Reference is shown on the next page.

The government's agenda was evident in the use of terms such as "performance", "efficiency", and "best practice". (We see the significance of these terms at the start of chapter 13). In essence, its concern was to reduce the railway deficits payable by governments, and perhaps also to lower the costs for freight shippers. However, there was no interest in improving the effectiveness of railways, i.e., how well they could meet the service needs of existing and potential customers, and possibly compete more effectively with road. The Terms of Reference perhaps revealed a bias in the Coalition Federal government towards roads and private sector activity, and against railways which were then still mostly public-sector activities.

5. Commonwealth Initiatives

The Terms of Reference

I, PETER COSTELLO, Treasurer, pursuant to Part 3 of the *Productivity Commission Act* 1998, hereby refer progress in rail reform to the Commission for inquiry and report within twelve months of receipt of this reference. The Commission is to hold hearings for the purposes of the inquiry.

Background

2. Australia's rail network forms a crucial part of Australia's transport infrastructure. Past reforms have delivered significant improvements in the operation of Australia's rail systems.

   However, the pace and nature of the reforms vary between systems. Performances in some areas continue to be below world's best practice. There is a need to undertake a stocktake of progress in rail reform to identify areas, including both urban passengers and freight, where further action is most needed. The Industry Commission last undertook a stocktake of progress in rail reform in 1991.

Scope of Inquiry

3. In undertaking this inquiry, the Commission should identify progress made in rail reform as well as areas which could be subject to further reforms and the benefits of pursuing further reforms. The Commission should also clearly differentiate its analysis of interstate rail operations from intrastate and urban rail operations.

4. The Commission should report on:
   (a) recent reform initiatives and their implications;
   (b) the current structure of the rail industry, including the regulatory environment;
   (c) structural and operational rigidities and impediments which constrain the efficiency and development of the rail industry;
   (d) the strengths and weaknesses of the Australian rail industry, drawing on international and intermodal comparisons where appropriate;
   (e) the operation of third party access regimes for the interstate and intrastate rail freight networks;
   (f) the implications of the changing role of the Commonwealth, the States and the private sector in rail operations and ownership;
   (g) the implications for rail transport services and the economy generally of regulations, charges and arrangements affecting competing and complementary modes of transport; and
   (h) international best practice in rail and impediments to achieving best practice in Australia.

5. The Commission should also:
   (a) report on implementation strategies for any measures recommended by the Commission;
   (b) take account of any recent studies undertaken; and
   (c) have regard to the established economic, social, regional development and environmental objectives of governments.

6. The Commission's recommendations will be considered by the Government and the Government's response shall be announced as soon as possible after the receipt of the Commission's report.

PETER COSTELLO
5 August 1998

The main topics

The PC inquiry was one of several undertaken into the structure and performance of the Australian rail industry during the 1990s, and it was probably the most thorough. It covered freight and passenger rail systems, and interstate, intrastate and urban rail operations, but with a key focus on freight rail. The PC considered previous studies. The scope of its inquiry did not need to be as broad as for the 1991 inquiry, because many of the 'low-hanging fruit' (such as inefficient work practices, poor asset utilisation, and the effects of regulations) had by then been picked off. It consulted widely, receiving 128 submissions from individuals and organisations during its inquiry[156], reflecting a broad range of industry experience and opinions. This resulted in some contradictory evidence, which it was able to rationalise and present in terms of what was suitable for some situations was unsuitable for others. Although the Terms of Reference did not include the word "competition", this topic dominated the PC's report, *Progress in Rail Reform (PIRR)*. Stemming from the National Competition Policy at the beginning of the decade, competition was still very much seen as the panacea for improving performance and reducing deficits in the rail industry. The PC wrote, in its Overview of *PIRR* [157]:

> "The emphasis in rail reform has been on introducing competition between train operators on the same track ... by implementing access regimes and reforming the structure of railways. ... But, access regulation and vertical separation may be less effective in markets where there is limited scope for more than train operator, effective competition from other modes of transport, and/or competition in downstream markets. ... No single structure or access regime is appropriate for all networks."

Competitive neutrality (another topic discussed in detail in chapter 13) was of concern to many in the transport industry

5. Commonwealth Initiatives

generally, and to the PC. In relation to the lack of competitive neutrality between rail and road, and its causes, the PC wrote[158]:

> "Government decisions relating to investment, taxes and charges, access regimes and safety regulations affect competitive neutrality between road and rail transport.
>
> There are still concerns over the different funding criteria applied to road and rail and the comparative levels of government investment in each ... evidence suggests there has been inadequate investment in some parts of the rail network.
>
> Notwithstanding recent reforms, heavy vehicle charges do not cover the full costs of road usage, including road and bridge wear, pollution, accidents and congestion.
>
> These factors disadvantage rail compared to road. But large subsidies also are provided to rail.
>
> Adopting a more commercial approach to the provision of both rail and road would overcome competitive neutrality concerns."

Given that the federal government's ostensible agenda was the reform of rail, it was perhaps surprising for the PC to include a whole chapter in its report on the lack of competitive neutrality between road and rail, leading to some general recommendations for the government to do something about the recovery of its costs for highways. (See in the next chapter, under *The Response from the Commonwealth Government*.)

However, what the PC failed to appreciate and comment on in its discussion about subsidies to both the road and rail industries, was the effects of those subsidies, and how they were much more effective in promoting the transport of non-bulk freight by road. The subsidies provided to road transport, then and now, were by way of investments in highways (without any direct recovery of costs from users) to create:

- strong pavements to withstand the potential damage caused by heavy axle-loads, and
- eased curves, multiple lanes and town bypasses, so that trucks could travel without hindrances, minimising their travel times from A to B, and maximising the distances travelled per driver-hour.

These investments were therefore **enabling** for the road industry: enabling technical efficiencies of longer vehicle combinations with heavier gross weights, and over time, enabling gains in driver productivity. By contrast, the subsidies paid to government-owned railways were mostly **retrospective**, to make up for the deficits incurred. These subsidies allowed the railway organisations to keep trading, but they were definitely not investments in infrastructure or assets. They achieved nothing toward the removal of the steep grades and the many curves of century-old railway route alignments, which necessitated that freight trains continued to run as slowly as they did generations before.

The recommendations

The recommendations in *PIRR* that relate to rail freight business reform, and their relevance follows.

- *"Recommendation 6.2: Train operations should be vertically separated from track infrastructure on the entire interstate network. The infrastructure should be managed by a single network manager."* In 1998/99 the ARTC had not yet negotiated leases from the States to be able to fully manage sections of the interstate network that it did not own, and the PC had heard the frustration of train operators having to negotiate interstate train paths with individual State-based railways. These issues were mostly resolved by 2004 when the ARTC had leased the main lines in the Victorian and NSW networks, and finally in 2010 when it leased the section of track from the Queensland/NSW border to Brisbane.

- *"Recommendation 6.3: Regional rail networks without market power should be horizontally separated from other networks and [should remain] vertically integrated."* The issue was to separate regional freight railways structurally for different treatment from urban rail operations and the interstate network. This had been done in New South Wales in 1996, South Australia in 1997, and was happening in Victoria in 1999, but had not at that stage been done in Queensland or Western Australia. It was not relevant to Tasmania.
- *"Recommendation 6.4: Regional rail networks with market power (the main coal lines) should be horizontally separated from other networks."* This applied to the Hunter Valley and what was subsequently defined as the Central Queensland Coal Network (CQCN). It was recommended in response to pressure from the coal mining industry which objected to State railways using revenues from bulk coal traffic to cross-subsidise other traffics within those networks. This separation of the coal networks took place in the Hunter Valley in 2004, and for the CQCN in 2010.
- *"Recommendation 7.2: All remaining government-owned freight operations should be privatised."* Privatisation had happened in South Australia and Tasmania in late 1997 with the break-up of Australian National, and later all but one of the other government-owned freight operations were sold as going concerns: V/Line Freight in May 1999, WestRail in October 2000, and Pacific National was formed from the joint sale of National Rail Corporation and NSW's FreightCorp in February 2002. Queensland Rail's freight operation became QR National in July 2010 and was floated on the stock market in November 2010, with the State government retaining a minority share.

- *"Recommendation 8.1: The pricing and allocation of train schedules should reflect the value that users place on the track. To encourage this, the Commonwealth Government should establish a process to investigate the feasibility of developing a market approach for allocating schedules or transferring capacity on the interstate network."* Unlike the majority of recommendations, this one was bizarre from a rail industry point of view. The PC included it in spite of strong opposition from rail industry participants. The only possible explanation is that it was ideologically motivated. The language used by the PC – *"establish a process"* to *"investigate the feasibility"* of *"developing a market approach"* – suggests three stages of tentative initiation, but nothing more. This sort of language is sometimes used to hide the lack of understanding of an issue.[159]

In the case of this last recommendation, its inclusion shows that the Productivity Commission believed that the theory of price-based competition should be applicable to the allocation of train schedules. It must have assumed that such competition would be based on scarcity of resource. Although railway line capacity is finite in the short term, it is easily substituted by the almost infinite capacity of the highways. Therefore, there is no scarcity, but instead an abundance of freight transport 'paths' in Australia. Hence "a market approach for allocating schedules" is unworkable. However, the PC clearly had no understanding of this, and no idea of its impracticality in the real world.

Why this theory would have been impractical, and even possibly destructive for the potential usage of rail networks, is explained in detail in Appendix 5, *Managing Access to Rail Networks in Australia*.

6. Procrastination and Evasion

At the end of the 1990s, the potential demand for federal rail funding was enormous. There were three major new rail proposals being aired:
- The Darwin to Alice Springs rail line through the Northern Territory, which would link with existing lines to provide a trans-continental connection to Adelaide
- The Inland Rail route to connect Brisbane to Melbourne, bypassing Sydney
- A Very High-Speed Train (VHST) to link Brisbane, Sydney, Canberra and Melbourne for passenger traffic.

In addition, of concern to the federal Coalition Government:
- the Neville Report had called for substantial federal government investment in the existing interstate network (not an acceptable idea to the Coalition Government)
- the Smorgon Report, "the private sector solution", had made many unacceptable recommendations,
- the ARTC was newly established and would need funding,
- the National Rail Corporation was still struggling financially, and
- the only Australian government railway to have been broken up and partly sold to the private sector at that time was Australian National (AN).

The response from the Commonwealth Government

In April 2000, the Coalition Commonwealth Government produced one written response to the three reports that it had received over a year before. This made sense because these reports had much in common in their recommendations on what should be done to assist the Australian rail freight industry. (A copy of the complex title page of the response document is on the next page.)

Its putative author was the Hon John Anderson, Deputy Prime Minister and Minister for Transport and Regional Services. He was also, since July 1999, the leader of the National Party, the party to which Paul Neville MP, chair of the House Committee that produced the first of the reports, belonged. Paul Neville was a senior MP, being the National Party Whip from 1998 until his retirement in 2013. Given that the Government's response rebutted many of the recommendations, one can imagine the robustness of the prior discussions that would have occurred in the Party Room.

The response document's format was six pages of preamble, in which the Government's policy position and direction for rail reform was stated, followed by formal response statements and comments on each of the recommendations made. Where the recommendations of two or three of the reports had much in common, they were clustered and responded to together.

The Government's preamble stated[160] its principles for land transport were to promote efficiencies, competition, and private sector investment in both rail operations and infrastructure. Its policy was not to own or operate rail services, and accordingly it confirmed that it intended to sell its interest in the National Rail Corporation. It would work with the States to achieve a more competitive and commercial national rail network, encouraging the States to deliver on their commitments to network investment, harmonisation, safety and access arrangements, made under the Intergovernmental Agreement for establishment of the ARTC.

RESPONSE OF THE FEDERAL GOVERNMENT TO

REPORTS OF THE HOUSE OF REPRESENTATIVES STANDING COMMITTEE ON COMMUNICATIONS, TRANSPORT AND MICROECONOMIC REFORM

'PLANNING NOT PATCHING' AND *'TRACKING AUSTRALIA'*

REPORT OF THE RAIL PROJECTS TASKFORCE

'REVITALISING RAIL'

REPORT OF THE PRODUCTIVITY COMMISSION

'PROGRESS IN RAIL REFORM'

THE HON JOHN ANDERSON MP, DEPUTY PRIME MINISTER,
MINISTER FOR TRANSPORT AND REGIONAL SERVICES

April 2000

The common themes in the recommendations of the three reports were:

- There was a need for a national strategic integrated land transport policy, with the Commonwealth government leading the policy development process; the hope was that investments in transport infrastructure could be more equitably spread

between road and rail to address the perceived lack of competitive neutrality between the modes;
- There was a need to upgrade the "substandard" national interstate rail network, to enable it to be competitive with the highway network, which had by then had billions of dollars invested in it since the 1980s, with this level of investment by the Commonwealth on-going;
- The Commonwealth government was urged to invest much more money ($billions) in the national rail network than the $250 million that was at that time already committed;
- There was a need to harmonise rail operational and safety standards across all States;
- There was a need for "road reform" leading to competitive neutrality if freight railways were to win more business, become profitable and attract private investment.

The Commonwealth Government's response to these recommendations was to oppose all but the fourth one. It declined to take the lead in strategic planning for national land transport, or to risk being seen to be dictating policy to State governments.

> "The Commonwealth pursues its policy objectives in land transport by investing directly in infrastructure ... By providing funding for these purposes, the Commonwealth does not assume responsibility for them, nor does it seek to direct where its money is spent." [161]

> "The Commonwealth provides the overall economic, competitive and fiscal framework for transport infrastructure provision through the tax system, management of the economy and the national competition policy." [162]

Clearly, the federal government did not accept any responsibility for the fact that the national interstate rail network had languished for want of investment while the National Highway System had flourished. At this time, the ARTC had yet to gain control of the sections of the national interstate rail network within New South Wales, Queensland and Western Australia, and had only recently taken over the standard-gauge interstate lines in Victoria, initially on a five-year lease. But the lack of investment in the national interstate rail network by the States (which are largely reliant on the Commonwealth for funds) was exactly the problem for which the three reports were asking, in effect, for a change of policy; i.e., for the Commonwealth to do for the rail network as it had done for the highway network – to fund substantial track upgrading, to enable train operators to compete more effectively with road carriers.

One positive outcome was that the response included an announcement that the ARTC would be asked to conduct an audit of the interstate rail tracks in year 2000, to quantify investment needs. (This is covered in chapter 9 under *The Interstate Track Audit*.)

On this issue of investment in the interstate rail network, the Government response was:[163]

> "The Commonwealth accepts there is an argument for investment in rail infrastructure to enable rail to provide interstate freight service levels comparable to road transport between the major urban centres. However, the Government is not convinced that responsibility for that investment should rest solely with the Commonwealth."

The response then fobbed off any responsibility by conflating the national interstate rail network (to come under the control of the federally-owned ARTC) with what was happening, or not happening, on the intrastate networks:[164]

> "Investing government money in rail infrastructure without other reforms is not sufficient to ensure rail sustainability and service competitiveness. Operational

> improvements are also required to improve service quality and reliability. The infrastructure in most States is owned by the State and is managed by State owned authorities or companies on a commercial basis. The Commonwealth has no control over that infrastructure and no assurance that reform of the sector will be pursued consistently. As such, the Commonwealth needs to be convinced that reforms are being achieved before considering investing additional funds in the rail track. Preferably, track owners should make investments from internal or debt finance, because track upgrades for inter-State rail freight should be commercially justifiable and track owners are best placed to make such decisions."

To expect that track upgrades could be commercially justified was unrealistic. (Why this is so is explained in chapter 15, under the heading *Why invest in rail network infrastructure?*) It was either a disingenuous response, or the government policy-makers were blind to the reality that rail network investment has to be considered in the broader context of land transport — something that the writers of the three reports wanted to convey, but perhaps were not sufficiently explicit about.

On the issue of lack of modal neutrality, and the Government's roles in influencing that, the response document was blatantly disingenuous:[165]

> "The Government supports the principle of competitive neutrality between modes of transport. However, the road and rail sectors have different usage, charging and funding structures. Road sector charges include registration charges, sales taxes, tolls, local government rates, parking charges and fuel excises. Rail charges include accreditation charges, access charges and fuel excises. ...
>
> Roads tend to be budget funded while access charges are charged directly by rail track management authorities and are re-invested directly into the track."

The recommendations in the three reports to achieve modal neutrality between road freight and rail freight were based on the existence of these differences, but the Government's refusal to change its policy position was also justified on the existence of these differences!

On the need for "road reform" to help achieve modal neutrality, the Productivity Commission had said, in a three-part recommendation:[166]

> **"RECOMMENDATION 10.4**
> The Commonwealth Government should establish a public inquiry into road provision in Australia. This inquiry should examine:
> - road transport planning processes;
> - methods of investment appraisal (including the evaluation and allocation of costs and benefits);
> - funding arrangements (including taxation, charges and grants);
> - the scope to improve road pricing; and
> - current institutional arrangements and alternatives."

Unfortunately, although the case had been made in the body of the report for "a more commercial approach to the provision of roads", including user charges for heavy vehicles as was done in New Zealand, the PC writers omitted this reasoning in its wording of this part of the recommendation, perhaps assuming some good will on the part of the Government to whom it was addressed. The response document reproduced only the last part of the recommendation, exactly as shown above, to take it out of context, then dismissed the whole issue with:[167]

> "The Commonwealth does not accept this recommendation. The Commonwealth is not convinced that there is a need for another public inquiry into road provision at this time."

There has been no effective change to the lack of modal neutrality between road freight and rail freight in Australia since then, and no implementation of axle weight- and distance-based road user charges for heavy road vehicles. (There is a full discussion of Competitive Neutrality in chapter 13.)

At the end of the 1990s going into year 2000, the Coalition federal government clearly had no interest in dealing with railways development. Whatever vision it might have had for the freight rail sector, it had to be subservient to the higher ideals of competition and privatisation. This can be gleaned from comments made by its Department of Transport and Regional Services (DoTaRS) in a submission made in November 1998 to the Productivity Commission, which was at the time gathering information for its 1999 report *Progress in Rail Reform*. DoTaRS stated[168] an intention that the Commonwealth would "extract itself from above-rail operations", meaning it planned to sell its part-ownership of the National Rail (NRC):

> "The newly privately owned above-rail operations should be characterised by high levels of investment, innovation, and customer focus. In line with other industries, commercial incentives and imperatives should be in place with revenues from above-rail operations able to cover all above-rail costs and all below-rail ongoing operating costs."

On the matter of investment in rail networks, it said:[169]

> "The Commonwealth's position on investment is that it should be undertaken jointly between the Commonwealth, the States and the private sector. Where there are commercial gains to be made from infrastructure investment, it should be undertaken by the private sector. Other investments provide benefits to track controlled by State Government owned entities which the Commonwealth has no jurisdiction over. These investments are more properly the responsibility of State Governments. The Commonwealth should retain responsibility for investment principally on track

that it manages through the ARTC where net national benefit accrues from the investment but for which there is not a commercial benefit to attract private investors."

At that time, the only tracks the ARTC managed were the interstate lines of the former AN network. Since then, it has acquired control of most of the interstate network, through long-term leases from the States, and the federal government has funded some upgrading of this network.

The Parliamentary Report – *Back on Track: Progress in Rail Reform*

Paul Neville chaired another Parliamentary Committee that looked again into progress in rail reform, particularly concerned to hear the rail industry's views. The official reason ("pursuant to Standing Order 324(b)") for the Committee's work was a review of the 1999-2000 Annual Report of the Department of Transport and Regional Services (DoTaRS).[170] This document confirmed the continuation of the Commonwealth Government's biased approach to land transport. It reported that during the year the Minister had approved $50 million for rail projects, from an existing four-year rail infrastructure program with a budget of $250 million. It also reported an allocation of funds for the year for the Commonwealth roads program, of $818.2 million, not including (additional) payments made under the Black Spot program (to alleviate local road design issues causing accidents). But under the heading of "Rail Revival", it stated:

> "The Commonwealth Government envisages a rail industry consistent with world best practice and delivering a high-quality service to customers. ... Two years into the program the Melbourne-Adelaide interstate rail track, which was speed-limited on 28 per cent of its length, now has speed restrictions on less than 3 per cent of track. Journey times have been cut from 13.5 hours to 11 hours"

"Rail Revival" was an exaggeration in the context of $50 million for rail projects. This was modest spending to fix a backlog of localised track deficiencies enabling the removal of temporary speed restrictions which still left the original century-old track alignment with its permanent speed restrictions. These are due to grades and curvature on the track alignment. They necessitate speed restrictions in the sense that trains could run significantly faster (on well-maintained track) if the alignment were relatively level and straight. It has been calculated[171] that each train between Sydney (Strathfield Junction) and Brisbane (Acacia Ridge) or vice versa has to travel around the equivalent of 177 circles, half to the left and half to the right. On the Melbourne to Sydney (Glenlee) route, the number of circles is 71. These railway routes were built this way before 1920 because going around hills, rather than through them, was the cheapest type of construction. The legacy is slow transit times for trains, and higher-than-average track maintenance requirements and fuel consumption. Both of these are due to much greater friction between wheels and rails, which increases the wear to both wheel flanges and rail edges, and causes the phenomenon of 'wheel squeal' heard when trains pass by.

By year 2000, these old railway lines also needed investment for once-in-a-generation 'Major Periodic Maintenance' and asset renewal: ballast cleaning, replacing deteriorated wooden sleepers with long-lasting concrete ones, and replacing worn rails with heavier rails that can support the heavier axle loads that became possible with later twentieth-century wagon design and construction.

6. Procrastination and Evasion

Speed-limiting curvature on a main-line route built over 100 years ago

Decades of investment to widen, flatten, straighten, strengthen and resurface the roads that had become the National Highway System, coupled with the lack of equivalent investment into the interstate railway routes, had made all these rail routes in the eastern States now uncompetitive with road in terms of transit times, capacity and reliability. They were and (despite improvements) still are far from "world best practice" for "delivering a high-quality service to customers". The 1994 BTCE report on the adequacy of the interstate rail network had estimated some $3 billion of investment over 20 years was warranted to address these service-disabling deficiencies in the four eastern States. Paul Neville's Committee was aware of this.

The Parliamentary Committee was clearly not satisfied with the slow progress in rail reform. It had held a seminar in November 2000 to gather input from industry stakeholders on progress of reform and issues that still required attention. The focus of the seminar was on the broad issues of strategic planning, Commonwealth and State relations, competitive neutrality, access to networks, and accreditation of train operators. It released its report in April 2001, to counter the stultifying effect of the Transport Minister's response to the three reports of the late 1990s. The report stated[172] "we want to help put rail reform 'back on track'."

Some of the issues that were seen then by industry stakeholders as a priority for reform, and which remain not fully resolved today, were:

- The need for a National Transport Strategy "setting out the Commonwealth's overarching policy framework, including policies governing investment evaluation." [173]
- The slow release of already budgeted funds for investment in rail networks, due to "significant delays in determining the most cost-effective improvements and in negotiating cost sharing arrangements between the NSW and Commonwealth Governments." [174]
- Sourcing funds for network capacity improvements to accommodate growth in traffic. "…with the current road-pricing regime, rail projects are unable to be self-funding. This means Governments will [need to reposition] their views of the industry, or all of the reforms to date will have been of little value as rail becomes incapable of growing due to lack of capacity."[175]
- The disincentive to private sector investment in rail infrastructure and rolling-stock, due to "policies which deny competitive neutrality to the rail industry". [176]

There were other issues around the difficulty experienced by train operators getting access to track, that have been largely resolved by the ARTC now having control of most of the interstate network. However, there are still impediments for intrastate train operators in dealing with more than one track provider. There remain three such impediments in New South Wales, and two in each of Queensland and Victoria. (This issue is discussed further in chapter 13, under the heading

Competition for Access to Networks.)

The Commonwealth Government did respond officially to the *Back on Track* report, but not till 26 March 2003, nearly two years later.[177] The Minister for Transport and Regional Services, still John Anderson, issued a statement which is no longer available. However, in the following year the government created a program that showed some recognition of the need for more investment in rail relative to road – AusLink.

AusLink

AusLink was a Coalition Government initiative announced in the Commonwealth Budget of May 2004 and described in a White Paper published in June 2004. The Ministers for Transport and Regional Services, and for Local Government, Territories and Roads announced it thus:[178]

> "AusLink will revolutionise the planning and funding of Australia's national roads and railways by taking a long-term strategic approach for our long-term future. It represents the most significant change since Federation in the way we tackle the national transport task. ... This White Paper, *AusLink: Building Our National Transport Future*, is the Government's formal policy statement on land transport. This framework will move Australia from a parochial and ad hoc system to a clear national land transport plan that all levels of government can support and deliver together."

A parliamentary analyst saw that what was intended did not meet this grand ambition. His Current Issues Brief, written at the time for Senators and MPs, stated:[179]

> "It is presented as the Government's 'national land transport plan'. ... But it might be more appropriately described as a federal land transport infrastructure financing plan."

The White Paper included the government's recognition of the uncompetitive state of the national rail network after decades of investment in building and improving highways:[180]

> "The National Land Transport Plan, in conjunction with the Government's substantial contribution to the Australian Rail Track Corporation, will begin to address the historical deficiency in the quality of rail infrastructure. This cannot be fully overcome in the short-term. But over time the AusLink framework will progressively improve the capacity of rail operators to effectively compete on their merits for a greater share of the forecast growth in freight traffic."

The plan brought together for the first time the existing road and rail funding programs and established a "National Network" of nationally-important transport corridors. Total funding over five years was to be $11.8 billion, of which rail would get 9%, or $1.05 billion.[181] This sum marked an increase in federal funding for rail projects compared to previous years. The majority of this sum was to be spent on upgrading the track between Sydney and Brisbane, and on building the Southern Sydney Freight Line (first funded under the *One Nation* program, and which was not completed till 2013). Rail links to ports in capital cities were also to be improved.

The White Paper had noted the need for successful planning and wise investment especially for the eastern seaboard north-south corridors linking Brisbane, Sydney and Melbourne, both for environmental reasons and for coping with the forecast increase in non-bulk freight.[182]

> "A continuation of current strong user preference for road transport would see the interstate non-bulk road freight task more than double by 2020. Given the distances involved on these corridors, rail has the potential to be more competitive than it has been in recent decades. An under-performing rail system is unacceptable and there

6. Procrastination and Evasion

is substantial scope to achieve a high-performing east-coast rail system."

However, there was no suggestion that the Commonwealth Government should or would do anything to encourage any shift from road to rail along these corridors, whether to reduce highway congestion or greenhouse gas emissions. Its view was

> "The potential for rail to increase its share of the non-bulk freight task depends on the appropriate level of infrastructure investment together with commercially sustainable operating practices."

There was no recognition that rail's commercial sustainability had to compete against governments' own lack of commercial sustainability for highway investments. Indeed, its outlook for rail was somewhat pessimistic:[183]

> "Given the forecast passenger and freight growth rates, even a significant improvement in rail's share of the long distance ... freight market will not avoid the need for progressive upgrading of key road links on these corridors. Substantial upgrading will be required to enhance capacity, safety and **transit times**." [My emphasis]

The unconscious bias in the thinking of federal government and/or its bureaucracy was revealed again – that is, it was the Commonwealth government's role to invest to enhance transit times for highway users, but to do this for railway users was not a priority. This was demonstrated in the following year, 2005, when the government found it had a budget surplus.

One of the touted features of AusLink was that all investment projects were to be rigorously assessed to improve strategic infrastructure planning and project selection across modes:[184]

> "A new, nationally consistent project assessment methodology will be adopted. The assessment methodology will enable projects to be compared in

> future plans in terms of value for money. This will enable a comparison of the relative merit of investment within, and between, land transport corridors."

However, according to a 2009 report, an additional $1.268 billion was spent on upgrading two highways without much assessment done, which exacerbated the competitive imbalance between road and rail on key arterial routes:[185]

> "... 'strategic infrastructure planning' was dumped for the convenience of the Government. In late 2005, the Howard Government, at the nadir of its fiscal discipline, realized it was heading for a massive Budget surplus, due not merely to the mining boom but its own inability to get money out the door quickly enough. Ministers were asked to hastily come up with new spending proposals that could be implemented before the end of the financial year.
> Transport officials suggested a $800m duplication project on the Hume Highway in NSW, based on what were by their own admission "necessarily fairly rough" calculations about the costs and benefits, and a $268m upgrade of the Bruce Highway. John Howard liked their suggestions and promptly gave the money to Warren Truss, who had succeeded Anderson in the portfolio."

The AusLink program was superseded in 2009 by the Labor Government's Nation Building Program. Under this latter program funding for rail included a $1.2 billion equity investment in the ARTC to help fund its $1.6 billion investment in track upgrades and construction,[186] and the upgrading of the Tasmanian and Eyre Peninsula (SA) networks.

The Productivity Commission's 2006 Report – *Road and Rail Freight Infrastructure Pricing*

The Terms of Reference

This report had its origins in a Productivity Commission review of the National Competition Policy Reforms, in which it recommended in part[187]

> "a national review into the requirements for an efficient and sustainable national freight transport system, encompassing *all* freight transport modes."

The resulting infrastructure pricing review was commissioned by the Commonwealth Treasurer Peter Costello on behalf of COAG. Its Terms of Reference included:[188]

> "The purpose of the review is to assist COAG to implement efficient pricing of road and rail freight infrastructure through consistent and competitively neutral pricing regimes, in a manner that optimises efficiency and productivity in the freight transport task and maximises net benefits to the community."

Unfortunately, "optimises efficiency and productivity in the freight transport task" is so vague as to be a meaningless objective. See the first section in chapter 9 for an explanation of why this is so.

The Terms of Reference stated also that provision of public infrastructure such as highways and railways should be priced for full cost-recovery:

> "The review will estimate the full financial costs of providing and maintaining freight transport infrastructure on major road and rail networks. It should be based on the principle that prices charged should reflect all costs in each mode".

Charges that "reflect all costs" imply there should be no subsidies, implicit or explicit. It is worth noting that the principle of charging freight transport users of the NHS to recover full costs had not been raised before, and was possibly contrary to one of stated objectives for the NHS:[189]

> "minimising the cost of the National Highway to the Australian community"

What the Productivity Commission found

The recovery of full costs was also much more than would be needed just to provide competitive neutrality in pricing between the rail and road modes for the use of their 'way'. (The contemporary meaning of 'Competitive Neutrality' is explained in chapter 13.) The Productivity Commission (PC) in its report side-stepped the issue of full recovery of costs by focusing on the issues affecting competitive neutrality in pricing of infrastructure. However, it was clear that railtrack providers could never recover long-term full costs wherever there was intermodal competition, and so the COAG requirement was not feasible, although this was never explicitly stated. (There is an explanation of why rail networks need government support in chapter 14, under *Other Consequences of Vertical Separation,* and in chapter 15, under *Most Vertically-Separated Rail Networks are Inherently Unprofitable.*)

The PC was not in favour of the resumption of governmental control of rail networks, even though it knew this was going to happen in Victoria and Tasmania in 2007:[190]

> "It is possible that where rail lines are heavily reliant on government subsidies, governments may prefer to own infrastructure or provide subsidies to vertically separated entities rather than being seen to support regional monopolies. Vertical separation may also enable governments to more transparently target subsidies to provision of below-rail infrastructure. However, it would seem perverse to maintain separation in order to

> transparently target subsidies if doing so increases co-ordination and other costs and, hence, the size of the subsidy required."

Although the PC knew of the deterioration of the vertically-integrated privatised rail networks in New Zealand, Victoria and Tasmania due to TranzRail's and Pacific National's priorities for ensuring profits, it still favoured vertical integration as a way to limit government subsidies for networks.[191]

> "Finding 11.3: The costs of vertical separation on regional rail networks are likely to be greater than the benefits where infrastructure providers are unable to exert market power."

The reality was that limiting subsidies was not the main issue at this time for each of these networks. The three governments acted to regain control of their networks to prevent a sudden collapse of rail services for all freight, and to begin many years of network restoration. (These stories are told in some detail in chapter 11.)

The PC devoted the majority of its report to issues of roading and trucking. It considered many submissions and various methodologies for estimating the provision and maintenance costs of highways and regional roads. There was some uncertainty about how much of these costs the road transport industry should be liable for. The PC's viewpoint was that road networks had much greater economies of scope than did rail networks.[192]

> "Road freight has an inherent advantage over rail in that roads are also used extensively by passenger and other light vehicles. This means that many costs which are 'common' or 'unattributable' can be largely shared with other road users. There is no 'right' way to allocate common costs"

Common costs were estimated to be about $4 billion out of a total of $10.4 billion.[193] How much of this the road freight industry should pay was therefore somewhat arbitrary, making it difficult for any road user charges to be verifiable and credible. Also, the cost allocation methodology used by the National Transport Commission, which the PC accepted as given, excluded $3.6 billion of the total $10.4 billion from any calculation of the liability of the road freight industry to pay. The reason for this decision was that the exclusion was for "local access" which was funded by local governments. The PC probably had in mind local access in urban environments, where heavy vehicles are less likely to visit. However, local access in a rural setting is very different. My contention is that heavy vehicles should contribute through user charges to the maintenance of lightly-constructed rural roads. Hence the share of total roading costs attributable to heavy vehicles should be larger. The lack of contribution to rural roads is felt especially in grain-growing areas, where the local shires are poorly resourced. This has proven to be a real problem in WA where 'tier 3' rail lines have been closed by Brookfield, the railtrack provider, forcing grain trucks onto local roads not built for them, creating maintenance difficulties for the affected shire governments. (There is more detail in chapter 11.)

Given these issues and exemptions, the PC's report found that the sum of total road costs attributable to heavy vehicles (including an allocation of common costs) was $1.63 billion.[194] It concluded then that the road transport industry as a whole had probably covered the operating costs (maintenance and management) attributable to its use of the nation's main roads and highways prior to year 2000. But increases in charges for road use had not kept pace with recent increases in roading expenditure, due to caps on annual increases applied by the National Transport Commission.[195] Road transport operators pay vehicle registration fees and a per litre diesel fuel excise. Both types of charge are effectively taxes, being paid into Commonwealth government's general funds, and so are not hypothecated for roading expenditure. Therefore, there is no linkage between economic demand for roads and highways, and the investment decisions affecting the supply of adequate roads and highways of durable quality.

However, the PC found that there was substantial cross-subsidisation within the road transport industry favouring 'B-double' rigs, because of the coarseness of the two types of charges. To summarise,[196] the sources of cross-subsidy were (and still are):

- By vehicle class – rigid trucks and road trains cross-subsidise B-doubles because the registration charges for each do not reflect their differences in capacity;
- By vehicle use – the vehicle registration charge does not distinguish between less-intensively-used heavy vehicles, typical of the ancillary fleets of manufacturers, distributors or grain growers, which
  — are usually empty on the return trip to base, and
  — travel shorter distances than average and/or
  — carry lighter loads and/or
  — are used mainly on a seasonal basis,
  — and the more-intensively-used B-doubles typical of the companies which compete in the interstate freight transport markets, which are
  — frequently loaded in both directions, and
  — fully loaded as often as possible, causing exponentially more road wear.

The National Highway System was built with extra lanes to enable heavy vehicles to share the roads with light vehicles travelling at faster speeds. Generally, all lanes were built with the deep pavements needed for the otherwise damaging impacts of heavy vehicle axle loadings. The increasing numbers of heavy vehicles led to a number of town bypasses being built. Similarly, heavy vehicles required stronger bridges than would have been in existence before. It is known that B-doubles are the most frequently used type of heavy freight vehicle used on the NHS, and that they compete most directly with rail services in the non-bulk interstate market. However, the PC took the view that the actual costs that B-doubles impose on the NHS would be lower than for other roads, because this network was built for them. Therefore, the cross-subsidisation that favoured B-doubles should not be seen as a serious issue. This indicates that the PC ignored the previous provision of the NHS as irrelevant to the issue of competitive neutrality between road and rail. Its finding was:[197]

> "The available evidence, while not conclusive, does not support the contention that road freight is subsidised relative to rail on either the inter-capital corridors or in regional areas."

This view was contrary to the position taken by Commonwealth Ministers two years previously, where the AusLink program sought to redress the previous imbalance of investments in highways and railways. (There is a more detailed discussion of the PC's perceptions of these issues in chapter 13 *Competitive Neutrality – Government Investment in Highways versus Railway Infrastructure*.)

An example of a B-double rig

6. Procrastination and Evasion

The PC recommended a change to the method of charging for freight moving on roads to one that reflected a 'user pays' principle, based on a combination of vehicle mass, distance travelled and location. There were three benefits of this method:
- it would remove the cross-subsidisation by vehicle class and usage,
- make possible the proportional distribution of funds to the various road providers, and
- make the basis of road user charges consistent with what is done for rail access.

But it also hedged this recommendation with doubts about the net benefits: [198]
- There would still be no mechanism to ensure that charges kept pace with road expenditure;
- The process for determining charges would still be open to political influence, conducive to lobbying by road and rail interests;
- Would the implementation costs be justifiable for the efficiency benefits?
- There was a likelihood that removing the cross-subsidies would leave regions paying more for road use than on the heavily used interstate routes, disadvantaging regional economies;
- The changed method of charging would incur new administrative and enforcement costs, and compliance costs incurred by truck operators;
- Depending on the level of charges set, registration charges and/or a fuel levy might still be needed to raise enough to cover the costs of road provision;
- Institutional reform in road funding and provision would be needed to gain community acceptance for the changes in road user charging.

For these reasons, the PC recommended a staged approach, overseen by COAG, to enable satisfactory resolution of issues. COAG next met in April 2007, accepting all of the recommendations, including a plan for a feasibility study into mass-distance location-based heavy vehicle charges, to be delivered by December 2011, almost five years into the future. (See chapter 7, under *Heavy Vehicle Charging and Investment Reform (HVCI)*.)

The outcome

With hindsight, an unfortunate bias can be seen, given the timing of the PC's study, when the provision of the National Highway System (NHS) was substantially completed. The NHS had been funded by general government spending, without any attempt at cost-recovery of the substantial investments. By contrast, funds from the AusLink program had just begun to flow

> "to address the historical deficiency in the quality of rail infrastructure". [199]

COAG accepted the PC's assertion that there was competitive equality between road and rail.[200]

> "COAG endorses the PC's view that the policy reform focus should be on enhancing efficiency and productivity *within* each of the road and rail sectors as the evidence presented suggests competitive distortions *between* road and rail have been limited and are not a significant source of market inefficiency."

Did the PC perform a very successful conjuring trick? It would appear so.

At the end of 2007, a Labor government came to power at the federal level, with a different focus – less about economic efficiency in land transport and more on the capacity and effectiveness of transport networks. It also founded Infrastructure Australia (see in chapter 7), which articulated a different point of view on transport priorities. In February 2011, Infrastructure Australia published a discussion paper *National Land Freight Strategy*. In its introduction it stated:[201]

"Rail and road freight infrastructure planning and investment can no longer be undertaken in isolation from each other, or worse, in competition with each other. ....."

"A new national freight strategy needs to be developed for our freight networks to improve planning, investment and decision making".

7. Transport Sector Reform by Commissions and Councils

Overview

It is a feature of Australian federalism that the relationships among the Commonwealth, State and Territory Governments are more equal than hierarchical. Various groupings have been created since 1990 to get high level agreements on changes where both levels of government have shared interests, such as in education, health services, and transport. For land transport networks, States still have responsibility for railways and regional roads, but the Commonwealth created and owns the ARTC (see in Chapter 9) and took responsibility for the creation and development of the National Highway System (chapter 4).

The grouping at the highest level was COAG[202] – the Council of Australian Governments: a bi-annual forum attended by the Commonwealth Prime Minister and Premiers of the State and Territory governments. Bodies under COAG with oversight in the transport space were:
- ATC, the Australian Transport Council, 1993 to 2011
- SCOTI, the Standing Committee on Transport Infrastructure, 2011 to 2013
- TAIC, the Transport and Infrastructure Council, 2013 to present.

Policy development and advisory bodies which provide advice to the above, include
- NRTC, the National Road Transport Commission 1992 to 2004, which became
- NTC, the National Transport Commission, 2004 to present
- IA, Infrastructure Australia, 2008 to present

To complete the survey of sources of rail reform, we look at the efforts of some of these organisations.

The National Transport Commission (NTC)

Establishment

The NTC had a former and primary existence as the National Road Transport Commission (NRTC), started in July 1992,[203] as an outcome of the Labor Commonwealth Government's push for microeconomic reform. (See in chapter 8, under *Slow progress in Road Reform*.)

In August 2002, the Australian Transport Council agreed that a National Transport Commission should be formed. It would be responsible for national approaches to rail and intermodal regulation, and take over the role of regulatory reform of road transport from the NRTC. However, a new body was not formed. Instead, in 2004, the NRTC was just renamed the National Transport Commission (NTC) to accommodate the inclusion of rail and intermodal transport into its existing mandate. Hence, the new NTC had corporate knowledge of the road freight industry, but not of the rail freight industry. My comments on the NTC focus on how effective it was for developing the rail freight industry.

The NTC's first achievement in the rail space was the drafting of an exemplary law covering rail safety, the intent being to harmonise such laws across Australia. At that time, no federal law would have been possible, because constitutionally, railways were (and are still) a State responsibility, so each State was encouraged to use the draft law to revise its own rail safety laws. Adopting this draft law turned out to be a slow process. The Rail Safety Act was passed in Victoria in 2006, followed by South Australia in 2007, New South Wales in 2008, Tasmania in 2009, and in 2010 – Western Australia, Queensland and the Northern Territory.

In the NTC's 2006-07 Strategic Plan, rail productivity was identified as a key work area as part of its Transport Efficiency objective, with the outcome being[204]

> "the identification of impediments to improved productivity in rail transport and progress towards removing these impediments"

A proposal for coordination in planning and policy

In January 2008, the NTC contracted John Hearsch Consulting to investigate and report on what rail operators saw as the industry's productivity problems and what the NTC could do to assist. In reporting the concerns of companies and individuals involved in the rail industry, Hearsch's first recommendation for the attention of government was:[205]

> **"Develop/facilitate the development of a national policy for rail**
>
> The most critical issue facing the industry, and that which is impacting on productivity, is the matter of a coordinated policy and vision for the future of rail in Australia. The current situation is a reflection of the past, however a coordinated national approach is required to maximise the potential of the industry and fully realise productivity gains.
>
> The NTC should take a lead role in the formulation of policy, working closely with the Commonwealth to bring about a strong vision for the future of rail. This must be linked to a strong policy that seeks to achieve maximum benefit from rail's potential strengths, not just

a collection of projects. This will stimulate productivity improvement activity within the industry, as greater surety of the long-term role of rail within the national economy will encourage investment."

Hearsch's observations were that there was a "policy vacuum" in that there was "no coherent vision ... at either Commonwealth or State level".[206] Such a vision would acknowledge that:

> "rail has a potentially significantly increased role to play in reducing urban congestion, improving road safety, freight and logistics efficiency and in addressing energy demand and climate change."

> "A visionary statement agreed between the Commonwealth and States for the future of rail ... would provide a highly visible initial framework for moving the industry forward. This then needs to be translated into clear policies for action that are more specific in terms of investment and other strategies that can demonstrate economic, environmental and social benefits not readily achievable by other means."

These comments echoed the pleas of the 1990s for Commonwealth leadership of strategic planning for land transport. (See in chapter 4, under *No Centralised Comprehensive Strategic Planning for Land Transport*.) The Commonwealth Government had refused in 1990 to take this up, on the grounds that it did not have a mandate to commit State governments to any course of action in their areas of responsibility. Not surprisingly, the Commonwealth did not agree with Hearsch's recommendation that "the NTC should take a lead role in the formulation of policy".

However, during 2008 the NTC initiated a rail industry productivity review to take forward some of Hearsch's other recommendations. This resulted in a Final Position Paper in August 2009. Given the very limited data available on the productivity of freight rail operations, it was aimed at[207]

> "identifying productivity impediments within the freight rail sector; and developing recommendations for government to effectively intervene in the rail sector to improve outcomes for the transport system as a whole. The review has therefore focused on the investment and regulatory frameworks that underpin the rail freight industry to determine where these create a barrier to rail businesses investing in more productive technology, assets and business practices."

We will see in chapter 9 that the notion of governments intervening to improve the productivity of rail businesses would have been heresy only a few years previously. But by 2009, the privatised Victorian and Tasmanian rail networks were back in government control, and most Australian governments had already been under pressure to invest in their rail networks.

Consultation with below-rail providers by the NTC for its 2009 Position Paper[208]

> "highlighted a lack of planning and policy direction from government for rail infrastructure and intermodal terminals as one of the major productivity impediments. Resulting infrastructure deficiencies and bottlenecks in urban areas were also mentioned as one of the impediments to improved freight rail productivity."

Reasons for this lack of policy direction included:[209]
- conflicting government objectives creating ambiguity: for example, Victorian rail policy had to fulfill State government transport policy objectives (including that for ports), and AusLink policy objectives, and also those of the Australian Transport Council (ATC);
- lack of coordination of planning for the longer-term: examples were 1) the State networks for grain haulage being undermaintained, leading to ad hoc investments in response to the threat of cessation of rail services, on Eyre Peninsula in 2006 and in NSW in 2008; and

2) the RailCorp network where passenger services increasingly take precedence over freight services in terms of scheduling and allocation of line capacity, leaving freight operators without confidence about the number of future train paths available;
- insufficient coordinated planning for land use and transport – particularly important for the development of urban intermodal terminals, and for servicing consolidated and enlarged grain receival and storage sites in the regions.

The 2009 Position Paper postulated also[210] that the use by governments of subsidies to rail network providers was another **reason for** a lack of policy direction. However, in my view, such subsidies were instead a **result of** the lack of policy direction, because such subsidies were typically ad hoc and spasmodic investments.

The NTC reiterated the Hearsch recommendation in its 2009 Position Paper that:[211]

> "NTC should work with state and federal governments to develop a national framework to overcome coordination failures for rail transport planning, policy development and investment across Australia."

That this never happened shows that the Commonwealth stuck to its earlier position of not taking a lead in federal/state relationships. Perhaps that is why the NTC was set up as an advisory body only.

Another proposal

A less ambitious recommendation was agreed to by the ATC:

> "NTC to develop a consistent framework for assessing and providing government funding to private and publicly owned rail businesses, and improved monitoring of rail businesses receiving government funding"

Over a year later, NTC produced a Discussion Paper in October 2010, titled *The Role of Government in Rail Freight Investment*. Its purpose was to:[212]

- "initiate a discussion concerning the range of issues that ATC has directed NTC to address in the development of a policy position paper with respect to the productivity of rail freight in Australia
- provide a mechanism for stakeholders to formally participate in the development of the policy to be submitted to ATC

  As this discussion paper is the first step in developing a policy paper, part of its purpose is to collect specific evidence and examples on the role of government in rail freight."

The way this discussion paper was written reveals that the NTC, and perhaps also the ATC, were still ignorant of, and naïve about, the Australian rail freight industry and its difficulties. Also, its language would have been obscure for most of its intended readers – it discussed issues and asked questions of its readers in the language of economics, such as:[213]

> "Parts of the rail industry may be characterised as an incomplete market (one where demand and supply curves do not intersect). In this case no production takes place unless government investment can shift the supply curve so that rail network access can be provided at a price that generates non-zero demand."

> "Question 2: What are today's objectives for rail freight?"

> "Question 3: Are there examples where productivity and efficiency objectives appear to have overtaken social objectives?"

> "Question 5: Where has government intervention in the rail freight sector corrected market failures?"

> "Question 6: What other forms of market failure should prompt government intervention in rail freight?"

"Question 7: When has government interventions (sic) failed to correct market failures in the rail freight market?"

Unsurprisingly, the policy position paper to follow this discussion paper never appeared. Instead, in 2013, a recommendation was made by the Transport and Infrastructure Senior Officials' Committee of the Department of Transport and Infrastructure:[214]

> "The NTC's work on supply chain reform and rail freight investment reform should be discontinued, unless the NTC is able to identify specific deliverables and timetables for SCOTI consideration"

After that, the NTC's projects were mostly road-related issues, apart from maintenance of rail safety national law, and the release of a revised National Standard for Health Assessment of Rail Safety Workers in 2016. One of the NTC's key roles of concern to road freighters is the annual determination of truck registration charges and the levy on fuel known as the road user charge. It emerged around 2015 that its model for these determinations was defective, which enabled the trucking industry to pressure transport ministers to freeze these charges at least twice.[215] Due to inflationary pressures, these freezes just worsened the lack of competitive neutrality between the road and rail modes (explained in chapter 13).

Review of the NTC's operational effectiveness

There is a requirement under the Act which created the NTC for it to be reviewed periodically[216] for:
- "evaluation of the current operational effectiveness of the NTC;
- consideration of the NTC's future role and relationships; and
- recommendations on the future work priorities and governance arrangements, if the NTC is to continue."

In 2015, the third such review was done by an expert panel. It reported that the NTC should continue its work in road transport, because the States and the road freight industry supported an on-going role for it. However, for the rail industry it stated:[217]

> "There are conflicting views on the future role of the NTC in strategic rail transport reform and there are concerns regarding the NTC's lack of expertise in this area. The Panel notes it may be difficult to define a role for the NTC in the absence of a nationally agreed policy agenda for rail."

The Panel recommended a remedy for this:[218]

> "The Council should charge the Transport and Infrastructure Senior Officials' Committee (TISOC) to develop a nationally agreed policy agenda for rail and recommend whether there remains a role for the NTC, or another suitable organisation, to progress further reforms in this area."

As a result, the Transport and Infrastructure Council published in 2016 its *National Rail Vision and Work Program*,[219] which is discussed below, in the section on TAIC. It appears that the NTC did no significant work in the rail space till after this program was adopted.

The National Rail Action Plan

In May 2020, the NTC announced its National Rail Action Plan, which set out actions for governments and industry to work together on projects "to lift the productivity and safety of rail." In August 2022, it produced a short document titled *National Rail Action Plan* which described three areas for cooperation:[220]

- recruiting and training people to reduce the national shortage of skilled labour in the rail industry, and increasing their portability of qualifications and experience

- developing national standards for rail industry engineering components, in an attempt to incentivise local manufacturers to supply, hoping that will reduce costs for a fragmented rail industry
- "improved interoperability" to "better connect a fragmented national rail network into a network that works as one system."

That these were still issues in 2020 stemmed from the historical development of the rail industry in Australia: its lack of unity, firstly due to the separate development of the State networks, then compounded by the divisive processes of privatisation and vertical separation, aimed at enabling competition, and hence greater productivity. As was seen in chapter 3 (under *A multitude of track providers*), there are now twelve separately-managed networks running freight trains, whereas under government control in 1990 there were six. Similarly, there are now twelve freight rail companies (see chapter 3, under *A who's who of current freight train operators in Australasia*), whereas under government control in 1990 there were five organisations. Because companies and other organisations tend to specify requirements and make purchasing decisions that will primarily support their own objectives, the NTC's Plan is a brave one indeed.

The most fruitful area for cooperation is likely to be in tackling the national rail skills shortage, although it will take years to fill what is estimated to be a gap of up to 70,000 skilled workers.[221]

The other two areas for cooperation, shown above, look harder to achieve. In 2023, the ARA published a study calling for an Australian national local content procurement policy (LCP), to replace the existing State-based ones.[222] The effect would be that when bids for rolling-stock construction are called by one State, potential suppliers in other States would be treated as local instead of foreign. In the ARA's example used to demonstrate potential benefits, the study found an estimated

$1.85 billion of foregone procurement cost savings over the previous ten years of State-based acquisition of passenger rolling-stock, comprising:
- "$717 million of savings from increased scale
- $811 million of savings from reduced complexity and planning and design, and
- $318 million of savings from major componentry harmonisation."

This suggests that developing national standards for rail industry engineering components will need to follow agreements on reduced complexity in planning and design of railway vehicles, signalling systems, and other types of assets, all of which are long-lasting, and replaced perhaps once in thirty to fifty years.

Getting successful cooperation and interoperability will be a big ask for the rail freight industry, given the timespans, in a country where interstate rivalry is ingrained, and in an industry that was deliberately transformed to be competitive not cooperative. Five priority areas identified as critical:[223]
- "identifying the best mechanism for codifying a small number of critical national standards and complementary rules to make rail more competitive;
- aligning train control and signalling technology on the eastern seaboard;
- reducing the burden on drivers, crew, and maintenance workers;
- streamlining rolling stock approval regimes and
- identifying the national/international pathways for digital skills required in Australia in the next five years."

The National Rail Action Plan now has the blessing of the National Cabinet[224] (the successor to COAG). The outcome could be that the governments will think they are providing support to the rail industry. That could deter the kind of support that would really make a difference: investment in rail networks to increase train speeds and network capacity, done with as much interest and enthusiasm as is done for highways. Investment in publicly-owned rail networks would be the most productive way to make the rail mode more competitive. But the NTC cannot recommend that: it is constrained by both its ignorance of the rail freight industry and by being a creation of Commonwealth governments that will not take a lead on rail industry issues.

Infrastructure Australia and The National Land Freight Strategy

Infrastructure Australia was established by the Labor federal government in 2008,[225] to provide advice to the Australian Government and to COAG. It is an independent statutory body with a mandate to prioritise and progress nationally significant infrastructure of all types across transport, energy, telecommunications, and water. As such, its role in relation to land transport is to provide better information and analysis of potential rail and highway investments, and to prioritise them within a national list of options for governments. With such information publicly available, it should make it harder, in theory, for governments to announce vote-buying highway projects ahead of analyses being done to show their economic justification.

In February 2011, Infrastructure Australia (IA) published a discussion paper about a proposed National Land Freight Strategy, seeking input on objectives, strategic directions and priorities, from all levels of government and private industry. In its introduction, it espoused what was then a somewhat radical view:[226]

> "Rail and road freight infrastructure planning and investment can no longer be undertaken in isolation from each other, or worse, in competition with each other. ..... A new national freight strategy needs to be

developed for our freight networks to improve planning, investment and decision making."

It was radical in the sense that transport policy was up till then segmented by jurisdiction and by mode (roads, railways, ports, etc). This paper led to the adoption and publication in 2012 by COAG's Standing Council on Transport and Infrastructure (SCOTI) of the National Land Freight Strategy.[227]

This document states that it is the first time a national approach for planning for freight has been jointly agreed by the Commonwealth, State, Territory, and local governments. Its purpose is to direct the efforts of all governments and industry towards the long-term vision. It identified six major challenges that require coordinated policy action and effort by governments and industry to:[228]

- "ensure there are long term and integrated plans in place for freight;
- invest in the right infrastructure at the right time;
- improve access, investment and charging arrangements for heavy vehicles;
- create better and more consistent regulation;
- enhance understanding of the freight task and its associated challenges; and
- build community understanding and support for the role of freight in society."

Infrastructure Australia now publishes annual Infrastructure Priority Lists and 15-year rolling Infrastructure Plans. The first such Plan[229] was published in 2016, recommending reforms to the funding and operation of major infrastructure. Under the heading of "efficient infrastructure markets" it advocated for full privatisation of the energy and water sectors, and "user pays" as a general principle for all infrastructure use. It offered no advice on possible reform of freight rail infrastructure, but for roads it said:[230]

"the transition to a more user pays approach would allow charging to be linked to funding and supply to be linked to demand. This will be fundamental to securing the required funding and sustainably improving the level of service."

This was theoretically sound advice, but as we will see in the next chapter, politically difficult to implement.

The Australian Infrastructure Plan of 2016 also called for the development of a National Freight and Supply Chain Strategy. Its purpose would be to define nationally significant freight corridors and precincts, and to identify priorities for Australia for the next 20 years which would improve freight and supply chain productivity, efficiency and capacity. The outcome was a report commissioned by the Commonwealth Department of Infrastructure and Regional Development in March 2017, with input from an expert panel.231 This report was published in March 2018, and is discussed below under *Changes in the focus of transport sector reform*. Its findings were endorsed and led to the publication of the *National Freight and Supply Chain Strategy* by the Transport and Infrastructure Council in August 2019.232

The Transport and Infrastructure Council (TAIC)

This Council was established by COAG in December 2013, and effectively replaced the COAG Standing Committee on Transport Infrastructure (SCOTI), which in turn had previously replaced the Australian Transport Council in 2011. The Transport and Infrastructure Council (TAIC) reports to COAG, although it was announced on 29 May 2020 that COAG would cease and would be replaced by a new National Federation Reform Council (NFRC), primarily to better respond to the Covid-19 pandemic.[233] The TAIC is chaired by the Commonwealth Minister for Infrastructure, Transport and Regional Development.[234]

Its other members are various State and Territory Ministers for Infrastructure &/or Planning &/or Transport &/or Roads, the president of the Australian Local Government Association, and the New Zealand Minister for Economic Development and Transport.

The scope of the Council is more proactive than was SCOTI. TAIC:[235]

- "Considers and develops responses to emerging issues in the transport and transport infrastructure sectors
- Supports an internationally competitive transport and transport infrastructure industry
- Pursues further opportunities for national consistency in regulatory and policy frameworks to improve safety, reduce costs and improve the operation of the transport and transport infrastructure sectors
- Delivers on responsibilities under legislation, national agreements, national partnerships and any other governance arrangements."

In March 2016, National Rail Policy was the subject of a workshop organised by the TAIC and attended by all jurisdictions and other interested groups such as the NTC and Infrastructure Australia. As a result, the Council produced a document *National Rail Vision and Work Program*,[236] which identified what were seen as the key topics for continuing rail reform to improve productivity:

- Access pricing and interoperability – wanting common pricing principles
- Safety and incident regulation – seeking harmonised standards across Australia
- Environmental regulation, planning and corridor protection
- Funding and investment – collaboration needed for most appropriate use of road and rail in grain-growing areas
- Performance measurement and management.

7. Transport Sector Reform

These topics were technically worthy but politically unchallenging. The 'national rail vision' did not include any changes to:
- the convention that the Commonwealth does not initiate policy for the rail industry
- the current situation of States' primary responsibility for railways, which inhibits development of national policies, and
- the existence of multiple rail network providers within the four most populous States, which inhibits rail operators' productivity and flexibility in responding to changes in their customers' needs, particularly in NSW and Victoria. (I will explain in chapter 9 how this situation originated, under *Division of the Rail Networks of South-east Australia*.)

Despite the call for integrated planning in SCOTI's 2012 National Land Freight Strategy, there was mostly no evidence in TAIC's Work Program of planning for railways and roads together, for the purpose of improving Australia's productivity, environmental issues, or its transport difficulties. The one exception was that the increased use of rail was seen as a means to alleviate congestion on city roads caused by movement of containers from and to the ports.

Changes in the focus of transport sector reform

The publication in March 2018, by the Commonwealth Department of Infrastructure, Regional Development and Cities, of the report *Inquiry into National Freight and Supply Chain Priorities* focused on planning for freight supply chains rather than infrastructure per se. It also highlighted a beneficial outcome of transport reform that had not been openly acknowledged before – improving Australia's position as a trading nation. The expert panel that wrote the report took the focus away from **efficiencies** in asset use to **effectiveness** of supply chains. (The difference between these two terms is explained at the start of chapter 9.) Here is the first paragraph from the report's Introduction:[237]

> "In order to secure the nation's productivity into the future, Australia needs to adopt a clearly defined goal of having a national and integrated approach to freight. Failure to have a national approach means higher cost of living for Australians and reduced competitiveness of Australian exports in the global marketplace."

The purpose of the Inquiry was made clear:[238]

> "The Inquiry will inform the development of a *National Freight and Supply Chain Strategy* to be considered by the Council of Australian Governments (COAG) Transport and Infrastructure Council in 2018."

The report referred to several reforms and strategies done with freight as the main focus in the previous six years, and pointed out that:

> "These previous reforms and strategies do not deal with the supply chain in its totality. A number of priorities/reforms identified in those documents are still to be implemented, and a number of the identified issues remain. Urgent action is now needed to facilitate the physical growth in the freight task, and to maintain and boost Australian competitiveness through productivity and efficiency enhancements which have been stalled in recent decades."

The expert panel's method of enquiry was to seek advice and submissions from a wide range of supply chain stakeholders, as well as having Supporting Papers prepared by the Commonwealth Department of Infrastructure and Regional Development. From all these sources, it was able to categorise thousands of supply chains into three types with common characteristics: [239]

- import/export freight, requiring better productivity at ports and intermodal terminals;
- inter- and intra- state freight, requiring good access to regional rail networks, particularly for the grain flows which are subject to large variations in annual harvest size;
- urban freight, the fastest growing type of any in Australia, increasingly experiencing congestion and 'first/last mile' issues, and requiring well-integrated transport and land-use planning. Short-haul freight trains between ports and suburban intermodal terminals are seen as a significant way to ease some of the congestion difficulties, but in the four main urban areas[240] there are conflicts with peak-hour passenger train operations to be resolved.

The Inquiry Report appears to have an immediate impact of benefit to rail – just two months after its publication the NSW government announced a major increase in funding for its *Fixing Country Rail* program. (There is a description of this program in Chapter 13, under *The NSW Experience*.)

In September 2018, the federal House of Representatives Standing Committee on Infrastructure, Transport and Cities published a report *Building Up and Moving Out: Inquiry into the Australian Government's role in the development of cities.* In one of its recommendations to the Australian Government, it wrote

> "Give priority to the development of a national freight network, with a view to creating a strong system of multimodal integration based on dedicated freight nodes, **prioritising the movement of freight by rail**, separating freight and passenger movements where possible" (my emphasis)

In its response,[241] the Government agreed in principle, citing the already agreed National Freight and Supply Chain

Strategy and associated National Action Plan as evidence of its recognition of the importance of freight. However, as usual, it did not comment on prioritising freight by rail.

The implementation and progress of the National Freight and Supply Chain Strategy can be followed at this website *https://www.freightaustralia.gov.au/* .

8. Australian Road Reform

The Australian Infrastructure Plan of 2016 recognized the validity of the many calls for a reform of the funding of roads and highways. The system in use then (and still now) created an inflated demand for highways, and a pricing distortion in the interstate freight market, to the detriment of the rail mode. All the aspects of what might need to be changed are generally grouped under the term "Road Reform". Because of the importance of this long-standing and still unresolved issue for the competitiveness of the rail freight industry, we take a brief look at what it's about.

The early development of the Australian road freight haulage industry is covered in chapter 2, under *Deregulation of Australian Road & Rail Competition*.

The truckies' blockades

By the 1970s, the bulk of interstate haulage by road was being done by self-employed owner-drivers, contracted to freight forwarders and other large companies. During the 1970s, owner-drivers endured a cost-price squeeze. Between 1973 and 1979, rates paid by freight forwarders to subcontractors increased by 45% while operating costs for owner-drivers increased by an estimated 110%.[242] Adding to these difficulties, the numbers of owner-drivers increased significantly from 1977 due to a change in tax policy — the introduction of investment allowances. The numbers of new trucks leased in the 1977/78 financial year also increased significantly[243] with new entrants to the industry wanting to take advantage of the 40% investment allowance. Some new entrants did not pick up enough business, and so made losses, not profits. Hence, they were unable to claim the investment allowance. With the increase in the size of the national trucking fleet, the prices for second-hand trucks fell, making it more difficult for marginal operators to sell and get out of the industry.[244]

One can imagine the accumulated frustrations, worries, tiredness and hopelessness among the owner-driver community. On 2 April 1979, six owner-drivers parked their rigs across the Hume Highway at Razorback, near Picton, in NSW. Within hours many more drivers joined the blockade, informed by the use of Citizen Band (CB) radios. Within two days other highway blockades were set up at three other sites in NSW, as well as in Queensland, Victoria, South Australia and Western Australia, each involving hundreds of trucks.

The demands of the owner-drivers varied across the country and over the following days, but the consistent one was the immediate removal of road maintenance charges, levied by the State governments at that time. On 7 April the federal and state transport ministers met and agreed to the abolition of road maintenance taxes from 1 July, along with other concessions. By eight days after the blockades started, all had been voluntarily removed, although under threat of arrest in NSW. A popular talkback radio host portrayed the blockades as a struggle of small business operators against bureaucracy, and for some, this image of heroism has become part of Australian popular history.

The blockades also showed the truckies how powerful they could be by acting together. In mid-July 1988 there was a spontaneous blockade on the Hume Highway at Yass protesting a proposed rise in truck registration fees imposed by the Commonwealth and calling for the abolition of the demerit points system under which truckies could lose their licenses.[245]

However, on this occasion, support from other truckies was lacking, so many of the thousands of trucks stopped at Yass were trapped there. However, the protesters won a promise to have truck registration fees frozen, and the blockade was lifted after five days.[246]

The blockades showed governments how difficult it can be to impose charges on owner-drivers, who constitute the majority in the road transport industry. On both occasions, the governments' responses were politically expedient. It was easy for them to yield, because there was no formal or legal linkage between these charges and government spending on roads and highways, and therefore no defensible legal justification for road transport charges. If there had been such, then all parties might have accepted that the charges paid by the road transport industry were for services and the use of assets provided by governments, and therefore a valid cost of doing business. In that case, the revenues and the expenditure could have been accounted for and publicised, even with multiple road and highway providers.

The need for Road Reform

In Australia, there is a strong tradition that roads and highways are provided and maintained primarily by governments, funded as part of the annual budgetary processes. These practices date from the era of Keynesian economics (approximately 1935 to 1980), and they continue despite the change to neoliberal economics from the 1980s. Neoliberal politicians apparently have not considered the potential to reduce government expenditures by selling off existing roads and highways to become businesses. One roading consultant thought this was mainly because roads are viewed as social infrastructure. It wrote, in 2012: [247]

> "Roads appear to be the last major infrastructure monopoly in Australia in which social and economic purposes are not closely defined."

However, for decades, there has been widespread agreement on the need for reform of the ways in which roads are paid for; only the road transport industry opposes such reform, being the beneficiary of the under-recovery of costs. The primary issues to be resolved in Road Reform are:[248]

- the basis on which the National Transport Commission (NTC) calculates the total cost of roading, because it omits 75% of the cost of urban local roads and 50% of the cost of rural local roads – hence it understates how much needs to be recovered from road users;
- the basis on which costs are deemed attributable to heavy vehicles or treated as common costs to be shared equally among all road users – this understates the real costs of maintaining highways and bridges for use by heavy vehicles;
- there is no recognition of the value to road freighters of historically provided infrastructure;
- the lack of any formal linkage between the money raised by taxing road users, and the money spent by governments on providing and maintaining roads and highways.

The under-recovery of roading costs incurred by heavy truck operations is the main reason for the lack of competitive neutrality between road and rail, described in chapter 13. This lack can be seen in a comparison between the two modes: in 2010, before the ARTC increased its charges to current levels, train operators spent 30-40% of their operating costs on rail access charges, while heavy vehicle operators spent only 5% of total costs on road user charges.[249]

The need for Road Reform has been a persistent topic in the national deliberation on land transport for over sixty years. In 1990, Dr Philip Laird, a prolific writer on land freight transport issues, found[250] fourteen papers and reports that wrote about hidden subsidies to the road freight industry, the

earliest published in 1956. The majority of these reports were by various government agencies and inquiries:
- the Bureau of Transport (and Communications) Economics, in 1984 and 1988
- the Inter-State Commission, in 1986, 1987 and 1990
- the Industries Assistance Commission, in 1986 and 1989
- the Business Regulation Review Unit, in 1988
- the House of Representatives Standing Committee on Transport, Communications and Infrastructure, in 1987 and 1989.

Significantly, all these reports were written in the decade after the first of the truckies' blockades in 1979, which resulted in the removal of road maintenance charges by State governments.

There have been suggestions since the mid-1980s that road user charges, based on vehicle laden weight and distance travelled, would be a better alternative in Australia for raising revenues for road spending than vehicle registration charges and the diesel fuel levy. It was noted that similar systems were already in use in New Zealand, Britain, France, Sweden, Finland, Austria and Portugal.[251] The reasoning is that such a system better aligns with the user-pays principle, and is therefore fairer to all road freight transporters. To the extent that B-doubles are subsidised by other types of trucks due to the registration system, vehicle-linked road user charges would also provide fairer competition for freight train operators by removing those subsidies. (See in chapter 6 for the details, under *Road and Rail Freight Infrastructure Pricing*.)

In the 1990s, Road Reform continued to be pushed by those concerned with Rail Reform. The Industry Commission in its 1991 report *Rail Transport* (see in chapter 5) included:[252]

> "Recommendation 5.1:
> The Commission recommends the introduction of road user charges which reflect more accurately the amount of road use and pavement damage caused by all classes

of vehicles. A national vehicle registration scheme is a key element in achieving these changes."

In 1992, the Industry Commission commented on the method of recovery of roading costs in the context of charges that had recently been set by the NRTC (see below in the next section): [253]

"Annual fixed charges are not efficient because costs vary with the distance travelled and the mass of the vehicle. The result is that some vehicles - the heaviest travelling long annual distances - will meet less than 20 per cent of their attributed costs. Charges for heavy vehicles that reflect costs they impose are essential to ensure best use is made of the nation's road and rail infrastructure ... Differences between the recommended charges and road-related costs are greatest for vehicles competing with rail. The charges, as recommended, will therefore potentially distort the long-haul freight market as rail reforms take effect."

In 1999, the Productivity Commission, in its report *Progress in Rail Reform*, noted:[254]

"The existing road user charging system for heavy vehicles underrecovers road costs attributable to classes of vehicles which compete directly with railways. This confers a competitive advantage on long distance road transport operators. ... The National Road Transport Commission should prepare — and recommend to the Ministerial Council for Road Transport for adoption — a revised schedule of heavy vehicle charges which ensures that each class of vehicle pays the full cost of its road use."

Similarly, the Productivity Commission in its 2006 report *Road and Rail Freight Infrastructure Pricing*, echoed the call for a change to the basis for highway funding:[255]

8. Australian Road Reform

> "Road pricing policies will be more likely to achieve efficient outcomes (strengthen market discipline, and influence supply and demand the most) when there is an explicit link between road-user prices, revenues received and decisions about future road expenditures."

In 2011, the need for reform of the method of charging for road use by heavy vehicles was raised by the Australian Treasury, in the context of a broad review of opportunities for tax reform. It wrote:[256]

> "heavy vehicles cause the great bulk of road wear. ... current arrangements provide inadequate incentives to operators to choose routes and vehicle configurations that minimise road damage and costs on others."

This discussion paper noted that reform of road vehicle charging was being considered at that time by COAG, which had received a feasibility study report,[257] originally requested in April 2007, which

> "found that a more direct link between the costs of heavy vehicle road use, heavy vehicle road use charges and revenues to road providers would promote long-term cost effective maintenance and investment in roads."

It is vital that the Commonwealth Government initiate any moves to Road Reform because of the fiscal imbalance; it has the power to tax or charge road freight operators, while the State and Territory governments have the responsibility for the great majority of spending on roads. Despite the many calls, listed above, for Road Reform to be implemented, there have still been no major changes (by 2023). Why, after more than four decades, is this so?

Slow progress in Road Reform

National Road Transport Commission

One increment of Road Reform, in its broadest sense, was implemented as an outcome of the early 1990s period of 'microeconomic reform' led by the federal Labor government. The National Road Transport Commission (NRTC) was established in January 1992[258] to work towards a national uniformity in the regulation of road vehicles and road use. Up to that time each State and Territory had had its own regulations, and there were major disparities in heavy vehicle regulation that were perceived to be affecting the efficiency of the interstate trucking industry. Disparities were many and varied:[259]

> "Many of the areas involved are highly technical and have ramifications for other aspects of regulation. Variations may reflect different judgements on empirical matters, different trade-offs between safety and efficiency, different operating conditions or the entrenchment of historical accidents."

The purpose of the NRTC was to develop legislation that could be agreed to and adopted by all the States and Territories. Areas of work included setting vehicle registration charges, vehicle safety standards, driver standards and licensing, traffic regulations, and dangerous goods regulations.[260]

The NRTC first recommended a national set of heavy vehicle registration charges in 1992, but the States and Territories took till 1995 (South Australia and Queensland), 1996 (Western Australia, Victoria, Tasmania and ACT), and 1997 (New South Wales and Northern Territory) to implement them.[261] A heavy vehicle registration scheme had been recommended in 1991 by the Industry Commission as a prerequisite for implementing a weight- and distance-based road user charges scheme.

During the next decade, nothing was achieved to contribute towards a change in collecting money for road maintenance

8. Australian Road Reform

and development, nor in the method of funding such, as indicated by the reports quoted in the previous section from 1999, 2006 and 2011.

Heavy Vehicle Charging and Investment Reform (HVCI)

However, following the Productivity Commission's 2006 report *Road and Rail Freight Infrastructure Pricing*, COAG established a group in 2007 called the COAG Road Reform Plan (CRRP).[262] In 2009, COAG approved this group to proceed with a feasibility study of options for heavy vehicle road access pricing, and the provision of roads to support freight. COAG received this feasibility study in 2012, and consequently established the Heavy Vehicle Charging and Investment Reform (HVCI) project to build on the work of the CRRP.[263] A significant finding from the feasibility study was that the reform of heavy vehicle charging would not deliver benefits without there also being reform of the 'supply side', i.e., the distribution of funds to roading agencies.[264] This finding immediately made the Road Reform project much more complex and cumbersome.

It is noteworthy that for the HVCI, the issue of competitive neutrality between road freight services and rail freight was not a policy consideration, because of the influence of the Productivity Commission's 2006 report *Road and Rail Freight Infrastructure Pricing*. This report had stated that[265]

> "The available evidence, while not conclusive, does not support the contention that road freight is subsidised relative to rail on either the inter-capital corridors or in regional areas."

(See in chapter 6, under *The Productivity Commission's 2006 report* for an explanation of why this PC finding was biased and misleading.) Indeed, this policy perspective might have made the HVCI's discussions with the road transport industry easier, by being able to provide assurance to the road industry that the proposed reforms would not benefit the rail industry.

In November 2013, transport ministers asked the HVCI to develop a detailed implementation plan[266] for consideration at the May 2014 meeting. Hence, as well as developing charging options, HCVI also investigated options for the structure and governance of an entity to collect and disperse roading funds, what its scope of operations might be, and issues such as the identity of a future economic regulator for heavy vehicles.[267] In 2014, it presented a proposal to the Transport and Infrastructure Council (TAIC) recommending mass-distance-location pricing, which would have required fitting trucks with monitoring devices to charge them based on the weight they carried, the distance they travelled and the roads they used. This proposal also had the full support of the National Commission of Audit (NCOA), on the basis that it would "reduce congestion and increase funding from those that directly benefit from road use."[268]

However, TAIC declined to implement the recommended new heavy vehicle pricing system. A former member of the Board of the HVCI Reform project explained:[269]:

> "We were asking too much of ministers... There is no appetite for big bang reform... The complexity and cost of implementing a new road pricing regime and the lack of industry support for it also influenced ministers' thinking."

This reluctance to proceed was made positive in the communiqué from the May 2014 meeting:[270]

> "The Council agreed that jurisdictions would commence work to implement initial heavy vehicle investment and access reform measures... The Council has also agreed that advice be prepared on possible next steps in heavy vehicle charging and investment reform for consideration at the next Council meeting. This advice will build off a plan prepared by the Heavy Vehicle Charging and Investment Board, which has now completed its work."

In other words, work could proceed on the 'supply side' issues, i.e., the way governments plan, govern and invest in roads. However, nothing was to be done yet to change the method of charging for road use. The HVCI Reform project ceased on 30 June 2014.

An inconvenient truth

Soon after the HVCI Reform project ceased, a report[271] was leaked as an "industry consultation draft", intended to be published by Infrastructure Australia (IA), but written by a consultant who had previously had reports published by IA.[272] Titled *"Spend more, waste more"*, it was highly critical of many aspects of the ways in which funds were collected and spent on roads:[273]

> "Australia has a true gambler's addiction to roads: the money spent is not a rational investment. Governments assume that major improvement is just around the corner, if they could just spend more."
>
> "The current Australian system assumes that roads are an answer to most transport problems and seeks more and more funding to that end, with little consideration of alternatives that most other developed parts of the world enjoy, such as significant heavy intercontinental rail networks"
>
> "The COAG Road Reform Project ... has achieved nothing, other than to reject outright some of the pillars of Australia's competition principles."
>
> "Barring some notable exceptions, the culture of road agency monopolies is extremely resistant to change – at times actively so. Crucially, this includes very strong resistance to private investment in and access to road infrastructure, which appears as much as anything to be a fear of loss of control."
>
> "The unhealthy focus of road agencies appears set on 'getting, controlling and spending' more taxpayer

money, rather than questioning efficiency or value to the motorist and governments."

The tone of these comments was altogether too provocative for some, and the CEO of IA ordered the report withdrawn within hours of it being leaked.[274] It has not been acknowledged since, although it contained much valuable analysis and comment. It argued for direct pricing of trucks on roads, as had been recommended in the Productivity Commission's Review of Road and Rail Infrastructure Pricing in 2006 (see in Chapter 6). It argued that achieving an "efficient road/rail mix" should be a major reform objective:[275]

> "Australia's ongoing failure to remove cross subsidies from the road freight sector *in those places where it competes directly with commercial rail* lies at the heart of seeing greater investment in Australian rail freight. Not resolving this issue – known as competitive neutrality – has strong potential to be keeping freight costs to the Australian economy artificially high."

An inconvenient truth indeed.

Heavy Vehicle Road Reform

By 2016, Heavy Vehicle Road Reform was the name given to the broader project that had evolved since the HCVI group was closed down. At that time, the TAIC had an article on its website that explained the purpose of Road Reform and what progress had been made.[276]

> "The ultimate goal of heavy vehicle road reform is to turn the provision of heavy vehicle road infrastructure into an economic service where feasible. This would see a market established that links the needs of heavy vehicle users with the level of service they receive, the charges they pay and the investment of those charges back into road services."

"Shifting to a system where heavy vehicle infrastructure is provided as an economic service will be complex and take time to implement. The reform requires substantial policy, financial, institutional and governance changes to be implemented by all levels of government. In addition, heavy vehicle users, and the industry more broadly, will need to understand and participate in new investment decision making and charge setting processes."

The website also provided more detail on what had been agreed at the TAIC May 2014 meeting as the next steps for the program:[277]

"Transport Ministers agreed that jurisdictions would work together to implement four heavy vehicle access and investment initial measures:
1. asset registers and assessments of road conditions according to agreed service level standards by the end of 2015;
2. improved data for demand forecasting by the end of 2016;
3. publish annual heavy vehicle expenditure plans, based on efficient costs and prepared on a consistent basis by the end of 2016; and
4. investigate practical ways for industry to negotiate and pay for improved access by the end of 2016."

Progress was reported on all of the measures above, together with a commitment by the Commonwealth Government [278]

"to work with states and territories to accelerate heavy vehicle road reform, including identifying potential steps to transition to independent price regulation for heavy vehicle charges by 2017-18."

The promised acceleration of heavy vehicle road reform was such that, by 2021, the successors to TAIC had produced a comprehensive plan[279] (reproduced on the next page) for yet

Pathway ahead: Heavy Vehicle Road Reform

INFRASTRUCTURE AND TRANSPORT MINISTERS

As governments proceed along the pathway, they may decide at any time whether to continue on the pathway, and whether to ultimately participate in the reformed system.

	2021 Identify	**2022 Prepare**	**2023 Setup**	**2024 Apply**

(Given the complexity of the reform, these dates are indicative only)

(A cascading roll-out, not concurrent commencement)

The four pillars:

1. National Service Level Standards for roads
- 2021: Finalise the framework (road categories, customer values, metrics), including specific reference to heavy vehicle application ▲
- 2022: Allocate roads to service level standard categories; begin collecting data on service levels ▲
- 2023: Negotiate then set level of ambition for standards; establish ongoing governance arrangements for reviewing and updating standards; (continue to collect data on service levels) ▲
- 2024: Use service level standards framework to help identify road investment priorities; prepare for ongoing review of service level standards

2. Independent determination of what expenditure is recoverable through heavy vehicle charges
- 2021: Agree a governance model for expenditure review; identify expenditure review body/ies
- 2022: Agree principles for expenditure review on which legislative drafting will be based; scope responsibilities and roles of expenditure review body/ies
- 2023: Start to draft legislation; agree national expenditure review guidelines; begin staffing investment review body/ies, who begin engaging with road agencies
- 2024: Investment review body/ies to determine cost-effective expenditure that is [reasonably] consistent with service level standards, providing guidance and feedback to road agencies on requirements

3. Independent setting of heavy vehicle charges
- 2021: Identify independent price regulator; agree high-level principles for charge setting and revenue implications
- 2022: Decide key settings for a forward-looking cost base (FLCB); agree a transitional path for charges/revenue ▲
- 2023: Start to draft legislation for independent price regulator; begin staffing independent price regulator; develop guidelines for charge setting
- 2024: Independent price regulator begins charge-setting process in line with agreed transition arrangements

4. Hypothecation
- 2021: Provide Ministers visibility of current funding arrangements, to compare to proposed reform
- 2022: Detail hypothecation arrangements
- 2023: Finalise implications for existing infrastructure commitments; consider reflecting reforms in LTIP National Partnership Agreement
- 2024: Hypothecation of charges revenue begins

▲ = Proposed public consultation point

more slow progress on the supply side issues. Note the get-out clause in the top left of the document:

> "As governments proceed along the pathway, they may decide at any time whether to continue on the pathway, and whether to ultimately participate in the reformed system."

The indication from this "pathway" document is that reform to the way heavy vehicles are charged for the use of roads and highways will not start till sometime after 2024, and possibly never in any States that choose to step off the reform pathway.

Infrastructure Australia in 2016 predicted the consequence for railways of slow progress in Road Reform, a consequence which will still hold true well into the 2020s:[280]

> "Competitive neutrality between road and rail freight is yet to be established. The absence of effective heavy vehicle user charging distorts the efficient movement of freight across the economy and undermines the economics of freight rail for some cargo profiles, meaning modal choices and pricing outcomes for freight are not always optimal."

It looks like Heavy Vehicle Road Reform has become a case of paralysis by analysis.

Part C:
Outcomes

9. How and Why the Rail Freight Industry Changed

10. Privatisation – Hopes and Outcomes

11. The Privatisation of Four Vertically-Integrated Railways

12. Competition Outcomes

9. How and Why the Rail Freight Industry Changed

Changes in railway ownership and organisation structures

For an industry that was stable for many decades, in terms of its ownership structure and purpose, the changes experienced from the 1990s onwards were disruptive and widespread, affecting every State's railway. It now appears that the industry has reached a new stability in these respects. What follows is an attempt to make sense of a stream of largely unrelated events by looking at common themes.

After the federal government closed the old and isolated narrow-gauge in 1976 North Australia Railway, every government in Australasia disposed of its freight railway system as a going concern. The circumstances of each railway's disposal are well documented elsewhere, so the events will just be listed and summarised. What are of interest are the reasons for these disposals, discussed below. The disposals mostly involved one of two different processes which characterised the instability in the Australasian rail industry over the transitional period – vertical separation and privatisation. Some railways were subject to both processes sequentially.

However, the earliest disposals, prior to the 1990s, required only the transfer of assets and operations to another government owned railway, in unique circumstances. In the early 1970s the Whitlam Federal Government offered for the Commonwealth to take over the state-owned railways, in an attempt to create one national railway. In 1978 the Tasmanian and South Australian governments took up the offer. As a result, these state-owned rail networks were absorbed into the recently formed Australian National Railways Commission (AN). The other State governments did not accept the offer, and the impetus to create one vertically-integrated national railway system dissipated.

Some railways changed control in their existing vertically-integrated form

This type of change meant that the whole of the business and all its assets (rolling-stock, tracks, yards, buildings and other structures) were included.

- The federally-owned Commonwealth Railways formed the core of what was intended to be another federally-owned but national rail system – Australian National Railways, in 1975.
- South Australian Railways and Tasmanian Government Railways were absorbed into Australian National Railways in 1978, but with TasRail operating as a necessarily isolated business.
- New Zealand Rail Ltd was privatised by its sale in 1993 to the Tranz Rail consortium comprising Wisconsin Central Railroad (in the USA) together with American and New Zealand investment bankers. The sale price was $NZ328 million, based on an 'enterprise value' of $NZ400 million minus NZ Rail Ltd's debt.[281] The sale included the network of fixed assets which had previously been legally separated from the land on which it lay, because the sale of any government land was a contentious issue at the time for other reasons. The rail corridor land was leased to the rail operator for $1 per year.

- The federal government privatised TasRail in 1997 when AN sold it as a going concern to Australian Transport Network (ATN) for $A22 million[282]. In 1998, ATN bought the privately-owned Emu Bay Railway in western Tasmania for $A7.8 million and incorporated it into the TasRail network. In 2004, Pacific National (PN) bought the whole ATN business, which then comprised the enlarged TasRail business and network, and some rolling-stock for grain haulage contracts in NSW and Victoria. The purchase price was undisclosed but estimated to be approximately $A13 million.[281]
- V/Line Freight Corp was sold in 1999 to Rail America (trading as Freight Victoria then Freight Australia) for $A163 million, with the Victorian intrastate broad-gauge rail network leased for 45 years.[283] In August 2004 Pacific National bought this business including the network lease for $A285 million.[284] Since then, there has been no separately identifiable Victorian rail-freight entity.
- WestRail Freight was sold in 2000 to Australian Railroad Group (ARG), partly owned by Genesee & Wyoming, for $A585 million,[285] including an up-front payment of the total rent for the rail network leased to it for 49 years.

Considering the hopes of the governments that sold New Zealand Rail, TasRail and V/Line Freight, the outcomes of these sales were ultimately failures. In contrast, the sale of WestRail Freight had a partially successful outcome for the WA Government. These four stories are told in chapter 11.

All the privatisations above were achieved by competitive trade sales, but in Queensland it was done differently. In 2010, the executive team of QR convinced the Queensland Government to sell its freight rail business by IPO. In preparation for this event, Queensland Rail was vertically and horizontally separated so that QR National (later named Aurizon) took the above-rail freight business and the below-rail Central Queensland Coal

Network (CQCN), while QR remained the network provider for the majority of the state's network and its passenger train operator. (See in chapter 12, under *How Competition Evolved - Queensland* for a fuller description.)

Some railways were vertically separated years ahead of privatisation of train operations

- The former State Rail Authority of New South Wales (SRANSW) underwent the most change. Freight Rail was created as a business unit of SRANSW in 1989. In 1993 the interstate traffic, plus some staff and rolling-stock, were transferred to the new National Rail Corporation (NRC). In 1996 Freight Rail was corporatized to become FreightCorp, while the NSW rail network was put under the control at that time of state-owned Rail Access Corporation (RAC), in anticipation of creating an open access regime. This was the first instance of an intentional vertical separation achieved in Australasia. In 2001, RAC was absorbed into the Rail Infrastructure Corporation (RIC). However, in 2004, management and maintenance of the NSW network was split into three jurisdictions (with consequences that are explained in Chapter 16, under the heading *The Legacy of the Reform Process in NSW*):
  — RailCorp, a vertically re-integrated rail system (of 672 route-kilometres) with a predominant focus on urban and regional passenger services, managed the Metropolitan Network, spanning urban Sydney and the Central Coast, Newcastle, Illawarra and Blue Mountains areas;
  — The ARTC leased the Interstate and Hunter Valley lines from the State for sixty years;
  — The remainder of the state network, known as the Country Rail Network (CRN), was owned

for the NSW Government by the Country Rail Infrastructure Authority (CRIA), which contracts out the management and maintenance functions. From 2004, the role of Rail Infrastructure Manager was contracted to the ARTC, then in 2012 this contract was awarded to the John Holland Rail Group for ten years. The CRN is not actually a conventional railway network; it is a notional network of eleven geographically separated sections of regional and branch lines, united only by its management. In 2004 it comprised 3110 kms of lines still used, and 2900 kms of disused (but not closed) lines.[286]

Meanwhile, the above-rail FreightCorp was sold in 2002, together with National Rail Corporation, for over $1 billion to become Pacific National (PN), a joint venture between Patrick Corporation and Toll Holdings.

- Australian National (1975 – 1998) had to transfer its interstate business and rolling-stock to NRC in 1994, then its South Australian and Tasmanian businesses were sold separately by the Commonwealth in 1997, while its mainland network became the core of the Australian Rail Track Corporation (ARTC) network in July 1998. There was therefore a partial and de facto vertical separation of AN, with open access on its network from 1993 to 1998. Both NRC and ARTC were government-owned, and ARTC remains a corporation owned and capital-funded by the Commonwealth Government (see below, from page 106).

Some railways were vertically separated after privatisation

- ARG reorganised itself in 2002 to become the Australian Railroad Group (ARG – the WA train operator) and WestNet Rail (the network operator). In 2006 ARG was bought by QR National, which later

became Aurizon. WestNet Rail was bought by Babcock and Brown, which in turn sold it in December 2010 to Brookfield Rail, a subsidiary of the international infrastructure holding company, Brookfield Infrastructure Partners, based in Bermuda.
- Tranz Rail was vertically separated in 2004 when the railway network was bought back by the New Zealand Government for $1 after ten years of inadequate spending on track maintenance and asset renewals under Tranz Rail ownership. Tranz Rail had been bought in 2003 by Toll Holdings, an Australian freight logistics company. In 2008, the government bought the above-rail business from Toll and re-integrated it as KiwiRail.
- In Victoria, after Pacific National had bought Freight Australia including the lease to the country intrastate network, it sold the track lease back to the government for an announced sum of $A133.8 million,[287] ceding the network in May 2007 while retaining the above-rail business.

Division of the rail networks of south-east Australia

The process by which the defined interstate rail network was created, eventually under the control of the ARTC, is described below. The Commonwealth Government had focused over many years on the completion of this network only, while the States retained ownership, but not always control, of the residual networks in their jurisdictions. The narrow-gauge networks of Western Australia and Queensland, which continue to service intrastate traffics mainly from the regions to the ports, remain the least affected by the creation of the interstate network. It was in Victoria and New South Wales that the impact was greatest, because the lines that came under ARTC control were and still are the trunk lines for each state's regional network.

In these two south-eastern states, the rail networks that had been part of a government-owned vertically-integrated railway, were each split into three jurisdictions after vertical separation.

The lines used by the capital city urban passenger services are controlled by State government authorities, the ARTC now controls the main lines, and other State organisations control the regional branch lines. This is the result of what has been described as "policy neglect"[288]. When decisions were made by various governments in the 1990s to implement the policy of competition, involving vertical separation and privatisation of train operations, little thought was given to regional lines and traffics. In both States, maintenance and upgrading of regional lines has been inadequate until recently, leading to some abandonments. The existence of three jurisdictions in each State still hampers train operators in ways that will be described in Chapter 13, under *Competition for Access to Networks – Obtaining Train Paths Across Multiple Access Regimes*. Suffice to say that train operators are not happy with this situation, and the network owners' lack of concern about it. In 2007, the Freight Rail Operators Group commented to the ACCC about inefficient train pathing across the 'borders':[289]

> "By refusing to formally recognise the need to work collaboratively across networks, network owners have created their own borders that are every bit as disruptive as the State borders that ARTC was supposed to eliminate."

By 2012, Transport for NSW had recognised the problem, because it was an impediment to increasing the volume of freight on its rail network:[290]

> "Depending on the circumstances, those operating rail freight services in NSW may need to negotiate with up to three different network owners, under three different access regulatory arrangements to operate across multiple networks. Network interface management is now a key challenge for operators and it's important that the future access regime supports the efficiency of the supply chains operating across these networks."

Both States are keen to increase the movement of freight by rail, particularly within their major cities. Perhaps because of the split provision of access to tracks, and the competition between train operators by market segmentation, there has been no unified marketing to freight shippers of their rail freight option until recently. However, the Victorian Government has in 2020 established a Rail Freight Working Group, combining government agencies with freight and primary industries, to identify rail freight network priorities that will increase the volume of freight on rail.[291]

Due to both policy neglect and maintenance neglect, some intrastate traffic has shifted to road over the last twenty years. However, the development of regional hubs is now slowly reversing this decline in rail traffic. Created by progressive logistics companies and by local shire councils, these hubs enable the intermodal transfer of freight onto the railway near to the sources of that freight.

An overview of the key events in the history of vertical separation, privatisation, and renationalisation

As the table on the following pages shows, the processes of vertical separation and privatisation were not a prerequisite for each other.

9. How and Why the Rail Freight Industry Changed

Steps in Vertical Separation and Reintegration	Date	Steps in Privatisation and Renationalisation
	Oct 1993	NZ Rail Ltd sold to a consortium led by Wisconsin Central Railroad; the business was later rebranded Tranz Rail Ltd
National Rail Corp (NRC) first operated its trains, meaning de facto open access in Vic & SA	Nov 1993	
Australian National ceded its interstate traffic to NRC, creating de facto vertical separation in SA	1994	
First formal vertical separation: NSW Govt created FreightCorp as above-rail freight business, and Rail Access Corp (RAC) to manage track access	July 1996	
Australian National remained as below-rail operator for interstate routes till these ceded to ARTC in July 1998	Nov 1997	Australian National sold its South Australian intrastate business to ASR, and TasRail to Australian Transport Network (ATN)
Victorian interstate standard gauge lines leased to ARTC in July 1999	May 1999	V/Line Freight sold to Rail America with long-term lease of Victorian broad-gauge network. In 2004, this business was sold to PN
In 2002, ARG vertically separated itself into two companies: ARG (above rail) and WestnetRail (below rail); each was later sold to separately	Oct 2000→	WestRail sold to Australian Railroad Group (ARG) with long-term lease on its network
	Jan 2002	NRC and FreightCorp sold jointly to create Pacific National (PN)
RailCorp formed by NSW Govt as a vertically-integrated, primarily passenger railway network	Jan 2004	

Steps in Vertical Separation and Reintegration	Date	Steps in Privatisation and Renationalisation
Tranz Rail, was vertically separated by agreement between Toll and NZ Government	July 2004	Railway network bought back by NZ Govt for $1, with promise of $200m new investment
TasRail was vertically separated because Pacific National was not maintaining the network	May 2007	Tasmanian government bought the island's rail network for $1
Victorian freight railway was vertically separated when Government bought back the lease on the broad-gauge network	May 2007	Control of the Victorian country network passed to V/Line (regional passenger train operator)
New Zealand's railways were re-integrated, adopting the name 'KiwiRail'.	May 2008	Toll Rail renationalised: NZ Govt bought back the above-rail business after under-payment of network usage charges.
TasRail became vertically-integrated again	Dec 2009	TasRail renationalised: Tasmanian Govt bought above-rail business after PN announced closure
Queensland Rail separated its above-rail freight business, and the CQCN for later sale; retained remainder of network and its passenger operations in government control	← July 2010. November 2010 →	CQCN and freight business sold by IPO, trading first as QR National, later as Aurizon

In addition to these key events, there were a number of other changes happening on Australian networks from 1995 onward. Several small freight train operators were started, and some of these have later merged or been consolidated into others. (There is more detail in chapter 12 *Competition outcomes*, in box 12/1.)

The Australian Rail Track Corporation (ARTC)

In the beginning ...

Up until 1998, the Interstate Rail Network was still managed by five separate rail systems. TNT, a freight forwarding company that ran its own trains from 1996 onward described the situation thus:[292]

> "there were no uniform pricing principles across States, no transparency of track management costs and access prices, no mechanism in any State to ensure costs were driven down to reflect efficient practice and competitive neutrality between State owned operators and private sector operators was not guaranteed."

In September 1997, Commonwealth and State Transport Ministers had met at the National Rail Summit. Agreement was reached for the Commonwealth to establish the Australian Rail Track Corporation as a single point of access for the Interstate Rail Network. Its functions were to: [293]

- "manage track maintenance and construction, train pathing, scheduling, timetabling, and train control on track it controls;
- develop and promote uniform safe-working, technical and operating requirements; and
- manage an interstate track investment program with commercial funding and grants from the governments involved, in consultation with rail operators and track owners."

Given the historical reticence of the Commonwealth Government to get involved with rail, its expectations for the ARTC in 1998 were consistent, but unfair to the rail industry given its continuing subsidies to the road sector through its funding of the National Highway System: [294]

> "Track access revenues will need to cover all below-rail ongoing operating costs and the ARTC will be required to act as a commercial entity with no ongoing subsidy from Government."

The ARTC started operating from 1 July 1998, with the lines ceded from AN, and the leased Victorian standard-gauge interstate lines from Albury to Melbourne and Melbourne to the South Australian border. By September 1999, ARTC had spent $20 million on infrastructure upgrade for the Melbourne to Adelaide line,[295] building two new crossing loops and extending five others, all to 1500 metres in length. In addition, maximum train speeds over most of this route were increased from 80 kph to 115 kph.

The ARTC outlined four key objectives for itself in its 1999 annual report:[296]

- Improve reliability
- Improve the yield[297] for train operators and the track infrastructure
- Improve transit times, and
- Establish the foundations for a 'one-stop shop', from Brisbane to Perth.

The annual report commented:

> "The improved transit time objective is primarily directed at achieving competitiveness over short haul routes against road. It is not aimed at matching road times per se, but rather achieving overnight service capacity and greater potential asset efficiency for rail operators."

> "An early target was to obtain a 10.5 hours transit time for premium services on the Melbourne to Adelaide corridor and 12 hours for superfreighters. The premium services have experienced transit time reductions from over 13 hours to 10.5 hours, while superfreighters have reduced from up to 16 hours to around 12 hours, with further consolidation of these gains by December 1999.

The average transit time for freight services on this corridor has reduced by 70 minutes."

The investments to improve the yield for train operators paid off, because over the first six-year period to 2004, freight hauled on the ARTC network increased 24% from 25.7 bgtk to 31.9 bgtk.[298] Also, rail's market share of the land transport market on the east-west corridor climbed from about 67% under AN control in 1998 to over 81% by 2004.[297]

The ARTC was also successful in reducing track maintenance costs compared to when AN managed the interstate lines, by outsourcing some of the work, providing 'competition for the market', instead of using its own maintenance staff 100% of the time. It formed alliance relationships with several specialised infrastructure maintenance providers. An example was a contract for maintenance and reconstruction on the trans-continental line across the Nullarbor Plain, where getting maintenance staff to and from remote work-sites was time-consuming and unproductive paid time. A small Western Australian operator, South Spur Rail Services, developed a caravan train which enabled track maintenance staff to be fed and rested on board when the train was parked at remote sidings closer to the work sites. By being a separate business from the ARTC, with its own industrial agreement with its employees, South Spur achieved greater efficiency and reduced costs, by reducing the amount of paid travel time for track workers.

The Interstate Track Audit

The ARTC had been asked in year 2000 by the Minister for Transport to conduct an audit of the interstate rail tracks, including those not yet under its control. It would involve:[299]

> "assessing network track performance, upgrading options that might increase rail's efficiency, and the business case for investment in ARTC and non-ARTC owned segments of the interstate track. Findings would be presented in a form accessible to potential private investors."

In May 2001, it released the audit results[300] in which it recommended an investment of $507 million. This investment would create benefits to the Australian community of $1500 million, in lower freight costs and reduced road accidents, road congestion, noise, air pollution and GHG emissions. Benefits included the transfer of two million tonnes of line-haul freight per year from road to rail, an increase of 38% based on year 2000 traffic volumes. $398 million of the proposed investment would be used to upgrade the east coast corridor between Melbourne, Sydney and Brisbane, where there had been the least amount of investment in previous decades, due to deferred major periodic maintenance (MPM) under the State governments. How this situation came to be is described in chapter 13, under *The Economic Appraisal of Rail Network Projects – The NSW Experience*.

In the Audit's recommendations, $146 million was proposed for the Southern Sydney Freight Line (SSFL). As a dedicated freight line connecting the ARTC interstate network with Sydney's Metropolitan Freight Network, it would enable freight trains to avoid being restricted by RailCorp's twice-daily curfews for freight trains on its passenger network. This project was first funded by the *One Nation* program in early 1990s. However, it was not completed until 2013 because it proved much more difficult and expensive than was first estimated to relocate the underground services within RailCorp's rail corridor. A line of just 36 kms, its final cost was $960 million.[301] Under ARTC control, it runs parallel to RailCorp tracks from Macarthur to Sefton Junction via Cabramatta, giving 24/7 access for freight trains to and from the Chullora intermodal terminal, Enfield Yard, the Sydney Ports intermodal terminal at Enfield, and Port Botany.

Expansion into NSW

Further growth of the ARTC network did not come till September 2004 when it took up a 60-year lease for the NSW Interstate and Hunter Valley lines, after three years of negotiations. ARTC would take full responsibility for the leased lines, including investment decisions and train control. As a part of the agreement between the Federal and NSW governments, the Commonwealth would invest $872 million through the ARTC between 2004 and 2009.[302] Of this, specific allocations were:

- $192 million to build the Southern Sydney Freight Line from Macarthur (the boundary) to Chullora (Pacific National's intermodal terminal) within the existing rail corridors, so that freight trains could avoid having to use the busy passenger lines and junctions;
- $152 million to upgrade the Hunter Valley coal network, to increase its capacity from 85 million tonnes of coal per year to over 100 million tonnes;
- $186 million to upgrade the Main South Line from Macarthur to Albury, to reduce freight train transit times;
- $54 million to upgrade the Albury to Melbourne line in Victoria, to reduce transit times;
- $119 million to upgrade the North Coast line from Telarah (the junction in the Hunter Valley) to the Queensland border, to reduce freight train transit times;
- $57 million to upgrade the lines between Cootamundra, Parkes, Dubbo and Werris Creek;
- $21 million to upgrade the line between Parkes and Broken Hill, to enable double-stacked container trains to operate, (and thence from Broken Hill across the continent to Perth).

When the ARTC took up the lease of the NSW interstate lines, rail's share of the intermodal Sydney-Melbourne market was estimated to be 11%.[303] With the investments made, it was expecting that this market share could be increased to 20% by 2010. A year later, it had increased this target to 30%.[304] In addition to track investments, the NSW lease created a need to develop and implement new information systems for payroll and personnel management, and train management.[305]

The ARTC was quick to make improvements to the NSW network, doing the previously deferred maintenance work to enable the removal of temporary speed restrictions (TSRs). It reported:[306]

> "The number of TSRs in place on the North Coast and Hunter Valley corridors has been considerably reduced following commencement of ARTC's New South Wales lease. ... The reduction in TSRs has been a major factor in improved transit times and on time running for the multiple users of the Hunter Valley network. ... TSRs on the northern corridor (Maitland to Border Loop) reached their lowest level for twenty years in March 2005 resulting in improved reliability and faster transit for trains between Sydney and Brisbane. Within the first two months of the NSW lease commencing, all TSRs in the Taree area had been removed, some of which had been in place for the past seven years."

In 2007, the ARTC published a Strategic Investment Outline for its North-South Corridor. It wrote:[307]

> "The focus of this paper is the general freight market between the three east coast capital cities. These markets represent the largest non-bulk movement of freight in Australia, are projected to grow at a rate above GDP growth, and offer the opportunity for rail to regain volume and market share.
>
> For the North-South corridor (Melbourne – Sydney – Brisbane) what ARTC is seeking to deliver is a step change in performance."

The ARTC calculated that the rail mode could achieve a significant increase in market share on the north-south corridor by improving its service quality. Improving the infrastructure contribution to service quality was therefore a primary focus of ARTC's strategy. However, there are complex and conditional relationships between any investment to improve a rail network in some way and the benefits such investment might generate. These are discussed in chapter 14, under *Investing for Capability Improvements to the vertically-separated Interstate Rail Network*.

The lease of the NSW interstate and Hunter Valley lines increased the ARTC's network by some 3400 kilometres, nearly doubling its size. For the first time, there was one track provider right across the continent between NSW and WA, although not yet between the Sydney and Perth freight terminals. The ARTC was able to negotiate rights to sell access to the standard-gauge lines in the WA network, but west of Kalgoorlie, the standard-gauge line remains under separate control.

In 2009, management of the Botany rail terminal (at Sydney's container port) passed from RailCorp to the ARTC, in anticipation of the transfer of the Sydney Metropolitan Freight Network to ARTC. This was completed in August 2012, and had been provided for in the 2004 lease agreement.

In January 2010, the ARTC leased the standard-gauge line from the NSW-Queensland border to the Acacia Ridge terminal in Brisbane, completing its interstate network in the eastern states.

The key projects in the North-South Strategy are identified in the following maps,[308] all intended to support the performance objectives of increasing line capacity and reducing transit times.

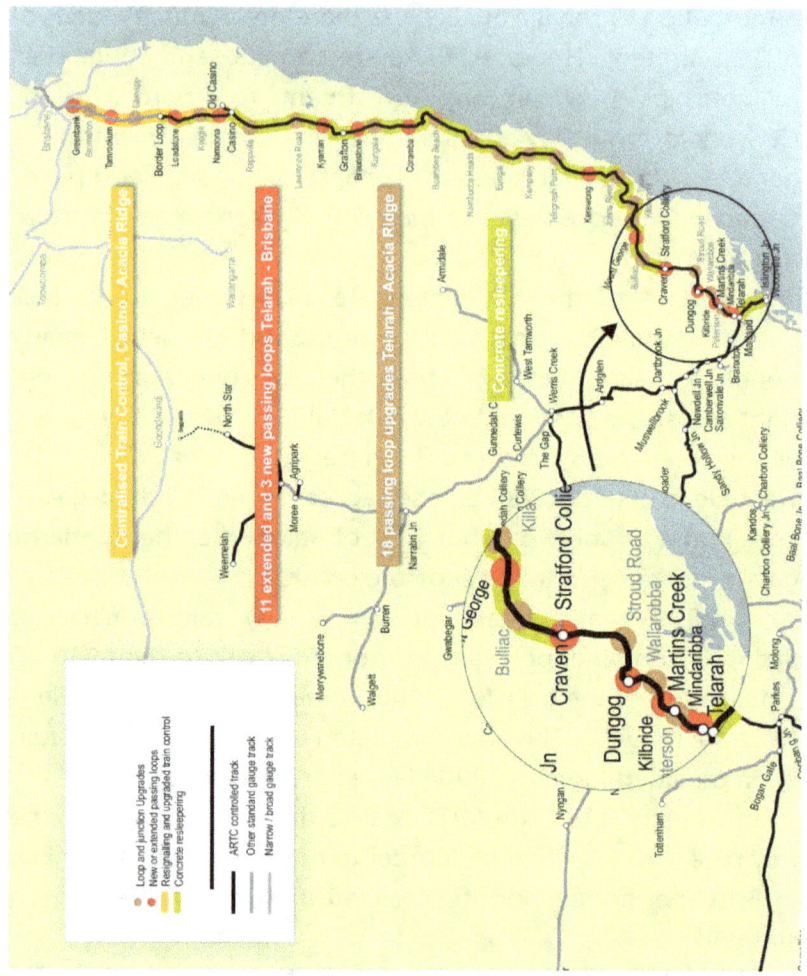

Sydney to Brisbane: ARTC projects in 2007 to enable traffic growth

9. How and Why the Rail Freight Industry Changed

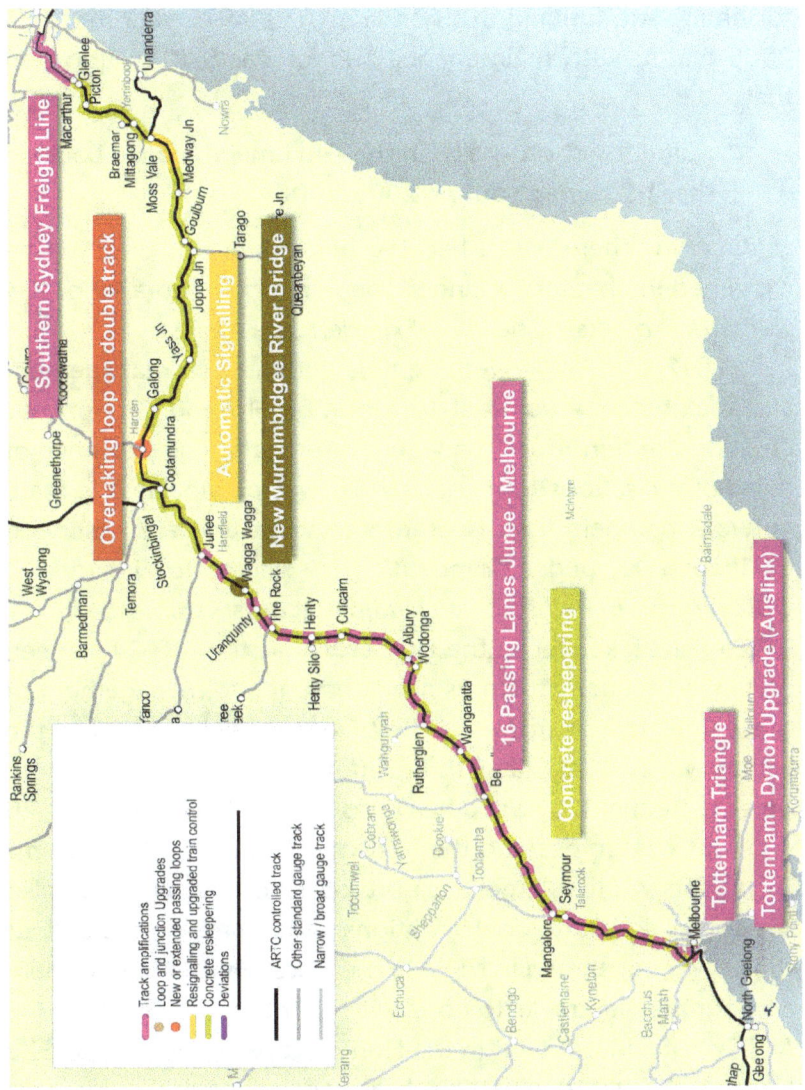

Sydney to Melbourne: ARTC projects in 2007 to enable traffic growth

In addition to the lease, the ARTC separately contracted with the NSW Rail Infrastructure Corporation (RIC) in September 2004 to manage and maintain the so-called Country Rail Network (CRN). The NSW government retained responsibility for policy and funding of these lines. The ARTC reported[309] in 2006 that its CRN maintenance budget was $110 million, and that

> "Significant progress on the CRN maintenance backlog has been made during 2005/2006."

Just why there was a backlog of work at this time will be explained in chapter 13, under *The Economic Appraisal of Rail Network Projects – The NSW Experience*.

In 2012, the NSW government passed the CRN management and maintenance contract to the John Holland Group, thus creating the third track manager in the State. The existence of three organisations to manage what was previously one State network hampers train operators in ways that are described in Chapter 13, under *Competition for Access to Networks – Obtaining Train Paths Across Multiple Access Regimes*.

Since its takeover of the Hunter Valley, the ARTC has been particularly successful in its development and management of these lines leased from the NSW Government. Known as the Hunter Valley Coal Chain, three different above-rail companies operate frequent long and heavy coal trains between about 20 different coal mines and the Port of Newcastle, which claims to be the world's largest export coal port. Coal trains also supply local electric power stations which provide the bulk of the power consumed in NSW. In the lower Hunter Valley, there are four parallel tracks to cope with all the traffic. By 2010, the ARTC's total investment in the Hunter Valley network was $1.3 billion.[310] Its stated objective then was to increase to increase the capacity of the coal chain from a current 97 million tonnes of export coal to cope with a projected 200 million tonnes per year by 2014.

However, the Hunter Valley route has never been just for coal exports, as is widely thought. It is also a part of the interstate network, and the regional network for north-west of NSW. Hence it carries interstate container trains that run between Sydney and Brisbane, seasonal intrastate grain trains to and from the Port of Newcastle, intrastate export container trains on scheduled 48-hour cycles between the north-west of NSW and Port Botany, regional passenger trains to and from Sydney, and local passenger trains operating from Newcastle.

Extended lease in Victoria

In May 2008, ARTC and the Victorian government signed an agreement to extend the 15-year lease of the standard-gauge interstate lines for another 45 years to 2059. The reason given by the ARTC Chairman for this extension was[311]

> "The length of this lease will allow sufficient time for ARTC to plan and implement practical, long term infrastructure improvements to the rail network in Victoria, so as to obtain a commercial return on its investment."

(The issue of gaining a commercial return on a rail investment depends in part on whether the economic appraisal allows for the long productive life of the railway asset. There is more on such issues in chapter 13.)

As a part of this agreement, the 200 km North-East broad-gauge line between Seymour and Albury (which was alongside the standard-gauge line opened in 1962) was ceded to ARTC and converted to standard-gauge, turning this segment of the interstate route into double track. This work, including upgrading with concrete sleepers, was completed in 2010, and a new bypass around Wodonga was opened that year also. Another addition to the ARTC network under this agreement was the standard-gauge branch line from Maroona (on the western interstate route) to Portland, which is a major grain export port serving western Victoria.

The conversion of the North-East main line to standard-gauge cut off the 125 km Benalla to Oaklands grain-only broad-gauge branch line. However, the Victorian government funded its conversion to standard-gauge, so that the grain from its extension into the Riverina area of NSW would continue to go to Melbourne. After that, the ARTC incorporated the line into its leased Victorian network.

Shifting priorities

These are revealed when one looks through the series that are ARTC's Annual reports. In the Report for 2003, this statement appeared for the first time in the preamble, and was repeated in 2004:

> "Australian Rail Track Corporation Ltd (ARTC) was incorporated in 1998 following an inter-governmental agreement (IGA) between the Australian Government and all mainland States **to provide a 'one stop shop' for access to the interstate rail network.** ...
>
> As part of the IGA, ARTC was also given the task of **improving the interstate rail infrastructure** to achieve a number of performance targets relating to reduced transit times, increased network capacity and improved reliability with the underlying aim of increasing the share of interstate freight carried by rail. Over the last five years, through targeted investment and improved management, ARTC has been able to achieve these targets." (My emphases)

In the Annual Reports for 2005 through to 2008, similar statements were made, but not from 2009, perhaps because traffic volumes had declined in the wake of the global financial crisis. The 2009 Annual Report showed a shift in priorities:[312]

> "The Board has adopted a Board Charter which, inter alia, embodies the aim of the company as;
> - to provide efficient and seamless access to the interstate rail network **and to operate the business on commercial principles;**
> - to implement a growth strategy for interstate rail through improved efficiency and competitiveness;

- to improve interstate rail infrastructure through better asset management and coordination of capital investment; and
- to encourage uniformity in access, technical, operating and safework procedures in the Australian rail industry."

From 2005 to 2013 inclusive, the ARTC had an agreement with its owner, the Commonwealth government, not to pay dividends. These were years in which billions of dollars were invested in upgrading the interstate and Hunter Valley networks, to a large extent funded by government injections of equity. However, by 2014 this period of catch-up maintenance, asset renewals and capacity enhancements was over, and payment of dividends resumed. This was reported in a matter-of-fact way in 2014. However, in the 2016 Annual Report, the tone was triumphant:

> "This year, ARTC produced a strong underlying profit, despite challenging market conditions. Following this result, the total dividend paid for the year to the Shareholders was $91.3 million, an increase of 59 percent over the prior year. We are pleased to deliver such a satisfactory outcome for our Shareholders."

Substantial dividends have continued to be paid in subsequent years, while at the same time the government has been investing billions of dollars for the construction of Inland Rail, by way of increasing its equity in the ARTC. (There is more on the Inland Rail project in chapter 12.)

In 2012, ARTC adopted a strategy to become more active in the market, including signing take-or-pay contracts with all the Hunter Valley export coal producers. This enabled more certainty about the pace of growth in exports, for which ARTC has, since its beginning, had a policy of developing sufficient capacity in the Valley network to keep ahead of expected demand.

The principal reasons for ownership changes

When governments sold all or part of their railway systems, there were many reasons for doing so. Some were stated explicitly, but others were not. Some of the stated reasons were based on political ideology and were therefore 'articles of faith', while other reasons were just pragmatic.

Faith in the benefits of competition

In Australia, the first time that changes in ownership of rail systems were mooted was in Prime Minister Paul Keating's One Nation document of February 1992. Its reasoning stated that railways (and other 'monopoly' government businesses) had inefficient performance due to lack of competition, which put Australia at a substantial disadvantage in its major export and import-competing sectors.

At the time, the National Rail Corporation had just been established to take over and develop interstate rail traffic, and all other railways were state-based, vertically-integrated systems. The lack of competition cited in the *One Nation* document was perceived to be within the railway industry, and the assumption was made (falsely) that this was critical. Railways did of course have competition for transporting freight – from road transport for intrastate traffics, and from sea transport for interstate traffics. That these forms of competition were ignored shows how much the railways were seen as government services, performing functions that other forms of transport perhaps could not or would not undertake.

The Commonwealth hoped the National Competition Policy (NCP) of 1995 would be a stimulus for the States to open up their railways to intra-industry competition. The first State to attempt this was NSW in July 1996 when it vertically separated its State Rail Authority into distinct units, to enable other train operators onto the State network. (See above, p.101, for the details of this development.) A short-line operator (NRR) started operating under contract to FreightCorp in September 1997, and therefore not in competition with it. Apart from the NRC, there was no other freight train operator on the NSW network until August 1999 when Silverton Rail started running 'trip trains' between Sydney suburbs and Port Botany.

The competition policy had been impeded by the high barriers to entry into freight rail transport. (We will look in Chapter 13 at what these *Barriers to Entry* were.) The first competitors to FreightCorp in NSW had enabling advantages that lowered these barriers:

- Because of its unique history, Silverton[313] already had accreditation in NSW and standard-gauge rolling-stock that it had bought at auction in 1994.
- ATN was a new company when it started competing in 2000 in the NSW grain transport market, but it had available the expertise of its overseas rail company owners. (ATN also operated in the Victorian grain market but only on the standard-gauge lines.)

However, it was not until the joint sale in 2002 of FreightCorp and the NRC, with the consequent bidding for surplus rolling-stock, that other train operators emerged on the NSW network. This left apparent competition between Pacific National as the main player, and several small rail companies. These small companies had overcome the barriers to entry by acquiring second-hand rolling-stock cheaply, and by employing experienced rail managers and workers who had been made redundant from FreightCorp, who therefore knew the network and the potential customers. However, as is explained in Chapter 13, this apparent competition between PN and the smaller operators on the NSW network was a mirage created by market segmentation.

When the railways in South Australia and Tasmania were privatised by the breakup and sale in 1997 of parts of Australian National, there was no attempt to create competition. When the broad-gauge railway serving intrastate traffic of Victoria was sold to Rail America in 1999 with a long-term lease enabling control of the network, there was no provision made for Open Access (to allow for competition) until 2001. However, no other train operator saw any opportunity to compete against the incumbent train operator on this network until December 2006. By this time, PN had bought the above-rail business, and the Victorian government had retaken control of the network.

The *Progress in Rail Reform* report of 1999 noted that intra-industry competition was of limited benefit to intrastate/regional rail services, quoting[314] a contributor who saw the false assumption for what it was:

> "Rail suffers from an excess of competition. ... Pro-competitive reform is designed to prevent monopolists setting prices too high in search of excess profits. This is clearly not the problem with rail."

In Western Australia, the Minister of Transport was reported[315] as saying at the time of sale that

> "selling the freight network was less about money that it was about ensuring the long term best interests of the State's industries and communities."

The vertical separation of the Western Australian network in 2002 saw ARG (and later Aurizon) as the only train operator on the State's narrow-gauge network for ten years until one of its customers (CBH) bought its own locos and grain wagons for $175 million and invited an American train operator (Watco) to provide its train operations in 2012. Evidently CBH responded to dissatisfaction with ARG, and the lack of a competing train operator, by creating the competition with ARG itself. CBH bought aluminium grain hoppers with less tare weight than ARG's steel wagons, thereby enabling an additional ten tonnes of grain per wagon[316] and reducing the transport cost to growers.

Queensland Rail (later QR National) remained a vertically-integrated government-owned freight rail operator without competition within the state until 2005, when the State government permitted competition on its network from PN. However, QR did provide competition in other States, through its subsidiary company. QR bought Northern Rivers Railroad (NRR) in May 2002 to create InterRail, gaining a number of standard-gauge locomotives and wagons. This enabled QR to haul Hunter Valley coal from March 2003, start a container train service in May 2003 from Casino in northern NSW to the Port of Brisbane, and start inter-capital container train operations in April 2004. QR bought ARG in 2006, gaining its customer contracts, rolling-stock and operating depots. This acquisition enabled QR to operate under the ARG brand in WA and in NSW grain haulage, and to expand its interstate intermodal operation in competition with Pacific National. However, competition from a state-owned rail operator was not the sort of competition that was envisaged and espoused by the federal government in the previous decade. QR National became privatised through an IPO in 2010, and later changed its brand to Aurizon.

It is of interest that Aurizon still contracts for bulk coal, minerals, chemicals and grain in three states, but in August 2017 it announced its withdrawal from intermodal operations, both interstate and within Queensland, citing financial losses over some years.[317] The CEO Andrew Harding was quoted as saying

> "The business has not been able to establish significant scale and a customer base to support a profitable business in such a highly competitive market."

In summary, competition within the rail industry, as a stimulus to efficiencies and a reason for structural reform, was an ideal which ignored the high barriers to entry into the industry for newcomers, and the existing benefits to rail operations from economies of scale. The push for competition within the rail industry was based on faith in the efficacy of a market that would emerge triumphant once it was unleashed. That this turned out to be largely a fantasy has been conveniently ignored by its proponents.

Competition within the rail industry was of no relevance to smaller networks. For this reason, it was never cited as a reason for reform in New Zealand where competition for transporting freight has always been between the railway and other transport modes. How 'competition' actually worked out on each of the Australian rail networks is described in chapter 12, under the heading *How Competition Evolved in Australia*. How the rail industry in Australia evolved to avoid direct competition is explained in Chapter 13 under the heading *The Perceived Need for Competition*.

Faith in the private sector and privatisation

For government-owned railways in the 1990s to benefit from intra-industry competition, it was seen as necessary that the private sector would provide it. The *One Nation* document stated:[318]

> "The Government has established a program of disposal of those businesses for which there is no compelling reason for Commonwealth ownership."

Furthermore, the private sector was expected to do better because of its abilities to be more customer-focused, to raise capital, and to make quick investment (or disinvestment) decisions. These were abilities that were seen as inhibited in government-owned railways, and hence railway prospects would not be changed greatly by limited reforms such as had happened with the creation of the NRC. There was also a concurrent disbelief, or lack of faith, that continuing government ownership could ever be beneficial for railways, enabling them to climb out of the financial situations they were in. NZR was sometimes described by concerned politicians and economists as a "money pit", implying a hopeless case. Certainly, governments had no expertise in turning around what they perceived should be profitable businesses, and no desire to tackle such formidable tasks.

However, one economist described the main concern to be using assets productively, rather than seeing railways as a means to provide services to the community:[319]

> "As with some other publicly owned infrastructure-intensive assets in some States, it became governments' view that these assets could be operated more productively as private companies, adopting the risk profile, economies of scope, and industrial relations practices of the private sector."

Certainly, asset utilisation was low then in government railways because, under the financial accounting methods then used, the costs of assets were seen as 'sunk costs'. Asset acquisition was outside of the annual operating budgets and therefore asset utilisation was not normally a managerial focus in a not-for-profit enterprise, as all the railway departments then were. Other reasons for low asset utilisation included the obligation to be common carriers, the obligation to have lines and enough rolling-stock specifically to handle the seasonal grain harvests, and the legacy of providing a transport service between the main centres and many regional and rural locations.

The faith in the private sector was shown by the willingness of governments to sell their railway systems, or at least the above-rail parts, to businesses or consortia with different views of railways. Many governments did this without understanding or caring what the implications would be for the regional economies, stemming from the changes that the new owners would make. In all the mainland States of Australia some freight shippers had to switch to road freighting at a greater cost, as a result of decisions made to improve profitability by the new owners of former government railways. (See in Chapter 13 under the heading *The Perceived Need for Competition*.)

Sale conditions usually imposed few obligations on the new owner, partly to encourage the best sale price. There was no thought about the possibility of rorting, and hence no conditions imposed to prevent this. For example, the Victorian Government had made no requirement for its leased non-passenger lines to be maintained to any standard.[320] The consequence was that the companies controlling these lines allowed the condition of the broad-gauge network to decline significantly.

The New Zealand Government asked only that Tranz Rail be listed on the stock market in due course, to enable local investors to participate in the prosperity. Although it knew that the investment bankers in the Tranz Rail consortium would sell down their shares sometime after the IPO, it probably did not anticipate that all the major consortium partners would use this means to quit their ownership after just a few years. Their absence of commitment may have contributed to the company's near-bankruptcy just before its purchase by Toll and the renationalisation of the rail network. (See in Appendix 1 for the details.)

One stated benefit[321] of the sale of any government assets to the private sector was the absence of any form of government guarantee. The new owners should not have had any reason to believe that, if they failed to operate profitably, the government would fund them to relieve their financial difficulties. However, for the governments of Victoria, Tasmania and New Zealand, their faith in privatisation turned out to be very costly for them in the longer term. Operators' profitability had been maintained by reduced spending on track maintenance and renewal. This rorting led to the imminent collapse or closure of their freight railways, which was a potential outcome that the governments definitely did not want. (See in chapter 11, under The Privatisation of Four Vertically-Integrated Railways.)

Other ideological and pragmatic reasons

Governments that sold their freight railway systems were motivated to improve their own financial situations. Their reasons included:

- Avoidance of future calls on capital funds for rail asset renewals to keep services operating,
- Avoidance of having to subsidise annual operating deficits, currently and in the future,
- Selling government assets was a way to reduce the overall government debt burden.

Although NZ Rail was not sold until 1993, the possibility of selling it was first aired in the second half of the 1980s, because at that time there were more than twenty government trading departments and enterprises seen to be running at a loss.[322] Together, the capital investment that was thought to be needed for these departments was greater than the whole government budget. Transport costs were rising faster than the rate of inflation and were blamed for making New Zealand's exports uncompetitive. Successive governments of both colours saw asset sales as the way out of their predicament. By 1993, NZ Rail had become marginally profitable despite a much-reduced annual revenue due to declining freight rates. In the context of the then prevailing neoliberal ideology of 'small government', it appears that the NZ government's primary reason for sale was avoidance of funding the future capital requirements. Ruth Richardson, the Minister of Finance was reported to have said in Parliament[323] the day after the sale that:

> "We know that, for New Zealand Rail to play a successful part in a growing economy, it will require hundreds of millions of dollars just from now to the turn of the century, and will require the thick end of $1 billion as we head to the year 2010. The taxpayer is not well placed to make that investment."

When Australian National (AN) was sold by the Commonwealth government in 1997, it was incurring huge losses because its most profitable freight contracts had been passed to National Rail. As a result of this change in structure that had not been adequately thought through, AN's 1995/96 deficit was $250 million.[324] AN was unbundled into four business units, three of which were sold for a total of $95 million. Clearly, the avoidance of ongoing deficits was the motivation for disposal of AN.

V/Line Freight was created when the State government broke up the Victorian Public Transport Corporation into separate businesses. Its profitability was marginal and the government decided to sell. Its financial objectives were[325]:

- "To maximise sale proceeds and minimise any associated long term costs to the taxpayer;
- To transfer risks to the private sector"

When the Western Australian Government Railway (WAGR) was sold in 2000 for $585 million,[326] it was noted in Parliament that the sale proceeds would allow the government

> 'to retire a significant amount of state debt, and reinvest in vital state social and economic Infrastructure.' [327]

It was stated that the size of the rail freight system debt owed to the State Treasury and the Commonwealth was approximately $1 billion.[328]

The Queensland Government developed seven criteria to guide the decision on the best privatisation model for QR National, of which the top three were:[329]

- Maximising sales proceeds;
- Minimising residual government risk;
- Facilitating private sector provision of infrastructure.

Benefits postulated as reasons for privatisation

In New Zealand, the Ministry of Transport was aware of the reductions in real freight transport prices that had resulted from the removal of restrictions on road competition with rail since the mid-1980s. Because the New Zealand economy is very export dependent, and NZ Rail had long been involved in haulage of New Zealand's main export commodities (meat, dairy products, forest products and wool), the Ministry could justify privatisation of the railways to lock in and further reduce freight rates, because this would enhance the country's competitive trade advantage.[330]

In Australia, the *Progress in Rail Reform* report[331] included comment from the NRC that it felt constrained in its decision-making by being government-owned. Its reasons were the need to get government approval for any company acquisitions or alliances it might want to make, and that gaining this approval could take many months. The NRC thought that such moves would need to be both covert and quickly executed to be successful, and that this was not possible at that time.

Analysts and commentators have postulated other reasons for privatisation, after the fact:
- To stimulate modernisation of railways,[332]
- To enable a change of culture,[333]
- To allow industry consolidation across state boundaries.[334]

10. Privatisation – Hopes and Outcomes

Privatisation as the solution to deficits

Privatisation was better than closure

By 1990, all the government railways in Australasia had been making losses, in conventional accounting terms, for many years. Why did governments not just wind up their 'unprofitable' railways, and sell off the assets?

This was a question that was rarely asked at the time, for good reasons. Firstly, there were expectations that there ought to be viable freight businesses that could be exposed and made more efficient if the social-service passenger operations could be separated off in some way. Secondly, many railway assets were fixed in place; these were sunk costs which would have little value for any other purpose. Rolling-stock might be sold in the international market, but in the 1990s, this market was undeveloped compared to that of today. Thirdly, railways were still hauling many millions of tonnes of freight, so their closure would have been very disruptive to the economy. Therefore, governments thought that sales of whole freight railway businesses to the private sector would rid them of railway problems, with the least disruption to the existing economic arrangements.

Privatisation of public assets and businesses was also an integral part of the neo-liberal economic theory that several governments in the English-speaking world adopted in the 1980s and 1990s. Its rationale was that government spending and taxation should both be as small as possible, as proportions of the total economy. Therefore, any government business that could be operated by the private sector should be operated by the private sector. Along with this approach, there was an often-stated tenet that the private sector would be more efficient and nimbler in the management of such businesses than the public sector could ever be. It was believed that the private sector would be less risk-averse, more innovative, customer-focused and profit-oriented.

Privatisation became increasingly popular as a solution for a number of government difficulties and problems, including railway deficits. As the author of the story of the privatisation of QR National (later Aurizon) wrote: [335]

> "After Thatcher had made privatisation fashionable, it became a popular tool for reformist governments across the world."

Proposals to privatise government railways in Australasia were initially statements of faith. There was a quasi-religious belief that privatisation would be the better option for railways than continued government ownership, because at the beginning of the 1990s, there were no precedents for such changes in ownership and control anywhere in the world.[336] It has been written[337] that "faith is belief without evidence". Faith was definitely the basis for the sale of New Zealand Railways, the first railway system sold in Australasia. First considered seriously in 1988,[338] it was sold in 1993. Evidence for the success of privatisation of government-owned businesses had come from other industries. The impetus for this privatisation was to build on the productivity improvements made while in government ownership, and to keep the railway operational without further government investment or subsidy. It was also suggested after the sale as the means to prevent future interventions by governments for politically expedient reasons.[339] However, a subsequent complaint about the government's "desire for political control" suggests otherwise (see below, in the next section).

Belief in the success of privatisation remained a matter of faith for some years. It took seven years in Victoria, and ten years in New Zealand, until it was demonstrated conclusively in each case that privatisation had been a poor policy choice (see in chapter 11), given that continuation of the service was an expectation (see below). In 2013, the failure of privatisation in New Zealand was spoken of in the Queensland parliament as an example of why not to privatise the Mt Isa rail line[340] (see in chapter 15, under *The phantom privatisation*).

The issue of land ownership in New Zealand

Significantly, in most cases when a rail network was privatised, its government retained ownership and control of the land underneath the track, yards and buildings. Certainly, in New Zealand, this was an insurance against the possibility of failure of the privatised rail company, when sale of core railway land might have been an option to pay off creditors. The retention of railway land by the government, especially in the cities where the land was most valuable, could enable new beginnings. Additionally, the alienation of government land would have been a political problem in a different context – the concurrent negotiations between the Crown and Maori tribes to redress historic confiscations of Maori-owned land.

For these reasons, the creation of NZ Rail Ltd in 1990 as a core railway business left the ownership of all railway land with the New Zealand Railways Corporation (NZRC), with a lease from the NZRC to the rail company to use just the land it needed. In 1993, negotiations between NZ Rail Ltd and NZRC took place to identify and release to NZRC any parcels of land that were agreed by NZ Rail as being surplus to core railway requirements. In anticipation of privatisation, this process

10. Privatisation – Hopes and Outcomes

assuaged a concern that the new owners should not profit from sub-leases of land, lest it be a distraction from turning the transport business around. Many parcels of surplus land were later sold by NZRC for redevelopment, or reallocated to other government entities for compensation to Maori tribes. All the proceeds of land sales went to the New Zealand Government.

This separation of land from the rail network that occupied it was misunderstood and criticised in a 2009 economist's paper arguing for the partial or full closure of New Zealand's rail system. In his purview:[341]

> "A (perhaps unintended) consequence of this separation of ownership and operation is that it undermined incentives to maximise the economic welfare from each railway line. Economic efficiency is maximised when land is used for its most productive use. If a railway operator can make a greater return from closing a line and selling the land for a more productive use then it is in the economic interests of both the operator and society for them to take that action. However the terms of the Core Lease meant that the railway operator would not gain the benefit of the sale value. **Their incentive was therefore to keep a line open** even where it was not economically efficient to do so. These incentives provide a partial explanation of the fact that the reduction in length of the rail network has stalled since privatisation."
> (My emphasis above)

Keeping lines open was exactly what the New Zealand Government wanted; this policy was made explicit as early as 2002. It was a recognition of any government's role to make transport policy, and to keep options open for the long-term future. That is why it is absolutely appropriate for any government to own railway land in perpetuity. It is not wise to sell the land of a practically irreplaceable national asset, such as a railway or a highway network, for short-term gain.

The economist quoted above speciously attributed the failure of the privatisation of New Zealand's railway to the government's "desire for political control",[342] which was therefore contrary to the neoliberal catchcry for 'small government'. See below for an exploration of what the "desire for political control" might actually be, under the heading *Hopes for Continuation with Improvements*.

His assertion that "economic efficiency is maximised when land is used for its most productive use" was, in my view, misguided. This truism is best used for short-term decision-making, such as "shall we grow carrots or potatoes on our land this year?"

The method of privatisation

All the vertically-integrated Australasian railway businesses were privatised by trade sales (with one exception, in Queensland). In New Zealand, Victoria and Western Australia the owning governments developed a competitive bidding process among a few interested companies or consortia, including a controlled 'due diligence' process in which all the potential owners were given the same information. The successful bidder was the one that made the highest unconditional offer. Thus, it was the bidders who decided what the purchase price would be, by their reckoning of what could be done to turn the railway into a profitable business. This method of determining the market price recognised that in each case, the businesses were functioning but loss-making at the time of sale. The purchase price always included the fixed and mobile assets, control of the rail network, a ready workforce, and a collection of customer contracts of varying durations.

This method of determining the price meant that the assets were sold at well under both their original purchase cost and their replacement cost. The reality of this was not a worry for the governments because their main concern was to quit the businesses and stop the cash outflows. Any possible intrinsic value of railways to the broader community and economy was ignored. The pattern was set as early as 1991 when the charter for National Rail Corporation was written, the primary requirement being commercial viability. There was no mention of economic development or public interest benefits as had been recognised for the National Highways.[343]

Unfulfilled hopes from privatisation

Hopes for continuation with improvements

Governments which sold their freight railways (instead of closing them) seemingly made a tacit assumption about the result. They hoped that the private sector owners would want to offer the range and frequency of services that governments had failed to do profitably, but would succeed by managing the railways differently. This was alluded to by a government transport policy manager in 1990, prior to the privatisation of NZR:[344]

> "Government policy has been consistently to withdraw from direct involvement, leaving individual operators with the prime responsibility to innovate, invest and operate, according to their assessment of the particular sector of the market in which they are interested"

The reality was that there was a substantial difference between this expectation of a government selling or leasing its railway, and the expectations of a company that bought or leased that railway. This difference was coyly explained in a parliamentary review of the management of the WA freight rail network,[345]

> "privatisation ... can create tension if the profit maximisation goal of business and the public interest goal of government are not aligned."

Rather naïvely, governments did not expect that the new owners would see opportunities to pursue profitability through various forms of deferring maintenance, asset stripping, and selective abandonment of services. However, these rorting activities were used wherever vertically-integrated railways were transferred to the private sector.

Prior to privatisation, there had been well-developed engineering practices that included a philosophy of planned preventive maintenance, which is a proactive approach to the maintenance of a railway network. The purpose then was on maintaining existing railway assets up to a level that delivered operational reliability, with cyclic asset renewals (such as locomotive rebuilds, ballast cleaning, and rail and sleeper replacement) programmed over long time-frames of 10 to 40 years. Under this approach, a small proportion of the assets would be renewed every year. This approach is deliberately incremental, to spread the financial burden and to provide a steady workload for specialised machinery and staff.

This practice was developed and refined by professional railway engineers over some decades. Its purpose was to keep the system operational in perpetuity, and to upgrade the assets where needed to provide for continuing business. It is evidence of organisational maturity, committing to preventive maintenance in order to reduce future corrective maintenance, which is operationally disruptive.

Where a government-owned freight railway had drifted into decline with a reactive management style, and had become a financial burden, its government could be motivated to privatise it. But the hope was that the private sector would be able to keep the system available, and do so profitably, because the private sector was believed to have abilities which governments lacked. Thus, each government must have expected continuation and improvement of its railway system, even if this was not made explicit at the time of privatisation; the alternative of closure had already been tacitly rejected, and 'managed decline' was never any government's policy objective.

By selling and/or leasing their railways, rather than closing them, Governments also sent a tacit message to the private sector that governments still valued railway services in the context of land transport policy. This told the private sector that, in effect, railways might be 'too big to let fail'. Hence governments exposed themselves to the possibility of being exploited in their future dealings with the new owners. In two cases (Victoria and New Zealand), this outcome became the reality years later when governments resumed control of their rail networks. And in Western Australia, the State government has twice been manipulated into providing funds, both for keeping grain lines in use, and for repair and upgrade of roads where railway lines have been closed. (These circumstances are covered in the next chapter, under *Western Australia*).

Evidence for hopes unfulfilled

There were five freight railway networks that were privatised as part of vertically-integrated railways. Two networks were sold in a package deal with the above-rail business, in New Zealand (1993) and Tasmania (1997). Three networks were leased long-term to the buyers of the above-rail businesses: Eyre Peninsula (1997), Victoria (1999) and Western Australia (2000). Four of these networks were bought by consortia that included a North American railroad company, and the Eyre Peninsula railway was bought by Genesee & Wyoming Australia (GWA). All these buyers regarded vertical integration as the normal (and preferable) structure for a railroad.

All five networks had been operated by government agencies for many decades prior to their privatisation. From the 1930s to the 1970s, they were reduced in size by closing some branch lines, in response to competition from road carriers. It is instructive to see how the governments responded to the way in which their former networks were managed after some years under private sector control.

Victoria

The Victorian Government expressed a hopeful expectation to the Productivity Commission in 1998, in anticipation of the sale of the V/Line Freight Corporation:[346]

> "The continuation of the privatisation program will build on the reforms undertaken since 1992 with quality and value given new emphasis in a competitive, transparent business environment. The Victorian Government will build on its existing high-quality service to create a prosperous, innovative and expanding rail industry."

The contrast between this naïve ambition and the outcome was significant. The private sector lessees of the country broad-gauge network (Freight Australia then Pacific National) chose to cut back on both track renewals and maintenance. This led to severe speed restrictions for safety reasons, and over a few years much freight traffic was lost to road haulage. To address this, the government bought the lease of this network from PN in 2006. However, in 2007, PN ceased operations and withdrew its rolling-stock after droughts had reduced the size of the grain harvests. (These events are covered in the next chapter, under *Victoria*.)

Western Australia

In 1999, the Western Australian government hoped for the following benefits from the disposal of its railway:[347]

- the introduction of 'an efficient, innovative specialist private rail operator committed to the sustainability of rail transport in a competitive market and willing to make the necessary investments to improve rail's market share';
- 'a renewed stimulus for increased rail freight tonnages, better services, decreased freight rates and increased investment in rail infrastructure and rolling stock';
- a reduction in the 'community costs', such as 'the environmental costs of greater fuel use and the

resultant pollution, higher road maintenance costs, and the social costs of road congestion and road crashes';
- the potential for rail to capture as much as possible of the forecast greatly increased bulk freight demand over the coming decade and so 'avoid a massive increase in heavy truck traffic'; and
- the 'potential to capture or recapture freight from road transport'.

(See in the next chapter, under *Western Australia*, for what actually transpired.)

Eyre Peninsula

The Eyre Peninsula narrow-gauge rail network has always been geographically isolated from other rail networks in South Australia. After it was sold as part of the Commonwealth Government's disposal of Australian National in 1997, GWA operated trains to Port Lincoln mainly for bulk grains. In 2005, the Eyre Regional Development Board sought Commonwealth assistance to have the deteriorating rail network upgraded.[348] From this, it can be inferred that GWA was not spending enough on track maintenance, despite this network being in poor condition when it was sold. In 2006/07, Commonwealth funds from the AusLink program were used to restore part of the network to an acceptable operating standard, with a maximum train speed of 60 km/hr. In 2018, a special study[349] of the future options for the transport of grain found that rail capacity had been reduced, by both accumulated speed restrictions due to poor track condition, and the withdrawal of one of the two grain trains in 2014/15.[350] Consequently, by 2018, more grain was being transported to Port Lincoln by road than by rail. The study described one of the main problems as:[351]

> "The existing rail network infrastructure requires capital investment to remain reliable and competitive with road transport. Equally, any significant capital investment on the rail infrastructure may result in an increase in rail

charges such that the rail rates may not be competitive with road transport."

In other words, it would be impossible for GWA to retain the grain traffic if it invested in track renewals to bring the network back up to an acceptable operational standard, and then operate it profitably, because the customer had the subsidised road network as an alternative.

In 2019, GWA and its one grain customer, Viterra, and the South Australian Government (as the network owner) jointly agreed that investment in the road network was a better option than any more investment in the rail network. The contract between GWA and Viterra, and the movement of grain by rail ceased on 31 May 2019. However, GWA still had 28 years left on its lease, and it considers the network still open. It still hauls gypsum 60km from Kevin to the port at Thevenard, at the western end of the network, while the remainder, the majority of the network, lies idle.

A Hope for Private Sector Financing

Mobile assets financed but generally not network assets

Closely linked to the hope for 'continuation with improvements' was the hope that the private sector would invest as much capital as was needed to provide that continuation. The private sector owners of rail businesses have shown some willingness to invest in new locomotives and wagons – the mobile and tradeable assets. However, there has generally not been a willingness to invest in network assets, except for Brookfield's investments in the WA rail network (other than for the grain-only lines) and Aurizon's Central Queensland Coal Network (CQCN). Significantly, both of these are monopoly trading situations, where it is possible to charge access fees that cover full costs over the long term.

In the later 1990s there was optimism that privatisation was working. The *Progress in Rail Reform* report in 1999 stated:[352]

> "There is evidence that regional rail networks which have been horizontally separated (and privatised) are being transformed from loss making businesses requiring government subsidies into commercially independent businesses (for example, Freight Victoria, ASR, and TasRail)"

In year 2000, the hope for private sector financing of railway networks appeared again. The Commonwealth government, in its April 2000 Response document[353] wrote:[354]

> "The Commonwealth ... will explore ways to involve private funding and achieve greater efficiencies in the provision and upkeep of the road network. The Commonwealth is also promoting private sector investment in rail operations **and infrastructure**." (My emphasis)

However, the Commonwealth's own agency, the ARTC, had advised the year before that:[355]

> "A significant impediment to private sector investment in rail infrastructure is the lack of recognition [by those who expect private sector investment] that such investments:
> - are long term
> - are illiquid (sunk) investments
> - often offer less than competitive financial returns ... but include social benefits which are often ignored."

The vertically-integrated new railway businesses in New Zealand, Tasmania and Victoria initially reported new business gained, and increased profitability. All made a show of their investments in track upgrades and rolling-stock.[356] However, by 2003, TranzRail was in financial difficulties, due partly to previous decisions made by its Board which favoured the companies that owned TranzRail before it was listed on the stock market. (An explanation of this is in Appendix 1). In 2004, both

Freight Australia and TasRail were on-sold to Pacific National (PN), which in turn struggled to make money from both these vertically-integrated railways in Victoria and Tasmania.

Little recognition of the government role of stewardship

Why did governments hold out hope for private sector financing of rail network assets? Was it just because governments wanted to avoid future capital spending and subsidies for rail operations? A possible answer is that there was some implicit hope or assumption that the private sector companies would see themselves as the successors to governments with regard to provision of capital. But that could not happen. Governments and companies have very different objectives for their rail networks, and different perceptions of opportunities. Significantly, governments should have a stewardship role, treating their rail networks as national assets, similar to roads, and this role of stewardship should not be delegated to the private sector. There must have been some tacit understanding of this, shown by the governments that privatised their rail networks, because they all retained ownership of either their network assets or at least the land of the rail corridors.

With a few exceptions, governments in Australasia originally built all the transport networks. Historically, all governments in Australasia built railways to serve the hinterlands of ports and later to connect the disparate lines into networks. Facilitating taxable economic activity was their motive. Similarly, a general objective of "facilitating overseas and interstate trade and commerce" [357] was and still is sufficient to justify the building and upgrading of the multi-billion dollar 18,500-kilometre Australian National Highway System from the 1970s onward.

Transport networks built by governments quickly became arteries for their economies, in the same way that fibre networks are doing now for the information flows of modern economies. Transport networks need maintenance and renewal, so it is governments' on-going responsibility to fund this. It is a responsibility to be an active rather than a passive steward – to manage and maintain these long-lasting public assets for use by future generations. Governments all across Australia and New Zealand, at all levels, accept without question their responsibilities for maintaining roads and highways. However, there has been a general lack of understanding until fairly recently that this responsibility applies also to railway lines and networks. The New Zealand Government, through its ownership of KiwiRail, has accepted this responsibility at least since 2019:[358]

> "As a landlord, a landowner and a protector of land for future generations, kaitiakitanga[359] is important to us. ... We take our role seriously as guardians of the rail corridor for future generations, securing and protecting active rail land"

The difficulty for governments, and hence for the rail industry from the 1990s onward, was that any understanding of governments having stewardship of rail networks, was by then lost. A likely reason for this is that rail networks had been managed for generations by the same organisations that used them, and those organisations reported their finances conventionally, as though they were for-profit businesses. Rail networks came to be seen as an integral part of railway transport, in a way that has never applied to highways and road freight transport. Hence some governments, influenced by the tenets of neoliberal economics, developed the expectation that by disposing of the whole of their railways to the private sector, they would be absolved of all their liabilities and responsibilities. Because governments had no understanding or recognition of their stewardship role, there was no obvious reason for them not to sell, for convenience, their rail organisations as vertically-integrated railways. Rail systems sold in this way were:

- NZ Rail Ltd, sold by the NZ government in 1993, with a long-term peppercorn lease of the operational land under the rail network,

- The South Australian and Tasmanian freight rail parts of AN, sold in 1997 by the Commonwealth government, with leases of land from the State governments,
- V/Line Freight, sold by the Victorian government in 1999, with a long-term lease of the broad-gauge network and associated land,
- WestRail, sold by the WA government in 2000, with a 49-year lease on the network.

The disposal of WestRail as a vertically-integrated business was more than convenient; it was a deliberate strategy to preserve (for the grain industry's benefit) the existing rail transport network at the new owner's cost. Vertical separation by the first private owner/lessee subsequently undermined that strategy. (This is explained under *Western Australia* in the next chapter.) The current lessee of the WA network, Brookfield (now Arc Infrastructure), has made major investments to upgrade the WA network over a number of years, but it has also asked for and received funding from the WA Government. When Brookfield refused to pay for any resleepering of the majority of the grain-only lines, the State government was coerced into providing $258 million for this work to keep these lines open from 2010.[360] Also, in December 2012, Brookfield Rail signed a 15-year agreement with the ARTC[361]

> "to jointly market the corridor to attract more freight to rail. As part of this agreement ARTC paid $55 million to assist Brookfield Rail to upgrade its network between Perth and Kalgoorlie"

NSW and Queensland were the only States that did not relinquish control of their railway networks, perhaps because both State governments operated regional passenger train services. To ensure that the networks remained in good enough condition to run these trains reliably, they accepted the responsibility and cost of network maintenance. NSW was also the first railway system to be vertically separated as a matter of policy to encourage competition among freight rail operators.

Assessment of the Maldon to Dombarton link line

Although the NSW government, through the RIC, owns and pays for the maintenance of all of the NSW network except the lines that RailCorp and the ARTC control, it was reluctant for about twenty years to invest in any new freight-only line. The thinking that prevailed was that investment in new railway lines was not a role for government; rather, this was a role for the private sector. The Maldon to Dombarton link had been started in the 1983 but construction was abandoned in 1988 after a change of State government, and "an economic downturn and the forecast growth in coal traffic not eventuating".[362] In 2011, the federal government had commissioned a feasibility report by consultants[363] that showed that a completed line would not generate sufficient benefits to cover its costs. Although it would relieve future congestion on the Hurstville to Wollongong passenger line and service an expansion of Port Kembla, its problem was the high construction costs due to the terrain. Nevertheless, by 2014 there was strong interest in having its construction finished. The NSW government appealed to the private sector to invest by calling for registrations of interest to design, build, operate and maintain this 35-km line. The NSW Minister Duncan Gay was reported at the time to have said:[364]

> "The 'Registration of Interest' process ... proposes an innovative, market-based approach where the private sector would take the lead in managing the freight demand to ensure it is a commercially viable rail freight line."

This expectation of a private owner "managing the demand" to ensure commercial viability was not realistic. Demand would derive from the freight traffic available, but also the competition from RailCorp and the ARTC for use of existing alternative lines. Unsurprisingly, no suitable offers appeared from the private sector, and this line has still not been finished. Transport for NSW reported on its website in June 2017:

"Transport for NSW undertook a comprehensive evaluation of the two proposals received which included advice from independent experts. Neither proponent was able to meet the RoI evaluation criteria. The RoI showed that the Maldon to Dombarton Railway **would need substantial ongoing State Government funding and policy support** to make it commercially sustainable and that the existing infrastructure is sufficient to manage the short to medium-term rail capacity requirements for the Illawarra." (My emphasis above)

The inconsistency of this decision seems to have eluded the NSW government. The reality is that it funds the great majority of the maintenance and upgrading of the existing rail network in the State,[365] most of which would be 'commercially unsustainable' if it were to be assessed on a similar basis. (This issue is covered in Chapter 15, *The Profitability of Rail Networks*.)

The better way to manage the demand might have been for the ARTC to own and manage the new line while RailCorp restricted access to freight trains to and from Port Kembla running on its passenger route between Tempe and Wollongong. It is not known why this option was not considered, given that the proposed new line would have linked two other lines both managed and maintained by the ARTC.

Unrealistic expectations exposed

The ideologically-based expectation that the private sector should, and would want to, invest in rail networks (as well as the above-rail businesses) has proven now to be largely unrealistic. Private sector investment in lines and networks did not happen except in the monopoly trading situations of WA and the CQCN, and one other exception – the Darwin to Alice Springs line, which started construction in 2001 and opened in 2004. However, after the FreightLink consortium that operated it became insolvent, this vertically-integrated rail business was sold in 2010, and its original investors lost about $A500 million. (See in chapter 12, under *The interstate intermodal sectors*.)

Because of the inadequate network maintenance by its lessees, and the consequential effect on grain transport, the Victorian Government paid Pacific National (PN) $133.8 million[366] to terminate the lease on the broad-gauge network in 2006, in order to regain control to begin upgrading the country rail network. However, it did not contract or oblige PN to remain as the principal operator on this network. In November 2007, PN announced that it would withdraw in March 2008 from grain haulage in both Victoria and NSW, proposing to sell or close its business, because it could not sustain it through years of drought and low volume of grains.[367] PN's Portlink rural container services in Victoria would also be sold or closed, leaving all of the State's rail intrastate freight to be moved by road. Consequently, since 2008, the Victorian Government has paid subsidies, through its Mode Shift Incentive Scheme (MSIS),[368] to freight shippers to put their export freight on rail. That initiative, and the reduction in network access charges to a negligible amount, has been successful in retaining the use of the country rail network. Its justification is both to reduce traffic congestion around the Port of Melbourne, and to protect the rural roading network from damage by some of the heavy vehicles it would otherwise carry.

For similar reasons, the NSW government instituted in 2016 its 'Fixing Country Rail' program. It is funding the reinstatement of unused grain lines and building extensions to sidings at major grain receival sites to facilitate efficient loading of trains.[369]

In 2007, the Tasmanian Government bought the island's rail network for $1,[370] rather than see the whole operation be closed by PN. Nevertheless, in mid-2008 PN announced its intention to withdraw from all above-rail services in Tasmania, resulting in the Tasmanian Government taking over the above-rail business from PN by December 2009.

In these cases where control of a vertically-integrated railway business passed to a company or consortium, the buyer saw a stream of revenue for itself that could be maximised by whatever means. The priority of 'maximising shareholder value' displaced the former objectives of long-term sustainability and providing consistently reliable services. Usually, cutting costs was seen as the quicker means to deliver increased profitability, rather than by increasing profits through chasing more business. Consequently, in the context of having to appease shareholders, the deferral of network maintenance and asset renewals became the way to deliver acceptable annual (and sometimes quarterly) results. The inevitable outcome of that choice was equipment and asset failures, increased operational unreliability, and later loss of revenue as customers diverted their freight to other modes, usually road.

In summary, governments that hoped for private sector financing had some rewards in relation to above-rail assets; but for rail networks, other than the two monopolistic ones, there was only disillusionment.

11. The Privatisation of Four Vertically-Integrated Railways

We have seen in the previous two chapters that four governments had faith that the privatisation of their railways as vertically-integrated entities was the best course of action, but that subsequently the outcomes did not meet their expectations. In this chapter, we look into what the private sector owners did to bring about the disillusionment of the governments, and what followed.

New Zealand

The detailed facts of NZ Rail's privatisation, listing on the stock markets, financial difficulties and two-stage renationalisation are told in Appendix 1. What follows is a summary and interpretation.

Tranz Rail, in brief

The sale of the railways in 1993 had been developed as a policy by the New Zealand Government since the late 1980s. It was part of a wider program of asset sales intended to raise money to pay off government debt. The sale was also intended to enable the government to avoid funding the investments known to be needed in the coming twenty years.

Despite these investment needs, the privatisation of NZ Rail Ltd (which became Tranz Rail) looked successful in the first few years, vindicating those who had promoted it. Freight tonnages increased from 8.5 million tonnes in 1993 to a peak of 14.7 million tonnes in 2000 (see table[371] below), a 72% gain but with reduced unit prices.

Tranz Rail Freight Volumes 1993 – 2003 (for financial years ending 30 June)

Financial Year	Net Tonnes (000s)	NTKs (millions)	Av. length of haul (km)
1993	8,514	2,468	290
1994	9,444	2,835	300
1995	9,584	3,202	334
1996	10,305	3,260	316
1997	11,525	3,505	304
1998	11,706	3,547	303
1999	12,900	3,671	285
2000	14,699	4,078	277
2001	14,461	3,942	273
2002	14,330	3,766	263
2003	13,702	3,692	269

This statement was made about Tranz Rail Ltd in 1996, three years after its privatisation:[372]

> "Since privatisation operating profits have risen substantially from $54M in 1993 to $105M in 1995 (adjusting for redundancy payments in the 1992-3 year). The operating ratio has improved from 88.9% to 81.1 % and productivity has improved 50% since privatisation."

But by 2003 Tranz Rail was heavily in debt, and the Government stepped in to provide $44 million[373] to prevent financial collapse, and the closure of the rail and ferry network. By this act, the NZ Government confirmed that the railway system was indeed 'too big to let fail'. (This vulnerability was discussed in chapter 10, under *Hopes for continuation with improvements*.) The New Zealand Government had shown its vulnerability to being pressed for subsidies in the future, until its tolerance for this behaviour ceased in August 2007.

11. Four Vertically-integrated Railways

An analysis of Tranz Rail's difficulties

Why was Tranz Rail not successful in the way that the government expected? The website of the NZ Ministry of Transport summarises it this way:[374]

> "The change [of ownership] appeared to bring benefits through the early years. Costs were reduced and freight volumes increased. But a recapitalisation, increased debt, and management changes combined to sap profitability and performance in the late 1990s and early 2000s. Growing levels of debt reduced the amount of capital available for investment in the network."

This explanation is glib, and possibly misleading. Apart from the unrealistic expectations (explained in the previous chapter under *A hope for private sector financing*) that NZ governments (of both the left and the right) had held of the new private sector owner, the failure was probably due to a combination of factors.

Change of ownership led to changes in company culture

When the Tranz Rail consortium took control of the NZ Rail Ltd, the culture of the organisation began to change. This was both intended and unintended. Someone[375] described the change as

> "going from an engineering business that ran trains, to a business focused on making profit by whatever means possible."

Firstly, the Tranz Rail Board were a much more proactive group than the NZ Rail Board, who had been effectively counsellors and mentors to the management team. The Tranz Rail Board instigated new strategies to give effect to the joint and separate ambitions that each of the three main companies in the consortium had for their new acquisition, and their investment in it. Initially, the dominant message about strategy given to staff was "to enhance shareholder value", leading up to the IPO planned for 1996. Hence these strategies included:

- focussing on core railway business, and disposing of other activities such as running buses
- paying off debts incurred by the consortium partners for the acquisition of NZ Rail
- "sweating the assets", because the consortium saw an opportunity to slow down the rate of spending on asset renewals, for both infrastructure and rolling-stock
- increasing the volume of business to grow revenue and profitability.

(There is detailed discussion of some of these strategies below.)

Other aspects of the culture changed. "Loyalty to the service" had been an acknowledged and common sentiment among operating and maintenance staff in the years and decades before privatisation. This motivated staff to 'go the extra mile' when mishaps or bad weather caused line blockages and train delays. But the increasingly frequent equipment failures caused by the Tranz Rail policy of sweating the assets sapped staff motivation. Tranz Rail made a conscious effort to recapture staff loyalty, using a different motivator. After the IPO, staff were each invited to purchase a parcel of shares at a small discount on the listing price of $6.19. About one third of the staff took up the offer, the majority of whom had probably never bought shares before. Tranz Rail's stated rationale was [376]

> "share ownership schemes give staff a stake in the business and align their interests with those of the owners."

By 1997, the share price reached a peak of $9.00, but after that it declined over the next seven years. Staff who were not canny enough to sell early would later view this statement about staff share ownership as a sophistry. The reality was that the original owners made millions in profits by quitting their shares at the right time, while many staff lost the bulk of their investments when the share price crashed to below $1.00 in 2003.

After the change of ownership, middle management vacancies ceased to be advertised internally. Instead, individuals were chosen, without any formal application and selection process, on the basis of their can-do attitude, and their likelihood of being loyal to the new owners and their strategic direction. When an offer came, sometimes out of the blue, there was strong pressure to accept it, because it was tacitly understood that to decline was a career-ending decision. As a result of this quick and efficient method of selection, there were some instances of mismatch of person to position, resulting in increased stress and sometimes a resignation. Over time, I observed that this appointment practice led to a collective disinclination to express alternative strategies and/or consider long-term consequences of strategies. As a middle manager at Tranz Rail, I was told by a senior manager "Let's not try to solve today the problems of the next generation", meaning "don't worry about the long-term effects, focus on the short-term gains". Twenty years later, this phenomenon has been widely observed in corporations, and given the label 'strategic ignorance'.[377]

By March 2002, all of Tranz Rail's original major owners had gone, selling out to more passive institutional investors. The business also had a new CEO, with yet another strategic direction being implemented. This strategy was to outsource all maintenance activities, to create a lean 'transport services management company'.[378] The intention was to turn the fixed costs of owning assets into variable costs. However, because the contracts with the international maintenance providers Transfield (for infrastructure) and Alstom (for locomotive and wagon maintenance) were multi-year contracts, these maintenance costs became committed liabilities. By 2003, the difficulty of paying these costs, in the context of insufficient revenue and high debts, brought Tranz Rail to its knees.

Accounting Changes Created Inflated Profits Without Reducing Spending

In early 1994, NZ Rail's new owners changed the method of accounting for track renewals, allegedly in line with the practice used at Wisconsin Central Railroad. Track renewals (on any rail network) include projects such as rerailing, resleepering and ballast cleaning. For any given stretch of track, such work is done at 25- to 40-year intervals, and normally some track renewal work is done each year somewhere in the network to spread these costs.

Prior to the privatisation of NZ Rail, the practice was to expense these project costs and deduct them against revenue. This was consistent with the long-term view that such work was maintenance. The change in accounting policy classed track renewal costs as capital expenditure.[379] As such, they became an addition to the value of fixed assets, and these costs were not deducted from revenue. Instead, they were depreciated on a straight-line basis over 40 years. This change reflected the new owners' shorter-term view that such work was an upgrade to the track, prolonging its economic life. The net effect of the change was to create an illusion of increased profitability when profits from before and after the change were compared. This change was consistent with "enhancing shareholder value", i.e., doing whatever was going to make the business look more profitable in the lead-up to the share float, planned for 1996.

Many future share investors would not have had an understanding of the financial impact of this change to accounting policy. However, an independent financial analyst later showed that this change created a 52% increase in profit:[380]

> "The change had an extremely positive impact on Tranz Rail's reported profit. Restated profits for the 1992 and 1993 year, shown in the 1996 IPO prospectus, showed net earnings of $80.9 million for the two years under the new accounting policies compared with $53.2 million under the old approach."

The Capital Investment Conundrum

The purpose of the strategy to sweat the assets, i.e., to keep using existing assets as-is, was to reduce the total cost for upgrading or replacing them. Despite this, capital investment during the Tranz Rail years averaged $100 million per year,[381] but operating profits did not support an adequate rate of return on that investment. The network was described in 2002 by a financial analyst[382] as "heavily over-capitalised". Therefore, from an accounting perspective, this capital investment of $100 million per year was too much; however, from an engineering perspective, it was too little, because by 2001 it had become obvious that the network (and the rolling-stock) was "run-down".

At least some of Tranz Rail's major customers understood the significance of this paradox – that a sustainable and profitable private-sector vertically-integrated railway in New Zealand was an incongruous impossibility. The Rail Freight Action Group (RFAG) was formed in 2002 to lobby for some type of involvement by the government. (There is more about this group in Appendix 1, under *The Tranz Rail Years, 2002.*)

In July 2002, Tranz Rail revealed[383] the accumulated capital investment in track since 1993 was $187 million. During this period, the major track projects were the redesign and rebuilding of marshalling yards and freight terminals in Wellington and Christchurch (at Middleton). These were valid capital investments with productivity and safety benefits. However, the $187 million also included the costs capitalised due to the change in accounting treatment of track renewals. At the same time, Tranz Rail announced a proposed write-down of up to $170 million on its total asset base of $933 million, but denied that any of these write-downs related to track infrastructure.[384] Also, it would not be changing its accounting policy for track investment.[385]

Debts, Asset Sales and Dividends

The members of the consortium that bought NZ Rail Ltd jointly contributed $NZ105 million for the purchase of 105 million shares at $NZ1 each, and Tranz Rail Holdings borrowed the remainder, $NZ223.3 million.[386] This action converted the majority of the equity, contributed by taxpayers, into debt owed by the rail company. These original shareholders had planned that the rail business would be able to repay this debt, as well as the existing debts of $NZ71.7 million that they took responsibility for.[387] Hence, the rail business valued at $NZ400 million started under its new ownership with debts totalling $NZ295 million. Consequently, the need for debt repayment was a major influence on how the railway was managed.

Tranz Rail sold a number of its assets over eight years, garnering more than $NZ380 million. These sales would have enabled debt repayments, re-investment and/or money to be taken out of the business by the owners:

- In 1994, the company sold its 15% stake in Clear Communications for $NZ72.6 million.[388] (Clear was a telecommunications business in which Railways had acquired shares in the 1980s by granting it the excess capacity of fibre-optic cables buried alongside rail tracks, particularly along the North Island Main Trunk.) This sale enabled a $NZ100 million capital repayment to the private shareholders in July 1995.[389] This was done via a buyback of 27 million shares from existing shareholders at $NZ3.70 per share.[390] At this price, the original shareholders were able to retain a majority of their shares while retrieving a majority of their original contribution. (See Appendix 1, under *The Tranz Rail Years*, for details.)
- In December 1996, Tranz Rail sold its DFT-class locomotives and some recently-purchased wagons for $NZ131.5 million to Chicago Freight Car Leasing (CFCL), and as part of the deal it leased them back for 12 years.[391] (At the end of the lease, KiwiRail took the option to buy these back for about $NZ36 million.)
- Soon after the introduction into service of the newly-

built rail-ferry *Aratere* in 1999, it was sold for $US55 million[392] (about $NZ104m then) to Wilmington Trust, an affiliate of Citicorp USA, and leased back for 15 years.[393] (However, Toll Rail bought out this lease in October 2003.[394])
- In 2001, Tranz Rail sold 50% of Tranz Scenic (its long-distance passenger business) to two directors of the Victorian rail operator West Coast Railway for $33 million.[395] This sale included long-distance passenger rolling-stock and ten diesel locomotives of the DC class, reclassified as the DCP class, and two EF class electric locomotives. (In 2004, this 50% share was purchased by Toll NZ.)
- The Auckland rail network was sold on 24 Dec 2001 to the NZ Government for $81 million[396] to provide a foundation for Auckland's suburban passenger services under a different operator, because TranzRail was unwilling to invest in new commuter rolling-stock.

The practice of sale-and-lease-back of assets (such as rolling-stock and the ferry) was essentially a rort. It has been described by an Accounting Professor as "really just a short-cut way to borrow money".[397]

Tranz Rail paid dividends from 1996 to 2001 at a rate of 8.5 cents per share every six months.[398] This meant approximately $NZ23 million per year was taken out of the company. After April 2001, Tranz Rail ceased paying dividends when it was experiencing financial difficulties. By then, the total paid out as dividends was about $115 million, of which $94 million had been borrowed.[399] Another rort.

Competitive Pressure

Tranz Rail actively sought to increase its traffic task. When NZ Rail Ltd was sold in 1993, it hauled approximately 2.5 billion (net) tonne-kilometres (btkm) of freight. By year 2000 it reached 4.1 btkm. However, to achieve this growth it had to compete with the road industry on price as well as service. Consequently, the average freight rate declined by 20% between 1993 and 2000 from 12.5c/ntkm to 10.0c/ntkm.[400] Hence, the business gained from new traffics, and/or existing traffics retained by rate reductions, was not as profitable as it had been before. In 2001, some freight was ceded to road carriers. The CFO Mark Bloomer was quoted as saying:[401]

> "We have had to take a hard look at some of our freight business to ensure that we were operating profitable services. This has been particularly so in forestry, where we have rationalised low-margin traffic that was not providing a sufficient return."

That rationalisation included ceasing to haul tissue paper from Kawerau in the eastern Bay of Plenty region. This was a legacy traffic from the 1960s, where KS-class box wagons were each loaded with three large rolls of tissue directly from the factory floor within hours of production of the paper. The wagons were then sent on mixed freight trains, via marshalling yards, to factory private sidings in Te Rapa (Hamilton) and Henderson (west Auckland). This factory to factory move, all on rail, was efficient for the paper company, but relatively inefficient for the railway. Scores of these wagons were allocated to this traffic to ensure that there were always enough of them ready to shunt into the Kawerau factory siding when required. They all had to be returned empty to Kawerau. Each KS wagon, with a tare weight of 8 tonnes, was volume-filled with a 3-tonne payload. Hence the load-to-tare ratio for this traffic was only 18.75% allowing for the empty returns. KS wagons were high-maintenance and hard to use because their steel sliding doors would often get stuck.

One of 1600 'Ks' wagons, made late 1960s, withdrawn early 2000s.

Quitting this traffic made sense. Tranz Rail reported the reduction in its forestry revenue for the 2000/01 financial year, but it would have been very difficult to identify the resulting marginal cost savings in fuel, shunting and wagon maintenance. The significant but unreportable cost saving was the capital not spent on new wagons[402] that might have been competitive against road transport, which by then was capable of getting full loads of 11 tissue rolls by double-stacking them on well-deck trailers.

While a vertically-integrated railway should seek as much business as its capacity allows, to spread its high fixed costs more widely, this is counter-productive if the marginal revenue does not cover its marginal costs. This may have been the situation for the tissue traffic, given that Tranz Rail had bought fleets of old high-maintenance locos and wagons, and was sweating these assets. For rolling-stock, this meant accepting higher-than-desirable rates of failure-in-service, having a higher proportion of the fleet out-of-service much of the time, and higher maintenance costs per wagon than would have been the case for a younger fleet. In addition, Tranz Rail bought fifteen second-hand locos cheaply from Queensland in 1995 to cater for increased traffic. These were rebuilt at Hutt workshops, but after a short period in service in New Zealand, they were sold in 1998 to ATN for use in Tasmania.

From 1992 onward, Tranz Rail also had to compete on its inter-island ferry operation, with its competitor adding more capacity every few years. This would have forced Tranz Rail to reduce both its freight and passenger charges for inter-island transport.

Vulnerability to External Events

All businesses are, to some degree, vulnerable to events beyond their control, affecting their revenues, costs, or both. How they survive such events depends both on the severity and duration of the events and how well prepared and financially secure the business is to cope with them. In New Zealand, the main environmental dangers are earthquakes, floods, and droughts. They are a fact of life, occurring every year somewhere in the country. In April 2003 Tranz Rail announced a shortfall of $11 million in expected revenue causing a fall in expected profit of $10 million, due in part to the effects of a drought and a strike at a pulp and paper mill.[403] Such was the precariousness of Tranz Rail's finances at that time, the announcement led to another downgrading of its credit rating, and the share price crashed to 30 cents by mid-April. It was reported then that "the company teeters on the brink of insolvency".[404]

Why and how the government took back the rail network

In 2003, the New Zealand Government was aware that the failure of the privatised railway system was an increasing risk to its National Transport Strategy. It decided to try to retake control of the railway network. In a memo for Cabinet outlining its options, the Minister of Finance summarised the current situation:[405]

"In the medium-term rail in New Zealand is not sustainable without government support, which necessarily involves a subsidy in one form or another to rail operators. Without this support it is likely that a commercially focused rail operator would reduce services, particularly on regional routes, and continue to run down the network, eventually making viable rail services unsustainable."

Confirmation of this came later from the World Bank. In 2005, it published a review of railway privatisation in Australia and New Zealand, focussing on the results from privatisation,[406] to discern

"the merits or otherwise of private sector participation in railways as a broader policy principle".

For Tranz Rail, it noted the deteriorating situation in its later years, as evidenced by this table[407] headed *Tranz Rail Key Financial Performance Statistics*:

	1996	1997	1998	1999	2000	2001	2002	2003
Operating Revenue NZ$m *	546	557	554	552	573	607	574	579
Operating Margin (percent)	24%	21%	19%	18%	20%	14%	12%	15%
Interest Cover (x)	3.5 x	7.9 x	7.0 x	2.6 x	2.6 x	1.3 x	0.8 x	na
EBITDA/Funds Employed	23%	19%	14%	11%	13%	10%	8%	na

* Passenger and Freight (including Ferry) Operating Revenues.
Source: TRH annual reports, TRH website

In its conclusions, the report said:

"The experience of the last five years would suggest that, in the current deregulated market, the medium/long term commercial viability of the NZ railway system in its current configuration is dubious. The viability of the system overall would improve if the Government were to significantly increase road user charges imposed on trucks (but noting that this would increase the costs of freight transport in general). However, in the shorter term, it has decided to contribute to the railway's commercial viability by renationalizing and providing funding for the rail infrastructure network."

In other words, the "private sector participation in railways" could be successful in New Zealand in the medium to long term, so long as the government provided financial help by one means or another.

Such an outcome was not what was hoped for when the government sold its railway in 1993, specifically to avoid on-going funding. By 2002, it was obvious to many that this privatisation was failing, in part because of the actions of the first owners. However, the government had no strategy for this scenario, because in the early 1990s it could see only the rosy future that the private sector owners would provide; failure of privatisation was unthinkable back then. Hence in 2003, the government had only ad hoc responses when Tranz Rail's imminent financial failure became apparent.

The opportunity for the government to regain the network came in 2003 when Toll (a large Australian transport and logistics company) decided to buy Tranz Rail through a takeover on the stock market. The government made an agreement with Toll before the takeover that it would buy the run-down network, all the 'below-rail' part of the business, for $1. By then, the reality was that the network was more of a liability than an asset. Hence the government also gave a public undertaking to fund upgrading of the network. However, despite the guile of the original owners of Tranz Rail, the Finance Minister showed continuing faith in private sector competence, sincerity, and ability to operate without any more government assistance. He was reported to have said when this deal was announced in August 2003:[408]

"We recognise [Toll has] the managerial and financial capacity to restore Tranz Rail to viability. Toll's strong balance sheets also mean that it will be able to put in the capital required to rebuild the rail fleet, and to pay full access costs for the rail network in the long term rather than rely on a subsidy from the taxpayer."

Why and how the government took back the above-rail business

After Toll bought Tranz Rail and sold the network to the Government in June 2004, Toll and the Government slipped into an uneasy interdependence. The two parties had signed the National Rail Access Agreement (NRAA) as the means to manage their relationship. The Government had bought the network to keep all of it open and operational, and depended on Toll to operate over all of it to fulfil its National Transport Strategy. By contrast, Toll saw an opportunity to enhance profits by depending on the Government for subsidies. It resisted paying the full access charges it had agreed to pay, suggesting in March 2006 to Government that it might cease to operate over about 40% of the network.[409] Consequently, the Government had to subsidise the costs of the restoration of the network for the whole period of Toll's ownership of the above-rail business. Therefore, a key requirement of the NRAA, from the Government's viewpoint (referring to the Finance Minister's quote above), was not fulfilled.

Toll also resisted investing in new rolling-stock, reneging on its commitment in the NRAA to spend $100 million on this. Moreover, during negotiations to find a more workable arrangement to replace the NRAA, it asked Government to purchase new rolling-stock and lease it to Toll. It also suggested sale and lease back of the whole fleet. By this means, it hoped to have the government carry the financial risks of the capital-intensive business while it retained the customers and cash flows. The government, having considered the possibility of a franchise deal and rejected it as too complex and risky, decided in October 2007 to buy Toll Rail. However, Toll was an unwilling seller, and for six months, confidential negotiations on a sale price were frustrated by arguments about how to value the company. These arguments derived largely from different assumptions about the future network access charges payable by Toll, which was the main issue in contention from the start. The government, mindful of New Zealand's international reputation as a good place for business investment, never considered using legislation to take back the railway business by force. Thus, in the negotiations, Toll had the stronger position, resulting in a final sum being agreed that was much higher than was generally considered to be the value of the assets.

Victoria

Privatisation and its outcome

Both the Victorian rail networks (standard- and broad-gauge) were separated from train operations by the State government in July 1997, and run by VicTrack, a government authority. In July 1999, ARTC took control of the interstate standard-gauge lines between Melbourne and the state borders of NSW and SA.

In 1998, the Victorian Government put State-owned V/Line Freight onto the market for sale to the highest bidder. Its initial motivation was to be seen to comply with the federal Competition Policy Reform Act 1995 (described in chapter 5 under *The National Competition Policy*) and to qualify for extra Commonwealth funds. However, its real aim was just to avoid the costs and risks of what was seen as a marginally profitable operator.410 The government's original intention was to privatise V/Line Freight as an above-rail operation only. However, after getting feedback from the market that it could achieve a higher price if track and train operations were available together, it offered V/Line Freight as a vertically-integrated freight railway, with the business for sale and the 'country network' to be leased for 45 years.411 For $A163 million, Rail America bought the freight business and leased the broad-gauge track. This made it effectively a monopolistic vertically-integrated freight train operator, just as the government-owned V/Line was previously.

What resulted from the privatisation of V/Line Freight, including the lease of the country broad-gauge network, was something very different from "a prosperous, innovative and expanding rail industry".[412] After privatisation in 1999, intrastate non-grain freight on rail declined by about 10%,[413] while grain tonnages fluctuated both with seasonal variations in the size of the grain harvest, and the abilities of train operators to service this very variable market.

Under the conditions of the 45-year track lease, no specific maintenance obligations for the freight-only network had been imposed on the new track managers.[414] Requirements for the lines used by passenger trains were defined only in terms of a ride quality index which did not necessarily correlate with actual track condition. Although maintenance cost-cutting had started under government control in the mid-1990s,[415] Freight Australia took the view that the network was over-maintained, and reduced its on-going costs by down-sizing maintenance resources, particularly those doing track renewal programs.[416]

> "The short-term perception was one of significant cost savings but in reality the asset base began to again degrade and retention of the network's capability increasingly relied on the redundancy installed with the earlier [1980s] maintenance catch-up program."

A review of the condition of the country network, done in 2007, found substantial degradation due to inadequate maintenance. Generally, two to three sleeper replacement cycles had been missed.[417] An example of the consequence was:[418]

"In the last ten years the container freight train transit time from Mildura [to Melbourne] has deteriorated from 10 hours to 16 hours on average. As a result, freight has transferred to road, including to Adelaide in order to meet shipping schedules."

Maintenance of the broad-gauge network under its two private sector owners had been much less than that required for continuing reliability. Rail consultant John Hearsch put this outcome as a criticism of the decision to privatise the network:[419]

"The final outcome of Victoria's infrastructure privatisation, at least for the freight-only network, is that the residual life of the asset has been largely consumed by its private sector owners. In other words, the railway has been "asset stripped", with much of its former value (at least until September 2004) flowing to Rail America's shareholders by way of maintenance expenditure savings and the significant proceeds from its sale to Pacific National."

In August 2004, Pacific National (PN) bought Freight Australia including the lease to the broad-gauge network. In 2006, PN was negotiating with the government regulator, the Essential Services Commission (ESC) about access arrangements. Initially the ESC rejected PN's proposal because it had failed to specify that the tracks would be guaranteed as being fit-for-purpose. However, after further negotiations, it relented. The outcome has been described thus: [420]

"Following the commissioning of a consultancy report on the 'fitness for purpose' issue, the final decision of the ESC noted that there were a number of potential trade-offs between track quality and cost, and that where track is not used intensively it may be more cost effective to require trains to travel at reduced speed and minimise maintenance costs. Based on this, the ESC was able to give conditional support to PN's revised minimum service standards."

Control of the country network retrieved

In 2006, the ESC realised that maintenance of the intrastate freight network at reasonable levels of service was unsustainable without on-going government support.[421] This support was in addition to the access charges payable by government-owned V/Line Passenger to PN for its regional passenger services. The Victorian Government was able to use a technicality, being the change in PN's ownership in May 2006, to trigger a termination of the lease.[422] However, to regain control of this network, the government had to buy back the lease for an announced sum of $A133.8 million; but later, the audited estimate of final cost to the Victorian Government after the sale was found to be $A214.5 million.[423] Negotiations to cede control of the intrastate freight network were agreed by November 2006, with the handover to occur in May 2007. Management of the country network passed to the government-funded regional passenger train business V/Line.

The termination of the lease on the Victorian broad-gauge network was an admission of policy failure, which should have been an embarrassment for the State government. However, the Coalition government that privatised the rail system had since been replaced by a Labor government with different priorities.

In early 2007, the State government urgently needed advice on how to rehabilitate its rail network. It appointed a Rail Freight Network Review (RFNR) Committee, with terms of reference that included:[424]

- potential future levels and composition of rail freight traffic
- the network's present physical condition and maintenance needs
- the network's future configuration from a public interest perspective including promoting economic

growth and any impact on the road network and grain handling facilities
- the relative priority of lines for upgrade and/or conversion to standard gauge
- the role government and stakeholders can play in contributing to the long-term network viability.

The *Rail Freight Network Review* (RFNR) group reported back towards the end of 2007, strongly supporting the retention, rehabilitation and development of the broad-gauge network for freight. It saw the alternative was to let it fall into disuse or be closed,[425]

> "accelerating a switch to road with major environmental, social and economic consequences."

It was known to this group that Pacific National was losing money in Victoria,[426] due to:
- 2007 being a second year of drought with a poor grain harvest, hence not enough business for the resources deployed,
- the concurrent deregulation and fragmentation of grain handling and marketing, disrupting previous transport arrangements and relationships,
- the poor condition of the rail network causing slow train operations, customer dissatisfaction, and poor rolling-stock utilisation, and
- relatively high network access charges. These had been set during the negotiations between the Government and PN for the return of the network lease, and were substantially higher than for ARTC lines or for the southern NSW branch lines, in a similar grain growing area.

Consequently, the RFNR recommendations[427] to the Government included that:
- network access fees be immediately reset at levels comparable with those of south-east NSW and the

ARTC lines for at least five years – this implied an acceptance that fees revenue would be much less than network restoration and maintenance costs for the foreseeable future
- the network be rehabilitated and restored to previous classes of speed as applied to arterial and branch lines, this work to be funded and done in an order of priority according to a proposed classification of lines
- after the restoration of lines, there be a commitment to annual routine maintenance beyond 2011, including major periodic maintenance such as sleeper renewals.

The report commented on the access charges and the issue of the subsidy involved:[428]

> "RFNR acknowledges the reduced access revenue from the reduced rates, but does not see the merit of setting access charges at levels which will not generate any revenue because the business has shifted to road."

> "If governments are concerned to reduce the subsidy inherent in this approach, the best way to solve that is for the very high subsidy in long range road transport to be progressively reduced so that rail access pricing with its triple bottom-line advantages over road can be given more pricing headroom. The current approach does not allow this and in fact is pushing customer substitution the other way, in sharp contrast to the Government's policy objective of 30% of port related freight on rail."

The Government accepted the RFNR recommendations because it was determined not to let the use of the rail network cease due to its previous neglect. Taking a holistic view, it was prepared to invest in the rail network in the public interest – particularly in support of the grain-growing industry, for maintaining the safety and condition of rural roads, and for reducing congestion around major grain export ports. Under these circumstances, the rail network's financial viability was not considered to be of any relevance. (Expectations of network profitability are discussed in chapter 15.)

The Victorian Government's decision in 1998 to gain more money by disposing of its railway as a vertically-integrated system, actually caused it to lose over $50 million on the disposal and network retrieval transactions. In addition, it subsequently had to invest $1.2 billion for rehabilitation of the network over the four years to 2011.[429] In November 2007, Pacific National (PN) announced its withdrawal from export grain and some intrastate services within Victoria from March 2008,[430] then took away all the rolling-stock. Altogether, the implementation of the Commonwealth Government's push for privatisation, private sector investment, and competition among train operators was a complete failure in Victoria. The successful revival of freight on rail in Victoria since 2007 is described in the next chapter under *How Competition Evolved in Australia*.

Tasmania

While the Tasmanian rail system was a part of Australian National Railways Commission from 1978 onwards, it recorded deficits every year, which the Commonwealth government financed. In 1991, it asked its Bureau of Transport and Communications Economics (BTCE) to assess the options of closure of TasRail or its retention with actions taken to improve its financial performance. In summary, the conclusions from the BTCE study were that it was likely that financial deficits would continue, but the social cost-benefit analysis showed that Tasmania would be better off if TasRail continued to operate. On that basis, it recommended retention, and the governments agreed.[431]

Nevertheless, as a part of the break up and disposal of Australian National by the Commonwealth government in November 1997, the Tasmanian railway system was sold for $A22 million.[432] Land under the network reverted to the Tasmanian government. The buyer of the business was the Australian

Transport Network group (ATN), owned 67% by TranzRail Ltd (New Zealand) and 33% by Wisconsin Central (USA). The sale commitments[433] included an agreement that ATN would maintain all existing operational lines for a minimum of five years, and would invest $A20 million over this time on locomotives, wagons and track. The locomotives supplied by ATN included fifteen second-hand narrow-gauge locomotives sourced from Queensland which had been rebuilt in New Zealand before shipment to Tasmania. Labour cost reductions in TasRail came from implementing driver-only train operations and remote-controlled shunting, using technologies already proven in New Zealand. New business was found, and ATN announced a profit of $1.2m for the first seven months of operation.[434] Financial results were not announced subsequently, but in 2004 the whole of ATN, including its mainland contracts and rolling-stock and TasRail, was sold to PN for approximately $13m. The sale at this price came about because by 2004, ATN had new owners; Toll had bought (the almost insolvent) TranzRail, and Canadian National had bought Wisconsin Central. Neither company wanted to continue ATN as a separate entity. PN then struggled to make an operating profit from TasRail even with reduced track maintenance. The Tasmanian government took control of its rail network in May 2007, and two years later it bought the above-rail business rather than let PN close it down.

The BTCE assessment of TasRail in 1991 had shown that while its retention was the best outcome for Tasmania, it was unlikely to become profitable. Therefore, for the Commonwealth government to expect private sector owners to make a profit, while investing to make up for past neglect of the whole system, was totally unrealistic. Hence the failure of this privatisation.

Governments to the rescue

The three governments (New Zealand, Victoria, and Tasmania) which were formerly the owners of these railway systems were clearly disappointed by the degradation of the rail networks under private sector management. Each government retrieved control of its network, with commitments to rehabilitate it, and these works are on-going more than a decade later.

The problem with maintenance deferral in railways is that it is easy to do and hard to catch up on. It takes many more years to recover from deferred asset maintenance than the number of years of deferral, because of limitations in financing, resourcing, and getting access to otherwise operational tracks. Railway track degrades with both time and use, and componentry in track is ideally maintained by planned or predictive maintenance in cycles that range from monthly to once in forty years. When planned maintenance is deferred, a greater proportion of the remaining maintenance budget then has to be spent on reacting to problems as they emerge. This means doing patchwork that keeps the line open, but with speed restrictions that increase train journey times. (In Victoria, the impact was greater for grain trains, because increased train journey times busted train cycle times, which reduced the overall capacity of the wagon fleet.) Hence, deferred track maintenance leads sooner or later to more freight carried on roads. Therefore, a failed railway privatisation is a serious setback for the affected government and state economy. It was an outcome that was never even considered possible in the fervour for privatisation in the 1990s.

In all three railways discussed above, private sector owners chose to put their own business profitability and shareholder dividends (or financial survival) ahead of sustainability of their railway networks, regardless of government wishes or public sentiment. They demonstrated that private sector ownership of government-built rail networks cannot usually make a business viable in the longer term. However, there is one exception to this, for exceptional reasons, in Western Australia.

Western Australia

The WA government deliberately disposed of WestRail as a vertically-integrated business in year 2000. It wanted to ensure that the rail network would stay intact under private control, in order to retain both its economic and social benefits for the State. The sale and lease of WestRail was a whole-of-business transaction, with buyer and the lessee being the Australian Railroad Group (ARG). The sale included the rolling-stock, current customer contracts, and a company which employed all the staff at the time of sale. There were two 49-year leases of the standard-gauge and narrow-gauge infrastructures, networks and associated land, for which ARG paid all the rent in advance. The government saw this method of disposal as the best way to retain the network in public ownership while enabling the new owner to access the benefits of a vertically-integrated business and contribute "capital investment in the infrastructure greater than government can provide".[435]

However, in 2006 the railway was vertically separated and resold as distinct above-rail and below-rail businesses, the latter being named WestNet Rail. That this vertical separation happened is a key to understanding why the outcome in WA was different from the outcome of the privatisation of vertically-integrated railways elsewhere. Multinational company Brookfield Infrastructure acquired 100% of the below-rail business in 2010, at a time when minerals traffic was forecast to grow rapidly. It has invested $2 billion upgrading the network since it took over.[436]

Historically, the WA railway network was built largely to serve the grain industry. Cooperative Bulk Handlers (CBH) is a farmer-owned grain consolidation and export business that owns hundreds of grain silos located at sidings across much of the rail network. Hence CBH is a significant customer for Brookfield Rail. Brookfield reports that of its 5500-kilometre network, some 2400 kilometres are used solely for grain transport.[437] However, from Brookfield's point of view, grain is now a minor component of its traffic task, being only 9% of GTKs moved.[438]

By 2009, WestNet Rail had told the State government that the grain lines were uneconomic and would need public funds for the next cyclic resleepering program. If this money were not provided, WestNet Rail would surrender these lines to the government, with the result that all the grain in the 2010 harvest would have to be moved by road. After months of negotiations, the WA government agreed to fund the resleepering program for tier 1 and 2 grain lines in order to keep them open. Agreed in 2010 at an estimated cost to the government of $258 million,[439] this work was completed in December 2013.[440] A program for the Tier 3 grain lines was not funded; these lines were the least intensively used, and the least maintained lines in the network.

In May 2013, the government published the Western Australian Regional Freight Transport Network Plan, outlining its priorities to 2031. Under the heading of Rail, it stated:[441]

> "The rail freight task on the State-owned rail network, managed by Brookfield Rail, will increase ... from 50+ million net tonnes per annum to more than 130 million net tonnes per annum.
>
> To meet potential demand, Brookfield Rail will need to invest substantial capital in order to create the required capacity in the rail network."

Its planning and policy priorities for the rail network included:[442]

> "Continuing to work with all parties to facilitate a sustainable arrangement to keep Tier 3 lines operational."

At the end of June 2014, the tier 3 branch lines were "placed into care and maintenance"[443] by Brookfield, which is a euphemism for barring access, effectively closing them. CBH protested, unsuccessfully. Brookfield also refused an offer by

CBH to sub-lease the tier 3 lines.[444] The Tier 3 lines comprise 509 kilometres of track, being 10% of Brookfield's total network or 21% of the dedicated grain network. This closure was against the wishes of the Western Australian Government, which legally still owns the network, and which is responsible for land transport strategies. This still unresolved dispute about the Tier 3 branch lines is an example of the divergence between a government's expectation that privatisation would enable continuation of its rail network, and the profit-motive of a private sector company. (Refer to chapter 10, under *Hopes for continuation with improvements*.) Brookfield, now called Arc Infrastructure, used a business strategy known as 'purposeful abandonment', espoused by business management guru Peter Drucker.

In June 2020, the State government published the *Revitalising Agricultural Region Freight Strategy*.

> "The Strategy identifies and prioritises specific infrastructure upgrades, and suggests regulatory and policy measures that will help make freight transport in WA's agricultural regions more productive, efficient, and safer." [445]

On the Tier 3 lines issue, it stated:[446]

> "Investment in State and local roads will have to compensate for increased road freight traffic in areas formerly served by Tier 3 lines."

This suggests that, in the six years since the closure of the Tier 3 lines, nothing had been done about the deteriorating road network, but the Government knew it would have to fund road repairs caused by Arc's closure of these lines. However, in September 2020, it was reported[447] that three of the Tier 3 lines could be reopened at a cost of $486 million. The Transport Minister was reported as saying:

"While the engineering report confirms restoring the entire [Tier 3] network would involve significant costs, there are arguably specific lines where the cost of investment could be offset by ongoing commercial and community benefits such as reduced truck volumes on local roads and cost savings to farmers."

In May 2022, after a record 24 million tonne grain harvest, the WA Government announced, under its Agricultural Supply Chain Improvement (ASCI) program, an initial funding of $200 million for works to improve the rail network.[448] These include siding extensions and upgrades at eleven sites, which will enable CBH to load trains more quickly, and the progressive reconditioning of one of the closed Tier 3 lines, from Narrogin to Kulin. This will reconnect six CBH sites to the rail network, and also service a new kaolin mine near Wickepin.

At the time of writing, no further decisions have been made, but it is now obvious that the State government has accepted that it must fund the refurbishment of either these grain lines and/or the wheatbelt roading network.

In summary, whether or not the privatisation of the WA railway network has been a success is dependent on the stakeholders' viewpoints:

- For Arc Infrastructure, it is a profitable business, helped in part by the closure of the Tier 3 grain lines, which reduced some of its cost of network maintenance for grain transport;
- For all train operators, there is now a heavy duty, reliably maintained network to use;
- For CBH, some of its silos were cut off from the rail network, leaving no option but to use trucking to shift bulk export grain to Kwinana, at a higher unit cost ultimately to grain growers (the owners of CBH);
- CBH has estimated that with targeted investments into the rail network, another 1 million tonnes of grain

could be moved by rail instead of by road[449] from an average annual harvest;
- The WA Government has succeeded in having a company facilitate and fund a major increase in the use of the rail network, but failed to ensure the continuity of all the grain lines, and has also failed in its intention to avoid future rail network maintenance and development costs. It has had little influence on how the annual grain harvest[450] is moved, despite having to fund the infrastructure required, both rail lines and roads.

12. Competition Outcomes

The significance of competition

In the 1980s and 1990s, governments in English-speaking countries, including Australia and New Zealand, were motivated by neoliberal economic thinking, in which competition, in all forms of economic activity, was a core value because it was expected to deliver efficiencies. The first stimulus for competition within the Australian railway industry came from Prime Minister Paul Keating's 1992 One Nation program of microeconomic reform:[451]

> "When this Government came into office the problem of inefficient performance was endemic in areas shielded from competition – including … railways."

Keating established the National Competition Policy Review, the recommendations of which were incorporated into the Commonwealth's Competition Policy Reform Act of 1995. (See chapter 5, under *The National Competition Policy*.)

This Act obliged the State governments to enact legislation enabling competition on their networks among different train operators. How this was to be achieved was for each State to decide. Hence, the actions of the federal and State governments were significant in assisting or hindering competition on their networks. The meaning of 'competition' in this chapter is in this fairly loose sense, that of train-operating companies sharing the markets for railable freight.

12. Competition Outcomes

There were different market sectors across the Australian continent, and still four separate State-based rail networks. In these State networks, the competition outcomes were quite different; hence, I will discuss the evolution of competition for each one individually, below. In summary:

- In NSW, competition for the market started in the same year (2002) that the government-owned train operators (NRC and FreightCorp) were privatised, and it has flourished since then.
- In Victoria, the Government was persuaded to sell its freight business and lease its broad-gauge network as one package in 1999, and did not seek any competition. No competition emerged until after the network was back under State control in 2007, and then it grew steadily.
- In WA, the Government deliberately chose to sell its freight business and lease its network as one vertically-integrated railway system in 2000; there was already some interstate traffic on the standard-gauge lines, but it did not want any competition on its narrow-gauge network, to protect services for the grain industry. However, in 2012, CBH (the sole grain marketer for the State) started in competition with the incumbent train operator.
- In Queensland, the rail system remained government-owned and vertically-integrated until 2010, although some competition within the State was permitted from 2005. There are now at least four train operators competing for the coal, grain and general freight markets.

Other aspects of competition in the freight rail industry will be explored in chapter 13.

The interstate intermodal sectors

The east to west corridor

The first rail operator on this corridor was Commonwealth Railways, then from 1975 the Australian National Railway Commission, operating between the SA/Vic border and Broken Hill (NSW) in the east, to Kalgoorlie in WA. The National Rail Corporation (NRC) was set up in 1991 specifically to take over interstate traffic from Australian National and the various State railways. The aim was to provide a much better standard of service and profitability in this sector than had been achievable previously. (See in chapter 4.) At that time, interstate traffic included dedicated train-loads of billet and coil steel from Whyalla (SA) to all mainland States for further processing. NRC became the first rail company to operate between the eastern States right through to Perth. In 2002, NRC was sold and became part of Pacific National (PN), which continued the services for general freight and steel.

In June 1995, the conversion of the Melbourne to Adelaide line from broad- to standard-gauge was completed, and this was the catalyst for the first competitor against NRC on its Melbourne-Perth route. Specialised Container Transport (SCT) was the first private sector company to venture into interstate rail competition. Based in Melbourne, it was a trucking and logistics company which bought National Rail's fleet of refrigerated and louvered vans and boxcars that it had been using as a customer of NR. In July 1995, SCT started its own freight-on-rail service between Melbourne, Adelaide and Perth, initially once a week each way. It contracted with V/Line Freight, later Freight Australia (Melbourne to Adelaide), and with Australian National (Adelaide to Perth) to haul these trains. From October 2000 Freight Australia (later Pacific National) provided the 'hook-and-pull' service for SCT all the way between Melbourne and Perth, by then operating several days per week. In 2007 SCT bought and leased a total of twelve locos from Pacific National, under conditions mandated by the ACCC, to operate its own trains. SCT had started operating trains also between Parkes (NSW) and Perth in 2006.

In June 1996, another freight forwarding company TNT (later known as Toll) started competing on the Melbourne-Perth route with its own trains, and in 1997 Patrick Corp started a container land-bridge train service between Port Melbourne and Port Adelaide. In 2002, both of these companies were absorbed into the newly formed Pacific National along with the NRC, so PN became the main train operator on the east to west route.

From 1995 to 2003, this east to west interstate route was the only one in Australia where competition between rail companies took place. Price competition in both directions between rail companies was possible here because rail had the advantage over road due to economies of scale and the length of haul. In addition, the majority of the traffic moved from east to west. Hence, producers in WA enjoyed cheaper backhaul rates for over two decades due to otherwise unused wagon capacity west to east.

In 2007, QR became the third competitor on the route, offering a Melbourne-Adelaide-Perth intermodal service, enabled by its purchase of Perth-based ARG the previous year. This continued through QR's organisational changes until Aurizon decided in 2017 to withdraw from all interstate intermodal business, citing persistent losses (more detail below, in the next section.)

After 2015, the market share of freight on rail from Sydney, Melbourne and Adelaide to Perth reduced year by year. Competition came from shipping, but not Australian shipping. The Commonwealth Government had permitted cabotage, where overseas shipping lines could sell their spare capacity east to west more cheaply than rail rates, to carry domestic containerised freight along with export freight. (The shipping lines did not have spare capacity in the west to east direction because containerised imports to the eastern States exceeded containerised exports.) By 2020, the historic freight imbalance on the rail route was reversed, with eastbound traffic then the dominant flow. Consequently, freight rates were increased significantly for producers in WA.

Understandably, PN and SCT were not happy about competition from cabotage, which they saw as an irrational federal government policy. The Managing Director of SCT has been quoted:[452]

> "The illogical part of all this is that the majority — if not all — of the price advantage that foreign shipping companies have over rail is achieved through avoidance of the track access charges and tax revenues that we pay to the government. It is difficult to see the logic in that for Australia."

With the advent of the Covid pandemic from 2020, overseas shipping patterns changed, reducing this form of competition for the rail operators.

The south to north corridor of the eastern States

Competition with NRC, which later became PN, in the north to south corridor did not start until May 2003. Freight Australia started a Melbourne-Sydney service for Colin Rees Transport Ltd (CRT), using CRT intermodal depots at Altona (Vic) and Yennora (NSW). However, in August 2004 PN bought out Freight Australia, and CRT switched to Interail. Queensland Rail, through its subsidiary Interail, had started a Brisbane-Melbourne service in April 2004, and with access to CRT's Yennora intermodal depot, Interail's service became Brisbane-Sydney-Melbourne. This developed over the years into daily Aurizon services each way. Much of its traffic came from freight forwarding companies. For some years, Aurizon's trains also included SCT's wagons in their consists until SCT started operating its own trains between Melbourne, Wodonga and Brisbane from January 2017.

12. Competition Outcomes

Queensland Rail had bought ARG in February 2006 for $446m,[453] acquiring rolling-stock, depots and contracts in WA and NSW. ARG continued to trade as a separate entity for some years, but QR's acquisition also enabled it to expand its interstate intermodal operations to include linking Brisbane with Perth via Melbourne. For some ten years, QR, known later as Aurizon, was a significant operator in all the interstate intermodal sectors. However, in August 2017 Aurizon announced its withdrawal from all its interstate operations, completing this in December 2017. Its CEO was quoted[454] as saying:

> "In making the decision to exit, we considered the significant financial losses that have been sustained year on year by Aurizon Intermodal. The business has not been able to establish significant scale and a customer base to support a profitable business in such a highly competitive market."

Was the federal government's competition policy too effective in this case? Withdrawal from the market was not an expected outcome, because that would have reduced the competition.

As a result of Aurizon's withdrawal, only two train operators, PN and SCT, remained in the interstate intermodal markets for the next five years. PN had acquired this business as a going concern when it bought National Rail, using intermodal terminals originally established for AN and the State-owned railways. In contrast, SCT had grown its interstate rail business step by step, adding new sectors as it developed its own intermodal terminals to operate from. Growth in SCT's traffic in 2017 between Melbourne and Brisbane was reported[455] to have come mainly from trucking rather than from the withdrawal of Aurizon from interstate operations. While SCT's trains necessarily travel through Sydney, SCT does not provide freight service by rail to and from Sydney because it has no access to an intermodal terminal there.

In November 2022, Qube started a thrice weekly return service to Melbourne, enabled by the opening of its Moorebank terminal in Sydney.

Historically, Sydney was not a major origin and destination for interstate railed freight for two main reasons. Firstly, rail's modal share of the Sydney-Brisbane and Sydney-Melbourne sectors steadily declined from the 1970s due to the Commonwealth Government's initiation of, and funding support for, the National Highway System (described in Chapter 4). Over the same time, the lack of developmental investment by both the Commonwealth and NSW Governments in these interstate routes left the privatised train operators with transit times completely uncompetitive against trucking companies, as the market had come to expect overnight deliveries, door to door. PN was the sole intermodal train operator servicing the Sydney-Brisbane and Sydney-Melbourne sectors. It recently estimated it has less than 1% market share of 20 million tonnes of palletised and containerised freight transported between Melbourne and Sydney.[456] The remainder moves on the Hume Highway in approximately 1000 B-double trips each way per night, nearly every night.[457]

Consequently, the Commonwealth Government's policy for competition within the rail industry became irrelevant, due to its development of the Hume Highway (see chapter 4, under *Creation and funding of the National Highway System*.) The current situation follows from this government's decision not to lead national transport policy development (see in chapters 4 and 6). It is an outcome of the unacknowledged and incoherent, but de facto, land transport policy that existed for many decades.

On the sector between Brisbane and Melbourne, the expected transit time is over two nights, or up to about 56 hours. PN (and previously Aurizon) can achieve this comfortably. It schedules its trains to arrive in the Sydney area, shunt Sydney wagons on and off, and depart, all between the morning and afternoon curfews[458], which is possible only if there is somewhere within the Sydney network to do this. Nevertheless, PN has only a minority market share of this sector.

The matter of where to shunt in the Sydney area was, and still is, a problem for any interstate freight rail company wanting to compete with PN. Because of the way in which FreightCorp and National Rail were privatised in 2002 (see chapter 9, under *Changes in railway ownership and organisation structures*), PN acquired the exclusive use of SRANSW's intermodal freight terminal in Chullora. Then in 2003, Freight Australia was able to provide a Melbourne-Sydney service to CRT only because CRT had depots at Altona (Vic) and Yennora (NSW) with rail sidings available at which to start and terminate these trains. When Interail (later Aurizon) became CRT's train operator, shunting its long through-trains at Yennora was not practicable because that terminal has only one north-facing connection to the main lines. The pragmatic solution was to shunt these interstate trains just south of the RailCorp area at Glenlee, and connect them with daily trip trains between Yennora and Glenlee and return.

The new multipurpose open-access freight terminal and rail yard at Moorebank in southern Sydney, being developed by Qube with some funding from the Commonwealth Government, should open Sydney to all freight train operators for the first time. In 2007 Aurizon took a strategic stake in Moorebank, holding a 33% share in the Sydney Intermodal Terminal Alliance (SIMTA).[459] However, in 2016, it sold this stake to Qube after it secured a 10-year lease at the nearby Enfield Intermodal Logistics Centre, owned by NSW Ports.460 However, in February 2018, a change of operator at the Enfield Intermodal Logistics Centre was announced, from Aurizon to Linz Cargo Care Group. This completed Aurizon's withdrawal from all its intermodal work outside of Queensland.

Inland Rail – the alternative south to north corridor for the eastern States

The Inland Rail route is planned to connect Brisbane directly to Melbourne, linking new and existing routes through north-eastern Victoria, central New South Wales and south-east Queensland, thereby avoiding the constrained capacity and difficulties of the existing 'coastal route'. When it opens in 2027,[461] it will cut about ten hours and 200 kilometres from the transit between Brisbane and Melbourne.[462] This will be made possible by trains not having to traverse the slow circuitous century-old route alignments north and south of Sydney, and by avoiding the congestion and curfews of the Sydney metropolitan network. Additionally, it will reduce the route from Brisbane to Adelaide and Perth by 500 kilometres, going via Parkes and Broken Hill instead of via Melbourne. Inland Rail will allow for trains up to 1800 metres long, with containers double-stacked; neither of these features is possible on the Brisbane-Sydney-Melbourne route. Consequently, when completed, it will be a step change in the productivity of inter-capital freight transport, enhancing rail's competitiveness against trucking, and enabling increases in rail's market share in the eastern States. This, in turn, will improve road safety and environmental impacts from land transport.

Removing the Queensland-Victoria through-freight traffic from the Sydney metropolitan network has benefits there also. Significant growth is forecast for both passenger traffic and import/export containers on rail from and to Port Botany. These will take up any line capacity made available in Sydney, and in the corridor between Sydney and Newcastle, where usage between 5am and 10pm has been nearly at capacity since 2012,[463] mainly due to the frequency of passenger trains.

Inland Rail was first proposed in the mid-1990s. Selection of the best corridor option was done in 2006, and planning the route alignment within this corridor was completed in 2010.[464] The Commonwealth Government committed to Inland Rail in 2013, the ARTC published its detailed Programme Business Case in 2015, and construction managed by the ARTC started in 2018, funded by the Commonwealth increasing its equity in the ARTC. Construction is expected to take ten years to complete. The business case for this project was based on capturing inter-capital freight from road transport,[465] and this market sector is expected to grow to 66% of the total NTKs moved on the new route.[466] For this reason, the decision was made before 2015 that a transit time of less than 24 hours for trains between terminals in Brisbane and Melbourne, and vice versa, must be reliably achievable in order to capture that new business. Consequently, the decisions on route alignment and engineering design are in support of that goal, to make the route as fast and as flat as possible. Suggestions that the line pass through Dubbo or close to existing grain silos were eschewed.[467] However, as construction progresses, Inland Rail is being criticised in the press for not being useful to agricultural producers along the route,[468] and is being subjected to various forms of 'nimbyism'[469] and lobbying for and against route adjustments proposed since the original plan of 2010.[470] This led to the routing of the new line becoming a federal election issue in 2022.[471] (There is more on this in chapter 16, under The national discussion on freight transport & infrastructure – The discussion about Inland Rail.)

It can be expected that PN and SCT will continue their intermodal competition on the new route, and that they or other operators will find opportunities to move coal, cotton and other regional agricultural products from northern NSW to ports in Queensland.

The Adelaide to Darwin corridor

In 1997, the Governments of South Australia and the Northern Territory created the AustralAsia Railway Corporation to oversee the design, construction and operation of a new line from Alice Springs to Darwin. It was to be the logical extension of the standard gauge line from Tarcoola (SA) (the junction with the east-west interstate route) to Alice Springs (NT), built in the 1970s, replacing a flood-prone narrow-gauge line that ran from Port Augusta. The vision was to create a new transcontinental route from south to north, creating the potential for Darwin to become an export port for South Australia. In accordance with the political thinking of the time, enshrined in the Commonwealth Competition Policy Reform Act 1995, this new line would be owned and operated by the private sector, under Open Access conditions. However, competition between train operators did not eventuate because the market was too small. Also, as explained in chapter 13, Open Access is insufficient to enable competition where there is an incumbent operator on a vertically-integrated network.

The Northern Territory, South Australian and Australian Governments contributed up-front funding of $165 million, $150 million and $165 million respectively, to ensure the project was commercially viable, recognising the social and economic benefits of the railway while passing on commercial risk to the private sector.[472] The remainder of the $1.3 billion design and construction costs came from the Asia Pacific Transport Consortium, the preferred bidder. The contract was a Build, Own, Operate and Transfer (BOOT), with the transfer back to the AustralAsia Railway Corporation due in 2054. Construction started in Alice Springs in July 2001.

The Consortium contracted another consortium known as FreightLink to operate the trains and maintain the assets, and the first freight trains ran between Adelaide and Darwin in January 2004. FreightLink owned the new line between Alice Springs and Darwin (on land leased from AustralAsia), and had a long-term lease from the ARTC on the line from Tarcoola to Alice. To run trains between Tarcoola and Adelaide, it paid ARTC for access as all other train operators do.

FreightLink was expected by all the government and business stakeholders to earn enough to repay the debts incurred for the construction of the Alice Springs to Darwin railway. However, while it covered its operational costs, it could not service these debts. FreightLink was placed into voluntary administration in November 2008, which enabled it to keep operating until it could be sold. In June 2010 the American short-line operator Genesee and Wyoming Inc (GWI) bought the assets of FreightLink for $A334 million,[473] with the long-term leases for the tracks between Tarcoola and Darwin. The private sector investors in the Alice Springs to Darwin line lost just under $A500 million.

Genesee & Wyoming Australia (GWA) became the owner[474] and could presumably operate the Adelaide to Darwin service profitably, although this has not been separately reported in its annual statements. The line carries general freight, bulk fuels and minerals, and its existence has enabled the development of mining and the export of mineral ores through both Darwin and Adelaide. It also has strategic value for transporting military equipment.

The whole GWA business was sold to One Rail Australia (ORA) in February 2020, which in turn was bought by Aurizon in October 2021.

Continued competition

On 20 February 2023, intermodal logistics provider TGE (formerly Toll Global Express) announced, with Aurizon, an 11-year partnership (estimated worth $1.8 billion) for daily containerised freight trains on both the east-west and south-north corridors, from Perth to Brisbane.[475] TGE stated that this created secure access to the rail mode, certainty of having line-haul capacity available, and the appearance of helping to address climate change. As TGE was up to this time a PN customer, its change of train operator indicates there had been service issues. For Aurizon, this enabled a secured re-entry into the interstate intermodal market nation-wide, with TGE estimated to fill an average 70% of each train's capacity,[476] leaving Aurizon to sell capacity to other customers, and expand its interstate business. Services started in April 2023, "with a ramp up to full service offering by April 2024".

New South Wales

The NSW Government was the only government to separate proactively its rail network from its freight train operator (FreightCorp), done in 1996 in anticipation of other operators wanting to compete. However, the first two private train operators on the NSW network did not compete directly with FreightCorp, but started services that were new to rail: Silverton in August 1999 and ATN in June 2000. Silverton had bought locomotives and various wagons cheaply at the SRANSW rolling-stock auction of December 1994, enabling it to compete for contracts in future years. It started the first short-distance intra-urban service for import/export containers, known as 'trip trains', running between Villawood and Port Botany. (FreightCorp did not start such a service until May 2001, running between Minto and Port Botany.) ATN ran trains from the Riverina area in southern NSW to carry export bulk grains over the State border to Port Melbourne – an innovation at the time.

The advent of Pacific National created opportunities for others

Conventional competition for the market started after the State-owned freight train operator, FreightCorp, was sold in February 2002 together with the National Rail Corporation (NRC) to become one combined train operating company, Pacific National (PN). PN was a joint venture between two large Australian transport companies Toll Holdings and Patrick Corporation. The latter company had significant stevedoring businesses at the container ports at Sydney and Melbourne and was already operating trains to support those businesses. Patrick Portlink (PPL), as it was known, continued to trade under the PPL brand until May 2010, when its remaining intrastate business (Sydney-Dubbo and Sydney-Narrabri) was picked up by PN.

Neither the National Rail Corporation nor FreightCorp had been profitable at the time of sale, so the first priority for the new owners of PN was financial survival. This was a rapid exercise in downsizing while concurrently integrating the two organisations. At the same time as making a number of staff redundant, PN abandoned some of the train services it had inherited. Hence several small train operators appeared, started by experienced railway people, using cheaply bought old rolling-stock, to pick up the traffic flows discarded by PN.

Much of this business involved container trains going to and from the congested Port Botany yard. These trains carry loaded export containers, each one planned to arrive at the port 'just-in-time' for a specific sailing of a specific ship going to a foreign port for delivery to the exporter's customer. (The exporter books the slots on the sailings and dispatches the containers accordingly.) The trains often have to be split and shunted into the private sidings of the stevedoring companies[477] – POTA and Patricks – because each stevedore deals with a separate range of shipping companies that trade to all parts of the world. Each stevedore allocates fixed dwell times of more or less one hour, called 'windows', to the train operator for it to place wagons off inbound trains for unloading, and then remove the empty wagons after unloading. Hence, it is a complex process to coordinate both companies' windows with scheduled train times for arrivals at, and departures from, Port Botany yard. These times are themselves complicated by the need to avoid Sydney's twice-daily curfew which gives absolute priority to passenger trains. (For more about the curfews, see chapter 2, under *Infrastructure constraints in New South Wales*.)

It is no wonder that those who were influential in Pacific National at the time of its formation in 2002, with experience from FreightCorp, wanted to minimise PN's exposure to export traffic going through Port Botany. This traffic was troublesome to manage at the port (without any extra recompense) when any aspect of operations went wrong. Relatively minor operational problems could create major problems for exporters if booked slots on sailings were missed, and the train operating company could easily be blamed. PN, as a new operator, would have wanted to avoid such reputational damage.

Under these circumstances in 2002, Silverton was able to expand its business, having gained the experience of managing trains into and out of Port Botany's stevedores since 1999. It started running whole trains of containerised export cotton for two customers: Namoi Cotton and Auscott, from Wee Waa and Narrabri (in north-west NSW) and Warren and Trangie (in central west NSW) to Port Botany, returning with empty containers loaded at the Cooks River container yard sidings. However, four years later, Silverton was sold to WA company South Spur Rail Services (SSRS), which brought in new managers who lacked experience of operating trains through Sydney. Silverton lost its cotton traffic in 2009. The combined SSRS business was bought out by P&O Trans Australia (POTA) in 2010.

A success for competition policy

Competition, as envisaged by the Commonwealth Government's National Competition Policy of 1995 (see in chapter 5), flourished in NSW, much more so than in any other State. As seen above, competition enabled both gaining certain types of traffic, and avoiding others. Apart from PN and Silverton, there were several other train operators in NSW. In the two decades since 1996, when the NSW Government opened up its railway to competition, there were start-ups, takeovers and some consolidation in the industry, as shown in Box 12/1 (over).

Box 12/1 – Freight rail companies in New South Wales

- Austrac started in 1997, based in Junee, hauling export grain. It failed financially in 2000.
- Lachlan Valley Rail Freight (LVR), the commercial arm of a heritage rail society, operated a container service between Newcastle and Port Botany. LVR was bought in 2006 by Independent Railways of Australia (IRA), which then operated from seven regional locations to Port Botany and return. IRA in turn was acquired by Qube Logistics in 2012.
- P&O Trans Australia (POTA), an integrated stevedoring and port logistics company was started in 1999, and operated trip trains from Yennora to Port Botany. It bought out SSRS in 2010, and was itself acquired by Qube Logistics in 2011. Qube focused on import/export container movement, initially in NSW, but has since expanded into Victoria and WA.
- Queensland Rail bought a NSW start-up in 2002 to create Interail, with the purpose of competing in the growing Hunter Valley export coal market, previously serviced only by PN.
- ARG started in WA as the company that bought WestRail in 2000, and was the sole train operator in that State for ten years. In 2003, it entered NSW when it took over the Manildra contract from PN, hauling bulk product from its mills at Gunnedah (in north-west NSW), Manildra (in central west NSW) and Narrandera (in the Riverina, NSW) to Bomaderry (south of Wollongong), and containerised products from Bomaderry. QR bought ARG in 2006, thus obtaining assets and network access in NSW outside of the Hunter Valley, and in WA. When ARG lost

the Manildra contract in 2008 to Patrick Portlink, ARG was able to keep going by hauling other grain traffic. Both Interail and ARG ceased to trade as separate brands in 2011, being absorbed into QR National (QRN). QRN adopted the name Aurizon in 2012.

- Freightliner, an offshoot of the UK train operator, started in NSW in 2009; it recruited executives previously with Silverton, and took over the export cotton traffic previously serviced by Silverton. It also contracted in that year with coal-miner Xstrata (now Glencore) to operate Xstrata's trains, becoming the third company operating in the Hunter Valley export coal market. A year later, the Freightliner group worldwide was bought by American railroad company Genesee & Wyoming, and consequently the NSW business came under Genesee & Wyoming Australia (GWA). In 2016, GWA bought Glencore's fleet of 30 locos and 894 coal wagons for $A1.14 billion, with a 20-year contract to haul 40 million tonnes p.a. In 2020, Genesee & Wyoming worldwide group was sold, and GWA was split off; it became known as One Rail Australia (ORE), and that company was acquired by Aurizon in 2021.
- Southern Shorthaul Railroad (SSR) hauls customer-owned intermodal trains (for Fletcher Industrial Exports, at Dubbo) and coal trains (for Centennial Coal) to export ports, plus infrastructure works trains, and bulk grain trains using its own fleet. Established in 2003 in Victoria, SSR continues to operate there and in NSW. In 2018, it became the fourth train company operating in the Hunter Valley export coal market.

Another line of business that was formerly FreightCorp's was hauling petroleum products within NSW. Freight Australia took over this contract with Shell to distribute bulk products in tank wagons from Sandown in Sydney. However, when PN bought Freight Australia in 2004, the contract was passed to PPL. It used one train of tank wagons to deliver products weekly to regional distribution depots in Canberra, Dubbo and Tamworth. In 2009, Shell announced it would cease using rail, because it was more efficient for it to close the regional depots and deliver direct to its customers in B-double road tankers.[478] Although not admitted by any party, it was also possible that the rail tankers and the rail loadout facility at Sandown all needed replacement or renewal, and no party wanted to make these investments. The NRMA protested about the added danger on the roads, environmental activists protested about the increase in emissions, and the NSW Government declined to get involved. The last rail tanker train ran in March 2010.

Despite the many traffic flows abandoned by PN, it remains a major player in the NSW market, and has picked up new business since its creation in 2002, including:

- a contract with Veolia to haul containerised compacted rubbish from Sydney to be buried at a former open-cut copper mine near Tarago on the line to Canberra;
- a contract with Northparkes Mines near Peak Hill to haul mineral ore to Port Kembla.

Victoria

Competition discouraged

The first private operator on the Victorian network was Great Northern Rail Services, providing infrastructure maintenance trains, as well as rolling-stock maintenance for other companies. It operated from December 1997 to November 2002, ceasing allegedly due to the cost of public liability insurance. It was a contractor, and was not competing as a train operator.

In 1998, the Victorian Government put State-owned V/Line Freight onto the market together with a long-term lease on the broad-gauge country network, for sale to the highest bidder. (The details are in chapter 11.) The way it was sold, as a vertically-integrated railway, all but guaranteed that competition on the broad-gauge network would not eventuate.

In May 1999, Rail America bought V/Line Freight, trading firstly as Freight Victoria then as Freight Australia. In June 2000, a minor competitor to Freight Australia appeared. It was ATN, the overseas-owned company which had bought TasRail, but which had had no prior experience of rail business on the Australian continent. It had won contracts with the Australian Wheat Board (AWB) to haul export grains from the Riverina in southern NSW and from western Victoria to the Port of Melbourne. These flows would use only the ARTC's standard-gauge lines within Victoria, so ATN was not challenging Freight Australia on its broad-gauge network. There is no way of knowing how profitable ATN was as a private company. It ceased to exist when Pacific National (PN) bought it in February 2004. PN then bought Freight Australia in August 2004, including the lease to the broad-gauge network, and thus it took the place of Freight Australia as the monopolistic train operator for intrastate freight. The ACCC investigated[479] whether a monopoly would exist but it did not oppose the sale of Freight Australia because of the dominance of road freight transport. The Victorian Government had not sought competition on its country network, and none existed for the first seven years after privatisation.

The effects of droughts

During this period of total private sector control, total net intrastate tonnage on rail declined by about 20%,[480] while the Victorian regional economy showed strong growth. Then in 2006 and 2007 Victoria suffered a drought which reduced the size of the 2007 grain harvest to 1.8 million tonnes, compared with a normal harvest range of 4 to 6 million tonnes.[481]

Normal domestic consumption was about 1.5 million tonnes, which left very little to be exported. Normally, trains carried mainly export grains because of the concentration of bulk flows to just two export ports, Geelong and Portland. In August 2007, a start-up company called El Zorro contracted with AWB to haul grain. Significantly, this was just three months after the Victorian Government had regained control of the broad-gauge network (See in chapter 11 for more on this event.) In November 2007, Pacific National (PN) announced its withdrawal from export grain and some intrastate services within Victoria (and NSW) from March 2008, because it was losing $3 million per month[482] after the years of drought. However, it would stay if take-or-pay agreements could be made with grain marketers, so that the risks of variability in harvest size from year to year would shift from PN to the grain industry.

Government incentives for rail use

The Government responded in February 2008 to both the RFNR recommendations (see in chapter 11), and PN's notice of quitting, by announcing a $20 million funding package to provide short-term support for rail over two years.[483] The 'Rail Freight Support Package' funds would be used to provide rebates to container terminal operators (on both broad-gauge and standard-gauge lines), and to reduce broad-gauge network access charges for exporting grain. Funding was continued in subsequent years, and in 2012 the program was renamed the 'Mode Shift Incentive Scheme' (MSIS). By this time, much of the grain exports were being packed in containers and moving through the Port of Melbourne, and the Government was keen to minimise road congestion close to the port. In 2014, the Government allocated a further $20 million over four years to continue the MSIS, and funding has been provided annually since then.

The Government's response in reducing track access charges and providing incentive payments to shippers to use the rail network, despite its poor condition, had the intended effect. Competition evolved in the form of market segmentation. (There is more on this phenomenon in the next chapter.) Although PN relinquished some traffic, it stayed in Victoria to some extent. In 2009, GrainCorp started running its own bulk grain trains in Victoria and NSW, using PN's crews and train operator accreditation.

In September 2008, El Zorro picked up a contract to haul containerised mineral sands from Portland to Melbourne, traffic previously on road. El Zorro was also awarded the contract vacated by PN in March 2008 to operate between Melbourne and Warrnambool in the state's south-west. However, it lost this contract only seven months later to Patrick Rail, allegedly because Patrick could provide exporters direct access to Melbourne docks.[484] El Zorro continued as a train operator in Victoria, hauling bulk grain for AWB Grainflow, until it was wound up due to financial problems in June 2013.

QR National started container train services between Horsham (in the west of the state) and Port of Melbourne in July 2008 on the standard-gauge line. Since 2011, SCT has been providing this service. P&O Trans Australia (POTA) had commenced hauling containerised rice for export from Deniliquin (NSW) to Melbourne by 2009. In 2011 POTA was merged into Qube Logistics, which continues to haul container and bulk grain trains on the broad-gauge country network today.

The deregulation of the Victorian export wheat market in 2008, and increased on-farm storage, resulted in many wheat marketers replacing the former Australian Wheat Board. This resulted in the transport of grains on road increasing by 2011 to about 50% of the export task,[485] as trucks are used to supplement rail capacity at peak times or transport grain direct from farm to port. In addition, only the largest grain marketers can afford to contract their own trains, at $2-3 million fixed cost per train, plus operating costs.[486] The reason for this is the train operators' requirements for take-or-pay agreements, to haul train-load consignments only. (It is explained in chapter 13, under *Barriers to entry*, how this outcome of privatisation limits on-rail competition and the volume of business available to the rail mode.) Of the 2011-12 Victorian grain harvest of 6 million tonnes, about 3.5 million tonnes was expected to be exported. For this, the three major exporters had contracted four broad-gauge and five standard-gauge trains, expecting to move about 3 million tonnes with these.[487]

The Victorian Government, and its track provider, V/Line, have a major influence on the competition between rail and road for grain movement. Since taking back the broad-gauge network in 2007, the Victorian Government had by 2011 invested $1.2 billion in track upgrading. This enabled quicker and more secure train cycle times from silo to port and return, thus reducing the operating costs for rail transport. It also increased the seasonal capacity of each train-set, other things being equal, thus increasing the return on the owner's investment in rolling-stock. Hence, in this case, it as government investments, and not competition among operators, that provided the efficiency gains that the rail mode needed.

How V/Line manages the risks of track buckling in the summer heat, can affect this planned capacity, resulting in less grain on rail, and more on the road, because the grain must move when planned in order to meet ship-loading schedules. (I have written about heat-stress management in chapter 14, under *Sharing line capacity and managing access to railway lines*.)

Western Australia

Under the State's Transport Regulation Act 1966, the Government had required the transport of grain by rail for decades. In 2008, a scheme was put in place to permit some licensed transport by road, if the government and the rail operator agreed. However, the scheme still sent a strong message to all concerned that the rail system would continue to be the primary means for grain transport, and in turn, this encouraged CBH (Cooperative Bulk Handling, the State's sole grain storage and marketing organisation) to invest in rail-served assets.[488]

Hence, despite the federal government's National Competition Policy of 1995, when the WA Government sold its railway system in 2000, competition for hauling grain (still then the major commodity) was not wanted. Already there were two eastern-based companies competing on the standard-gauge interstate line to Perth, hauling intermodal traffic. Because the Government sold its network as a vertically-integrated package, its narrow-gauge network was therefore monopolised by just one train operating company, ARG, (then Aurizon) for more than eleven years. (There is more detail in chapter 13, under *Barriers to entry: Control of rolling-stock and facilities by the incumbent operator*.) Any competition was not introduced until 2012, by CBH, which up till then was an Aurizon customer. CBH bought 28 new locos and 574 lighter tare grain wagons, and invited US short-line operator Watco to operate them. After nine years, CBH went back to Aurizon to operate and maintain its trains, with a 6+2+2 years contract, in time to transport the 2022 harvest.[489] With the major growth in other traffic in the 2010s, both Watco and Aurizon continue to operate non-grain trains, hauling coal, minerals and bulk chemicals.

Since 2007, the WA Government has subsidised short-haul trains primarily for imported containers from Port of Fremantle North Quay to either the Forrestfield or Kwinana Intermodal Terminals, in order to reduce truck congestion at the port and around Fremantle.[490] Watco previously operated these trains but now Qube has the contract.

Queensland

Queensland's was the last freight rail business in Australasia to be privatised; Queensland Rail (QR) remained a vertically-integrated government-owned organisation until July 2010. QR was then split: the freight above-rail business and the Central

Queensland Coal Network (CQCN) became a company called QR National, while the remainder of the network, and all the passenger operations, remained as QR, a government organisation. This split enabled QR National to be privatised by IPO later that year.

By that time, coal had been growing in volume and had become over 90% of QR's freight.[491] It was known by the Government that QR National's focus would be on the coal business, so in order not to see non-coal customers abandoned, it contracted with QR National to operate minimum numbers of freight trains per year on the non-coal lines.

However, some years before the split, the Queensland Government had created a third-party access regime on its rail network, in order to comply with the Commonwealth Government's National Competition Policy. Thus, QR had permitted a new train operator onto the network. In 2005, Pacific National Queensland (PNQ) won a contract to carry the Toll Group's containerised freight between Brisbane and Cairns, and the major centres in between. To do this, PNQ equipped itself with a new fleet of narrow-gauge locomotives and wagons, a sizable investment that few other companies could have considered. In 2009, PNQ won take-or-pay contracts with three large mining companies in the Queensland coal market,[492] again taking the business away from QR. Again, it required a large investment in new (electric) locos and wagons.

Thus, by the time of the split, competition for the railed freight market was well established on both the CQCN and the QR networks. However, because QR National was given the whole of QR's freight business and assets, and contracted by the Government to provide general freight trains, the possibility of any more competition was inhibited for nearly a decade. Indeed, Aurizon itself, as the incumbent operator, was able to stifle any new competition that might want the locomotives it declared surplus to requirements – it shipped them all to South Africa. (The details are in chapter 13, under *Barriers to entry: Control of rolling-stock and facilities by the incumbent operator*.)

QR National was privatised by the IPO in November 2010, and in 2012 it rebranded to become known as Aurizon. It inherited all QR's freight train schedules, its staff and assets (locos and wagons, rolling-stock workshops) and the Acacia Ridge terminal in South Brisbane. Thus, there were essentially seven elements to the QR National / Aurizon business when it was established, as shown in Box 12/2.

In 2017, soon after a new CEO took over, Aurizon announced persistent losses from its interstate intermodal business, and its proposed closure. (See above, under *The south to north corridor of the eastern States*.) Simultaneously, it also announced the proposed sale to a consortium of PN and Linfox, of its Queensland intermodal business and the Acacia Ridge intermodal terminal. In addition, Aurizon stated that if the ACCC opposed the sale of the Queensland Intermodal business to PN, it would simply close that business down. Because these proposed sales would eliminate competition on the QR network, the ACCC took the case to the Federal Court in July 2018 to try and prevent both the sales of the Queensland Intermodal business and of Acacia Ridge.[493] It also obtained an injunction from the Federal Court restraining Aurizon from closing its Queensland intermodal business. That prompted Aurizon to change tack.

Before the Court ruled, Aurizon sold its Queensland Intermodal business for $7.3 million[494] to just Linfox, thus preserving competition with PN. The handover date was 1 February 2019, and the deal included leases, access to freight terminals, trucks, trailers and intermodal wagons, forklifts, gantry cranes, and the transfer of 190 staff.[495] As a part of this deal, Aurizon agreed to a ten-year 'hook and pull' contract to haul Linfox trains between Brisbane and Cairns, and to act as the accredited train operator. Aurizon thus achieved its objective of quitting the State's possibly unprofitable intermodal business while gaining a profitable haulage contract. It must have been profitable for Aurizon, otherwise it would not have been agreed to.

12. Competition Outcomes

> **Box 12/2 – elements of the QR National business when it was established in 2010**
>
> - The management and maintenance of the CQCN, which is now the Aurizon Network division
> - The heavy-haul coal export trains from multiple mines linked to the CQCN, to export ports, which are contracted by various coal-mining companies
> - The operation of bulk product trains, contracted by industrial companies (e.g., sugar refineries, mineral ore miners) on the QR network
> - The Queensland Intermodal business, including the services provided for the Queensland Government, under the Regional Freight Transport Services Contract (624 services per year) and the Livestock Transport Services Contract (300 cattle train services per year from regional hubs)
> - The ownership and maintenance of all the former QR locomotive and freight wagon fleets, together with rolling-stock workshops
> - The operation of QR's former freight ventures in other states, including
>   — Interail's export coal contracts in the Hunter Valley (NSW),
>   — ARG's grain and other contracts in WA and NSW,
>   — an import/export terminal at Enfield (Sydney) with trip trains between there and Port Botany, and
>   — the interstate intermodal trains operating between Brisbane, Sydney, Melbourne, Adelaide and Perth.
> - The Acacia Ridge intermodal terminal and marshalling yards, a 66-hectare site where the narrow-gauge Queensland network meets the standard-gauge interstate network. Acacia Ridge was open access, used initially by both QR National and Pacific National.

The legal dispute over the $205 million sale of Acacia Ridge to PN continued. In May 2019, the Court ruled in favour of the sale to PN proceeding, because of an undertaking given to the

Court by PN on the last day of the hearing. Pacific National had offered a court-enforceable undertaking not to discriminate in providing access to other rail operators at the Acacia Ridge Terminal.[496] The ACCC rejected this undertaking because it would not protect potential entrants from discriminatory conduct in the terminal's day-to-day operations. In the ACCC's Rod Sims' words:[495]

> "An owner or operator has so many subtle ways of discriminating against, or damaging, another user of the terminal. Such an undertaking would not be enough to give a would-be entrant sufficient confidence to make the significant investment necessary to actually enter the market."

The ACCC was right about this. The day after the Court's decision was made known, Qube announced it would not be seeking to enter the long-haul freight market in Queensland, nor the national intermodal rail business, because of PN's control of the Acacia Ridge terminal.[497] The ACCC appealed to the Full Federal Court, but the decision was upheld, and furthermore this Court found that no undertaking was required of PN. The ACCC then sought leave to appeal to the High Court, but this was refused. The sale was finalised in March 2021. Predictably, no train operator has since tried to contest the duopoly of PN and Linfox in the Queensland Intermodal market.

However, there was competition from new entrants for hauling bulk commodities. In 2018, Watco won a contract with GrainCorp, displacing Aurizon, to haul grain from south-east Queensland to the ports at Brisbane, Gladstone and Mackay, using a fleet of new wagons purchased by GrainCorp.[498] Due to the lag time for delivery of new locos to Watco, this work did not start till 2019.

Watco also took over the Queensland Government contract to operate cattle trains. This is the only remaining haulage of livestock by rail anywhere in Australasia.

In July 2021, Qube was advertising for experienced crew in Mt Isa, Hughenden and Townsville; in anticipation of a contract to operate on the Mt Isa line.

Rail competition with road in New Zealand

In New Zealand, inter-regional trade by coastal shipping came first, and its competition with the railways continues today. There has always been just one organisation (in various forms) providing rail freight services. It has experienced increasing competition from trucking companies since the 1970s.

After corporatisation in the mid-1980s, NZ Railways began the development of new wagon types better designed to meet particular customer requirements, with more efficient loading. The details of these are in Box 12/3. This policy of providing specialised wagons to attract and hold major customers continued after privatisation, up to about 2001. There were advantages and disadvantages with this policy:

- quicker turnaround at unloading sites with direct despatch of empty wagons, often marshalled in unit trains which avoided marshalling yards, but usually returned empty, whereas general purpose wagons might have been back-loaded
- specialised wagons tended to have more complex designs, and were more expensive to build and maintain than general purpose wagons
- when major customers temporarily ceased to load freight due to production problems, the specialised wagons dedicated to these customers would usually remain idle
- thousands of four-wheeled wagons could be withdrawn and scrapped, reducing the total size of the wagon fleet and enabling reduced maintenance forces and shunting in yards; the wagon fleet utilisation statistic also improved because these old wagons were moved on slower low-priority trains, and were allowed to be loaded and unloaded at the leisure of minor customers – less than one productive trip per week

was not uncommon when carrying agricultural lime or fertiliser for farmers, or scrap iron from country towns.

> **Box 12/3 – specialised wagons for particular customers and freight**
> - covered wagons ('Zg' and 'Zh' classes) with a wider deck and fibreglass plug doors, for palletised freight, to replace box wagons with steel sliding doors
> - concertina-top wagons (the 'Jp' types) for loads that previously would have been top-loaded onto general-purpose flat wagons and covered manually with tarpaulins
> - bottom-dumping high-capacity bogie wagons for bulk granular commodities such as export coal and fertilizer, to replace four-wheeled 'highside' wagons
> - end-loading double-deck long (25m) 'Gt' motorcar wagons, fully enclosed to protect cars from opportunistic vandalism and to shield car surfaces from the damaging particulates of locomotive exhausts, built in 1988 but withdrawn in 2014 when KiwiRail exited this traffic
> - container flat wagons with greater maximum axle-loadings, built for heavier import/export containers
> - 'RoadRailer' vehicles, for quick transfer between being articulated road trailers and rail vehicles mounted on special-purpose bogies (built in 1990, but withdrawn in 1999 due to limited load capacity and high maintenance needs)
> - 'swap-body' curtain-sided frames fitted to flat wagons, with a lighter tare than other covered wagons, made from around 1994 onward, to enable access to the whole deck for loading by forklift; these were particularly suitable for paper and pulp products, being easier for opening and closing, and more water-tight
> - new 'Fb' log wagons built in 1992 for full-length logs only, with slender lighter-weight underframes; these wagons quickly became obsolete because the log markets required most felled trees to be cut into shorter logs of various grades, which therefore needed log wagons with four, six or eight pairs of stanchions. However, in 1996 these 'Fb' underframes were fitted with aluminium tanks to become 'Om' bulk milk tank wagons for a totally new traffic.

After the new CEO started in 2001, a new type of service was introduced for the inter-city container market, dubbed the Intermodal Transformation Project.[499] This used fixed-capacity trains direct from loading siding to unloading siding, thereby eliminating the time and cost for shunting. The downside initially was being seen to be moving empty wagons in the direction of the predominant freight flow, if not all the container slots were filled by departure time.

When Toll Rail was renationalised in 2008, much pressure was applied to the new KiwiRail by the new government to reduce the perceived losses quickly. As a part of the buyback agreement, Toll had retained the rail business's fleet of several hundred contracted trucks, plus its depots on railway land in the cities, and thus Toll kept all the high-value LWL/LCL traffic that Tranz Rail had handled directly, i.e., separate from other freight forwarders' traffic. The quick fix to reduce the losses was to accept only containerised freight, or palletised freight that could be loaded into high-cube curtain-siders, and bulk products. All box wagons with steel or fibreglass doors were then made obsolete. Many were scrapped, or sold for storage on farms or industrial sites. Some bogie box wagons were rebuilt to add to the fleet of log wagons. Later, in 2014, KiwiRail adopted a policy of operational simplification, and withdrew from the transport of motor vehicles and bulk fertilisers, retiring the relatively modern but high-maintenance wagons needed for these products. Such selective abandonment of traffic reduced KiwiRail's staff needs for wagon design and maintenance, terminal operations, and shunting at private sidings in rural locations to deliver bulk fertiliser.

The competitive position of New Zealand's rail system after some 15 years of private sector control was summarised in a report researched and written in 2011 for the NZ Treasury:[500]

> "Prior to 2004, investment in the rail network and associated rail services was minimal, leading to deterioration in the network and decline in service

quality. According to the company, the condition of the below-track infrastructure and rolling stock continues to present material fit-for-purpose issues. The combined effect of ownership discontinuity and low reinvestment is that rail has lost relevance as a time-dependent freight option and has seen its share of the total freight task decline from around 19% (on a NTK basis) in 1993 to around 15% in 2007."

The loss of LWL/LCL traffic greatly reduced the competitive pressure for overnight intercity services. KiwiRail became a carrier of freight in bulk, serving many industries that work 24/7, carrying exports in particular. Its freight today includes import/export containers, coal, steel, logs, pulp and paper, industrial gases, bulk milk and wine.

Part D
Analyses

13. The application of economic concepts to Rail Reform

14. Vertical integration versus vertical separation

15. The profitability of rail networks

13. The Application of Economic Concepts to Rail Reform

'Efficiency', 'Effectiveness', 'Performance', 'Best Practice'

What these terms mean

Many commentators confuse **efficiency** (how well were available resources used?) with **effectiveness** (how well was the work done relative to agreed or expected performance?). Organisations can be both efficient (from the provider's point of view) and ineffective (from the customer's point of view). Efficiency is not an end in itself. It is one means by which an organisation can deliver effective service at an acceptable price for its customers, or funders.

Efficiency and Performance were major themes in the Industry Commission's 1991 report *Rail Transport* and in the Productivity Commission's 1999 report *Progress in Rail Reform*. Efficiency is about improving the value or quantum of outputs relative to the inputs. In the context of railways, it can be applied at any level across all aspects of railways operations and investments. Unless there is reference to specific types of inputs and outputs, discussion on improving rail efficiency and performance can be vague and imprecise, as was mostly the case in the reports cited above. Take this example: [501]

"Participants argued that urgent investment was needed in railways, including rollingstock, track and signalling equipment. The condition of these was seen as an impediment to improving the efficiency of the industry."

There is no doubt that investment in rolling-stock, track and signalling equipment would improve efficiency in the sense of greater productivity of labour used for maintenance activities, but the greater benefit to the rail industry could come from improved effectiveness. With fewer infrastructural failures, performance would be more reliable because more trains would arrive on time, and track investment could even enable faster inter-capital transit times.

Efficiency in service industries means focusing on the inputs to the service process, but which inputs need to be used more efficiently can change over time. Therefore, railway efficiency is not a uniform concept. Because there are many resources used in railway operations, there are inevitably trade-offs available for the use of these resources. Sometimes these trade-offs are made explicitly, sometimes not. Perceptions of efficiency at any given time will depend on which of the resources is seen as the most costly, or the most constrained in its availability. This means that measures of efficiency adopted today can be obsolete tomorrow.

A classic example of this is in the history of train operations on the central section (between Hamilton and Palmerston North) of New Zealand's North Island Main Trunk line (NIMT).[502] Appendix 2 tells that story.

'Performance' is a word with at least two meanings, even in the context of railways. The railway owner's concern is financial performance, whereas the customers' concerns are service performance, and price. The Productivity Commission was referring to poor financial performance in the comment below, but this is, in part, a consequence of poor service performance:[503]

> "During the 1990s, there has been a change in emphasis with governments according greater weight to improving the efficiency and financial viability of their railways. The focus on efficiency stems from the relatively poor performance of government-owned railways in the 1970s and 1980s."

Spending on rail infrastructure and rolling-stock is always needed and can improve both

- efficiency (reflected in lower charges to the customer, and/or improved railway company financial performance) and
- effectiveness (delivering adequate service performance to the customers, and offering more competitive services than before, and/or versus road carriers).

Best practice – the pot of gold at the end of the rainbow

The Productivity Commission was asked, in its 1999 terms of reference, to report on

> "international best practice in rail and impediments to achieving best practice in Australia."

The notion of Best Practice requires comparisons between railways about their performance and efficiency, a technique which is sometimes called 'benchmarking'. In practice, it is fraught with difficulties and caveats due to the inherent differences among railways in their sizes, histories, initial design standards, terrain, cultures[504], mission statements, accounting practices, regulatory environments and traffic task mix. Thus, the notion that railways' International Best Practice can be found is a figment of the imagination, like the pot of gold to be found at the end of a rainbow.

The Productivity Commission described this futility more tactfully:[505]

> "An important objective of reform is to improve the performance of the rail industry by creating an operating

environment which encourages efficiency and the adoption of best practice. ...

There are limitations on the extent to which assessments of rail performance can be used to make judgements about the effect of rail reform and the achievement of best practice. In particular, the attribution of changes in performance to specific rail reforms is difficult. There are many factors, in addition to rail reform, affecting the performance of railways simultaneously. These include the demand for rail services, mix of freight traffic and passenger services, technology, managerial decision making, input markets and competition from other transport modes.

The degree of comparability between railways can affect how differences in performance are interpreted, particularly in international comparisons. Railways operating in different environments often face different constraints affecting the level of efficiency achievable. Broader policy parameters such as labour market regulation or competition policy, the price of inputs, population size and density, a country's resource base and geography, and the technical characteristics of infrastructure and production, can all affect performance. ...

Performance comparisons need to be treated as broadly indicative rather than precise indicators of relative performance. The apparent links between performance and reform should be interpreted cautiously."

Railways as a monopoly?

Submissions to the 1991 Industry Commission inquiry into the inefficiencies of the Australian railways attacked the 'monopoly' of State Railways in hauling bulk commodities at freight rates that enabled the Railways to cross-subsidise other rail services.

That there was cross-subsidisation was true, but the assertion that railways had a monopoly on freight transport was not true. It helps to separate out these two issues.

Historically, cross-subsidies were both normal and invisible. Government Railways traditionally accounted for their spending by input functions, such as track maintenance, station operations, train operations, workshops. Railways have high levels of both fixed and shared costs, so there was no way to allocate these meaningfully to particular railway lines, to lines of business, or to particular customers. Railway freight rates were set at levels that were estimated to be 'what the market will bear.' Hence cross-subsidisation existed but it was unseen. If it was considered at all, it was seen as inevitable and unknowable, and therefore normal. However, the coal and mineral producers had no knowledge of the limitations of railway management accounting, and they argued that they were being charged 'monopoly rents'. They saw cross-subsidisation as a market distortion. The NSW coal industry described the SRANSW as lacking "a commercial approach to the setting of coal freight rates."[506]

State Governments had for some decades regulated that bulk commodities, such as coal and grains, be hauled on rail. This policy was to protect government-owned assets; both the sunk investments in their railway networks, and their rural roading networks which would have suffered cumulative damage caused by frequent use by heavily laden trucks. The 'monopoly' that railways had was therefore due to government policies but limited in extent.

However, there was a wide-spread perception up to the mid-1990s in Australia that railways had a 'natural monopoly' and were using their market power against their customers. 'Natural monopoly' was defined by the Productivity Commission[507] as

> "where economies (of scale) make it possible for one firm to supply the entire market more cheaply than a number of firms".

13. The Application of Economic Concepts

In reality, there were hundreds of companies supplying transport services. There had always been competition between rail and coastal shipping, and that continued. The true monopoly that the railway industry had enjoyed in land transport had been destroyed by the rise of trucking in the 1920s and the availability of many young men returned from World War I with recently-gained truck-driving experience. By the 1990s, competition with railways from road carriers was very strong for all types of freight except bulk commodities. Such competition had led to the closure of many rural branch lines from the 1950s onward. It was therefore a fallacy that railways still had a natural monopoly. Although government railways had a monopoly on the provision of the rail mode, the rail industry definitely did not have any monopoly power in freight markets.

The 1999 report *Progress in Rail Reform* confirmed this reality when it exposed as a furphy this belief that monopoly rents in rail rates resulted where railways were the sole transport provider:[508]

> "Despite the lack of intermodal competition highlighted by RAC, there is no evidence of railways extracting monopoly profits from customers in New South Wales. An important fact underpinning this position is the high level of competition in the final markets of these commodities. Commodities such as export grain face strong competition from alternative suppliers on international markets. Thus there are no monopoly profits to be earned by grain farmers in final markets to be extracted by the providers of inputs, including transport."

It is interesting to note that the coal and mineral industries, which were the most dissatisfied with the alleged monopoly by the rail industry in the 1990s, now have to deal with rail network providers in Western Australia and the Central Queensland Coal Network which **are** monopoly suppliers. (This was covered in chapter 12.) These private-sector network providers are the outcomes of two decades of rail reform. There is no cross-subsidisation, and these companies are very profitable.

The concept of competition in the Australian rail industry

More competition between rail and road was not intended

The National Competition Policy (NCP)[509] was designed to remove legal barriers, at both Federal and State levels, to business competition across a range of sectors in which governments had some influence through legislation, regulations and registrations. These sectors included:
- gas trading and pipeline access
- electricity generation and retailing
- water entitlements, trading, reticulation and resource management
- road transport – transport of dangerous goods, vehicle operations, heavy vehicle registration, driver licensing, and compliance and enforcement

The application of the NCP to railways was about the principles of:
- restructuring of what were perceived to be 'businesses', in monopoly positions,
- providing 'third-party access' to rail infrastructure, and
- removing the advantages that government railways had versus privately owned transport.

The NCP in land transport was designed to release the freight markets from perceived shackles, in the belief that unfettered market behaviour would produce the best results. The NCP was not proactive in the sense that it might address the 'uneven playing field' in land transport, which stems from the differences in capacity available for users of highway and railway. These differences were created by the combination of the Commonwealth Government's large spending on highways, and the State Governments' lack of sufficient upkeep and development of their railway infrastructures. Hence there was no intention to facilitate competition between rail and road, which might have achieved real productivity gains for the Australian economy, based on rail's inherent labour and fuel efficiencies on a 'per net-tonne-kilometre' basis. (There is more on the uneven playing field below, under *Neutrality between road and rail modes*.)

Thus, the potential economic gains for land transport users were and are much more limited than they could have been, because NCP reform was applied only to break the supposed monopolies of government-owned rail businesses.

The perceived need for competition

In his 1992 One Nation document, Prime Minister Paul Keating described Railways as one of a number of industries where

> "the problem of inefficient performance was endemic in areas shielded from competition".[510]

In 1993, Australian railways were included in the Hilmer Report, the wide-ranging review of competition law and conduct rules, by virtue of being 'government-owned businesses'. But the Hilmer report described rail tracks as a facility "which cannot be economically duplicated".[511] This report therefore supported the continuing monopoly ownership or management of rail track by government railways, subject to access to lines being assured to 'third parties' via an Open Access policy. Furthermore, railways would not become more competitive without investment. To quote from a paper assessing Australian rail transport policy after the Hilmer report: [512]

> "... for the potential of the Hilmer reforms to be fully harnessed, rail track infrastructure should be upgraded where economically justified to levels competitive with the National Highway; rail needs to be able to attract

and hold new private rail operators and to provide a realistic alternative to other modes of transport."

Under the National Competition Policy from 1995 onward, the objective for the public sector was reform, to minimise restrictions on competition and to promote 'competitive neutrality'. (What this term came to mean in the railway context is explained later in this chapter.) There was a widely-held view that competition in the railway industry would mean that private sector rail companies should compete with one another for the traffic already on rail, and that this would lead to efficiencies and lower freight rates. This type of competition was identified in the report *Progress in Rail Reform* (described in chapter 4) as 'competition in the transport market'.[513] Such competition is now seen only in specific markets where there are multiple customers, and a large volume of business to sustain more than one train operator providing services on a daily basis. These markets are in interstate containerised traffic, and the export coal flows from the Hunter Valley (NSW) and the defined 'Central Queensland Coal Network'.

The expectation of direct competition between railway companies for the same traffic has not been met elsewhere. This may be because the expectation ignored the fact that each competitor could not possibly have the same economies of scale as one provider has with a natural monopoly. The Commonwealth Government's 1990s belief appears to have been that somehow the advent of competition would deliver reduced freight prices across the whole rail industry, that the 'monopolistic' government-owned providers were not doing. This did not occur.

Open Access was insufficient to enable competition

One submission to the 1999 Productivity Commission inquiry for *Progress in Rail Reform* wrote that the policy for mandating Open Access to enable competition between rail companies on intrastate networks was misconceived:[514]

"If rail faces strong competition from road ... then we should not be treating rail as a natural monopoly. It may involve the technology of natural monopoly but there is no scope for this to provide for monopoly exploitation because of the inter-modal competition. The correct policy position ... would thus seem to be to remove regulation, and to remove third party access requirements, since these will not produce efficiency gains."

At the time this was written, the only examples in Australasia of private sector operation of formerly State-owned railways were all vertically-integrated, and therefore lacking intra-industry competition:
- ATN in Tasmania,
- TranzRail in New Zealand,
- Australian Southern Railroad (ASR) in South Australia, and
- in Victoria the government was in the process of passing control of the broad-gauge country network and rail freight business to Rail America, trading as Freight Australia.

Although Open Access had been mandated by the State government of South Australia to enable competition with ASR, none had emerged by 1999, and did not until 2003. In Victoria, the government did not establish an Open Access regime for its already-leased intrastate network until July 2001, and then only in response to pressure from the National Competition Council.[515] However, no company was prepared to invest time and money to compete on a rail network controlled by an incumbent train operator. Not until after the Victorian Government retook control of its country network in 2006, did a small train operator, El Zorro, challenge the incumbent train operator (by then it was Pacific National) for the haulage of some grain traffic. However, El Zorro folded in 2013.

The fault with trying to engender competition between train operating companies in an Open Access regime is that the vertically-integrated operator is obliged to release only what it defines as its **spare** line capacity. This therefore gives the incumbent the first choice of train paths, and it can protect them for as long as it likes, which gives the vertically-integrated incumbent a very significant competitive advantage. In any competitive bidding for new or existing traffic, the non-incumbents cannot have any certainty about the availability of suitable paths when they submit their bids to the potential client. Thus, they cannot promise better service as part of the bid, only better pricing. For these reasons, the requirement for Open Access in a vertically-integrated network to stimulate competition is usually ineffective.

Market segmentation evolved instead

Instead of direct competition, what evolved in each State, and to some extent in the interstate market also, was a form of market segmentation and product differentiation. Each train operator was usually a sole provider within its segment of the market, contracted with one or a small number of customers to provide regular whole-train services over a long term, typically five to ten years. This provided certainty for all concerned by reducing the operational risks, and by this means train operators were able to maintain profit margins by not competing with each other on price, except when it was time for contract renewal. Having these commitments and consigning only whole train-loads was administratively efficient, and it enabled some new small rail companies to enter the market. *Progress in Rail Reform* identified this situation as 'competition **for** the market',[516] involving occasional competitive tendering for contracts. The irony is that, for the rail companies, it was and still is an effective way to avoid the risks of direct competition. It even engenders co-operation among rail companies, such as short-term hiring of locomotives and crews to one another to meet exigencies.[517]

This would not happen if there was direct competition.

The government-owned railways in each State had been able, up to the 1990s, to accept almost anything presented for transport, although in the years of bumper grain harvests, resources were stretched and delays occurred. Thus, what the railways carried in the 1990s defined the size of the market for railed freight when competition was mandated. After competition was started and this market was segmented, some traffic ceased to move on rail. Initially, all the train operating companies in NSW and Victoria chose not to compete for the smaller market segments (typically less than a regular train-load). These market segments were abandoned, left for road carriers because the rail companies selected only the easiest to manage and/or the most profitable lines of business. Often there was only one road carrier serving a particular district. The result was that removing the allegedly monopolistic government railway to foster competition on the rail network left these former rail customers with Hobson's choice and higher transport costs. However, since about 2010, there have been increasing numbers of regional inter-modal hubs established, where such traffic can be attracted back to rail by being consolidated into train-loads.

Pacific National took the practice of abandonment further by actually withdrawing from traffic it had previously been carrying, that it had acquired with its purchases of the smaller companies ATN and Freight Australia. In March 2008, PN ceased hauling grains and running other intrastate trains in Victoria, and withdrew its (formerly V/Line and ATN) rolling-stock to use elsewhere.

Not surprisingly, some former rail customers entered the market by investing in and managing their own rolling-stock, where there were bulk commodities to move in a 'just-in-time' manner to meet production and shipping schedules. Ownership ensured continuity of wagon supply and train services, thus reducing the risks of contractor failure. Such former rail customers include CBH and Mineral Resources (both in WA) which own their own locos and specialised wagons. By providing their own rolling-stock, they have reduced the scope of services required from rail companies to just the supply of crews and managing the relationship between the train operator and the track provider. In the east, GrainCorp (in NSW and Victoria), Centennial Coal (in NSW), and Manildra Group (NSW) provide their own wagons, and contract in the loco power, crews and train management.

How competition actually resulted on each of the Australian rail networks is described in Chapter 12.

Competitive Neutrality

Neutrality between government and private sector

The term 'competitive neutrality' was first introduced into the lexicon of Australian land transport in the context of the National Competition Policy in the mid-1990s. There was recognition that government-owned businesses might have advantages over private sector business by virtue of being government-owned. Different regulations might apply, and government-owned businesses were not liable for taxation. Indeed, some had their annual operating deficits subsidised by their government owners. While these differences existed, there could not be competitive neutrality between the public and private sectors operating in the same space.

In the railways context, the National Rail Corporation (NRC) was at this time still having its financial losses reimbursed by its government owners while it faced competition on the east-west interstate corridor, from established transport companies SCT and TNT. In September 1999, a competitive neutrality complaint was lodged with the Commonwealth Competitive Neutrality Complaints Office (CCNCO)[518] against NRC by Capricorn Capital, an investment advisory company specialising in emerging markets. The basis of the complaint was that NRC had not earned a commercial rate of return on its assets in the previous three financial years, and would not do so in the foreseeable future. The CCNCO ruled that a breach of the competitive neutrality guidelines had not occurred because the NRC was at this time still in its five-year establishment period. Nevertheless, this situation must have been embarrassing for the Commonwealth government, which was both the proponent of the National Competition Policy and NRC's primary owner. The intention to sell NRC had been announced in 1997, but this did not actually happen until 2002.

Many submitters to the PC's 1999 *Progress in Rail Reform*[519] inquiry noted that State-owned freight railways, even though corporatized, were still vertically-integrated and therefore retained effective control of these networks. This was a sufficient deterrent to entry by the private sector into the rail industry, and therefore constituted another form of competitive inequality between the public and private sectors. This was of course a transitional issue that should have been resolved by 2002 (and 2007 in Queensland) by the sales of these organisations and/or the vertical separation that occurred in all mainland States. However, it turned out that government ownership was not the problem. (This is explained below, under *Barriers to Entry*.)

Neutrality between road and rail modes

By 1999, the term 'competitive neutrality' had acquired a second meaning which had become more common. The Productivity Commission (PC) received many comments from rail industry participants about the lack of competitive neutrality between rail and road transport,[520] stemming from various government policies and processes, and the fundamentality of this issue to rail reform. Its 1999 report *Progress in Rail Reform* devoted a whole chapter to this issue.

The ways in which this lack of competitive neutrality was evident then are largely unchanged now, and show the extent of changes still needed:

- What the ARTC identified as "imperfect and inconsistent project cost benefit analysis and evaluation",[521] which intensified the disparity in investments in highways and railways since the 1970s, creating a marked difference in the quality and capacity of the interstate highway and railway networks, reflected in travel times. This is documented in chapter 4.
- There is a significant difference in cost recovery methods for the use of 'way' – road carriers do not pay directly for the provision and maintenance of highways, while train operators do pay track access charges which contribute at least a proportion of the costs of the railed 'way'. This difference is seen to favour the road transport industry greatly.
- There is no recognition of the hidden costs of 'externalities' (such as air pollution, resources consumed by accidents and road congestion) which therefore ignores the potential benefits to the community from sending proportionately more freight by rail and less by road.

There is yet another less obvious way in which interstate rail operators have been for decades at a disadvantage versus road.[522] Under the Australian federal registration charges regime for interstate vehicles, lighter trucks cross-subsidise heavier trucks because the charges under-recover the cost of the damage that the heavier trucks cause to road pavements. Significantly, it is these subsidised larger heavier trucks ('B-doubles') that are used to compete against railways in interstate haulage. (There is a fuller explanation of this cross-subsidisation in chapter 6, *The PC's 2006 Report – Road and Rail Freight Infrastructure Pricing*.)

13. The Application of Economic Concepts

Government investment in highways versus railway infrastructure

The difference in levels of investment by governments in highways versus railway infrastructure was documented in the PC's 1999 report *Progress in Rail Reform*. This gross disparity in investments from the 1970s to the present time still remains the source of much of the lack of competitive neutrality between road and rail in the eastern States. There is no need for equal amounts of investment, but something more proportional to the potential capacities of the routes of each mode is needed. Insufficient investment has left railway routes stymied by uncompetitive transit times compared to highways, and in some areas, there is insufficient line capacity and a lack of intermodal transfer sites to enable business growth.

The Commonwealth Department of Transport and Regional Services[523] submitted the following in 1999 to the PC as to why investment had had to be directed to highways, and the PC reproduced it uncritically in *Progress in Rail Reform*:[524]

> "The rail network was largely developed before the advent of heavy vehicles on roads. Consequently the rail network represents a mature network with the focus of works on maintenance and realignments, while the road network has until recently been under development to meet current demands placed on the network."

This statement was disingenuous. The highway network was also developed from "a mature network" of existing roads, with deviations and by-passes built where advantageous to users. The rail networks were also built "before the advent of heavy (rail) vehicles", and so they need development to meet current and potential demands for higher speeds and heavier axle-loads. For example, the grain networks now have to accommodate increased axle loadings, due to the replacement of old 4-wheeled bulk grain wagons with 8-wheeled bogie wagons, each built to contain about four times the load of two 4-wheeled wagons. In many places, and particularly in the vertically-separated networks of WA, NSW and Victoria, modern grain trains are required to run slowly along branch lines because these tracks have not been upgraded to take heavier wagons.

The PC was well aware of how the lack of investment in railway infrastructure created a competitive impediment for the railway industry. In 1999 it wrote this in *Progress in Rail Reform*:[525]

> "low quality track has adverse consequences for rail costs and productivity. This is manifested in terms of slower train speeds, lighter axle loads, longer transit times, higher crew costs and higher fuel costs. Inadequate track capacity also impinges on rail performance. The lack of passing loops constrains traffic along a given line and short passing loops limit train length. Such deficiencies are likely to undermine the ability of railways to compete with road transport operators and contribute to modal substitution."

However, in 2006 the PC, in its report *Road and Rail Freight Infrastructure Pricing*, was constrained by its Terms of Reference to consider only operating costs and pricing issues. Hence it stated: [526]

> "The nub of concerns about whether there is competitive neutrality between road and rail lies in the question of whether the differences between the charging arrangements and related ownership structures in each mode systematically favour one mode over the other — specifically, road over rail."

In the Overview section of this 2006 report, the PC implied that there was indeed competitive neutrality on the North-South interstate routes between road and rail:[527]

> **"What are the implications for competitive neutrality?**
> The Commission has not found a compelling case that

heavy vehicles competing with rail freight on major north–south corridors are *relatively* subsidised. Corridor-specific data that are available are consistent with logic in suggesting that the unit costs of use of these 'built-for-purpose' routes are lower than average network costs and, for many heavy vehicles, are likely to be below current charges. For rail, significant government financial contributions allow access charges to be set below the long-run economic costs of providing freight services on major corridors."

In its 2006 study, the PC had compared costs and access charges of both modes, and found that both were subsidised in general. However, the B-doubles using the National Highway System (NHS) (which compete against trains) were not seen to be subsidised because the maintenance costs of their using 'built-for-purpose' highways were lower than for other roads. The PC had ignored the sunken costs of the previous investments in the NHS which created these 'built-for-purpose' highways. In 2006, it apparently considered what it knew in 1999 to be irrelevant, i.e., that for decades there had been a disparity in levels of investment by governments in highways versus railway infrastructure. The reality was the interstate rail network had never received any degree of investment equivalent to the NHS, on a per route-mile basis. Therefore, the interstate rail lines cannot be considered 'built-for-purpose' to provide private sector train operators with competitive transit times and reliability.

The "significant government financial contributions" the PC referred to (in the quote above) included ARTC projects to remedy deficiencies, upgrading projects under the AusLink program, and long-overdue major maintenance projects in Tasmania and the isolated grain lines of the Eyre Peninsula (SA).[528] Shortfalls in revenues of the State networks in Victoria, New South Wales and Queensland were and still are funded by their governments. Even in Western Australia where the rail network is leased to a profitable company, the State government was forced to pay for the resleepering of the tier 1 and 2 grain lines to keep them open. (See in chapter 15, under *The Western Australian Experience* for the details.)

In 2006, the National Transport Commission (NTC) stated its view on competitive neutrality:[529]

> "At the heart of the competitive neutrality issue is the disparity in investment between road and rail."

At that time, track providers were newly created after vertical separation, and were trying to follow what they assumed was good business practice. The outcome was that few rail infrastructure investments could be 'justified' using business-like Benefit Cost Analyses (discussed in the next section below) while highway investments continued. This disparity is explained below, under *The NSW Experience*.

In 2008, the NTC undertook some work to identify "impediments to improved productivity in rail transport".[530] This resulted in a Position Paper published in 2009, in which the NTC used the PC's 2006 logic to (unwittingly) undermine the Productivity Commission's finding of 2006,[531] that

> "The available evidence, while not conclusive, does not support the contention that road freight is subsidised relative to rail on either the inter-capital corridors or in regional areas."

Acknowledging and following the economic thinking of the Productivity Commission, the NTC Position Paper stated that[532] subsidies to rail included tolerance of low rates of return on infrastructure investment, and grants where any return on investment was not expected by the governments as shareholders. If we accept this logic, then the extension must be that the road transport industry is also subsidised, because all governments provide roads and highways without any return on investment being expected by them as shareholders/owners. Given the disparity in governmental investments in highways and railways over the last fifty years,[533] the road transport industry has been, and still is, heavily subsidised. Hence, the lack of competitive neutrality between the road and rail modes is very real.

The economic appraisal of rail network projects

A note on terminology: Cost Benefit Analysis (CBA) is sometimes named Benefit Cost Analysis (BCA). It is the same process. In quoting various writers below, I have kept whatever term they used.

Inconsistent project cost benefit analysis between the modes

In 1999, the ARTC identified "imperfect and inconsistent project cost benefit analysis and evaluation"[534] as one reason for the long-standing lack of competitive neutrality between rail and road modes. The Bureau of Transport Economics (BTE) also confirmed in 1999 that there was a difference in practice. The BTE wrote that Cost-Benefit Analysis (CBA)[535] was usually used for road infrastructure projects, but[536]

> "outside the road sector, public provision of transport infrastructure is quasi-commercial, and the authorities generally perform financial analyses, rather than BCAs, for internal investment appraisals."

This statement implies that the key difference between the two types of analysis was the inclusion, or not, of data about externalities. The effect of the commercial approach on rail network projects was that any customer, social or environmental benefits were not usually included in the analysis because the focus was on the 'economic efficiency' of the investment for the track provider.

After the vertical separation of Australian railways in the 1990s, the Commonwealth Government was prepared to fund gauge conversions on the interstate network, but not to upgrade the quality or the capacity of these lines. Financial justification of investments for the renewal and upgrading of railtrack was problematic. There was a belief that such investments had to be treated on a commercial basis, as if the investment were being made by the private sector with the expectation of a financial return. Hence, there were no significant upgrades until after the ARTC took over the degraded interstate lines in NSW in 2004, and no new lines built until the completion of ARTC's Southern Sydney Freight Line in 2013, which was built to separate freight from the busy RailCorp passenger routes. The approach now espoused (see below) was unthinkable for governments and their bureaucrats in the 1990s.

At the same time as rail networks were being starved of capital, the non-profit National Highway System had been the beneficiary of Commonwealth funding of projects worth billions of dollars. CBAs for these included the unbankable sum of the value of time that could be saved by all its users, both the trucking industry and private motorists, because this was seen as a social benefit. The Federal Department of Transport and Regional Services attempted to justify the lack of a consistent set of criteria for evaluation of road and rail projects in a submission to the PIRR:[537]

> "The critical difference between road and rail project assessment is the social criteria and time savings benefits that are evident in assessing roads projects which do not occur to the same extent in rail projects. This difference occurs as a result of the road transport industry sharing the asset with private motorists whereas railways do not have to contend with a similar element of private use."

By the confused logic of this argument, the time and fuel saved by truckers moving freight for commercial purposes on new or improved highways was a social benefit, but the time and fuel that might be saved by freight train operators on improved ARTC lines was not. This logic fits with the furphy often seen on signs alongside Australia's roads: "Without trucks Australia stops".

13. The Application of Economic Concepts

In 2014 the successor to the BTE, the Bureau of Infrastructure, Transport and Regional Economics (BITRE) published, on its own initiative, a paper *Overview of Project Appraisal for Land Transport*:[538]

> "This paper outlines first the broader appraisal process in which CBA sits, and second, CBA itself with the recent developments of **wider economic benefits and productivity metrics**." (My emphasis)

This reflects a change in approach from its 1999 position for publicly-owned rail infrastructure projects, making the appraisal much more similar to that for highway projects. In particular, the new approach now allows for projects to be considered that stimulate economic growth. For those with multiple potential users, there can be a role for government to fund all or part of the project. Since the publication of this report, it is noticeable that Commonwealth funds are being committed to major rail projects that will create wider economic benefits, for example:

- Inland Rail, connecting Melbourne to Brisbane while bypassing congested Sydney,
- the Murray Basin project to convert tracks to standard gauge and at the same time upgrade several of the lines in north-west Victoria,
- duplication of the line to Port Botany (the major container port for NSW),
- various projects to add line capacity to the northern Sydney shared passenger and freight route between Strathfield and Hornsby.

The application of benefit-cost analyses

BCAs are a mathematical method of assessing whether a project is worthwhile. When the inputs and outputs related to a capital spend are quantified by year, they can be discounted to determine the net present value of the opportunity at the time of the decision. The method appears objective and gives the impression of analytical rigour. However, the numbers are always based on the input of analysts: assumptions about the future, arbitrary and/or creative decisions about what factors to include and exclude, and how to calculate the time value of money. Hence there is always the possibility of unconscious bias influencing the results. Sometimes there is a blatant bias.

In the view of two transport researchers, the political nature of transport planning in Australia, particularly for road projects, sometimes means[539]

> "that decisions on infrastructure projects are made by sovereign fiat, not rationality: basically what the policy makers think is good, not what falls out of rational calculation. Rationalization follows decision. The role of BCA is to legitimate decisions not to guide them."

Peter Martin, the Australian economics writer, has described this use of BCAs more colourfully:[540]

> "very often they are conducted as an "add-on"; financial bling to be sprinkled over the project after it has been approved and announced."

For government-owned rail network projects, there appears to be an acceptance now that such networks are not profit-making, but they are a necessity for relieving pressure on the highways, at the very least. A recent example is a $28 million project to build a direct rail freight line between the Port of Melbourne and the manufacturing hub of Dandenong South, in Melbourne's eastern suburbs.[541]

> "The project will be funded by the Federal and Victorian governments and is the next step in the Port Rail Shuttle Network to remove congestion around the Port of Melbourne and cut freight transport costs by as much as 10 per cent. The savings the project would deliver would boost the competitiveness of Victorian businesses."

Reduction in highway congestion is an easily seen result of having rail passenger networks in the major cities, but this result applies to rail freight networks as well.[542] Therefore, BCAs need to include all the social and environmental benefits that publicly-owned rail network projects create, relative to moving all freight on highways. BCAs also need to allow for the long lives of railway assets in the calculations, together with a realistic choice of discount rate.

The significance of the CBA discount rate

The setting of the discount rate is perhaps the most critical element in a CBA.[543] It is necessary to use some discount rate in order to convert the future flows of benefits and costs to a common basis – the 'present value'. This process assigns a smaller weight to benefits and costs that lie further in the future than to those that are more imminent. Normally the funds for investment in a project have to be borrowed, so discounting is warranted because real interest rates are normally positive: benefits that come sooner rather than later have an interest-earning advantage.

The discount rate should be set to reflect the opportunity cost of the funds to be applied to the project, and in my view the rate should also reflect the investor's position on the spectrum between self-interest and altruism. Typically, the private sector, being profit-oriented, will use a higher discount rate than is needed for a public investment. However, an arbitrary figure is usually applied to both public and private, often in a deliberate non-recognition of this distinction. The current situation in Australia is:[544]

> "Infrastructure Australia asks for CBA results at a 7% discount rate in real terms, that is, adjusted to remove the effect of inflation, and sensitivity tests at 4% and 10% (IA 2013b). The Department of Infrastructure and Regional Development asks for CBA results at 4% and 7% in real terms. The 4% rate is intended to represent a level not far above the risk-free rate for the 'social opportunity cost of capital'. ... The 7% rate has long been the traditional discount rate used for transport projects

in Australia and approaches the 8% rate recommended ... for the social opportunity cost of capital based on the long-term before-all-tax real rate of return earned by private capital in Australia. **Economists are unable to arrive at a united position on the choice of discount rate, so there can be no universally accepted 'correct' rate.**" (My emphasis)

The Grattan Institute has confirmed[545] that regardless of the real borrowing rates available to governments in Australia, government agencies have chosen to keep their discount rates at 7 per cent since at least 1989.

One economist identified the criticality of the CBA discount rate setting when he spoke to the 2016 AusRail Conference about the effect of the choice of discount rate on the appraisal of rail projects, and how a change from the traditional would benefit the industry:[546]

> "The current discount rate used in Australia, typically 7%, is not representative of the opportunity cost in the current economic climate. At the time of writing, the Australian interest rate, as set by the Reserve Bank of Australia, is 1.5% and has not been 7% since 2008. Perhaps a better measure of the opportunity cost is the 15-year Australian Government bond which currently has a yield of around 2.3% while long term bonds in Germany and Japan now have negative interest rates! Moreover, discount rates are significantly lower in other places around the world. For example, guidance for economic appraisal in the United Kingdom stipulates a discount rate of 3.5% for years 0-30 of a project, 3.0% for years 31-75 of a project and 2.5% for years 76-125 of a project. This is significantly lower than in Australia and the impact on a long-term project is marked.
>
> Take a hypothetical project with a capital cost of $1bn and a three-year construction period which then

produces a $50m per annum economic benefit for the following 100 years. Using the Australian approach to discounting results in a Benefit Cost Ratio of 0.67 and a Net Present Value of negative $313m. Whereas, adopting the UK's discounting standards results in a Benefit Cost Ratio of 1.40 and a Net Present Value of positive $389m. Thus, this project, which could very well be a rail project, appears to be a value-for-money opportunity in the UK yet an identical project would be very unlikely to obtain funding in Australia."

This shows how the choice of the discount rate is absolutely critical for determining whether project benefits outweigh costs or not. It also has the effect of changing perceptions of the relative values of projects to the economy.

The Grattan Institute showed this effect in comparing four recent Australian rail projects at different discount rates, illustrated by the chart[547] over:

- the Canberra Light Rail project (urban passenger)
- the Murray Basin (Victoria) rail standardisation and upgrade project (regional freight)
- the Melbourne Metro project (urban passenger), and
- the Inland Rail project connecting Brisbane to Melbourne directly (interstate freight).

Chart: Benefit-cost ratio of selected projects at discount rates of 4, 7 and 10 per cent

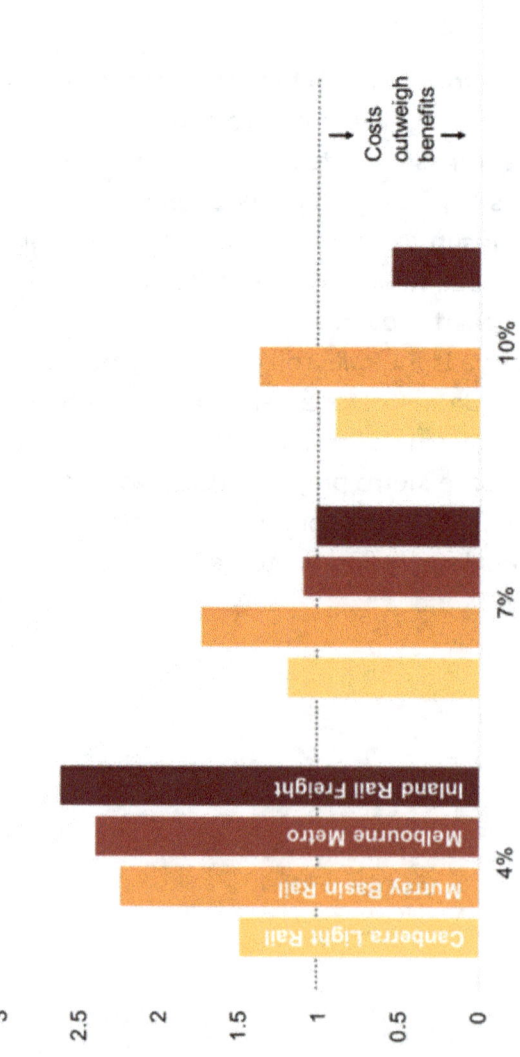

Sources: Australian Capital Territory Government (2014), Victorian Department of Economic Development, Jobs, Transport and Resources (2015), Victorian State Government (2016), and Australian Rail Track Corporation (2015).

At a discount rate of 4 per cent, Inland Rail has the highest benefit-cost ratio (shown on the y-axis), more than the other freight project, Murray Basin. But at a discount rate of 7 per cent, Murray Basin has the highest benefit-cost ratio, and Inland Rail has the lowest. At 10 per cent, the only viable project appears to be Murray Basin, because it will have the most immediate benefits.

As a general rule, projects with deferred benefits are hit hardest by high discount rates because decision-makers prefer projects with more immediate benefits. In the annual de facto contests for land transport funding, highways have usually looked more attractive than rail network projects when the historically traditional discount rate of 7% has been applied. In rail projects, the complex and conditional relationships between making the investment and reaping the benefits can have a lag time of years before the benefits begin to flow. (See in chapter 15, under *Investing for Capability Improvements to the Interstate Rail Network*.)

The legacy for future generations of Australians, resulting from the 7% discount rate being applied uncritically for some twenty years, is transport networks that will generate higher levels of GHGs and noxious diesel particulates for decades to come. If the BCA discount rates had been kept in line with the reducing costs of investment funds to governments, the legacy would have been quite different.

The NSW experience

The commercial approach was initially used for investment in the NSW rail network after the vertical separation of the NSW government railways in 1996. Two years later, FreightCorp said this[548] about the NSW network in its first submission to the 1999 PIRR inquiry, that the Rail Access Corporation (RAC) had funds to invest but

> "there aren't very many profitable opportunities for investment."

Then, in a later submission[549] it referred to current railway infrastructure being of

> "poor quality that is due to past years of low maintenance expenditure."

It seems that some types of MPM work were being tested for profitability and being rejected by RAC due to a lack of sufficient return on investment within the bounds of its business. One wonders how they factored in the increased risks to train safety due to maintenance work not being done. The operational benefits for FreightCorp were ignored because that was now a separate organisation from RAC. (It will be shown in chapter 15, under *The Western Australian Experience,* how vertical separation can change the perception of profitability of parts of a rail network.) In NSW, the consequence of insufficient maintenance was a gradual degradation in track quality. The ARTC took a long-term lease on the NSW interstate routes and the Hunter Valley in 2004. In 2007, it confirmed[550] that it was

> "addressing the significant maintenance deficit inherited in the NSW rail infrastructure."

The NSW Government now controls the remainder of the NSW rail network through a government statutory authority, Transport for NSW. Clearly it understands now that rail projects create prosperity for the regions by reducing the cost of freight transport to markets, and its assessment of rail projects is the opposite of what it was in the 1990s. In 2016 the NSW Government announced a program called Fixing Country Rail,[551]

> "to improve the economic growth and productivity of NSW".

The assessment criteria under this program for rail projects include a wide range of benefits for not just the State, but also the businesses and communities of NSW. The factors a BCA will consider positively include:[552]

- increasing the capacity of the rail network
- encouraging mode shift of freight from road to rail, with a consequent reduction of the number of long-distance heavy road vehicle trips
- improved efficiency and/or productivity of the rail network, such as longer and/or heavier trains, and better asset utilisation and improved cycle times
- improved safety on road or rail
- lower maintenance costs for road or rail assets, rolling-stock or other equipment
- lower transport costs and reduced freight rates for freight shippers
- lower externalities costs for communities, e.g., congestion, noise or emissions.

In May 2018, the NSW Government announced it would spend $137 million from this program on eleven projects to strengthen regional lines enabling heavier axle-loads and faster train speeds, with one of the touted benefits stated as shifting freight onto rail and removing trucks from the roads.[553] In another similar announcement the local MP is quoted in a media release as saying:[554]

> "It's just sensible investment, so producers and businesses in the Riverina will benefit from a more efficient and lower cost logistics chain, improving their domestic and international competitiveness, as well as create benefits to our consumers at the till of their local supermarkets."

Barriers to entry

'Barriers to entry' is a term in the theory of competition that refers to the costs and other obstacles facing new entrants to a market that the existing participants in the market do not have to deal with.

One of the difficulties unforeseen by those in the 1990s who were promoting competition within the rail industry, was the high level of difficulty for newcomers to the rail industry in getting started. With the benefit of hindsight, it is possible to identify some of the barriers that were faced.

Too many unknowns created too much risk

A major barrier for any company wanting to start up and compete as a hire-and-reward train operator was the number of unknowns they faced, including:
- what regular traffic flows could be secured, from other train operators or from road?
- what operational sites were obtainable, or even accessible?
- what rolling-stock would be needed, what was available to buy or lease, and how much investment was needed for rolling-stock?
- what was the availability of crews with current knowledge of both the routes and the locomotives to be used?

Many factors had to be put in place for a successful launch. Consequently, the levels of uncertainty were high, and this itself was an effective barrier to entry for any companies that did not have already some familiarity with the rail industry and/or the freight transport market. As the ARTC advised the PC for its *Progress in Rail Reform* report:[555]

> "Uncertainty creates risk; therefore high uncertainty creates high risk. High risk demands a higher rate of return to compensate for the increased risk. Uncertainty then, becomes a disincentive for investors seeking lower risk investment."

There was much uncertainty in the industry when this was written in 1999, not just about the unknowns listed above, but also who would be competing in the market in the future:
- it was known that the Commonwealth government wanted to sell the NRC, but not known how or when

- the sales of the government-owned State railways NSW FreightCorp, V/Line Freight, and WestRail had not yet happened.

The ARTC itself was newly established, with control at that time of only the former AN interstate lines. It had still to implement its 'one-stop-shop' concept for the interstate network, to lower the barrier to entry into interstate operations caused by inconsistent operating procedures and standards among the State railways.

Two decades later, little has changed. The knowledge needed by existing operators to expand their scope, or by new operators wanting to compete with them, is formidable. Here is an assessment written in 2022:[556]

> "A potential barrier to market entry [relates] to the complexity of rail versus road. If you would like to establish a new rail operation, and in particular new rail infrastructure, the pathway to do this is protracted and complex. For example, gaining the required approvals and consents to develop and connect a new rail terminal, or alter existing connections is a protracted and expensive task.
>
> This is exemplified by the long lead times for new rail interface developments such as SCT Altona, Salta Properties in Altona and Dandenong South, Austrak in Somerton, InterlinkSQ in Toowoomba and many more. Gaining physical and operational access to rail is complex, timely and expensive. These market entry and expansion challenges appear to serve as very real barriers to rail growth."

The ineffectiveness of the Open Access policy for vertically-integrated networks

Where rail systems were privatised in vertically-integrated form, and competition between train operators was wanted, mandating an Open Access policy was thought to be sufficient. However, as was seen in South Australia and Victoria, the incumbent operators had to release only what they deemed to be spare capacity on their networks. They could claim as much network capacity as they wanted, and this made a barrier to entry big enough to deter any other train operators for some years.

Contracts for regular train-load consignments

Vertical separation and privatisation together created a new barrier that could not have existed when most State railways operated. In those times, freight could be accepted onto rail in single wagon-load consignments, and the government railway was able to consolidate these with other larger consignments into train-loads. After vertical separation and privatisation, this type of freight service was considered too uncertain, risky and/or bothersome. Train operators considered that they needed the certainty of consistent, point-to-point, whole train-loads to be viable, and this became the basis of new contracts. This increase in minimum traffic volume constituted another barrier for any new entrants, the barrier being the difficulty of finding a residual market opportunity after the incumbent operator in each State had secured its contracts.

Traffic flows of sufficient volume to justify regular full trains were hard to find unless the incumbent operator deliberately avoided or relinquished them. When Pacific National was created, it was not interested in containerised traffic going to Port Botany (NSW), perhaps because of the difficulties of operating in the Sydney area with its curfews, and coordinating train schedules with the stevedores' schedules. However, this opened up opportunities for several other companies including Patrick Portlink, Silverton, and Lachlan Valley Rail Services.

In a rare instance of innovation brought about by vertical separation, ATN Access found a new market hauling grain for the Australian Wheat Board (AWB) across the border, from the standard gauge branch lines of the Riverina (NSW) onto the ARTC's standard gauge line to Melbourne. However, to fulfil this contract it had first to buy second-hand locomotives and import 44 new grain wagons from China to start these operations in June 2000.[557]

Control of rolling-stock and facilities by the incumbent operator

In regimes where there was full vertical separation, and in theory all operators had equal access to the rail network, the established train operators retained a distinct advantage because:
- they already had rolling-stock to access the network with, and
- they had occupancy of the existing terminals, sometimes exclusively.

When governments privatised their railways, it seems that they overlooked ensuring equitable access to all the existing locations on the networks where support for rail operations was provided. Such places included intermodal terminals, locomotive depots for refuelling and resanding, rolling-stock workshops, yards for parking wagons during periods of business inactivity. The National Transport Commission (NTC) identified this as a high priority issue still to be resolved in 2009:[558]

> "Inconsistent access to strategic intermodal terminals can be an impediment to rail competition."

Victoria

After the Victorian government bought back the country network from PN in 2007, PN still controlled the majority of the broad-gauge rolling-stock. When PN withdrew its services from Victoria in March 2008, it converted its rolling-stock to standard-gauge to use elsewhere. Hence any new entrant faced the barrier of converting other rolling-stock, leasing, or buying new, to operate on the only broad-gauge freight network left in Australia. When El Zorro contracted with AWB to haul grain from August 2008, it was AWB which invested in its own fleet of new grain wagons, so that no train operator could desert it again as PN had done.

New South Wales

Barriers to train companies other than Pacific National (PN) operating to, from or within Sydney were particularly high, because of the way that FreightCorp was privatised. When PN was created, all the major ancillary facilities for freight in Sydney were included:

- the intermodal terminal at Chullora, and the locomotive servicing depot at Enfield known as Delec were included in the sale, and
- the marshalling and holding yards at Enfield and Clyde were leased by the NSW government to Pacific National for ten years.

Although this lease required PN to allow other companies to use these yards, PN charged them a per-train entry fee, and could deny access if it deemed the yards to be too full. This situation left all the other train operators without the possibility of an operational base in Sydney, even though their trains might start or terminate there. All had to make their NSW bases elsewhere:

- Interail based its operations and maintenance at Broadmeadow yard in Newcastle,
- Silverton based its operations at Broadmeadow and rolling-stock maintenance at Parkes,
- Southern Shorthaul Railroad based its operations and maintenance at Lithgow,
- Independent Rail was based at Minto (southwest Sydney); it is now part of Qube, which will presumably base its rail operations at Moorebank when this intermodal terminal opens,
- Australian Railroad Group (ARG) had a small locomotive refuelling and stabling area leased at the

eastern end of Clyde yard, but also refuelled at the RailCorp fuel point in Bomaderry. When necessary, it did light maintenance of rolling-stock at its customer's private sidings, and for heavy repairs, it sent rolling-stock to its base in Adelaide.

Silverton Rail was in a unique position in NSW as an already established rail operator in Broken Hill when the rail networks of NSW and South Australia were apparently made available under the Open Access policy. It was the first company to compete against FreightCorp, running a daily trip train between Villawood and Port Botany. Yet in its submission[559] in 1999 to the PC for its *Progress in Rail Reform* report, it told how difficult it was to have open access to the railway lines but no access to operational infrastructure such as refuelling facilities and terminals. In NSW, almost all such facilities were under the control of FreightCorp, and subsequently Pacific National. Silverton operated for some years by refuelling its locomotives directly from road tankers at various sites around NSW that were accessible from the road, often done while its wagons were being loaded or unloaded.

Western Australia

In WA the government chose to dispose of its railway via a sale-and-lease agreement, where the purchaser of the rail operation and the lessee of the rail infrastructure were the same company, the Australian Rail Group (ARG). The government's objectives were to keep the network in public ownership while enabling coordinated investment from the private sector. This was to maintain the extent of the network in support of the grain industry, while enabling rail to cater for a forecasted large increase in traffic from mining and industry. The government was not interested in fostering competition on the rail network, and although there was a barrier to entry for any other rail operator this was not an issue then. The government had perpetuated its benign monopoly.

However, ARG subsequently vertically separated itself, and in 2006 its owners sold the above-rail and below-rail businesses separately. The above-rail business was sold to Queensland Rail (QR) which later became Aurizon, and crucially the sale included various types of infrastructure needed to support this business – marshalling yards, intermodal terminals, workshops and depots. This high barrier to entry continued as Aurizon continued as the monopoly operator. When CBH became dissatisfied with Aurizon, its only option for change was to become a de facto train operator itself to surmount the barrier. It bought all new locomotives and wagons, and contracted an American short-line operator, new to Australia, to crew its trains.

Queensland

In Queensland, the government-owned railway remained vertically-integrated until 2010. Hence all freight rolling-stock was owned by QR. This meant that when PN captured a contract in 2005 to haul intermodal traffic for Toll on the Queensland narrow-gauge network, and again in 2008 when it captured its first export coal contract, it had to purchase new locomotives and wagons. Few train operators could have financed such purchases to compete in the Queensland freight markets. Not until 2019 did a third train operator start on the Queensland network, again by purchasing new rolling-stock – it was Watco, hauling bulk products for GrainCorp which previously used Aurizon for this traffic.[560]

When the State government split QR in 2010, all freight rolling-stock was vested in QR National. This became a publicly listed company a few months later, and two years later it changed its name to Aurizon.[561] In subsequent years, Aurizon rationalised its locomotive fleet, offering surplus and old locomotives for sale on the world market. These had seen service in Queensland, NSW and WA, with many coming from the former WestRail and ARG fleets. In January 2015 a shipload of 17 locomotives sailed from Fremantle (WA) to Durban (South Africa), having been bought by Apex Industrial.[562] Interestingly, there is a website called *locomotivesforafrica.com* which self-describes as "a portal for Apex Industrial Pty Ltd ... based in Brisbane, Queensland".[563] It shows pictures of locomotives for sale, located in South Africa, mostly with ARG livery. The significance of this is that Aurizon appears to be strategically controlling surplus locomotives to prevent any Australian-based companies using these to start or expand their own freight rail operations.

The road transport industry

The strength of the road transport industry presented a barrier to entry for any train operator wishing to compete for general freight between adjacent State capitals. For a combination of reasons, rail was not competitive on service or price before 1990. By the 1990s, the road transport industry was well-established, particularly in the interstate sector. This position had resulted from a Privy Council decision in the mid-1950s that there should be no restrictions under the Constitution to interstate trade. (See in chapter 3, under *Deregulation of Australian Road & Rail Competition*). The Bureau of Transport Economics, in its 1979 and 1993 studies of the road freight transport industry, described how competition within the industry was very strong leading to extensive price cutting. It found there was a disequilibrium between the demand for and the supply of line-haul services, described as an "over-supply". A significant reason for this was the ease of entry and difficulty of exit for owner-drivers.[564]

> "The line haul trucking sector consists mainly of owner drivers, who form independent small business units, operated mainly as sole proprietorships or close family partnerships. Studies of the industry (BTE 1986;NRFll -1984) had found that it was relatively easy to enter the line haul trucking business as an owner driver, as long

as the necessary collateral could be provided. Often, the collateral provided consisted of the owner driver's home. In this situation, an economic downturn would make it difficult for some owner drivers to leave the industry, this action could result in the loss of the family home. Such a sequence of events presented the owner driver with few options, except to stay in the industry, even for very low returns. In such circumstances, a situation where the supply of line haul services outstrip demand could easily develop."

Four decades later, this situation still applies. As owner-drivers withdraw from the industry due to retirement, bankruptcy or serious accidents, others appear willing to buy rigs at depressed prices and chase contracts with the major players, such as supermarket chains, product manufacturers and distribution companies. These companies like to use owner-drivers. This enables them to take advantage of the over-supply while also avoiding the overhead cost of staff management. They can also avoid having to manage driver fatigue, caused by the long hours that owner-drivers typically work to make a meagre living.

In 2012, the Gillard Labor federal government set up the Road Safety Remuneration Tribunal (RSRT) to set minimum pay rates for independent contractors who own and drive their own trucks, and to provide paid time for breaks and maintenance. It was set up after the National Transport Commission found in 2008 that there was a link between driver remuneration and safety outcomes for truck drivers.[565] The mission of the RSRT was challenged in the courts, and the Tribunal did not make its first minimum-pay order until 2016. As the day for implementation approached, many owner-drivers alleged that they were being told not to show up for work because the big transport companies could not afford to use them at about 30% more than their current rates.[566] Hence they would be out of work, but many would still have debts to service on their trucks and houses. With combined pressure from owner-

13. The Application of Economic Concepts

drivers, the National Roads Transport Association and the Australian Logistics Council, the Coalition federal government rushed through legislation to abolish the RSRT, thus retaining the status quo.

Consequently, owner-drivers in the Australian road freight line-haul industry are a modern form of bonded labour. They still have low earnings and high working hours, resulting in low prices for road freight customers. Driver fatigue is still a reality which creates conditions that put at risk their own lives and the lives of other road users. (By contrast, train operations are very regulated for safety. It is the norm that freight train drivers do not exceed their rostered hours or take less than their mandated rest periods between shifts.)

In 2023, it was reported that truck drivers profit margins were being squeezed down to 2.5%, and there was a national shortfall of 24,000 truck drivers, resulting in unused trucks being parked up.[567] Also, nearly 200 transport companies became insolvent in the last year. A contributing factor is the imbalance in negotiating power between the major customers (listed as retailers, manufacturers and oil companies) and small trucking operators. If market forces prevail, there should be consolidation in the trucking industry, increased earnings for truck drivers, and/or a gradual switch of long-haul freight to the rail mode, to reduce the need for truck drivers. Perhaps the Feb 2023 agreement between intermodal logistics provider TGE and Aurizon enabling improved access to the interstate rail network for TGE is evidence of a switch by freight shippers away from the choked-off interstate trucking industry? (See chapter 12, under *The interstate intermodal sectors: continued competition*).

14. Vertical Integration versus Vertical Separation

The current situation

Vertical integration in any business means that it supplies most of its own process inputs, and management requirements such as information technology, accounting, marketing, legal and human resources functions. For historical reasons, vertically-integrated railways have been and still are the norm around the world, despite some recent instances of separation in Europe. The railways of Australia and New Zealand used to be very much vertically-integrated as government departments. Now, most of the mainland railway systems are vertically-separated, the main exception being the line from Darwin to Tarcoola (SA), operated by Aurizon. Only in New Zealand and Tasmania have the railways been vertically reintegrated, in the sense that the same organisations again control both the majority of above-rail and below-rail operations, after a period of separation in each case.

So, which is better – vertical integration or vertical separation? The obvious appeal of separation is that it enables multiple train operators to share rail networks. However, as will be seen below, there are several disadvantages that need to be managed.

Organisational benefits from vertical integration

Businesses that are vertically-integrated usually have been this way from the beginning. The need to supply their own inputs has usually arisen because of the absence of other suppliers. This was definitely the case for the railway systems of the Australian and New Zealand colonies. Initially the supplies of rails and rolling-stock were shipped out from Britain, then the 'mother country', or the USA as the only other English-speaking country with the manufacturing capability. Sleepers and ballast were obtained from local forests and quarries, and once good quality materials were found close to the expanding networks, the railways came to own their own timber mills and quarries. The distances, time lags and expense involved in getting mechanical maintenance work done overseas saw the early development of local workshops and foundries to support railway activities. Usually, the railways were the first in each area[568] to need such 'heavy industry', so it was natural that they became part of the railway organisations.

In economics terms, vertically-integrated railways have benefitted from both
- economies of scope, from minimising transaction costs among the different parts of the organisation, and having guaranteed supplies, custom-made when required, and
- economies of scale or density from being the single operator, enabling its network, traffic management, crews, locomotives and many wagons to be shared for any customer's traffic.

Vertically-integrated railways can have collaborative managerial relationships if staff morale is good. Operationally, there are three ways these have an effect:
- In the co-ordination of planned track maintenance, particularly for those activities that require track

closure for days at a time; this normally occurs when there is the least disruption to normal commercial operations, in order to minimise disruption to customers, but at the added cost of doing track maintenance on weekends and public holidays
- When derailments occur or there are other reasons for a temporary line closure, the focus is on restoration of services as quickly as possible; a sense of brotherhood is often expressed as a motivating factor to achieve this (see below for a discussion of the alternatives)
- The response to temporary line closures is prompt and cohesive decision-making. An example of this was seen after heavy flooding in northern Tasmania in July 2016. TasRail chose not to invoke the 'force majeure' option in its contracts. Instead, it used the quickly repaired sections of its rail network in combination with a temporary intermodal terminal and road freight connections to the north to continue providing a seamless service to its customers.[569] Such a response is likely to be much more difficult in a vertically-separated network, because of the need to negotiate contracts and prices before repair work starts.

ATN, in its submission to the PC for the *Progress in Rail Reform* inquiry, drawing on its experience of managing TasRail (and no doubt also its owners' experience in New Zealand) summed up the benefits of vertical integration this way:[570]

> "In an integrated railway we can readily identify the problem, take responsibility for it, and deal with it. In a separated model, either there is an artificial division of primary responsibility, and later debate and settlement; or the prospect of litigation and significant costs."

From an investment analysis point of view, vertical integration enables a direct linkage between proposed track investments and expected operational gains. Examples of these are faster

train speeds, heavier axle-loadings, and operational reliability from improved track availability. Usually, the known potential operational gains are the primary reasons for making the investment in infrastructure. Examples of past major projects of this type include:
- the extensive grade and curve easements followed by electrification of over 2000 kilometres of track in the Queensland network, completed by QR in 1989
- the curve and grade easements of the mid-1980s, made on the New Zealand North Island Main Trunk before its electrification,
- the two major mainline deviations in Western Australia, done as part of standardisation of the line between Perth and Kalgoorlie in the later 1960s.

Significantly, all these projects were justified by government-owned railways at times when there was never any consideration of future privatisation. They are now sunk costs, with their operational and financial benefits continuing still many decades later.

Vertical separation led to market fragmentation

There is no doubt that full vertical separation of the former State railways (except in Tasmania) was a necessary prerequisite for enabling multiple train operators to provide services in the same network. As explained in chapter 13, legislating for tracks to be Open Access was insufficient.

With full vertical separation, train operators compete in the rail freight market in a general sense. Proponents of vertical separation would say therefore that competition improves the performance of the railway industry, and is justification for vertical separation. However, direct competition for the same commodity flows and the same customers was generally not the result.

One of the unexpected outcomes of vertical separation was fragmentation of the rail freight market, particularly the intrastate markets. Some companies specialised to cater for just one or a few segments of the freight market, defined by commodity or area, while avoiding other segments. Examples of such market segmentation are:

- Grain, where companies such as GrainCorp and CBH invested in rail assets to haul their own traffic, while Aurizon (as ARG) and Pacific National withdrew from much grain haulage
- Hunter Valley coal, which was one of only two market segments that Freightliner[571] operated in, the other being export cotton from the north-west of NSW to Port Botany
- Coal originating in NSW outside of the Hunter Valley, which is a Southern Shorthaul speciality
- Containerised import/export containers, mostly hauled by Qube in NSW and Victoria
- Inter-capital intermodal traffic, only ever hauled by the three largest rail companies, and avoided by the smaller rail companies which lack the necessary financial and organisational capability to operate interstate.

Another market segment was less-than-trainload consignments. This was avoided by all train operators in NSW and Victoria from the demise of the State-run rail services around year 2000 to at least 2010. Due to the vertical separation and fragmentation of the rail industry, rail services for wagon-loads ceased between State capitals and regional cities and towns, such as Armidale, Tamworth, Parkes, Goulburn, Wagga Wagga, Bendigo, Ballarat, Wangaratta, Bairnsdale. Freight shippers were left with only a limited number of road carriers operating to each regional centre, and transport charges were somewhat higher than had been the case when rail service was an option. In South Australia and Western Australia, the process was different because of the marked concentration of each State's population in the capital cities, and consequently the small volumes of general freight to be transported to the regions. Those government-owned railways had already withdrawn general services to all country centres prior to privatisation and vertical separation. In Queensland, general rail freight services to the regional centres remained, because of the way that rail freight service was privatised. The Queensland Government contracted Aurizon to provide a core network of 624 general freight services per year, and over 300 cattle trains per year from regional hubs to abattoirs.[572] The general freight services are now contracted by the giant transport company Linfox.

In other networks such as New Zealand, Tasmania and the Eyre Peninsula (SA), where the practicality and prospect of there being multiple freight train operators was and is very unlikely, vertical separation was of no economic advantage. The OECD described this "policy option of vertical separation [as] a relatively significant regulatory intervention for relatively little gain." [573]

Vertical separation for network recovery

In New Zealand and Tasmania, the railways systems were each vertically separated for some years, but not by the choice of this policy as such. After more than a decade of private sector ownership of their railways, these governments decided to resume ownership of their networks, while train operations remained in private ownership. In each case, network assets had become degraded because the vertically-integrated private sector railway companies chose to cut back on network maintenance for a number of years, to achieve minimal profitability. (See in chapter 11 for the details.) It appeared to the governments that breakdown leading to closure of the networks was increasingly a risk.

Later, in each case after the resumption of government ownership of the whole railway business, each railway was vertically re-integrated.

These two instances of vertical separation created unequal relationships – between governments wanting to see rail services continuing for transport policy reasons while not wanting to be seen subsidising a company, and companies keen to minimise their costs. In New Zealand, the advent of vertical separation created adversaries. For three years, the government and the train operator could not reach any agreement on the details of network access charges. The issue was partially resolved only by using an independent auditor. (There are more details of this in Appendix 1, under *The Toll Rail Years*.)

The locus of vertical separation

There is an apparent simplicity to the logic of separating the railways' above-rail operations and assets from those of the below-rail, at the interface between wheels and rails. This locus of organisational separation has been consistently used wherever in the world there has been vertical separation. It separates one part of a railway that usually has been proven not to be suitable for privatisation (the networks of tracks and other fixed infrastructure which once built are mostly 'sunk costs') from the other part of the railway that is able to be privatised because its assets and operations are changeable, saleable and movable.

However, from an engineering viewpoint, it is a particularly sensitive locus at which to pull a railway organisation apart, because of the interdependence between the technologies of rail vehicles and infrastructure. The wheel-rail interface is, as one analyst described it:[574]

> "where so much of the investment, so much of the efficiency, and so much of the safety depend on the exact point of intersection between the steel wheels of the rolling stock and the steel rails."

The wheel-rail interface is the focus of much research and development in the rail industry:[575]

> "An examination of the railways trade press reveals that a large portion of the discussion of possible technological

improvements in the railways sector is focused on the ways that differences in rolling stock design and wheel design affect track wear, track maintenance requirements, and optimal track design, as well as the converse – the ways that track design and maintenance may affect rolling stock. Some examples are instructive:

"The modern railway environment of increasing axle loads, faster and longer trains, higher-adhesion locomotives, and greater cant deficiencies are all increasing the demands on the wheel/rail interface." ("Stress Reduction, Railroad Style," Railway Age, July 2002)

"The point where steel wheel meets steel rail is about the size of a dime, but bad profiles on one or both can lead to millions of dollars worth of problems for railroad car and maintenance-of-way people." ("Where Steel Meets Steel," Railway Age, May 2002)

"Vertically-integrated railways offer an excellent opportunity to optimize the 'total system' by ensuring that each element and each component is combined in sub-systems that work together and optimize the whole. An example is the optimization of the wheel-rail contact by establishing mutually compatible profiles that minimize contact stresses and wear while balancing curving and running stability performance. Optimizing contact surface friction through lubrication and restoration of rail profiles, and wheel profile maintenance enter the equations. At the next level, [freight and passenger car] suspension systems are tuned and modified to complement both curving and stability performance while accommodating track geometry and ride quality demands." ("North American Railfreight Benefits from Technical Advances," International Railway Journal, August 2002)"

Steel on steel: the wheel-rail interface, and the locus of vertical separation

Different approaches to managing care of the track

Sometimes, on any railway, wagons develop 'flat wheels' as a result of skidding along the rail track because the wagons' brakes have become locked-on during train braking. Flat wheels can be readily identified in moving trains, because they emit a rhythmic and continuous 'clunk-clunk-clunk' sound as the train passes by. Unfortunately, flat wheels are much less easy to detect when a train is stationary. If loaded wagons with 'flats' are allowed to continue to run, there is a risk of damage to the rail head, creating hair fractures that can grow if left unattended. The eventual result can be a suddenly broken rail, then a potentially serious derailment. Flat sections on wheels are removed on a specialised wheel lathe that has the wagon sitting stationary while one wheelset is spun and re-profiled. Such machines are expensive and are few and far between, so there can be days of wagon-time lost in getting wagons to a lathe and waiting for processing. Hence, a train operator who becomes aware of its wagons running with flat wheels faces service disruption and extra operational costs if the wagons are 'marked up' for repair at the next terminal. It has been estimated that 40% to 50% of wagon maintenance costs, and 25% of locomotive maintenance costs are related to wheel maintenance.[576]

In a vertically-integrated rail organisation, track maintenance costs are above the bottom line. Hence there is a shared responsibility between the operating and maintenance divisions for preserving rail integrity. Consequently, one could expect the organisation to be vigilant about detecting wagons with flat wheels in operation, having sufficient wagons in the fleet to replace temporarily withdrawn wagons, and providing the shunting resources to extract the offending wagons from trains. However, in a vertically-separate regime, the train operator lacks the incentive to remove wagons with flat wheels, because track providers do not impose a financial penalty when wagons run with flat wheels. In my experience of managing freight trains in the vertically-separated NSW network, the commercial imperative was to keep the trains running and to defer wheel maintenance to sometime in the future.

In Britain, after the vertical separation and privatisation of British Rail, the same phenomenon of lack of economic incentive to repair flat wheels was noted:[577]

> "While wheel irregularities are known to lead to track damage... there is less evidence that they adversely affect the vehicle structure... Thus in a railway system where vehicle owners and maintainers are insulated from direct track damage costs (such as the situation that now exists in Britain), there is less pressure on the mechanical side to maintain wheels in good condition."

The consequence of this practice of reducing the frequency (and costs) of rolling-stock wheel maintenance is that the separated track provider must become more vigilant in monitoring rail condition everywhere on its network. Specialised track recording vehicles have largely replaced visual inspections, with better results. They can gather a wealth of data on both rail condition and track geometry, for later analysis. The ARTC has also installed track-side monitoring devices to detect wheel defects in passing trains.[578]

When there is a derailment and, as is often the case, some uncertainty about the cause, (which may be track defect, rolling-stock defect, or some quirky interaction at the interface between wheel and rail), two different responses are possible. In a vertically-separated environment, blame-shifting and litigation are likely to occur, possibly lasting months and diverting management time from more productive use. In a vertically-integrated rail organisation, such negative activities can be avoided. (I have listened to this uncertainty of cause being discussed between mechanical and track engineers, as friendly lunchroom banter.)

Managing railway lines in summer

Managing access to lines on hot sunny days is an issue that many railways face. In times long past, track was laid with rails in standard lengths as they came from the manufacturer, and fastened together with bolted joints. Gaps were left between the ends of rails at the joints to allow for their extension in the heat. These gaps were the reason that trains could be heard making the characteristic 'clickety-clack' sound as they passed by. However, as train wheels passed over these gaps, they impacted the rail ends. The greater stresses at the rail ends could lead to fractures and eventually broken rails if they were left unattended. To avoid this risk of derailment, and to reduce the cost of track maintenance, the solution world-wide has been to weld lengths of rail together to create long lengths of continuous welded rail (CWR). When continuous welded rails are fastened to the sleepers, it has to be done when the rails are already extended, so that they will not suffer excessive compression when heated by the sun. This is easier said than done, and here is not the place for a technical explanation.

On many branch lines where the flow of traffic is heavily in one direction, the phenomenon of 'rail creep' has been observed. The wheels of the loaded wagons push the rails along in the direction of travel, perhaps as much as 10cm per kilometre of track. This seems a small amount, but issues arise when the creep is stopped by a fixed structure in the track, such as a bridge abutment, a turnout or a level crossing. Over a period of months, the continuing creep causes compression in the rails where it has been stopped. On hot days, the temperature in the rails is about twice the ambient air temperature, so the rails expand further, closing the gaps and causing more compression. In the heat of the afternoons, the risk of track failure, (called 'developing lateral misalignment') is greatest, whether the track is bolted rails or CWR. Under these conditions, the vibrations from a train passing can cause straight track to buckle. The straight track suddenly becomes an S-curve underneath the train, and a derailment of several wagons is often the result. How this risk is managed can vary from one network to another. It is not unusual to restrict train speeds, not so much to reduce the risk of track buckling, but to reduce the risk of any derailment being catastrophic.

A track buckle due to the combination of rail creep and heat-stressed track.

On 8 December 2016, V/Line (the Victorian government-owned vertically-separate country network track manager since 2007) issued without warning, a ban on trains running between noon and 10 pm on branch lines in the north and west of Victoria, on days when air temperatures reached 33 degrees Celsius.[579] There had been two derailments in this area in the previous summer, but the investigations to determine the cause had not by then been completed, and it appears V/Line acted out of extreme caution to protect its network (and its budget).[580] Air temperatures over 33 degrees were normal, so the ban would apply on the majority of days during the summer season of transporting the grain harvest. The disruption to planned grain train cycles probably had costly consequences:

- for grain growers and the grain marketing companies who were having a bumper harvest,
- for train operators and port operators who had all their people and equipment in place ready to move the harvest expeditiously,
- for road freight companies who were called upon at short notice to provide extra haulage,

- for other road users who faced increased risks from trucks on narrow rural roads, and
- for the track manager V/Line, which suffered loss of revenue.

This decision was that of a self-focused track manager in a vertically-separated environment. A vertically-integrated rail organisation with a known heat-stressed network would probably have managed the risk differently, because it would have been more aware of the consequences. Instead of eliminating the risk with a ban on train running, it would have implemented speed restrictions for trains over sub-standard track. It might even have planned for summertime, when the need for speed restrictions was predictable, by implementing network timetables incorporating reduced train speeds. By this means, the planned use of both the company's and the customers' resources would have minimised the extra costs, and kept the freight moving in a way that would enable all parties to plan their use of resources.

In response to customer complaints, V/Line announced that for the summer of 2017/18, it would impose speed restrictions on trains (but not temporary line closures) when air temperatures reached 36 degrees Celsius.[581]

Differences in sharing line capacity

In a vertically-integrated rail system, sharing the use of lines is done according to conventions about the relative priorities of different train types, where freight trains provide services from A to B and are not necessarily identifiable with just one customer. Train schedule adjustments are made iteratively to balance out competing priorities, and only then, to optimise use of finite line capacity.

By contrast, in a vertically-separated regime, train paths are negotiated and agreed in some detail, and become fixed in the short term at least, by being the subject of contracts between train operators and the track manager. Consequently, the latter has much less freedom to change agreed paths in order to accommodate new requests. This leads to inefficient use of potential line capacity, and in order to honour commitments, and prepare for traffic growth, line capacity should be augmented earlier than otherwise. But the very uncertainty of future new traffic makes it difficult to financially justify investment in new line capacity. (There is more on this in chapter 15, under *Government investment in rail network infrastructure*)

Investing for capability improvements to the vertically-separated interstate rail network

In 2007, the ARTC published a Strategic Investment Outline for its North-South Corridor. It explains very well both what it saw as its future mission, and the complex and conditional relationships between investments to improve the network, and the benefits such investments might generate.

The key characteristics of railway lines for freight train operators are – transit times from A to B, the reliability of those transit times, and line capacity. All are interdependent. The Outline explains:[582]

> *"Transit time*
>
> Reducing transit time is a critical input to a range of other important market outcomes.
>
> Reductions in transit time:
>
> • Improve [freight] availability, that is, the ability of rail to offer cut-off and delivery times that meet the needs of the market.
>
> • Increase capacity, as shorter track occupancy allows more trains for a given level of delay.
>
> • Reduces costs, directly for crew and indirectly where shorter transit times increase [train operators'] asset utilisation.

Transit time is a function of two things:
- Raw transit time, which is the time a train would take if it did not encounter any other trains, and
- Crossing delay, which is the amount of time that a train is delayed crossing oncoming trains (and to a much lesser extent where it is delayed by a train in front, or held to allow another train to overtake).

Reliability

The end-market for rail freight consistently identifies reliability as the key non-price consideration in decisions on modal choice. Poor reliability results in significant additional costs where, for instance, trucks are left to wait at a terminal for hours awaiting the arrival of a late running train. As unreliability is unpredictable, this further compounds the impact on cost and generally induces inefficiencies through the supply chain."

The ARTC (and any other separated track provider) will increase its revenue if it can attract more trains to its network. The key characteristics it can offer its train operating customers are competitive train transit times, and reliability of those times, because these service factors are important to freight shippers. To do this, it must have sufficient line capacity, not just for resilience in coping with short-term disruptions to planned operations, but also to accommodate future growth in traffic whenever new traffic presents itself. If it is not 'ahead of the game' in this way, the lead times involved in increasing capacity can be years, so it would take a very determined freight shipper to stay committed to using rail while waiting for capacity to be developed. Prospective intermodal and general freight shippers will not tolerate any delay in the availability of train paths. If a new train service cannot be organised within a month or so, the opportunity for new traffic on rail is lost.

Hence, a growth-focused track provider should always have some surplus line capacity:

- to enable growth in railed traffic as and when it presents,
- to reduce train transit times by reducing or eliminating train crossing delays en route,
- to give it resilience to provide high levels of reliability despite disruptions, and
- to avoid the disproportionate increase in its coordination costs as demand for train paths approaches practical line capacity and there is an increasing need to manage congestion.

In line with the above, the ARTC's stated business strategy in 2007 was[583]

> "to pursue growth for the rail industry on the North-South Corridor to assist in improving the role of rail in the Australian land transport task. ARTC believes that its success in growing the rail volume will flow through to increased revenues that will underpin the long-term sustainability of the business. ... To achieve a growth led business model means that the strategies for investment in the network must be driven by market need, not by what might be engineeringly elegant. This means that the focus of the company is very much on identifying what the market will respond to and developing the infrastructure to suit."

If this strategy seems familiar, it is. This is how new highways and highway deviations get identified, planned and funded. They do not rely on the certainty of a revenue stream to justify the investment. They ignore all the future uncertainties in factors that might affect usage levels. They consider only the benefits to potential users, and assume these will be used. (I wrote about the changed approach to CBAs for rail projects in the previous chapter – *The Economic Appraisal of Rail Network Projects – Inconsistent Project Cost Benefit Analysis Between the Modes.*)

15. The Profitability of Rail Networks

In Australia and New Zealand, highway networks are not expected to be profitable entities. Railways are an alternative and competing mode for freight on the highways. Yet often in the last forty years, railway networks have been expected to be profitable. In this chapter, I look at one instance where this expectation is reasonable (in WA), and others where it has been shown to be unsustainable, and why. But firstly, a little history on this topic.

Profitability of lines in former government-owned vertically-integrated railways

The Brew Report of 1996, on the options to deal with the financial situation of the vertically-integrated Australian National Railway, referred to 'unprofitable lines', as though their profitability was knowable and known.[584] Such was not normally the case. Normal railway accounting practices at that time meant that the profitability of individual railway lines within any network was rarely considered, because they were never separate accounting entities. This became an issue only when the possibility of closure was raised, because operations had declined or already ceased, and money had been saved by deferring maintenance of the fixed assets for many years. In that situation, a special study might be called for to determine the revenues, and the operating and maintenance costs. This was not usually a straightforward exercise, because it involved debatable assumptions and estimates.

Historically, in vertically-integrated railways, the revenues derived from hauling freight were never directly related to the costs, partly because many actual maintenance costs were unknowable on a line-by-line basis, being shared across the network and across many years. Accounting for such expenditure was done for the function, not the individual line. Thus, the normal practice for freight rates was based on charging 'what the market will bear' for different commodities and consignment sizes. (Even today, contracts between freight shippers and train operators retain some of this independence from actual costs, particularly when road haulage on subsidised highways is an alternative for the shipper.) Historically, data on rail freight revenues were associated only with the locations of traffic origin, so there was no routine allocation of revenue to each line that freight travelled on. Assessments of profitability were therefore necessarily arbitrary.

For rural branch lines that had lost originating traffic to competition from road, the majority of their remaining freight was inward, having originated elsewhere in the network. Hence revenue associated with the branch line would appear to be very low. As traffic levels on branch lines declined, annual costs were usually reduced by reducing frequency of service and by deferring maintenance of track and other assets. Decisions about closure or retention therefore took into account the potential cost of refurbishment of the track and other facilities, needed after years of maintenance neglect. Thus, these decisions were really predetermined by the previous decisions made to reduce costs in response to declining traffic volumes.

The Western Australian experience

The sale and lease arrangements for the privatisation of WestRail revealed, with hindsight, something about rail network profitability that has only more recently become clear. Whether

15. The Profitability of Rail Networks

lines are perceived to be profitable or unprofitable depends not so much on freight levels or absolute maintenance costs, but rather on the structure of ownership or control of the lines. In framing the Rail Freight System Act 2000, the WA government was determined that its rail network, including the less-used lines, should continue as it was for the benefit of the grain industry and rural communities. Hence it chose to dispose of its asset as a vertically-integrated rail system. (Some detail on this is provided in chapter 10 under Unfulfilled Hopes from Privatisation – A Hope for Continuation with Improvements.) The sale-and-lease was a whole-of-business transaction, with the buyer and the lessee being the Australian Railroad Group Pty Ltd (ARG). ARG was initially a joint venture between Wesfarmers and Genesee & Wyoming Inc. It comprised two separate legal entities: Australian Western Railroad (the buyer) and WestNet Rail (the lessee).

The lease agreement[585] included a formula for determining whether individual lines were economic:

> "in determining whether the maintenance of a line was uneconomic, the Avoidable Costs of maintaining that line for a three year period needed to be exceeded by 'all the additional revenue reasonably expected to be derived (directly or indirectly) by the Network Lessee and its Related Entities from the use of the Line'. The avoidable cost of a line is the difference between the long-term maintenance costs of the entire network and the long-term costs of the network not including the line in question."

Thus, the ARG corporate structure, and the words "and its Related Entities" mandated that freight revenue must be included when assessing whether a line should be regarded as uneconomic under the lease. However, when the WA rail network lease was sold as a separate entity in 2006, there ceased to be a 'Related Entity' of the lessee. Hence, the definition of revenue became limited to the revenue from access charges, which was a fraction of the former definition of revenue. In 2009, WestNet Rail claimed that most of the grain-only lines were uneconomic.[586] Negotiations led to the State government funding the resleepering of Tier 1 & 2 lines at a cost of $258 million,[587] in order to keep them open. However, it did not fund any work on the Tier 3 lines. The change in the structure of control of the network later made it possible for Brookfield to claim that the Tier 3 lines were uneconomic to maintain, enabling it to deny access to them by its customer CBH.

The Western Australian rail network is exceptional because it is the only vertically-separated one in Australasia that is managed by a private sector company. Therefore, to continue to operate, it must operate profitably. Two factors enable this situation. Firstly, all the freight moved intrastate is bulk commodities that, because of distances and/or volumes, would be much less economic to haul by road. In addition, these commodities are the shippers' inputs or outputs – they are not being shipped by third parties under competitive conditions. Hence, it follows that these commodities can only be moved by rail if the track provider can make a profit. Secondly, when Brookfield took over the network in 2010, it changed the contracting model. Previously (and still everywhere else in Australia where there is vertical separation, except where bulk coal is hauled) the track provider contracted only with train operators in relation to network access for trains. Now Arc Infrastructure (previously Brookfield Rail) has access agreements with 13 customers who are freight shippers, as well as with 6 train operators.[588] It has stated[589] that no two customers have the same terms and conditions. Arc Infrastructure's contracting model means:

- terms and conditions for the right to access the network are specific to each freight shipper, reflecting the customer's priorities
- Arc is able to tailor its investment to meet the operational capacity required by the customer,

particularly when new traffic is involved, and thus the access fees can reflect the full long-term cost of infrastructure provision
- access fees are a more transparent element of freight cost, are independent of the train operator's costs, and can be influenced by each customer's specific requirements
- freight shippers can more easily change their train operator, because train paths are an element of the customer's access agreement – instanced by CBH quitting the service and rolling-stock provided by Aurizon, and hiring Watco to operate CBH-owned trains.

In summary, the Western Australian rail network is a unique situation in Australasia. The commodities carried on it are all bulk flows (or long-distance interstate intermodal freight) for which transport by road is mostly not a realistic economic alternative. These freight flows enable Arc Infrastructure to operate profitably, and it has enhanced its profitability by making the tier 3 grain lines unavailable to use. Thus, Arc has pushed some bulk grain flows onto the road network, at a higher cost to CBH and its farmer-shareholders, the shires (as the road providers) and the environment (more GHGs than otherwise).

The Mt Isa Line experience

This section shows how the Queensland government's expectation of profitability changed, along with its perception of its own role in the provision of the rail network; also, how it resolved its policy conflict with its support for the regional economy in what is called the North West Minerals Province.

The phantom privatisation

Queensland Rail (QR) is a State Government entity. It owns and manages about 6,600 kms of track, the majority of the State's rail network. (The Central Queensland Coal Network was segregated and privatised in 2010.) The QR network includes the Mt Isa line which extends about 1000 kms west from Townsville in the north of the State. This line carries mineral concentrates, refined metals, fertiliser, mining inputs, bulk sulphuric acid, and cattle.[590] Train operators using the line are Aurizon, Pacific National Queensland, and since 2021 Qube Logistics trading as Progress Rail.

In January 2012, the Queensland Premier (of a Labor government) announced the findings of a preliminary evaluation study into the proposed Townsville Eastern Access Rail Corridor (TEARC) project.[591] The study's findings showed that a proposed $300m upgrade of the rail freight line between Mount Isa and Townsville could be built, would be profitable, and would deliver far-reaching benefits to North West Queensland. The TEARC project involved building a new 6.5km line connecting the Port of Townsville with the North Coast and Mount Isa lines in order to accommodate trains of 1400 metres in length. The government was seeking expressions of interest from private sector operators who would build and operate the new rail link.

Later in 2012, QR published a Rail Infrastructure Master Plan[592] for the Mt Isa line, which outlined possible scenarios for significant growth of line capacity to cater for possible new mining in the Mt Isa region. However, even for the base case of 8 mtpa, QR had a planned program to upgrade infrastructure. This included replacing steel sleepers with concrete sleepers and replacing lighter weight rails with heavy grade rail (60 kg/m). At that time, 380kms of track with 41kg/m or 47kg/m rail on steel sleepers remained, consisting of 116km in crossing loops and 264km on open track. The Master Plan stated that track maintenance expenditure would be funded from access charges, but funding of this track renewal expense was less certain:

> "Queensland Rail aims to continue the resleepering and rerailing to complete the transformation of the entire system to concrete sleepers and heavier rail. ... The

current timing of the program is dependent on sufficient growth occurring on the line to provide the additional funding for these works."

In other words, at current traffic levels with no traffic growth, this renewal program could be put on-hold due to funding restrictions.

On 30 April 2013, the State MP for Traeger, the electorate that includes most of the Mt Isa line, stated in Parliament that trains were travelling slowly because QR's cost-cutting on routine track maintenance was causing speed restrictions, which consequently reduced line capacity. This meant that some mineral ore traffic that was previously railed was now moving by road, at three times the cost to the miner of using the railway, because it could not get access to the railway. He said, in effect, that saving money on maintenance was reducing the effectiveness of service to freight shippers.[593]

> "The endgame here is to provide an efficient [sic] rail service, not to have an affordable rail service. Infinitely more important is that this critical asset is run as efficiently [sic] as possible to service all of the different industries along the line"

Of course, he meant that the line should be run **effectively** for all the freight shippers' benefit. (See the first section of chapter 9 for the distinction between efficiency and effectiveness.) He also spoke against the intention to privatise the Mt Isa line and the Port of Townsville as one entity, and cited the failed privatisations of railways in New Zealand and Tasmania.

In October 2014, the Queensland Government (then Liberal-National) announced its intention to award a long-term (50 + 49-year) lease to operate state-owned assets including the whole Mount Isa line and the associated port of Port Townsville.[594] The Treasurer was reported to have said:

> "Leasing some assets is the strongest and smartest choice because it will generate the funds needed to

bring the state's debt back under control, while ensuring Queenslanders always retain ownership."

Clearly the State Government's expectation at that time was that the private sector would value the opportunity to invest in this degraded line, operate it profitably, and relieve the government of financial pressures. (See in chapter 6, *Unfulfilled Hopes from Privatisation*.) There is no record of any private sector interest in this offer.

The benefit of State ownership

In December 2015, during the wet season for Northern Queensland, there was a train derailment on the Mt Isa line near Julia Creek. An Aurizon locomotive and all 26 wagons carrying sulphuric acid derailed where floodwaters had overtopped the track. The floodwaters had scoured the ballast and deformed the track. Hence, the track could not support the weight of the train.[595] One wagon leaked acid, causing environmental contamination.

Queensland Rail, still the owner-manager of the Mt Isa line, responded promptly but had to wait until the area dried out. It constructed an 800-metre deviation track to reopen the line by mid-January, bypassing the derailed rolling-stock which would be recovered later.[596] Media releases indicate that QR was under pressure from miners and other freight shippers.

> "We know that Queenslanders rely on the Mount Isa line for rail services and our priority is to build the deviation as quickly and as safely as possible to ensure we reopen the line."
>
> "We recognise the importance of the line to the local economy and shipping freight to port."
>
> "We are in regular communication with freight operators to ensure they are well informed of the progress of recovery works and to ensure we can process outstanding movements as quickly as possible."

15. The Profitability of Rail Networks

Sulphuric acid train 9T92, derailed near Julia Creek, Mt Isa line, on 27 December 2015.

The statement "We recognise the importance of the line to the local economy" represents an about-turn from the previous approach, that of maintenance cost-cutting then abandonment by privatisation. Certainly, by this time the State government was once again under the control of Labor, with a different view of the role for railways. In 2017, this government announced a $50 million investment in the Mt Isa line for rail replacement, new sleepers and ballast, new and improved passing loops, and upgrades to bridges. The purpose was to improve the capacity of the line and protect it against flooding.[597] In the 2018/19 State budget, the government confirmed an intention to spend $380m over five years on track maintenance and upgrades on the Mt Isa to Townsville route.[598]

Unfortunately for users of the line, it was hit by a bigger flood in February 2019, described as a once in 500 years event.[599] This caused erosion at 204 sites spanning 307 kms of track, including 40 kms of major washouts.[600] A PN train carrying zinc concentrate was stranded and damaged. QR mobilised a 400-person task force of contractors and its own staff from elsewhere in Queensland. Because of the remoteness of the

357

damaged areas, it created two temporary accommodation camps for workers, one near the site of the stranded train. It also constructed a 1200m deviation around the stranded train to allow for later retrieval and remediation work. The line was re-opened after twelve weeks, and the cost of this recovery effort was over $53 million

Flooding of the Mt Isa line in February 2019

One can only speculate what might have happened if the Mt Isa line had been transferred to private sector control before these flood events occurred. Possible outcomes:
- If the track provider had decided to reopen the line, there would likely have been weeks or months of delays in organising a recovery response, due to insurance assessments, budgeting and securing funds, and sourcing and contracting in all the necessary resources that the operator alone would not have had to call on from elsewhere in the QR network.
- If the track provider had decided that the cost of reopening the line was uneconomic, it would have had to call on the government to bail it out, and/or abandon its business and its customers, leaving the government to decide how best to respond. Resolving these issues could have taken many months

of optioneering and negotiations before any recovery work could start.

Fortunately, QR was resourced and able to get the line reopened as quickly as physically possible, because customer service, not profitability, was its priority.

In the 2019/20 State budget, the government announced a subsidy for freight on the Mt Isa line,[601] because trucks were using the parallel highway at no cost.

> "We ... will now provide $80 million over four years to reduce rail access charges on the Mount Isa Line, to drive the shift from road to rail."

This was tacit recognition that the profitability of the Mt Isa line was now considered irrelevant, because it has a vital role in enabling mineral exports worth billions of dollars annually. In December 2021, the Government announced it would fund a complementary freight coordinator service:[602]

> "Many smaller mining operators still rely exclusively on road transport. We want junior miners and potential new ventures, including in agriculture, to have access to the same efficiencies through freight trains that larger resource companies enjoy."

> "Taking more freight off our roads and onto the Mount Isa Line rail corridor would boost the productivity of our existing rail assets in the north-west and reduce road maintenance costs in the region."

One might say that the value of the Mt Isa line to Queensland, and to Australia, has now been recognised as almost priceless.

Most vertically-separated rail networks are inherently unprofitable

The current reality

Now that the majority of railtrack on the Australian continent is vertically-separated, it has become very obvious that most railway networks would be unprofitable in the long-term as business entities, in a strict accounting framework where a return on investments is expected. This is largely due to the competition from the extensive network of already-provided highways, where truckers contribute only a portion of the costs of highway management and maintenance, and not to their construction. Given the high degree of competition between road and rail for interstate general freight, road effectively sets a low upper limit to rail's access charges. In 2008, the ARTC was explicit about the access fees it could then realistically charge train operating companies:[603]

> "Price levels on the interstate network are constrained by the need for rail to remain competitive with road and sea. The current quantum of prices is essentially the residual left over from the cost of above rail operations. This price level was originally set at the time the transition was made to vertical separation and there has been little movement in those prices in real terms since that time."

Only where the private sector manages heavy haul networks (Arc Infrastructure in Western Australia and Aurizon on the Central Queensland Coal Network) are railway networks able to be profitable. Not coincidentally, these are natural monopolies, where bulk commodities are moved long distances in the millions of tonnes annually, and where shippers do not have a realistic option of moving such volumes of freight by road, or conveyor belt, at a lower cost. Hence, these shippers must pay the full long-term costs for using the rail network.

However, it has been reported that due to the difference between access charges of ARTC and Arc Infrastructure in

15. The Profitability of Rail Networks

WA, some intermodal freight from the eastern States is being off-loaded at the boundary between the two jurisdictions and on-forwarded by road to Perth,[604] some 550 kilometres. Arc's access charges are clearly too high for some interstate freight that can be moved by another mode.

Most State networks are subsidised

In Queensland, New South Wales and Victoria the State governments still own and pay for upkeep and upgrading of their vertically-separated regional lines. This is partly because they choose to operate regional passenger services, but also in recognition that, if this is not done, freight traffic will flow by road instead, which just increases their expenditure in other sectors (road maintenance, policing, and hospital costs). In 2012, the NSW government was quite explicit about this situation on its Country Rail Network:[605]

> "Rail operators can only compete with road because of the high level of subsidy paid by Government for the network."

In Victoria, the need for subsidy was learnt the hard way. The Victorian broad-gauge network was privatised by long-term lease in 1999, then largely neglected by the lessees. It came back into government control in 2007. (This story was told in chapter 11, under *The Privatisation of Four Vertically-Integrated Railways.*) Consequently, in 2007, the State Government, for the first time, had to deal with setting network access charges. A study report disclosed[606] that the first attempt had the charges set at a level that was thought to be able to recoup 40% of the efficient cost of managing and maintaining the network for freight in an average grain year. However, this was 250% higher than the lessee (PN) had been charging, and was found to be high enough to divert grain off rail and onto the roads. As a result, the study group recommended an immediate drop in access charges so the government could achieve its wider objectives of moving the grain harvests efficiently, protecting the fragile rural road network, and reducing road congestion around export ports. Up until this time, the marginal costs for grain exporters to ship grain by road were only fuel and wages. There was no additional cost for using the road network itself, whereas to ship by rail they had to pay an additional cost represented by the access charge. This charge negated the economies of scale offered from moving grain in train-loads. Illogically, the Government had expected grain shippers to contribute to the maintenance of the rail network, but not to the regional road network.

The lesson learnt here is that the Victorian country rail network would be very unprofitable as a trading entity, just as the regional road network would be if it were also a trading entity. However, taking the broader view, railing as much as possible of the grain harvests to export ports and urban flour mills is the lowest-cost option in the long run for the Victorian economy. It aids the export of millions of tonnes of Victorian grains at competitive prices, where the competition is against grain exported from other Australian States, and from overseas producers, such as Russia. In 2020, the Victorian Government set up a Rail Freight Working Group to focus on the future priorities for the rail freight network, stating[607]

> "Continued investment in rail freight infrastructure across Victoria will drive economic growth – creating important regional jobs and providing a major boost to the state's transport industry, agricultural sector and regional communities."

We saw in chapter 11 how, in Western Australia, the State government in 2010 agreed to pay for major periodic maintenance (resleepering) on the grain lines, so that they remained open for the benefit of the grain growing and marketing industry, and Arc Infrastructure could manage them profitably. Such payment for asset renewal is simply a subsidy; what was different was that that payment was made in response to coercion from the private sector company.

15. The Profitability of Rail Networks

In Tasmania and New Zealand, the unprofitability of the rail networks is somewhat hidden by the rail systems being vertically-integrated, although KiwiRail can show[608] that its above-rail operations make surpluses that only partially fund the cost of maintaining the network. Consequently, KiwiRail has been reliant, until recently, on an annual subsidy from the New Zealand Government. It also gets funded for capital works such as the rebuilding of the Picton to Christchurch line after the 2016 earthquake, the 2020 upgrading of the Northland line to convey high-cube containers on standard wagons, the proposed branch line to Marsden Point (Northland's port), and the repair and reopening of the previously-mothballed Napier to Wairoa line for the forecasted volumes of export log traffic in the 2020s.

The unprofitability of the railway networks in Australia and New Zealand should not be a surprise to their government owners, even if this is politically unpalatable. The World Bank, a bastion of capitalism and private enterprise, wrote this in 2011:[609]

> "International experience has demonstrated that full infrastructure cost recovery directly from railway users is infeasible in most countries, except those with highest density of traffic flows, particularly of freight traffic. Full cost recovery would include total capital costs of building, renewing, or expanding railway infrastructure networks. But similarly, full cost recovery is neither possible nor expected for national road networks, other than for trunk routes."

The ARTC's impossible mission

The ARTC was created to facilitate and grow the market share of interstate trade on rail, and it was also mandated to do so profitably. (How this occurred is described in chapter 9.) Over time, it has become increasingly clear that these two objectives are incompatible.

Having started in 1998 with the takeover of Australian National's lines, the ARTC leased the interstate lines in Victoria (1998), then in NSW (2004). To succeed in attracting more freight to rail, it invested continuously to upgrade these previously neglected lines. It spent a lot of money in just a few years that was not expected to have payback until decades into the future. Consequently, in 2005, the ARTC was assessed by or for the OECD as[610]

> "unlikely to meet long term network costs unless significant volume growth eventuates and generates significantly greater revenue to off-set current price settings."

The ARTC had adopted an approach to pricing that supported its objective of growing the volume of freight on rail, which had been endorsed by the ACCC. As it explained to the Productivity Commission in 2006:[611]

> "ARTC has sought to set access pricing at a level that will enable rail to be competitive with road in markets served by the interstate network. With the current level of utilization of ARTC's network, however, pricing at this level results in the amount of revenue collected by ARTC not being sufficient for the long-term economic sustainability of its network. It is ARTC's strategy to grow volumes in the long term, such that rail can remain competitive and achieve long-term sustainability of its asset.
>
> ARTC considers that this strategy is the only realistic one available to achieve long term sustainability of the interstate rail freight industry in an environment where its main competitor (long haul, heavy road transport) is not paying for the full economic cost of the infrastructure it uses."

In 2006, the Productivity Commission (PC) was keen to show that doubt about long-term sustainability of the ARTC's

15. The Profitability of Rail Networks

(and State Governments') rail networks was evidence for their being subsidised:[612]

> "Finding 6.5: Rates of return on rail infrastructure have generally been low. If sustained, at some point tolerance by government of low returns amounts to implicit subsidisation. Based on available evidence, it is difficult not to conclude that subsidisation through this means is already occurring."

The PC's implication was that the ARTC was expected by its owner (the Commonwealth) to be a profitable business, and therefore it was irrational that it be subsidised by its owner. In my view, the real risk was that the expectation of profitability would be revealed as unsustainable. For this reason, the ARTC changed its focus.

As we saw in chapter 9 (under *The Australian Rail Track Corporation – Shifting Priorities*), from 2009 the ARTC declared that it would "operate the business under commercial principles". Access prices have since been steadily increased, and the ARTC is now able to cover its operating costs, and pay tax and dividends to the Commonwealth government. However, rail's market share of interstate intermodal freight in the eastern States has dropped markedly; on the Sydney-Melbourne sector it was 11% in 2006,[613] down to 1% in 2019.[614] The CEO of Pacific National alleged this was the result of increasing rail access charges after the Transport & Infrastructure Council agreed to freeze heavy road vehicle charges in November 2015, and again in 2017[615] for two more years. The ARTC still carries lower-value freight on parts of the Sydney-Melbourne sector, such as bulk and containerised grains and mineral ores, but these originate in the regions, sometimes on State-owned branch lines. This traffic is not the interstate containerised general freight that the ARTC was originally set up to capture.

There is no reason why the ARTC could not be successful, except that its owner still expects it to be profitable. In this case, success and profitability are not the same. The Commonwealth is the only government rail network owner in Australia with this expectation. Apparently, it cannot see that profitability is a poor measure of success for a rail network that must compete for traffic with what would be a hugely unprofitable National Highway System if the same measure were to be used.

The ARTC is still reliant on equity investments or grants from the federal government for funding new lines and upgrades to existing lines. For example, in 2017 it created a 20% increase in the capacity[616] of its single-track Melbourne to Adelaide line, by increasing the lengths of six passing loops to enable trains up to 1800 metres long to operate.[617] However, this project had to wait until the Commonwealth granted $15 million for this project, a paltry sum in the overall scheme of things.

The ARTC's major project in recent years has been the Inland Rail route to connect Melbourne and Brisbane directly. Projected in 2015 to cost $4.7 billion, the estimate in 2020 had risen to $20 billion.[618] The Commonwealth's funding method is by injections of equity over several years. In the lead up to the 2019 federal election, the Labor party was supportive of this project, but critical of its financing:[619]

> "Albanese has been highly critical of the Coalition's decision to move Inland Rail's funding off Budget, meaning the project will need to make a return on investment.

[Anthony Albanese was reported to have said:]

> "The CEO of the Australian Rail Track Corporation delivering this project, John Fullerton, conceded to us in Senate estimates that [Inland Rail] wouldn't produce a return"

The problem here is unrealistic expectations. Investment in a railway line such as Inland Rail is not a conventional business investment. It is a nation-building economic enabler, like a highway or a nationwide communications network, built for the benefit of the whole community. Clearly, there is still some confusion in Canberra about the purpose of the project and of the ARTC.

Should the Commonwealth have sold the ARTC?

The proposition and response

In 2014, the National Commission of Audit (NCOA)[620] included in a wide-ranging suite of recommendations to the Commonwealth government that the ARTC should be sold. The government had been seeking advice on how to reduce expenditure in a sustainable way, and that included the possibility of privatising its assets and businesses. The ARTC was one of ten government-owned bodies about which it wrote, from an ideological perspective:[621]

> "The Commission considers that Commonwealth bodies that operate in contestable markets should be privatised."

Its qualifying comments about the ARTC included:[622]

> "ARTC's policy objective is to encourage modal shift of freight from road to rail. ARTC manages two distinct operating businesses, the interstate network and the Hunter Valley network, which provide train operators with access to move passengers and a range of commodities ... ARTC derives over 55 per cent of its revenue from its Hunter Valley network. The Commonwealth could privatise either all of ARTC, or just the Hunter Valley network."

The government undertook to conduct a scoping study to determine options for the future management, operation, and ownership of the ARTC, together with the implications for ARTC's track leases and wider issues to do with the intergovernmental agreements that established the ARTC. It authorised this scoping study from consultants in December 2015,[623] but the study result appears not to have been made public, so the outcome is unknown. However, the government quietly announced its decision in the 2016 Budget. The Finance Minister was reported to have said [624]

> "We will retain the ARTC in the hands of the Australian Government ownership to enable the [Inland Rail] project to access funds at the lowest cost to the taxpayer."

Given that the Inland Rail is a ten-year project, the question of selling the ARTC has been deferred for a later government to deal with, if the question arises again.

It is worth noting that the scoping study was not asked to address the political question whether the ARTC **should** be privatised, but rather to address the pragmatic and legal matters to answer the question, **could** the ARTC be privatised? These two questions are not the same, the answers being dependent on different criteria.

In its brief assessment of the ARTC, the NCOA approached its task with a predetermined objective (that the Commonwealth should not own trading businesses), sought and found 'facts' that suited its objective, sufficient to justify its recommendation that ARTC be privatised. (See below, under *Why invest in rail network infrastructure?* for an explanation of one of its false assumptions.) The Commission did not acknowledge taking any advice from the ARTC; it just demonstrated its ignorance of the purpose and work of the ARTC. Therefore, its recommendation for privatisation was naïve and lacked credibility, and ultimately it was rejected.

Would a sale of the ARTC to the private sector have been realistic?

Given what we now know about the economics and profitability of rail networks, should a future sale of ARTC need to be seriously considered, or is its retention by the Commonwealth

15. The Profitability of Rail Networks

Government a 'no-brainer'? The ARTC is the only one of the government-owned vertically-separated rail networks in Australia that was set up as a for-profit business.[625] This was from its inception in 1997, and that requirement has not changed.[626]

> "The ARTC will be required to act as a commercial entity with no ongoing subsidy from Government."

However, since its creation it has received financial support every year, mainly for capital works. Is that support the equivalent of subsidies? Is over two decades of government support sufficient evidence that the ARTC cannot exist as a fully self-supporting commercial entity? If the ARTC were sold, would the government want to be seen continuing to provide subsidies to provide profit for a private sector company? Not likely. If there were no subsidies, would the new owner want to invest in assets that become sunk investments with no resale value? No. As we have seen in the previous section, as the ARTC raised its access fees to maintain profits, so rail's market share of interstate containerised freight dwindled. How sustainable is that?

It is clear that the ARTC cannot be operated as a conventional profit-making business, and that should make it unsaleable. However, that does not deem it to be a failure. It is just a public service with inappropriate expectations currently being placed on it.

Apart from its unprofitability, it also has a reason-for-being that makes it incompatible with private sector ownership. The ARTC is the outcome of previous federal government attempts to commercialise the railway industry. It has been used to support the vertical separation of the rail industry. However, in addition to its functional purpose of maintaining and managing the interstate network for all who seek access to it, it has another intrinsic function. It has a moral obligation, if not a legal one, of guardianship – the preservation in perpetuity of the past investments in railway routes by various State governments. These investments were made not for profit, but done on behalf of the community at large, in the same way and with the same purpose as investing in roads and highways, i.e., to facilitate transport and trade. The ARTC shares this function of guardianship of the nation's railway networks with various State-based organisations, whether or not this function is explicitly acknowledged – by Queensland Rail, Transport for New South Wales, the Victorian Rail Track Corporation, the Western Australian Public Transport Authority, and TasRail.

Government investment in rail network infrastructure

Why invest?

Given that all but the heavy-haul rail networks are unprofitable, governments and the public need to know why they should continue to invest in their freight rail networks.

The first and obvious answer is to maintain the networks that are now carrying millions of tonnes of freight in bulk (grains, coal, mineral ores, logs and manufactured goods) lest they degrade and become unusable, and the freight pours onto the roading networks. No-one wants the added cost, congestion, noise and other pollution that would result. Governments have understood this as a political reality from the 1970s onwards. Hence the provision of subsidies that all State Governments, and the New Zealand Government, have made in various ways over the decades through to the present time. We saw in chapter 5 that the subsidies paid to government-owned railways in the 1970s, 1980s and 1990s were mostly retrospective, to make up for the deficits incurred. These subsidies were therefore not productive, not enabling improvements in the rail systems, and therefore an unsustainable waste of public money.

Rail network organisations are now much more labour-efficient than they used to be thirty years ago, through mechanisation of maintenance tasks, and automation of signalling and of data collection about asset condition.

15. The Profitability of Rail Networks

Government financial support for rail networks nowadays is not to keep them going, per se, but to promote railways as enablers of efficient economic activity.

Investment purposes

There are two main purposes now for governments to invest in their rail networks:
- major periodic maintenance (MPM), which addresses the reality that rail assets slowly degrade with time and normal use, and
- increasing line capacity to enable traffic growth.

MPM investment is especially needed because of the deferral of this type of work during the years of privatisation in Victoria, Tasmania and New Zealand; also in NSW where the first separate network owner (the Rail Access Corporation) was assessing maintenance projects as though it were a private sector company. (See in chapter 13, under *The economic appraisal of rail network projects – the NSW experience*.) MPM work, such as replacing wooden sleepers with concrete ones, should lead to a reduction in network operating costs, and hence a payback. The gain is in the reduced costs of inspection and replacement of sleepers, because wooden ones have a working life of about 15 to 20 years, depending on both use and climatic factors. By contrast, concrete sleepers can have an infinite life of at least 70 years, which is therefore the actual payback period for the investment. Long payback periods have not usually been considered in conventional cost/benefit analyses that incorporate discounted cash flows, but the reality is that many railway assets have long lives.

The second type of investment **cannot guarantee any financial return**. It is the same situation as for building new highways and deviations. For rail networks, investments in track and terminals add capacity, and hence potential value for the network's customers; investments such as curve easements, better signalling, rerailing with heavier rail, extending crossing loops. These create potential benefits that the train operators can use to improve their operations, and in turn, use for their marketing: better average train speeds, higher axle-loads and better load-to-tare ratios, longer heavier trains. These, in turn, can make rail services and pricing more attractive to freight shippers, or their agents the freight forwarding companies. Thus, in the vertically-separated environment, there are sequential stages of potential gains, tenuously linking three groups in the transport supply chain, that connect the investment with the payback of more business on rail. It looks like this:

The ARTC (or any other track provider) invests in some kind of track improvement, so that

- Freight trains can run faster and more reliably, so
- Train operators may save on crew and fuel costs, enabling reduced prices, and
- The train travel time gains may have commercial/marketable value, which
- Freight shippers may or may not like, compared to using trucking.

If all these potential gains are realised, then the ARTC will get a payback in the form of having more GTKs on its track, for which it will be paid through track access charges. The payback may come weeks or years after the investment is completed, because of the time it can take to make all the connections above, and the ARTC has no control over this. If the ARTC had been privatised, its new owner would not tolerate such uncertainty about its investments, and therefore it would not make such investments. Only governments can make this kind of investment, because enabling improved productivity in the economy is part of their function. Why else do governments build highways to enable heavy road freight vehicle use, and (mostly) allow their unrestricted access?

The following is an example of confusion between the two purposes for rail network investment. In 2012, the ARTC invested in concrete sleepers on the Parkes to Broken Hill line, which runs through territory that is remote and therefore expensive to put maintenance crews into. This MPM project was criticised in the National Commission of Audit (NCOA) report (see above, under *The proposition and response*) because it[627]

> "had marginal benefit-cost ratios, [was] not needed to meet future demand projections or did not effectively address expected capacity constraints".

The criteria the NCOA used were based on expectations of traffic growth.[628] In its ignorance, the NCOA had judged an MPM project by criteria suitable for the second type of investment described above. This is like saying: "It's a waste of money keeping a Clydesdale horse because it will never win the Melbourne Cup."

Combined purpose investments

Often, rail investment projects combine the two purposes described above. In March 2016, the Commonwealth announced a three-year track renewal program for the 600 kms between Adelaide and Tarcoola, fully funding its $252 million cost.[629] The Whyalla steel mill[630], close to the section of line to be re-railed, would supply 60kg rails to replace the existing 47kg rails on this line. Infrastructure Australia describes this project thus:

> "The project represents an acceleration of phase one of the 25-year long, phased re-railing program outlined in Australian Rail and Track Corporation's Asset Management Plan. The project will bring forward the upgrade of 600 km of track from 23 Tonne Axle Load (TAL) capabilities, to 25 TAL, to completion by 2019. This will support the operation of double-stacked trains at speeds of up to 115 km/hour between Adelaide and Tarcoola. ... The project will deliver economic benefits through reduced travel time for interstate freight, and increased reliability on the east-west rail corridor. The proponent's stated benefit-cost ratio for the project is 1.1 (7% real discount rate)."

These financial benefits will go largely to ARTC customers. This is asset renewal and upgrade being funded as though it were a highway upgraded from a regional road. Without any fanfare, the Commonwealth changed its approach to funding railway infrastructure, no longer expecting the private sector to invest, and not expecting to make money as a stand-alone business would. Hence it now sees its role to include funding the Inland Rail project (briefly described in chapter 12).

The major benefits from this new line connecting Brisbane and Melbourne directly will not be seen in the ARTC's bottom line. It has been estimated[631] that 80% of the total financial benefits from such projects accrue to the train operating companies, in the form of crew-time and fuel savings, and train running time savings, which can make them more competitive against road carriers. Ultimately, the freight shippers and the Australian economy stand to get the long-term benefits.

Inland Rail is not the only major rail project that could benefit the interstate transport markets. There are still major deviations needed to remove the steep grades and curvature, built by State railways over a century ago. Today, these severely limit train speeds. Some were identified for deviations well before the ARTC came into existence in 1998:

- On the Melbourne to Adelaide line: between Geelong and Ararat in Victoria, and in the Adelaide Hills of South Australia,
- On the Sydney to Melbourne line: Menangle to Aylmerton, Breadalbane to Yass, and Bowning to Cootamundra[632],
- On the Sydney to Brisbane line between Hexham and Stroud Rd[633].

New Zealand: ways used to fund the railway network

User pays: one access agreement with two interpretations

We saw in chapter 11 that the New Zealand government moved to vertically separate and take over the rail network, when the imminent financial collapse of Tranz Rail Ltd threatened to halt rail operations and effectively close the network to freight shippers. It was acknowledged that the network was run-down from insufficient maintenance, particularly of those assets that required periodic repair or renewal at multi-year intervals, such as timber bridges. As assets deteriorated, train speed restrictions would be applied for safety reasons. This slowed average train speeds, insidiously affecting the quality of customer service, but enabling Tranz Rail to report continuing profitability. By this means, and with the corporate 'strategic ignorance' [634] engendered by the dominant accounting view of the business, the inherent unprofitability of the rail network could continue unrecognised for some years, but not forever. The Tranz Rail strategy of sweating the assets failed as a long-term strategy, but it is clear now that the first owners of Tranz Rail intended that a long-term strategy would be someone else's problem. (The benefits and consequences of sweating the assets was covered in chapter 11, under *New Zealand: An Analysis of Tranz Rail's Difficulties*.)

As a result of the government's acquisition of the rail network, it was managed as a vertically-separated network from 2004 to 2008. It had only one freight rail customer, Toll NZ Ltd. The two parties agreed to the concept that Toll should pay an access fee to ONTRACK, but they never reached agreement on the components. (See in Appendix 1, under *The Toll Rail Years*, for the details.) A dispute resulted, which eventually went to mediation. The basis of the dispute was the differing objectives of each party. ONTRACK wanted to maintain the network to a standard suitable to last for future years, and also to meet the government's requirement to cease needing subsidies eventually. Hence, its access fees for future years were based on budgets that met these objectives. Toll had a current-year focus, and wanted to avoid any track expense that was more than absolutely necessary in the immediate future. The Independent Auditor's comments in the resolution of the dispute were illuminating with respect to long-term sustainability of the rail network:[635]

> "I accept Toll's point that it should not be required to pay more for maintenance **than it would as part of a vertically-integrated business**, and that consequently the maintenance charge should not be increased through ONTRACK adopting a role as guardian of the network. Commerciality should prevail." (My emphasis)

Presumably his understanding of a vertically-integrated business was as a private-sector business, as Tranz Rail had been since 1993. It had been considered good business practice by Tranz Rail and Toll Rail to use the remaining life of some assets without renewal, the strategy of sweating the assets. Clearly, the Independent Auditor thought it was solely the role of the government to protect the future of the rail network, as its owner and guardian, and that this was a non-commercial issue. This would put it on the same basis as for the highway network, the construction and maintenance of which was funded by the government.

Although the dispute about how to set the access charge was resolved by mediation, the causes of it remained unresolved. The only agreement between the two parties was that the National Rail Access Agreement was unsatisfactory for both. The Government saw itself having to continue to subsidise an Australian-owned company due to its partial payment of access fees; if no change could be achieved, this outlook was unacceptable. Thus, it began an exploration of options that would lead to the eventual return of the above-rail operations to government ownership. (This is covered in Appendix 1, under *Rethinking the Relationship Between Government and Rail,* and *How the Government and Toll Reached a Sale Agreement.*) The deal was announced in May 2008, with the start-up of KiwiRail under government control from July. In November of that year, the Labour government, which had just bought back the railways, lost the election to the right-wing party that had sold the railways in 1993. (The change of ownership of railways was not a significant electoral issue in this change of government.)

Drip-feed, with reluctance

The new government still had an unwavering belief in the virtues of private enterprise, and consequently, it had little interest in owning, let alone restoring, its run-down railway system. Also, after the Global Financial Crisis, it was very focused on paying down public debt. Reluctantly, it continued subsidies for network maintenance, but put KiwiRail under strong and continuous pressure to work towards profitability, or at least to be as efficient as possible. The Transport Minister was quoted in 2015, after announcing funds from the Budget, as saying:[636]

> "KiwiRail must continue to drive significant efficiency and productivity improvements to reduce an ongoing level of Crown funding required."

(A fuller story of this fraught relationship appears in Appendix 1, under *KiwiRail.*)

Over some years, KiwiRail responded by mothballing 335 route-kms of two lightly-used lines, after damage done by a derailment and a storm. Also, it ceased hauling bulk fertilisers, because the variable costs of carrying this traffic were too high; fertiliser was corrosive for the specialised wagons, and the service required trains to shunt at rural locations where otherwise there was no need to shunt. This was an efficiency achieved by strategic abandonment – let the traffic go by road, at someone else's cost.

Funds from annual government budgets to support KiwiRail continued over the nine years of the right-wing government, totalling nearly $5 billion.[637] The Finance Minister was quoted as saying[638]

> "It would cost a couple of hundred million dollars a year, but the public wanted it. [It] wants the … Government to own a rail company and to have rail, because they regard the alternatives as putting too many trucks on the road."

This drip-feed method of support meant that KiwiRail could not plan longer-term capital projects with any certainty of having funds available. That this annual response kept happening indicates that this government was stuck in the belief that a vertically-integrated KiwiRail **should** be profitable, and therefore it **must** be so eventually. It was a paradigm that obscured the reality. (The evidence for this is in Appendix 1, under *KiwiRail: Government Expectation of* Profitability and *The Plan for Eventual Profitability*.) The government had maintained KiwiRail as a State-Owned Enterprise (SOE) which, under the SOE Act, required it to be profitable as if it were owned by the private sector. However, the funding provided year by year by government was clearly inconsistent with the intent of the Act. Not until 2017 was the Transport Minister reported[53] to have hinted at the option of

> "removing the requirement for KiwiRail to be commercially viable and to make a profit".

It is likely that he knew by then the value of KiwiRail should not be measured solely by profitability.

Change the perception of railways in the economy

The 2017 election saw a new pro-rail government in office. Soon after the election, a report was released that had been suppressed for a year by the previous government. Commissioned by the NZTA, it was a study conducted by the professional services firm Ernst & Young (EY)[639] that looked at some of the wider economic benefits the rail network brings to New Zealand. It stated[640]

> "The areas where rail is delivering for New Zealand include cutting congestion, reducing greenhouse gas emissions, improving safety on our roads and lowering spending on road maintenance and upgrades.
>
> "These benefits do not show up on the balance sheet, but they are very real, and they make a huge contribution to New Zealand.
>
> "They need to be considered when choices are made about the transport options available, and how to allocate resources."

While many of these quantified benefits came from the operation of passenger services in Auckland and Wellington, there was still a net benefit from freight rail operations of $354 million[641] per year, which was well above the size of the annual subsidy the government had been paying towards track maintenance.

In 2019, the government used this new knowledge to announce boosted investment in KiwiRail over the next two years. Here is an extract from the Finance Minister's Budget speech in parliament:[642]

> "Mr Speaker, rail has huge benefits for New Zealanders' wellbeing, including unlocking regional economic growth, reducing emissions and traffic congestion, and preventing deaths and injuries on our roads. The previous Government took a hands-off approach and left rail in a state of managed decline.
>
> Today we begin to turn this around.
>
> Budget 2019 invests more than $1 billion over the next two years in modernising KiwiRail. These are the first steps in implementing our Future of Rail programme. This includes $375 million for new locomotives and wagons,

$331 million to invest in track and other supporting infrastructure, $300 million from the Provincial Growth Fund for regional rail and $35 million to begin the process of replacing current ferries that are nearing the end of their life."

Later that year, the government announced a significant change to KiwiRail's capital funding,[643] enabling it to access the National Land Transport Fund, which up till then had been used primarily to fund highways. This change enables multi-year investment programs to be approved, and allows KiwiRail to plan for long-term investments. These include the design and acquisition of new larger interisland road-rail ferries, and the new berths that will need to be built in Wellington and Picton specifically for them.

At the time of writing, KiwiRail is still a State-Owned Enterprise, for want of some more appropriate structure. For that reason, it is still reluctant to invest in some asset renewals. In July 2020, it announced it would close the last remaining branch line in Southland if $5 million could not be found to refurbish the line, including the old timber bridge at the Oreti River.[644] The line goes to just one customer, a coal mine shipping 150k tonnes per year. The mine's alternative would be to be to truck the coal to Invercargill to load onto the railway there. Faced with this expense, the coal miner agreed to provide the $5 million for line maintenance.[645]

Postscript, July 2024

In October 2023, the Labour-led government lost the general election. It has been succeeded by a coalition government of three right-wing parties. Early indications are that this new government will restrict capital funding for KiwiRail sourced from the National Land Transport Fund in the future. This is a rejection of the funding procedure devised by the previous government, which was an attempt to "level the playing field", i.e. to reduce the competitive inequality between road and rail.

15. The Profitability of Rail Networks

The new government has also announced that it will not fund the planned new larger interisland road-rail ferries, and the new berths that would be needed for them, due to a blowout in projected costs. Months later, in mid-2024, there has been still no announcement about any future ferries. Furthermore, there appears to be no interest by the Government in maintaining the rail connection between the North and South Islands, which has existed since 1962.

As a result of the withdrawal of funding, any program to replace KiwiRail's interisland ferries has been set back by some three years, due to long lead times. Consequently, KiwiRail will need to keep operating its existing ferries beyond their thirty-year design lives, with increasing risks of failures in service.

These politically-driven changes are typical of the existential problem for railways in New Zealand, one that has existed since the 1980s. The influence of politics on railways is described more fully in the first section of Chapter 17.

Part E
Epilogue

16. Some observations

17. Summing-up

16. Some Observations

What follows in this chapter are some personal observations about the transformation of the freight rail industry not covered elsewhere.

Simplification of the traffic task

In the last four decades, during which the freight rail industry in Australasia has been transformed, one common feature has been a major reduction in the variety of traffic and wagon flows to be managed, defined by the total number of origin-destination (OD) combinations. For example, on the New Zealand network, there were about 10,000 OD pairs experienced in the year 1983, with about 400 of these being regular moves.[646] Despite KiwiRail now carrying twice the net tonnage that NZR did in 1983, the number of regular OD pairs nowadays is about 300.[647] Traffic flows on all networks are so much more concentrated now, enabling a majority of point-to-point trains in the operating plans which can bypass intermediate marshalling yards. Many of these trains move one commodity for one customer. This, and computerisation, has made routine tasks such as customer invoicing and wagon fleet management very much simpler and cheaper.

This simplification of traffic task enabled many continuing efficiency gains, both before and after privatisation, by reducing the need for all types of operating resources. The closure of little-used private sidings, branch lines and rural stations enabled a big reduction in staff, both in the regions, and at shunting yards in the cities because train marshalling became much less complex. After these closures, turnouts to sidings could be replaced (wholly or partly) with straight rails, thus removing maintenance hotspots, and enabling gradual reductions in track maintenance forces.

A partial replacement: This turnout on the main line to an abandoned private siding has had its frog replaced by a piece of straight rail. The frog is the most maintenance-costly component of a turnout.

Private sector freight train operators that took over government owned rail organisations were quick to apply the 80:20 rule; i.e., to rid themselves of the 20% of traffic that took 80% of the effort, including wagon-load and less-than-trainload traffic. Pacific National, from its beginnings, chose not to take on some smaller traffic flows that were part of FreightCorp's business in NSW. Typically, their destinations were Port Botany, which required extra work to manage train arrival times to suit the stevedores for unloading containers at wharf sidings. This enabled some of the small companies to pick up these contracts. (More of this in chapter 12, under *How competition evolved in Australia – New South Wales*.) In another example of

PN discarding less-than-trainload traffic, it abandoned all train its services on Victoria's Portland branch in 2004 during a poor grain harvest, because the other traffic, that it had inherited from Freight Australia, (aluminium ingots) was too sporadic.[648]

In NSW, train operators were essentially wholesalers of rail transport, providing whole trains of fixed capacity for one or two customers. They had replaced the retail services of FreightCorp, and in so doing, had greatly simplified train marshalling, contract administration and marketing. Selling whole trainload capacity was and is far easier than catering for occasional or exceptional traffic. This was especially so in the new environment of vertical separation, where trains operated on a shared rail network. For the train operator, this meant having to book train paths and schedule trains, sometimes in advance of having secured the traffic that would be moved on each train. Hence the only customer worth dealing with was one who could provide train-loads of freight on a regular basis.

The trend for train operating companies to chase only regular traffic flows also affected the grain industry. Its traffic flows in each State could be millions of tonnes, but with variability in the size of grain harvests from year to year. State governments had previously invested in rail lines and rolling-stock, to move at least an average-sized harvest to cities and ports. Their reasons were to preserve fragile rural roads and to support the rural and regional economies. Poor utilisation of rail assets in poor years was less of a concern than good management of harvest transport in good years. After privatisation, grain marketing companies still wanted to use railways, but they experienced some frustrations. PN abandoned the Victorian grain traffic in 2007 following two years of drought and small harvests. GrainCorp in NSW, and CBH in WA, invested in their own rolling-stock, partly to ensure that rail transport of the grain harvests could continue regardless of the size of the annual harvest, as well as to better control the costs. (The detail of this development is in chapter 11, under *Western Australia*.)

TranzRail continued NZ Rail's strategy to exit minor traffics and to cease servicing small towns and rural locations. However, it did not have the luxury of abandoning some traffic flows because, although there were train-load quantities of coal, logs and milk, many major customers used the rail system to distribute products to several destinations, or to consign empty containers to multiple destinations. Shipping companies also used the railways to consolidate export containers, from multiple points of origin, into specific ports for specified ship sailings. Hence, wagon-load business still constituted the majority of business available to Tranz Rail in the 1990s. Wagon-load consignments are more complex to manage than whole train-loads; information systems are required to keep track of, and link, individual containers and consignments to individual wagons, and to move them all expeditiously on sequences of interconnected trains.[649]

The legacy of the reform process in NSW

The consequences of the division of the State's rail network

Prior to the start of Rail Reform, there were five separate vertically-integrated railway systems on the Australian mainland. The three in the eastern States were effectively broad service organisations transporting all types of freight, except that separately and jointly they did not service interstate freight at all well. Breaks-of-gauge at the State borders were the physical expression of severe limitations in the service offering.

With the creation of the interstate standard-gauge network, and of the ARTC in 1998 to be a "one-stop-shop" for servicing the users of that network, the Commonwealth Government assumed it had solved this problem. There were two outcomes from this assumption.

Firstly, upgrading of the interstate rail network was grossly under-funded for many years, while the national highway network was continuously funded. Consequently, the ARTC was left unable to offer freight shippers an attractive alternative to the highway system, and the intercity market share on rail steadily declined over the next twenty years. Secondly, the creation and expansion of the ARTC split the previously unified managements of the State networks in NSW and Victoria. This left the intrastate branch lines as State responsibilities, administratively disconnected from the trunk lines and each other. As a result, a few State borders were replaced by many more jurisdictional borders, called interfaces.

Network interface management became a complex issue for train operators in three ways: negotiating train paths across the interfaces, contingency planning because contiguous network providers do not coordinate the timing of their track possessions (see below), and in daily operations. Delays in progressing trains from one jurisdiction to another sometimes lead to further delays, which can create crew fatigue management problems, and/or potential safety issues.

For example, RailCorp in NSW has a strict curfew on weekdays that excludes freight trains from its metropolitan passenger network (MPN) twice a day, for a total of seven hours. Freight trains paths are planned to precede or follow the curfews. RailCorp has long refuge sidings located where freight trains approaching the MPN can be parked for the duration of the morning curfew period. However, if a late-running overnight train cannot exit the MPN by 6am onto the metropolitan freight network (MFN), managed by the ARTC, Rail Corp will stop it at an outer refuge siding from 5am onwards. The crew has to stay on board and wait until at least 9/30am to proceed. Frequently, they have to be relieved by another crew to avoid 'busting their hours', i.e., exceeding their maximum period of duty, prescribed by NSW law. The cost of providing an extra relief crew to ensure the completion of the train's trip can negate the profit to be had from running it.

The map on the next page shows the division of the NSW rail network from January 2012, after the transfer of the country network (CRN) from ARTC management to the John Holland Group (JHG).[650]

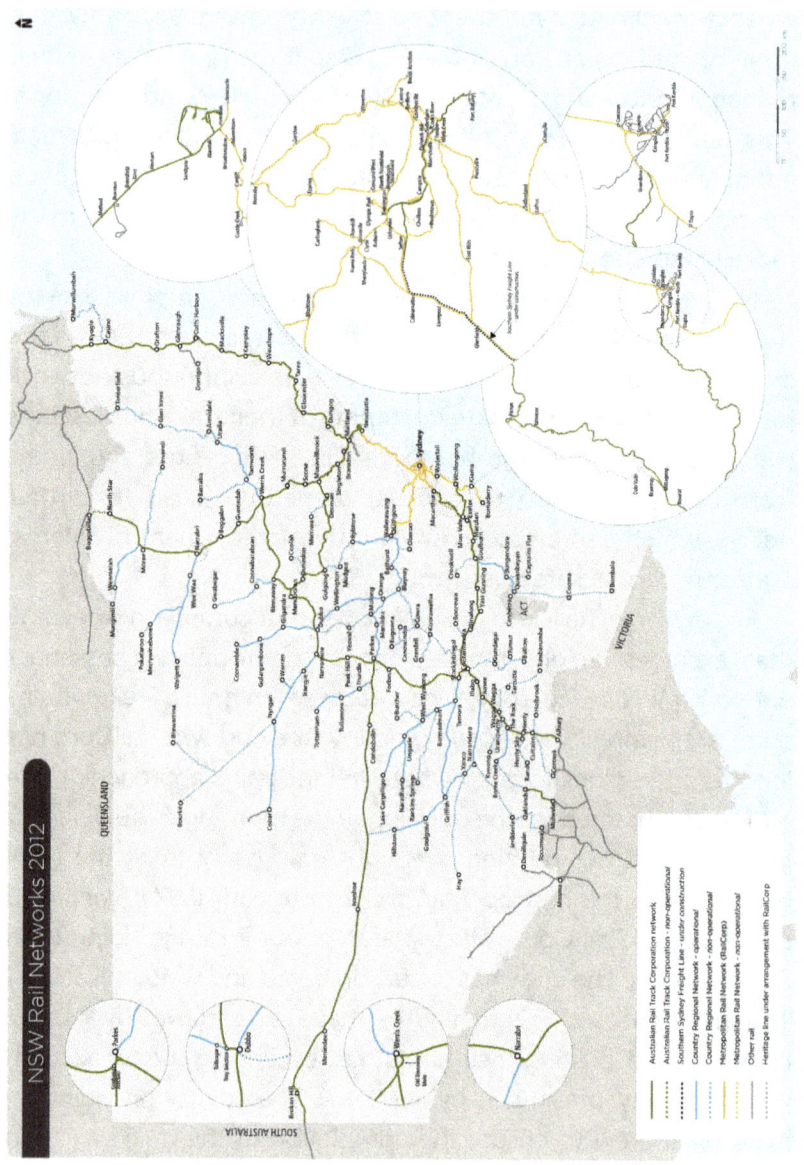

The Fragmented NSW Rail Network, 2012

16. Some Observations

For an illustration of its complexity, let us trace the progress of a train loaded with containers of export cotton from Warren (in the central west of the state) to Port Botany:

- Warren to Narromine, via JHG
- Narromine to Dubbo, via ARTC
- Dubbo to Lithgow via JHG
- Lithgow to Flemington Junction, via RailCorp
- Flemington Junction to Port Botany, via ARTC.

It is easy to see how inconvenient it is for a train operator when contiguous track providers do not coordinate their track possessions, meaning that part of a train's route is closed and part is not. In these circumstances, cancelling the train and losing the revenue from it is a normal outcome for the smaller operators. Only PN has sufficiently widespread resources to divert its trains through alternative routes.

In NSW, the two busiest track providers, RailCorp and the ARTC, both plan their track possessions efficiently. We saw at the beginning of chapter 13 that the understanding of efficiency depends on the context. For RailCorp, the key metric guiding efficiency in planning track possessions is to minimise the disruption to passenger services. Hence, its preferred times are overnight (10pm to 4am) when freight trains would be running, or for MPM work that requires days of continuous track closure, the weekends are best, especially public holiday weekends, such as Easter or King's Birthday (midnight Friday to midnight Sunday or Monday). However, for the ARTC, the cost of labour, its own and that of its contractors, is the key metric. Hence, avoiding the extra labour cost of working nights and weekends is preferable for economic efficiency. In the Hunter Valley, the ARTC often plans track possessions from Monday night to Thursday night, giving 72 hours of continuous possession, in which several different projects may be progressed simultaneously by different work teams. That is efficient use of precious time. Thus, for RailCorp and the ARTC to agree on a simultaneous track possession for any one route, such as for the Warren to Port Botany service above, one of them would have to compromise its own efficiency. That does not usually happen.

That this situation was allowed to develop, of a formerly unified network inadvertently becoming broken up into three jurisdictions and many segments, has been described as "policy neglect".[651] The way it hampers train operators planning new services for potential customers is described in Appendix 5, under *Obtaining Train Paths Across Multiple Access Regimes*. This network fragmentation still exists in 2023.

In 2014, the NSW government actually tried (unwittingly) to introduce a fourth network jurisdiction, when it appealed to the private sector to build and operate a new line[652] that would link two parts of the State network managed by the ARTC. The ARTC was not asked to be involved because the State government was trying to entice the private sector to invest. Fortunately, the two bids it received were not realistic. (See in chapter 10, under *A hope for private sector financing*.)

The disposal of FreightCorp, and RailCorp's dominance

State-owned FreightCorp was sold in 2002, together with the federal government's NRC, as an all-inclusive deal: existing contracts, staff, wagons and locomotives, access to and control of Sydney's marshalling yards, the Chullora intermodal terminal and the Enfield loco servicing facility. As was shown in chapter 13, this created a high 'barrier to entry' for any other train operator to base itself in Sydney. Pacific National's rapid simplification of its traffic task also meant that former servicing of private sidings in the Sydney area ceased.[653]

RailCorp's control of the majority of the urban network and its almost total focus on being the region's world-class commuter railway means that it will always be difficult to develop new rail freight business at industrial sites linked by private sidings. In the days of State Rail there were private sidings directly off the main line that would have been shunted outside of the commuter peaks. Such an activity is unthinkable now, because the frequency of passenger trains even between the peaks is such that there would be no time gap for any freight service to stop and shunt from the main line. RailCorp would consider this a major risk to on-time running of passenger services. To shunt such a siding at night regularly would not be reliable, because of RailCorp's regular need to close the lines for overnight maintenance of track and other infrastructure. Hence, the minimum requirement for a private siding now would be to have a track parallel to the main line where a freight train could pull in and stop, clear of the main line turnouts.

The Rooty Hill Regional Distribution Centre private siding is a rare example of what can be achieved. Two parallel sidings were built adjacent to, but well-separated from, the main lines, with access and egress both through the same turnout on the main line. Trains, carrying bulk quarried construction material in bottom-dumping wagons, arrive from the east and berth on the unloading siding. After unloading, the loco uses the other siding to run around the train, reconnecting at its eastern end, ready for the emptied train to depart eastward. To achieve this new form of private siding, the project needed

- a length of clear land adjacent to the rail corridor for the parallel sidings
- several million dollars of private sector money
- commitment to using rail transport over the longer-term, when road transport would be the easier, but not the cheaper, way to meet the industry's needs
- much time; this private siding project took ten years, from an environment report in 2005 to the opening of the rail sidings in 2015.

Another completely different consequence of the sale of FreightCorp was the abandonment of electric locomotives for hauling and banking freight trains. SRANSW had bought ten class-85 electric locomotives in 1979 and fifty class-86 locos in 1983, mostly for use on heavy freight trains going across the Blue Mountains, and coming into Sydney from the north; climbing from the Hawkesbury River to Cowan. When National Rail (NRC) was created in 1993, all these locomotives remained with SRANSW/FreightCorp because NRC did not want to change locomotives en route on its interstate trains. When FreightCorp was privatised in 2002, the electric locomotives passed to Pacific National (PN), but by then about half the fleet had been withdrawn from service with cracked frames; PN declined to use the rest for the same reason as NRC had. Operational efficiency was preferable to tractive efficiency. Possibly also, PN wanted avoid negotiating with RailCorp on a price for electricity; a complication not wanted during PN's establishment period.

Passive resistance to growth within the rail freight industry

A focus on cost reductions and compliance with industry regulations

During the 1980s and 1990s, all government-owned rail freight operators had a primary focus on cost savings, through "down-sizing", "right-sizing", "repositioning", "restructuring" or "rationalisation" to rein in the deficits, mainly by reducing staff numbers. When parts of these railways became private sector businesses, this culture of cost reduction was reinforced by the profit motive. Slashing staff numbers was not such a productive strategy as it had been, but the culture of cost reduction remained predominant. For at least the first decade in the new era of competition, most rail freight companies approached the future with caution rather than confidence. They operated with old rolling-stock and/or hired what they needed. Purchasing new rolling-stock was out of the question then, even for PN.

Some train operators had a culture of compliance with industry regulations, minimising operating costs by striving to reduce the incidence of reportable 'incidents', rather than focusing on how to maintain the quality of service to customers. Thus, for managerial action to achieve 'quality', it was seen as sufficient to meet the accreditation requirements and the minimum standards prescribed by the safety regulators. The only occasions when operational defects were investigated for rectification were when they were seen as safety breaches. Operational defects affecting customer service were not investigated systematically, because they were accepted as instances of "shit happens". Proactive contingency planning to maintain customer service, and budgeting for contingencies to provide service resilience, was rare.

Fragmentation of the rail industry created a more inward focus

Fragmentation of the industry initially led to each company acting in its self-interest, locked into semi-adversarial relationships with both its suppliers and customers by means of their contracts. This made it harder for rail companies to see themselves as part of the wider logistics chain for contestable freight, involving the shippers, freight forwarders, intermodal yard operators, train operators and track providers. However, this inward focus has now changed.

A number of the smaller rail companies, initially operating into Port Botany, were taken over by the two stevedoring companies operating there then – P&O Trans Australia (POTA) and the Patrick Corporation. In 2011, Qube Logistics bought POTA, and bought other small operators subsequently, and now it has become the dominant rail company in the import-export container market sector. It has developed some regional hubs to win new traffic to rail, and developed the Moorebank intermodal terminal in Western Sydney, initially to cater for containers railed to and from Port Botany. Qube has also expanded into Victoria and Western Australia.

Fragmentation of the industry impeded workforce planning. The freight rail industry is known to have an aging workforce, yet there was no planning for its rejuvenation until 2017 when the Australasian Railway Association (ARA) held a forum [654]

> "to discuss both the opportunities and the barriers in harnessing the workforce of the future".

The lack of skills training

The former government-owned railways did much of their own skills training, especially on-the-job training, because many skills they needed were particular to the rail industry. This applied to infrastructure construction, manufacturing, maintenance of assets, and rail operations. When these railways were vertically separated and privatised, skills training was largely ignored. As time went by, train operating companies, the ARTC and engineering firms competed among themselves to get qualified staff. The continued demand for experienced staff, both operational and engineering, to work on the private iron ore railways of the Pilbara in WA also added to this competition. For four decades, these mining railways had been able to attract experienced people from the eastern States and from New Zealand with their high wages available.

The Commonwealth Government, as instigator of the National Competition Policy and all the changes that followed in Australian rail, was confident that if there was a need to help the industry, 'the market' would provide it. However, the only appropriate industry skills training are basic introductory certificate courses, or a Masters program through the University of Central Queensland, for which there are specific conditions for the three-year program:

> "For acceptance into the program, students must be employed within the industry sector and have employer support, including the allocation of a work-based course mentor for the duration of the study period."

There was a lack of definition as to what skills were needed across all levels, and in what quantities. Industry members convinced the ARA to act. In 2018, the ARA commissioned a report on behalf of its members to look into what appeared to be an increasing shortage of skills right across the rail industry, relative to a growing demand for rail projects, particularly for urban passenger transport. The report, from a workforce capability analysis, was completed in November with a strong call for action. The chairman of the ARA wrote in the report's foreword:[655]

> "Rail investment stagnation, start-stop funding cycles and short-term cost cutting have been a feature of the Australian rail sector since the 1980s. And one of the consequences has been the collapse in investment in training and skills development of the people to build our infrastructure and to operate and maintain first class rail services. This is a clear case of market failure."

A key message from the report was:[656]

> **"The rail industry in Australia and New Zealand is already experiencing skills shortages as investment grows in new rail infrastructure and rollingstock and operations expand**, with the number of train drivers, controllers, track workers, signalling engineers and technicians, maintenance workers, electrical technicians and tunnellers not keeping up with growing demand. Just as importantly, from a future skills perspective, the industry is also suffering a chronic shortage of trainers and assessors."

And a major conclusion was:[657]

> **"With key risks to workforce capability driven by the presence of market failures in the industry now, and over previous decades** – including local monopoly characteristics which prevent easy movement of skills between jurisdictions, the lack of economies of scale, externalities in training and operations, as well

as network effects – the solutions necessarily imply a role for an formally structured body or taskforce to work in partnership with government, the rail industry and the education sector to redress suboptimal market outcomes."

The outcome has been an agreement among governments and rail industry to form working groups to deal with the three priority areas for the industry: skills and labour, common standards, and interoperability. The National Transport Commission has been asked[658] to develop a National Rail Action Plan spanning these areas. (See in chapter 7, under *NTC: the National Rail Action* Plan). Hopefully, it will be able to determine what skillsets are needed, how best for them to be provided, and how to attract young people into the industry and get appropriate qualifications and experience.

The consequences for State governments of ceding control

The making of transport policy has always been the prerogative of State governments in Australia. However, the Commonwealth's decision in 1974 to fund and create the National Highway System, followed by its introduction in 1992 of the *One Nation* program of economic reform, and then the National Competition Policy in 1993, gave State policy makers some overriding considerations for transport, particularly railways. The pressure was on to dispose of some or all of each State railway system.

In particular, the disposals of V/Line Freight in 1999, and WestRail Freight in 2000, both as vertically-integrated rail systems, led to the State governments becoming ineffectual in relation to network serviceability. In both States, bulk grains formed a major component of their rail systems' traffic at the time of disposal. Both governments had developed and supported their railways for generations, to support the grain growing industries, to help them be internationally competitive. Certainly, when they disposed of their rail systems, much money was needed for their rejuvenation. But with faith in the private sector, the governments appeared to believe they were doing the right thing for their rural communities. In WA, the Minister of Transport was reported[659] as saying at the time of sale that

> "selling the freight network was less about money that it was about ensuring the long term best interests of the State's industries and communities."

> However, as told in chapter 11, both governments were not pleased with the decisions of the companies that controlled their networks.

The WA Government was coerced into funding the resleepering of the Tiers 1 and 2 grain lines, undertaken from 2010 to 2013, because Brookfield could threaten closure for safety reasons if this work was not done. Then in 2014, the Government, which is still the legal owner of the network, was unable to have any influence over Brookfield's decisions both to prevent the Tier 3 grain lines from being used, and to refuse to sublease them to CBH to operate. In 2020, the Government published its Revitalising Agricultural Region Freight (RARF) Strategy, in which it was hinted that any future investment in grain lines would need government involvement.[660] It would support upgrading projects on the (still open) Tier 1 and 2 grain lines, and have business cases prepared for reopening some of the Tier 3 lines. Costs for these lines to reopen are estimated to be nearly $500 million.[661]

In Victoria, the two private sector lessees (Freight Australia then Pacific National) used up the residual life in the broad-gauge network, to the point that trains were forced to run very slowly to avoid the tracks collapsing under them. Freight customers were turning to trucking to get reasonable service. Rather than see the network collapse, the government bought back the network lease for much more than the whole vertically-integrated system had been sold for, so that it could begin to restore its rail network.

Both governments were pressured to pay hundreds of millions of dollars to keep their rail networks operating for the benefit of their grain-growing industries. With hindsight, it is obvious that at least the Victorian government would have been financially better off not to have privatised its rail network.

Bearing the risks of year-to-year changes in grain harvests

For reasons mainly to do with the variability of climate and weather, the size of the harvests in the grain growing areas of continental Australia vary from year to year and area to area. When State governments (and ANR in SA) provided the means (with rail networks and specialised rolling-stock) to transport the harvests to the cities and the export ports, it was they who bore the transport-associated financial risks of variability in harvest sizes. And given that there were (and still are) three gauges of rail networks servicing the grain growing areas, making sharing of rolling-stock impractical, State governments bore these risks individually.

However, over time, this has changed. With both the deregulation of grain marketing, and the vertical separation and privatisation of the rail systems, it is the grain marketing companies which now bear these risks. The two major groups, GrainCorp in the eastern States, and CBH in WA, both acquired locomotives and wagons so that they could have greater certainty of equipment suitability and supply. Competition on rail, in NSW and Victoria, and the lack of it in WA, did not serve them well enough. They now have much greater ability to integrate the management of grain storage in their networks of grain silos, with transport. Similarly, Viterra, operating on both sides of the Spencer Gulf in South Australia, has chosen not to use rail transport altogether, rather than rely on, and have to pay for, the under-maintained lines, rolling-stock and services previously supplied by GWA.

The national discussion on freight transport and infrastructure

Politicians' influence on investment decisions

Land transport in Australia has long been a 'wicked problem': complex, ambiguous and value-laden. Wicked problems are difficult to define and cannot be solved by traditional analytical approaches. They are societal problems where information is limited and confusing, where there are many stakeholders with conflicting values.[662] Hence, solutions may be untested in their effect, but still seen as detrimental by some stakeholders. Finding and implementing appropriate responses to climate change is both a classic example and the major wicked problem of our times. Other examples that governments experience are:

- setting a tax policy that everyone can agree with,
- trying to change the health system.

That land transport in Australia is also a 'wicked problem' is one reason why there has never been a coherent national strategic plan, or planning organisation and process, for land transport across Australia. Another reason is the chronically uneasy relationships between the States and the federal government. The absence of a national strategic plan was seen as a significant issue by the federal parliamentary committees that produced three reports between 1997 and 2001, and also the Productivity Commission in its 1999 report *Progress in Rail Reform* (see in Chapter 5). The lack of such a strategic plan is still cause for complaints. Actually, what is most missed now is a national infrastructure plan, which would logically be derived from the national land transport strategic plan, if it existed.[663]

At the same time, Australian society is wary of centralised planning. The term still connotes Soviet-era authoritarianism with its accompanying spectacular failures, such as overproduction of unwanted industrial goods, or agricultural underproduction, inducing famines.

Tapping into this wariness, the Australian Broadcasting Corporation (ABC) in 2014 and 2015 showed a quasi-documentary TV series called *Utopia* which satirised the concept of centralised planning. It took place at the fictional Nation Building Authority, where major infrastructure projects were always frustrated by bureaucracy, political self-interest and constant changes in priorities. What this TV series did, apart from entertain, was show up the Commonwealth of Australia's failure to develop a harmonious, integrated, non-political way to plan, fund and build major infrastructural projects for long-term prosperity. This failure particularly affects energy production and land transport.

Given all of the above, most people who participate in the national or state-based discussions about freight transport and infrastructure have at best a partial view and often a partisan understanding, be they politicians, economists, engineering consultants, business people or political commentators. Assumptions and misunderstandings occur frequently.[664] Proposals, academic papers and commentaries are spasmodic and scattered through the media. Hence the discussion is confused and confusing, and does not make progress.

Transport infrastructure projects have long been political footballs, kicked about to gain advantage or for point-scoring. It seems that, more often than not, politicians promise transport infrastructure projects that have vote-gaining value, but which do not have, at the time of the promise, clear and positive economic benefit/cost ratios. In the 1950s, 60s and 70s, politicians could justify such projects as 'progress', which meant improvement over time to public assets, for the betterment of all. However, the ethos changed in the 1980s, the decade in which privatisation and 'small government' began to be espoused. Given that these arguments negated the notion of government spending for the betterment of all, politicians became more focussed on their own survival than before. Hence transport infrastructure projects had to be visible to the electorate to be supported. Typically, such projects are now therefore limited to roading developments or urban public transport.[665]

Research[666] has shown also that projects that are announced prematurely by politicians are more likely to be built even if the cost-benefit analysis shows they are not worth it. These projects are more likely to have cost blowouts because the announcement fixes the projected cost based on preliminary estimates. It looks as if the Inland Rail project, discussed below, is an example.

Governments and their technical advisers have strong incentives to find benefits to justify what politicians want to do. This situation was summarised in 2010 thus:[667]

> "It means that decisions on infrastructure projects are made by sovereign fiat, not rationality: basically what the policy makers think is good, not what falls out of rational calculation. Rationalization follows decision. The role of BCA [benefit cost analysis] is to legitimate decisions not to guide them."

Projects that would be beneficial to freight railways are largely invisible to the electorate, and do not easily get political support. The only exceptions are rail projects that are so expensive, such as the Inland Rail or the ETTT (Epping to Thornleigh Third Track, in Sydney), that they have political value for the numbers of jobs they create, or the value of construction contracts available for the private sector to take up, in addition to their intrinsic value for improving the economics of freight transport.

The power of federal politicians is now endemic in the Australian infrastructure decision-making process, as part of the ethos of governments managing the national economy. There is an expectation that when the federal government wants to counter a recession by increasing its spending, there will be "shovel-ready" projects available to start at short notice. Shovel-ready implies that a project's planning and design work is done, with consents obtained, and its most expensive phase of construction can begin. In this environment, the rail mode has been seen as unready to participate in what is a kind of lolly scramble:[668]

> "With the federal government looking to states to nominate infrastructure projects that are ready to be rapidly implemented, a lack of ready to go projects is hampering rail's ability to capitalise on current funding offers."

However, a shovel-ready status for any rail infrastructure project would not be easy to achieve: funding would need to have been authorised and committed for at least

- determining and agreeing the need or opportunity, the operational concept design, land requirements, scoping and preliminary costs for the project
- preparation of the cost-benefit analysis followed by approval by Infrastructure Australia, and
- all design work commissioned, done and approved by the project sponsor.

If capital funding of rail network projects by lolly scramble is to be the new normal, then the ARTC and State governments will need to budget millions of dollars for preliminary work on projects that may in the end never be delivered. Or find a way to fund projects that bypasses the lolly scrambles.

The discussion in economics and policy commentaries

Economics and policy arguments are never objective. They are always based on some particular worldview, and supportive of some type of ideology, even if the economist or policy analyst making an argument is unaware of this.[669] Western economics is based on the idea of 'how would a rational person act in a market situation?'. Thus, it incorporates a Western worldview that an individual (and by extension a company) always acts rationally when acting in the market for his narrow self-interest, and that the values and rights of the individual are therefore the best basis for economic understanding. Actually, Western economics has hijacked this concept of rationality. Individualism is a Western cultural tenet in its origins, which spread around the world with the expansion of European empires and influence, and it largely smothered other worldviews. Nevertheless, people in African and Pacific cultures still understand that rational economic behaviour should promote reciprocity, co-operation and collaboration, not individualism and narrow self-interest.

In Australia and New Zealand, the issue of 'what may be best for society as a whole' was seen until the 1980s as the province of politics rather than economics. However, since then, 'managing the economy' has become a preoccupation of politics. Consequently, the 'rational' thinking of Western economics has greatly influenced political thinking, and the assessments of potential investments with public money, based as they are in the worldview of Western economics.

One might ask why this is relevant to discussions about land transport for freight in Australasia. It is relevant because the production of land transport, and particularly rail transport, is a much more collaborative and co-operative endeavour than we normally realise. The collaborative nature of transport systems spans both space and time. Typically land transport infrastructure is part of a network, and it is long-lasting. Viewing proposals for new infrastructure for transport using the techniques of modern economics usually downplays these collaborative and co-operative aspects. This problem particularly affects the railway industry with its long-lasting infrastructure. Modern economic analysis techniques, incorporating the concepts of the time value of money and discounted cash flow (DCF), and often with an unrealistically high discount rate, make potential investments in railway infrastructure look unattractive compared to other investments with more immediate returns. Hence, they ignore the fact that railway infrastructure can still deliver value many decades after it is built, and for reasons unforeseen at the time. In reality, it is easy to find railway infrastructure built eighty or more years ago, including tunnels and bridges, that are still in use today, providing value for current users. As an example, the picture below shows the Makatote viaduct on New Zealand's NIMT, built 1905-1908, with structures for electrification added in the 1980s, undergoing a $13 million refurbishment in 2016.

The Makatote viaduct, still in daily use, undergoing refurbishment 108 years after being built.

The problem with much of the discussion about the usefulness of, and role for, freight railways is that is it analysed in terms of conventional economic thinking and techniques, including in Australia a 7% rate of return required for rail projects. There are three reasons for the unsuitability of applying such thinking to the freight rail industry:

- The longevity, and on-going value of railway infrastructure, particularly when it is maintained in operable condition
- The tendency for economic analyses to ignore or dismiss the externalities[670] associated with railways, (see *The discussion in relation to environment aspects* below)
- The use of an arbitrarily high expected rate of return on investment that favours fast payback projects; most rail projects cannot deliver returns that quickly, and so get discarded. (See in chapter 13, *The economic appraisal of rail network projects*.)

Contrast this conventional Australian view of investment in railways with this comment by the Austrian federal transport minister, Jörg Leichtfried, in announcing a €15.2 billion framework plan of investments in rail infrastructure projects for the years 2017-2022, where the key objective is the modal shift of freight from road to rail:[671]

> "With our investments we create value for generations. Every year we earmark about €2 billion for the further expansion of the railway, securing more than 40,000 jobs"

The discussion about Inland Rail

One way to demonstrate the partial and partisan perceptions that many have of the freight rail industry and its infrastructure projects, is to look at some criticisms of the Inland Rail project. (There is a brief description of Inland Rail in chapter 12.)

In 2007, when Inland Rail was just a visionary idea, the so-called Centre for Independent Studies (CIS) published an opinion piece under the emotive heading *Cargo-Cult Railway Proposals*.[672] It tried to denigrate the project with some uninformed comments about how it would be a waste of money. It predicted the project as one in which "vested interests may stand to make large gains if railways are built", as though this was something unique to this project, rather than being applicable to all types of large infrastructure projects, including highways. CIS is a pressure group that advocates strongly for 'small government', in the hope of gaining reduced taxation. Therefore, its opposition to the Inland Rail project was based on its ideological position on government spending, not because it had any particular expertise in transport matters.

In 2015, after the Commonwealth government had made a commitment to the project, a political commentator and blogger attacked the proposal, under the inflammatory heading *Inland fail: the $10 billion rail line to nowhere*.[673] His comments indicated a lack of understanding of several factors – particularly the role of the ARTC as the federal government agency tasked with building, extending, upgrading, managing and maintaining the interstate rail network, for the economic development of Australia. He criticised the ARTC "which stands to benefit significantly from designing and building the project" for developing the business case, but this was done at the behest of the government.[674] He criticised the use of a 4% discount rate in the business case, which delivered an acceptable benefit-cost ratio of 2.62, instead preferring the conventional 7%. However, as we saw in chapter 13 (under *The significance of the discount rate*), a 4% discount rate is very appropriate for an infrastructure project that will deliver benefits for fifty years and more. Faced with a well-reasoned business case document of nearly 400 pages, the blogger's response was[28]

> "The problem is, inland rail is a dog, even under the optimistic ARTC business case."

He criticised the ARTC's assumption that the parallel Newell Highway would not be upgraded. However, the Inland Rail Business Case states[675] that one of its benefits is that the Newell Highway will not need to be duplicated to cater for future freight traffic growth. Since 2011, the NSW and Commonwealth Governments have been funding over forty overtaking lanes on this highway,[676] but these add capacity which benefits car users much more than heavy trucking.

The Senate inquiry into Inland Rail

In September 2021, the federal Senate instructed a committee to inquire and report on:[677]

> "The management of the Inland Rail project by the Australian Rail Track Corporation and the Commonwealth Government, with particular reference to:
> (a) financial arrangements of the project;
> (b) route planning and selection processes;
> (c) connections with other freight infrastructure, including ports and intermodal hubs;
> (d) engagement on route alignment, procurement and employment;
> (e) urban and regional economic development opportunities;
> (f) collaboration between governments;
> (g) interaction with National Freight and Supply Chain Strategy; and
> (h) any other related matters."

The Senate report was titled *"Inland Rail: derailed from the start"*, but it was not as one-sided as the title might suggest. It reflected concerns about two main interlinked issues: the scheme's increasing cost, and that their regional and rural constituents' issues were not being properly addressed.

The first 'desktop estimate' of cost in 2010 was $4.7 billion; in 2015 the estimate was $9.9 billion; and by 2019 the Commonwealth Government had committed $14.7 billion,[678] with still some costs not fully known and therefore some certainty of a further blowout. At first sight, the cost escalation looks alarming, and one submission to the Committee argued[679]

> "the budget overrun was grounds for the removal of the Inland Rail's CEO and project manager."

That did not happen. However, the escalation is explainable in part by the large size of the project and the process by which costings had to be developed and refined over a multi-year planning period, as the details of alignments were decided, and engineering designs were done.

A significant issue for some submissions to the Senate committee was the fundamental objective of the project, called the Service Offering. This was the capability to run trains, each way reliably, in less than 24 hours between terminals in Brisbane and Melbourne. This was advised to ARTC, as early as 2010, by potential intercapital customers such as freight forwarders and supermarket chains, as being the key to being competitive with road, along with price and availability.[680] Consistent achievement of this Service Offering would be the key to capturing the intermodal traffic from trucking, and this would in time be the major traffic on the line. This Service Offering has been a critical consideration in route selection, and this fact was conveyed to the Senate Committee in various submissions by the ARTC.[681] Nevertheless, the Senate report refers five times to that objective (a transit time of less than 24 hours) as being "arbitrary". This seems to imply that the objective was an unreasonably rigid commitment that should instead be negotiable, in order to accommodate the wishes of rural and regional communities wanting alternative and longer alignments. In its view[682]

> "Had the Australian Government [i.e., the ARTC] established a more flexible time parameter at the initial stages of this project, then many of the [implementation] issues faced by the ARTC today could have been avoided."

It is hard to tell whether this statement is political bloody-mindedness or routine truculence. In my view, the Senate Committee noted the Inland Rail project team's "could do better" performance on negotiating with landholders whose land was being compulsorily taken, and conflated it with regional envy about federal money being spent on a project that will benefit 'big business' and the residents of Brisbane and Melbourne. The outcome would be to convert a complex infrastructure project into a 'wicked problem' with multiple competing objectives. Fortunately, the ARTC, and the Australian Government, have not wavered from pushing on with the project, on the basis that it is in line with the National Freight and Supply Chain Strategy. (See in chapter 8, under *Changes in the focus of transport sector reform.*) This Strategy is preparing transport infrastructure for an expected freight volume increase of up to 35% by 2040.[683]

Discussions in relation to environmental aspects

The public awareness in the last thirty years of many kinds of environmental damage stemming from business activities has not led to the adoption of effective ways to account for it in commerce and in macro-economic measurements. Railways are the least polluting, most fuel efficient, safest form of land transport for freight that there is. But the Commonwealth Government's wilful blindness of the externalities of land transport has robbed the rail industry of the validity of some of its intrinsic efficiencies. In addition, this robbery has been compounded since 2010 by the federal government's disregard for, and lack of effective action on, the future dangers to the world caused by increasing levels of atmospheric CO_2.

What was common knowledge in the 1990s about rail being more fuel-efficient than road transport, and therefore a policy option for reducing greenhouse gas emissions, has been forgotten since then in the environmental debate in Australia. Instead, the debate has been focused on the electric power generation industry, which is dominated by coal-burning power stations. (By contrast, in New Zealand, where the bulk of electricity generation is already hydroelectric and geothermal, modal shift of freight transport to rail is seen as a positive move, and is a basis for the government investing in rail infrastructure since 2017.)

In 2013, the Coalition federal government introduced a scheme to put a cap on emissions from the biggest industrial sources of greenhouse gases, called the Safeguard Mechanism. It turned out to be a failure, because it was not properly enforced.[684] In 2023, the Labor federal government sought to revamp the scheme, targeting over 200 of the largest emitters to reduce their emissions or buy carbon credits. Either way it could be a cost increase for these companies. Unfortunately, this scheme includes Australia's two biggest rail companies, Pacific National and Aurizon. These rail operators have advised the government that if no exemptions are made, there will be unintended consequences, "a perverse rise in road congestion and emissions".[685] These two largest of rail companies offer the government the opportunity to reduce the emissions from the much larger road freight industry, in the contestable interstate intermodal freight market. However, if there is no change to what is planned in 2023, it is possible that rail freight costs could increase due to the Safeguard Mechanism, while road freight costs do not, simply because truck operators are too small to be included in the scheme. This lack of recognition by the federal government that the rail freight industry could be its ally in the effort to reduce overall emissions is (enter your own adjective here).

17. Summing-up

New Zealand: privatisation and renationalisation

The influence of politics

Governments in New Zealand oscillate between centre-right (led by the National Party) and centre-left (led by the Labour Party). The National Party is supported by business and farmers, and is a strong voice for the virtues of private enterprise. Despite espousing the notion of small government, it considers itself to be the better party to "manage the economy". The Labour Party is a voice for economic cooperation, promoting collective strength. The economic system should serve society, not the other way around. Since 1990, the fortunes of New Zealand's rail system have changed with whichever party is in power.

It was a National government that privatised the railways in 1993. The next Labour government retrieved control of the rail network in 2004, in order to rehabilitate it after many years of underinvestment. It bought the above-rail business in 2008 after a dispute about network access charges, and settlement followed a drawn-out negotiation with the owner about the valuation of the business. It re-established a vertically-integrated business, calling it KiwiRail. In November 2008, the National Party was returned to power, and it kept tight control on subsidies for KiwiRail, while insisting that KiwiRail must become profitable. Under these conditions, KiwiRail had to adopt a strategy it called "managed decline", allowing a gradual reduction in track quality, and continuing to use locomotives and wagons mostly dating from the 1970s. However, a Labour-led coalition was returned to government in 2017, and over the next few years it allocated billions for renewal of rail infrastructure and rolling-stock.

The outcome of privatisation was both success and failure

Around 1990, the New Zealand Government was pursuing a policy of selling its assets to pay down debts, in accordance with the tenets of neoliberal economics that it was influenced by at that time. New Zealand Railways was seen to be a chronic "money pit", which required deficits to be funded from the Government's budget. It was known also that perhaps a billion dollars was needed for asset renewals in the coming decades, so selling the railways in 1993 was quite openly a way for the Government to avoid that expense. (See chapter 9, under *The principal reasons for ownership changes*.) The productivity improvements of the 1980s had failed to make railways profitable, but that was largely due to price competition with the road haulage industry following the lifting of restrictions. There was faith that the private sector could do a better job of making a profit.

Six groups were shortlisted as potential bidders (see appendix 1, under *How NZ Rail was privatised*.) Five of them included New Zealand port companies and/or shipping companies, or logistics companies involved in road freighting. The Government was wary that such groups might take away NZ Rail's customers and traffic flows, diverting them to other modes. However, one bidding group could have no such ambitions; the chosen bidder was a consortium of Berkshire Partners (American investment bankers), Fay Richwhite (New Zealand investment bankers) and the Wisconsin Central Railroad (a successful American railroad company), whose chairman would ostensibly lead the consortium. It created an expectation that this group

17. Summing-up

would bring both money and railway business expertise to New Zealand Rail.

As it turned out, the consortium financed its purchase almost entirely with borrowed money. It created Tranz Rail Holdings Ltd, then cleverly had this company borrow the majority of the money needed for the purchase of NZ Rail. Thus, a railway system with a need for substantial reinvestment funding became a new company with a starting debt of $295 million. (See chapter 11, under *An analysis of Tranz Rail's difficulties*.) The need for debt repayment became a major influence on how the company was managed. After the first sale of Tranz Rail assets, the owners paid themselves back by having Tranz Rail buy $100 million of its own shares at $3.70, that two years earlier had been bought by the owners for $1 each. (See appendix 1, under *The Tranz Rail years – 1994, 1995*.)

One of the few requests that the Government asked of the consortium was that there be a future public share offering. The consortium happily obliged in 1996, floating Tranz Rail on the New Zealand and American NASDAQ stock exchanges. In the three years prior to this event, Tranz Rail appeared to be doing well by the usual measures for a company, but to some extent this was illusory. It had changed, not illegally, some accounting policies re track renewals, and assumptions for asset depreciation, both of which enlarged reported profits. After the float, there was a period of rising share prices, which enabled Berkshire Partners to sell most of its shareholding, retrieving up to eight times its original investment. (See appendix 1, *The Tranz Rail years – 1996*.) This banker had bought into a railway business, but it could have been any business, because its intention was to simply to play the stock markets for gain. Its involvement with Tranz Rail was very successful. The other two members of the consortium retained most of their Tranz Rail shares at this time.

From 1996, Tranz Rail profits were boosted by the sale-and-lease-back of rolling-stock, which was a way of borrowing from future revenues to pay down external debts. There were other forms of asset-stripping, exploiting the past and the future. In the later 1990s, the old rails at disused sidings and closed stations were dug up and sold as scrap iron, a valid harvest. However, in 1999, Tranz Rail took delivery of its newly-built rail-ferry *Aratere*, then soon sold it and leased it back, borrowing from future revenues again. (See appendix 1, *The Tranz Rail years – 1999*.)

By the year 2000, the remaining primary shareholders had substantially reduced their shareholdings, the original chairman had had to resign for external reasons, and Tranz Rail's CEO since privatisation had retired. The new CEO announced a radical downsizing by shedding various vertically-integrated functions, so that fixed costs would be reduced and Tranz Rail would become a 'transport services management company'. While this had been a successful strategy for the new CEO in his previous role managing a shipping line, because it could access services globally, it was a disastrous choice for the only railway business in an island nation. Companies able to provide track maintenance, workshops products and rolling-stock maintenance all had to come from Australia, and to start in business in New Zealand they needed multi-year contracts to justify this. Consequently, the CEO's move to reduce fixed costs resulted in swapping Tranz Rail's staff and facility costs for quasi fixed costs for services provided by others, with a profit margin added in.

In February 2002, the original shareholders sold their remaining shares as packages to institutions and pension funds at a tidy profit. For these original shareholders, the game was over, and they had done very well financially. Wisconsin Central had seen itself as a long-term investor, but in 2001 it was bought out by Canadian National, a huge North American railroad that did not want to be involved in New Zealand.

For the new owners, and the small investors and staff who still held shares, worse was to come. The share price rallied

17. Summing-up

briefly to $4 then slid downwards over the next 2 years to below $1. Tranz Rail was floundering: the strategy of being a 'transport services management company' was not delivering profits, the company was increasing its debts, its credit ratings were downgraded, it had almost run out of saleable assets, and a grouping of major industrial and exporting customers were lobbying for some kind of government involvement to fix Tranz Rail's problems.

The National Government's privatisation of NZ Rail had gone from an initial success to an abject failure in the ten years since the sale. One might say this was no fault of that government. However, it appeared to be oblivious to the capability of investment banks to chase profits through financial dealing, and hence it appeared unconcerned that the railway might be asset-stripped. Perhaps its faith in the private sector made it blind to the reality of rational economics, resulting in a New Zealand asset being laid open to exploitation by the more financially sophisticated. (See chapter 9, under *The principal reasons for ownership changes – faith in the private sector and privatisation*.) One wonders what might have happened had this government still been in power when Tranz Rail was about to collapse. (See appendix 1, *The Tranz Rail years – 2003*.)

Keeping the rail network open was a key decision for the future

By May 2003, Tranz Rail was nearly insolvent even after various asset sales had raised some hundreds of millions, and heavily in debt. Financial collapse looked imminent. Although the Labour Government had stood back during Tranz Rail's troubles in 2002, it made the key decision early in 2003 not to allow even a temporary closure of the rail system, that might result from Tranz Rail being forced into receivership. This government understood how disruptive that could be for the New Zealand economy, and particularly for the exporters who were reliant on rail, with a flow-on effect for some regional economies.

The Government rescued Tranz Rail from insolvency in June 2003. Then began a five-year battle for control and reinvestment, firstly of the network, then later of the above-rail business. (These events are fully documented in appendix 1.) During these years in which a government organisation (ONTRACK) managed the network and an Australian company (Toll) ran the above-rail business, a dispute about access fees continued. An independent audit led to a settlement in 2007 that incorporated a new perspective; that it was the Government's responsibility to fund the development and renewal of rail network assets, not that of the train operator. This led eventually to an acknowledgement in 2018 that the network and the above-rail business were separate parts of the railway system; the former always needed government support, and with that, the latter could reasonably expect to be profitable.

Years of grudging support and 'Managed Decline'

That this new perspective took a decade to be openly discussed was due to the change of government in 2008. KiwiRail came under the control of the National Government, an owner that was, at best, uninterested. (See appendix 1, *KiwiRail*.) Supporting KiwiRail was not part of its blinkered vision for land transport. It largely ignored the existence of KiwiRail's rundown network and fleet. It insisted that KiwiRail must become more efficient to be profitable (as an integrated railway). Hence, the notion that it was the government's responsibility to fund the development and renewal of rail network assets was unthinkable. This government was much more interested in funding new and improved state highways, through its Roads of National Significance program from 2009 onwards.

In 2014, after several unexpected setbacks, KiwiRail conducted a study of its potential profitability over a thirty-year planning horizon, incorporating all the capital requirements needed to keep it going. Four different network size scenarios were modelled, including an exit option, i.e., completely closing the business. (See appendix 1, *KiwiRail, the Commercial Review*.) Because there was no scenario that showed KiwiRail could ever reach financial sustainability, both the Board of KiwiRail and The Treasury recommended the Exit option, "as the highest value option for the Shareholder".[686] In other words, the most logical option for the Government, arising from the review using rational economics, was to close KiwiRail and dispose of the assets.

This was the third occasion on which the New Zealand Government had the option to close, or let close, the nation's railways, and decided not to take that option:

- Around 1990, closure of the "money pit" was an undeclared option, albeit not an attractive one, because then, Railways was a collection of assets and an on-going business that the Government believed the private sector should have been able to operate profitably;
- In mid-2003, the imminent financial failure of Tranz Rail as a listed company would have resulted in a catastrophic closure – which the Government chose not to permit, in order to prevent damage to and uncertainty for the New Zealand economy;
- In 2014, as the most rational economic option resulting from the Commercial Review.

Why this Government did not seize upon the recommendation, to close down KiwiRail in an orderly manner, and put an end to its financial losses, is not known. The Minister of Transport at that time was Simon Bridges, who was never supportive of rail. Perhaps the Government did not want to admit that the rail system was financially unviable because it had been run down by its private sector owners; that would force it to concede the ultimate failure of its 1993 privatisation. Perhaps it was an awareness that the ports and big industrial businesses would oppose this move, because it would add to their costs. Perhaps by then someone had read Sandel's 2012 book,[687] which explains that due to the ubiquity of 'market reasoning', non-economic values get disregarded, but not vanquished. The Government would have been aware that closing down KiwiRail would have been very unpopular among the public, because motorists put value on not having roads and highways dominated by trucks. Did political reality prevail over economic rationality? Did the Government realise that the economic analysis, however technically sound, was illogical for the viability of New Zealand as an exporting nation? One can imagine some kind of collective cognitive dissonance in the Cabinet. Whatever, the Government chose to keep the rail network as it was, untrimmed. However, it demanded yet more efficiencies and productivity improvements from KiwiRail, in order to reduce the amount of government support needed, and perhaps to assuage the cognitive dissonance. This response indicated that it still did not have any better policy for the run-down railway system it had inherited six years earlier. However, the Labour opposition transport spokesman expressed a then radical view that KiwiRail was two businesses – freight and lines – which should be treated differently.[688]

KiwiRail responded to the pressure from Government by abandoning some customers, to become more efficient by "simplifying our business" and "standardising our assets".[689] Abandoned traffic included bulk fertilisers and agricultural lime, which had been staple traffic for at least seventy years. In 2016, its strategy of 'managed decline' became public knowledge (see appendix 1), but this appeared to have been in use for some years. It looked similar to Tranz Rail's strategy of 'sweating the assets', only with a different motivation.

The evolution of a new perspective on rail network value and funding

The election of a Labour-led coalition government in 2017 brought a changed perspective of the potential and value of

New Zealand's railway system. It was a paradigm shift. KiwiRail remains vertically-integrated, but in 2021 was acknowledged to be "not a viable commercial business"[690] in that form. The railway and highway networks are now both funded by the National Land Transport Fund, with both track users and road users paying user charges. KiwiRail reports the finances of above-rail and below-rail operations separately, and has to be profitable with only its above-rail business.

To illustrate the New Zealand Government's 2022 positioning on transport, here is a quote:[691]

> "What is the role of government in the freight and supply chain system?
>
> Supporting what is needed for commercial activities to occur. The government ... invests heavily in public infrastructure such as roads, bridges, tunnels, and railway tracks."

Outcomes in Australia

Competition and Privatisation

In early the 1990s, the Commonwealth Government and four State Governments were all still subsidising their various railway organisations by funding their chronic deficits. In 1992, Prime Minister Paul Keating saw a need for all inefficient government businesses to compete, to stimulate a more commercial approach and realise greater efficiencies. Initially, competition did not require privatisation (see below), and conversely, at the first two sales of State Railways (in Victoria, May 1999, and in WA, October 2000) competition was not wanted by the State Governments. In both cases, they avoided competition by selling and leasing their railways as vertically-integrated operations, despite the requirements of the federal Competition Policy Reform Act of 1995.

Competition against the Commonwealth's interstate rail business, National Rail Corporation (NRC), started in 1995 on the east-west corridor from the eastern States to Perth. It came from established freight logistics companies (SCT, Toll, Patrick Corp), setting up their own train operations, gradually building up their service frequencies. In NSW, small companies competed on the State-owned network from 1997 onward, mainly by capturing traffic flows off road.

It was not until the joint sale of the loss-making train operators, NRC and FreightCorp, to create Pacific National (PN) in 2002, did privatisation become a catalyst for competition, particularly in NSW (see chapter 12, under *New South Wales*.) The NSW network had been separated from FreightCorp in 1996. This, together with PN's initial shedding of staff and troublesome traffic as a path to profitability, created suitable conditions for smaller companies to compete for, and secure, segments of the intrastate market. In 2010, there were ten of these smaller companies. By 2022, despite a number of company buyouts and consolidations, there were still five companies operating freight trains within NSW in 2022 (PN, Qube, Aurizon, SSR, Linx), plus SCT on the interstate through route.

The Commonwealth Government had expected in the 1990s that the privatisation of government railways would deliver efficiencies and competitiveness. The sale of railway businesses and assets started in Victoria in 1999 and concluded in Queensland in 2010. It was a rather haphazard process to separate freight operations from passenger operations, then to privatise the freight railways, either as vertically-integrated businesses or just as above-rail businesses. Separating out and subsidising the clearly loss-making but essential urban passenger railways did not necessarily leave the freight railways any more profitable.

There was never any analysis of options of how best to restructure a rail freight industry stuck in its ways, with State-based ownership and increasing deficits. Indeed, the concept of a rail industry was largely unrecognised outside of the industry itself. The only option seen by governments was to pass ownership to the private sector which would then provide its own solutions. This at least was consistent with the National Competition Policy prevalent at the time.

In this context, the notion of having a national strategic integrated land transport policy was irrelevant for Commonwealth governments of both persuasions. They could not see the need for it, even to bring about competitive neutrality between rail and road modes. (See in Chapter 13, under *Competitive Neutrality*.) In the late 1990s both the Neville and Smorgon Reports, and the PC's *Progress in Rail Reform*, all urged the Commonwealth government to take the lead in strategic policy development and planning for land transport, but the government's response was to dismiss the notion as politically undesirable. (See in Chapter 6, under *The Response from the Commonwealth Government*.) The outcome was noted by one Canberra transport policy person in 2013:[692]

> "The expectation by governments that privatised rail systems could improve their performance and shift freight from road to rail, without reform of transport policy to more accurately price the costs of heavy vehicles on the road network, appears to mark another area of failure in the rail privatisation experiment."

The push for privatisation and competition within the industry had some unintended side effects. It showed up barriers to entry not previously thought about (see chapter 13), it reduced rail organisations' economies of scale, and enabled strategic abandonment of former rail services by private sector companies. Their pursuit of profits came at the expense of the environment to the extent that some traffic switched from rail to road. The neglect of rail infrastructure by companies in pursuit of profits was at the expense of the State governments that had to fund upgrades later on (in Victoria, Tasmania and WA). These various consequential effects were unforeseen by governments, because privatisation was an act of faith founded on the belief in private sector efficiency. However, company efficiencies did not necessarily deliver rail industry efficiency, because their sets of objectives were sometimes incompatible.

Intermodal competition and the outlook for interstate rail

There is a peculiarity about interstate freight in the eastern States of Australia – how little of it travels on rail.[693] It does not make sense to people in the industry, who know how labour-efficient and fuel-efficient rail is for interstate traffic, particularly between the State capitals. The MD of one of the two rail companies remaining in this market sector wrote in 2020:[694]

> "High levels of taxation and track access charges are making rail freight uncompetitive with other modes, even on long hauls where speed and volume should give rail a natural advantage."

The track access charges component is due to the ARTC's problematic situation – more on that at end of the next section. The ARTC does claim to have spent $7 billion upgrading its network (which includes both the interstate network and the Hunter Valley) from 2005 to 2020,[695] specifically to enable more freight on rail. However, there are other contributing reasons for the underuse of rail.

Recognising that little progress has been made on some of these issues, the ARA launched its Rail Freight Action Plan in 2021[696]

> "to support greater use of rail to meet our current and future freight needs"

> "The ARA is embarking on a range of actions to shape policies and complete research on key issues affecting the rail freight sector. We have already established three new working groups with industry leaders to explore opportunities for modal shift, competitive neutrality and interoperability."

17. Summing-up

The issue of lack of competitive neutrality has been discussed at least since 1999 (see chapter 13, under *Neutrality between road and rail modes*). It is a wicked problem because it includes the unequal capability of highways versus railways, that resulted from fifty years of Commonwealth investment in highways while States were not maintaining and investing in their rail networks. (See chapter 13, under *Government investment in highways versus railway infrastructure*.) This problem is compounded by the totally different and incomparable ways that road and rail vehicles are charged for use of their 'way', and by the complexity of the issues around changing the means by which road freighters are charged. These were described in a 2006 report from the Productivity Commission (PC), *Road and Rail Freight Infrastructure Pricing*. I reviewed this report in chapter 6, and it appears to me to be an exercise in obfuscation. In it, the PC ignored the decades of unequal investment between highways and railways, and reached a flawed conclusion that the road mode was not more subsidised that the rail mode. Yet previously, in 1999, the PC had alluded to a subsidy in its *Progress in Rail Reform* report:[697]

> "The existing road user charging system for heavy vehicles underrecovers road costs attributable to classes of vehicles which compete directly with railways. This confers a competitive advantage on long distance road transport operators."

Another reason for the underuse of rail for intercity freight is the fierce competitiveness of the road freighting industry. This competitiveness is based in part on five market distortions:

- The existence of the service quality disparity between highways and railway lines, based on fifty years of unequal funding for route and quality improvements
- The under-recovery of costs for the use of highways by heavy road vehicles, noted above
- The predominance of owner-drivers in the sector, with their artificially low wages caused by their "over-

supply" since the 1970s, and their long working hours, (see chapter 13, under *Barriers to entry – the road transport industry*)
- The effects of a 1977 change in tax policy that allowed owner-drivers to claim an investment allowance, causing a sudden increase in the size of the national truck fleet and a drop in prices for second-hand trucks, making it easy for owner-drivers to get into the industry and hard to leave it (see in chapter 8, under *The truckies' blockades*.)
- The complete absence of any charge to take account of the environmental degradation caused by having too many trucks on the highways, compared with the lesser effects that would result from the greater use of railways.

It has been recognised that changing the many issues that impede greater use of interstate rail will not be easy. Indeed, getting the federal government to accept that there is a problem, or even a missed opportunity to ameliorate Australia's current level of GHG emissions, has been a barrier to progress, particularly when both the major political groupings have been disinclined to act to reduce emissions.

The ARA, following up its Rail Freight Action Plan, announced in February 2022 that it had joined with the Freight on Rail Group of Australia (FORG) and with the federal Department of Infrastructure, Transport, Regional Development and Communications, to fund a new study to "unlock policy gridlock".[698]

> "Are we going to capitalise on the next cycle of post-COVID economic growth with efficient supply chains that add great value to Australian industry and exports? Or are we going to languish with policy settings that fail to harness the opportunities that rail freight provides?"
>
> "What is required is an evidence-based assessment of the key impediments to rail and identifying practical policy

17. Summing-up

changes that improve the productivity of rail freight and allow the industry to bring more freight onto rail where rail offers safety, economic and environmental benefits for customers and for the community."

Unfortunately, this initiative followed a succession of attempts to understand and reform the land transport sector, detailed in part B of this book. They include:

- The Neville Report of 1998, and the Smorgon Report of 1999, both of which had many valid recommendations that were ignored then dismissed by the Commonwealth Government (see in chapter 5)
- The Productivity Commission's 1999 report *Progress in Rail Reform*, which had several valid recommendations for rail which were later implemented, and for road reform which were not implemented (see in chapter 5). Also, using economic theory as its frame of reference, it seriously misunderstood the issues around line capacity, (see in appendix 5, *Managing access to rail networks in Australia*) and reached conclusions about how to manage the interstate rail network that were bizarre, and therefore incapable of being implemented
- The creation of the National Transport Commission (NTC) in 2004, and its attempt in 2009 "to develop a national framework to overcome coordination failures for rail transport planning, policy development and investment across Australia",[699] which was suppressed because the Commonwealth did not take the lead in federal-state relationships in relation to land transport (see in chapter 7)
- The *Rail Productivity Information Paper* of 2008, commissioned by the NTC, written by John Hearsch Consulting, that was shelved by the NTC. It had identified a "policy vacuum", because there was "no coherent vision ... at either Commonwealth or State level".[700]
- The creation in 2013 of the Transport and

Infrastructure Council, and its 2016 *National Rail Vision and Work Program*,[701] which was worthy but limited in its ambition. It failed to include, for example, any reference to the on-going lack of a national plan for rail transport (see in chapter 7).

Looking back over the litany of inquiries, studies and reports done in the last three decades, from the Industry Commission's 1991 report *Rail Transport* through to 2022, it is obvious how little real progress has been made. It seems that the main impediment is the intransigence of federal politicians and their advisors. They have taken an ideological stance that favours the economic well-being of some individuals and companies over the collective well-being. Also, the decisions made prior to federation in 1901 have cast long shadows; the States' continued control of their railways and the federal government's unwillingness to lead in the land transport policy area. That the ARA and FORG are pushing to get policy impediments identified and cleared, says that there is still a long way to go.

Network Issues

All the former government-owned railway systems were vertically separated at some time before or after their privatisation; only in Tasmania has the railway been reintegrated, because that is the most practical for a small and solitary rail system on an island. The process of vertical separation uncoupled the cost of infrastructure investment from the payback derived from operational service gains, thus making rail network investments unjustifiable in conventional BCAs. (See chapter 15, under *The Western Australian experience*.)

After thirty years of Rail Reform, there are (in 2023) ten administratively separate rail networks in Australia on which freight trains operate:
- The ARTC standard-gauge interstate network, stretching from South Brisbane through NSW (including the Hunter Valley), Victoria and South

17. Summing-up

Australia to Kalgoorlie in WA
- The narrow-gauge and standard-gauge networks of WA, managed by Arc Infrastructure
- The narrow-gauge lines of the Eyre Peninsula, now mostly unused except at the western end, operated by Aurizon (formerly by GWA then ORA)
- The line from Tarcoola (SA) to Darwin, operated by Aurizon as a vertically-integrated rail business connecting Adelaide and Darwin.
- The broad-gauge and standard-gauge lines of the 'country' network of Victoria, managed by V/Line for the Victorian Government
- The suburban and interurban passenger network in and around Sydney, previously the RailCorp network, now managed by Transport for NSW
- The notional Country Rail Network (CRN) of NSW, which is a collection of separate branch lines that link to the ARTC network &/or the RailCorp network, managed for the NSW Government under contract by the UGL Group (and previously by the John Holland Group)
- The Central Queensland Coal Network (CQCN) owned and managed by Aurizon
- The Queensland Rail (QR) network comprising all other narrow-gauge lines in the State (excluding the very narrow-gauge sugar cane railways).
- TasRail, owned again by the State Government, and operating as a vertically-integrated rail business on its narrow-gauge network.

While there is no reason why rail networks should be more integrated than they are, except in NSW and Victoria (see chapter 9, under *Division of the rail networks of south-east Australia*), it is interesting that the various Rail Reform processes collectively created these ten networks out of the five government-owned railway organisations that existed in 1990.

Network owners' current expectations of profitability of these ten networks are very different:
- Three of them are a part of vertically-integrated businesses where network profitability is likely not to be measured as such, and not relevant. (Eyre Peninsula, Darwin line, and TasRail)
- Four of them are government-owned networks, where freight trains are charged a small fee for network access, but there is also a large element of willing subsidy for other reasons; indeed, the Victorian and Queensland Governments pay some freight shippers an inducement to use the railway; hence profitability of these networks is not expected and not measured. (Victorian country network, NSW RailCorp network, NSW CRN, and QR)
- Two of them are heavy-haul rail networks, where long-term profitability is vital for the business and the network's existence (Arc Infrastructure in WA, and Aurizon's CQCN)
- One has a public benefit mission, "growing the volume of freight on rail",[702] but it is also expected to be profitable – the ARTC.

The two clear lessons from Australian Rail Reform are that the above-rail businesses can be profitable, but where the largely unrecoverable costs have to be incurred is below-rail, the railway networks. Profits are made only on the two heavy-haul networks (WA and the CQCN) where there is no effective competition from road transport for the millions of tonnes of bulk commodities. Elsewhere, it is a fact of life that no rail network can be operated profitably, in the sense that as a trading entity, it will provide a measurable and direct return on funds invested. Governments, that two decades previously sold or leased their rail networks to avoid making the necessary investments,[703] now accept that funding the maintenance and renewal of their rail networks is a responsibility similar to

17. Summing-up

funding regional roads. Both are prerequisites for productive economic activity and a more prosperous State.

Only the Commonwealth Government continues to insist that the ARTC shall be profitable, even when it is easily demonstrated that that strategy makes highways more attractive to freight shippers than rail. The ARTC gives an appearance of profitability in its annual accounts, but it is totally reliant on its owner to fund its improvements (except for the Hunter Valley Coal Chain), and its access charges are now high enough to drive away the interstate intermodal traffic it was set up to capture. (See chapter 15, under *The ARTC's impossible mission*.) Is it rational to allow virtually free use of the interstate highway network but not the interstate railway network? Given the Commonwealth Government's on-going investment in the ARTC, by increasing its ownership equity to fund the construction of Inland Rail, it is certain that ARTC will never be a profitable company in a conventional sense. Yet it has enormous value for Australia, with its potential as a more economic and environmentally sustainable means of land transport than highways are.

The Commonwealth Government needs to find some more appropriate entity form for the ARTC than being a company, and release it from the obligation to be profitable on its interstate routes. However, this cannot happen until the absurdity of its current situation is admitted openly. The ARTC could then charge only nominal access fees, comparable to those of the eastern State networks, to gain a significant increase in market share of the eastern States interstate market. (For the purposes of climate change amelioration, this would be using existing assets to reduce Australia's GHG emissions, which is one of the easiest ways to achieve such reduction.) The access fees need to be sufficient only to deter any opportunist from detrimental competition, i.e., buying up all its line capacity without intending to use it, just to gain market dominance among train operators. (See in appendix 5, under *Railway line capacity is a unique offering*.)

Conclusions

Short-sighted governmental decisions

Governments that sold in the 1990s the whole of their railways, or sold with a long-term lease of the rail network, did so for ideological reasons and/or to improve their budgets. (See in chapter 9, under *The principal reasons for ownership changes*.) These sales were for both short-term gain and longer-term avoidance of expenditure, but they were essentially short-sighted decisions.

There was no analysis of what roles they wanted for their rail systems in the future, because that was for the new owners to decide. There was no understanding that governments might have a role of guardianship of the community's assets, because under neoliberal economics and market reasoning, governments were certain that they were the exclusive owners of these assets, as much as companies might own assets, and therefore were at liberty to dispose of them. There was little analysis of what might go wrong after the sales, because governments thought that they would be freed of any obligations or concerns.

There was never any recognition that railways might have some value for the economy, in addition to that of the assets; therefore, there was no allowance made for any future government to take the view that railways were too big to be allowed to fail. Indeed, it was unthinkable at the time of sale that privatised railways might fail. However, these four governments[704] found years later that the assumptions of their predecessors at the time of sale were no longer valid. All found that a resumption of funding was needed to continue railway operations over the grain lines (in WA and Victoria), or over the whole network (NZ and Tasmania). With hindsight, it is now understood that freight railway networks are too valuable to State and national economies, and for the environment, to be handed to private sector companies to manage in their own interests.

One former government-owned railways sale that succeeded was that which created Pacific National (PN), now one of the largest rail companies in Australia, and possibly the largest in the interstate market. A significant difference from the four sales referred to above was that this one involved only the above-rail businesses and assets. Both NRC and FreightCorp had been separated years before their sale from their formerly-associated rail networks, therefore the new company did not have network assets to mine for profitability. However, the sale of NRC and FreightCorp was carelessly done, for governments that should have been concerned about creating the conditions for competition. PN was given control of all of FreightCorp's operational infrastructure (yards, terminals and refuelling points) in Sydney. As a result, all the other companies that began operations on the NSW network had to make their bases elsewhere in the State, which put them at some operational disadvantage (see in chapter 13, under *Barriers to entry; control of rolling-stock and other facilities by the incumbent operator; NSW*).

Government funding of freight rail networks is now an accepted necessity

It is now obvious in the grain growing areas of Australia that if that industry is to continue and survive the large variation in crop sizes from year to year, due to vagaries of weather and climate, the transport systems must be kept available for use after each harvest. The eventual failure, shown in 2006-2008, of the 1999 privatisation of the Victorian freight operation and country network (see in chapter 11) is a situation that all grain growing areas should be wary of. Grain marketing companies now own their own railway rolling-stock fleets so that they can be certain of rolling-stock supply. Governments must ensure that grain lines are kept up to a standard that will enable grain trains to run efficient cycles to port and back, providing turnarounds comparable with what road transporters can do.

Keeping lines open but with restricted train speeds is not good enough. Governments, as track owners, must carry the risks of climate variability on behalf of their communities. Expecting the private sector to do this would be inviting another market failure.

This gives governments which own rail networks the role of guardians of these networks, efficiently ensuring track quality and continuing line availability without regard to profitability, as though railway lines were roads. Of course, there will be years in which government finances will be squeezed, and governments can justify better uses for money that might be spent on railway upkeep, as happens with roads. The benefit of government control is that sooner or later these shortfalls in track maintenance and renewals must be addressed, because the guardian role does not disappear. The disbenefit of private sector control was that underspending on maintenance and renewals was easily justified by the profit motive, and easy to do because the consequences did not show up till years later. Ultimately, abandonment is always an option for the private sector, seen even as a sensible business decision, because the consequences are external to the company. Abandonment of rail lines due to neglect is less easy for governments if there is still a need for railway service.

There is an unexpected outcome from the various privatisations of freight rail networks. The need for governments to be guardians and funders of their rail networks is now more visible than it was in the 1990s, when all rail networks in Australasia were government-owned. The manifestations of this acceptance are various:

- The WA Government has its Agricultural Supply Chain Improvement (ASCI) program, through which it funds works to improve the rail network still controlled by Arc Infrastructure;
- The NSW Government instituted its *Fixing Country Rail* program in 2016, particularly to fund the upgrading of grain lines and silo sidings;

- The Victorian Government invested $1.2 billion in the four years after regaining its country network in 2007, and subsequently has invested heavily in upgrading and converting the Murray Basin lines from broad- to standard-gauge;
- The New Zealand and Tasmanian Governments have both committed to upgrading their rail networks since regaining ownership and control;
- The Queensland Government split QR in such a way that although the freight business was privatised, its non-coal rail network remained in government control, enabling on-going maintenance and renewal.

Industry Outlook

Technological developments in road freighting will challenge the need to get more freight on rail. The extent to which they will be permitted should be up to government-run regulatory agencies.

Electrically-powered trucks are not far over the horizon in 2023. These will be used to argue against a need for any transfer of freight to rail because the emissions from the tractive units will be seen to be zero. However, on the Australian continent at least, the batteries for these tractive units will be recharged by mains-power made mostly at coal-burning power stations. Hence, the emissions reductions could be somewhat illusory, depending on the efficiency differences between power plants and internal combustion engines.

Another development will be self-driving trucks, with various combinations of linked trailers, as now. The appeal to regulatory authorities to allow these will be based on not having drivers on board, and how that efficiency will flow through the economy to benefit everyone. If a safety case can be made, and approved, self-driving trucks would be allowable on multi-lane highways, if not everywhere.

The real game-changer would be the combination of self-driving trucks with the capability of platooning them. By using Wi-Fi to connect sequences of vehicles, a new type of road train would be possible, at least on the NHS where the roads are high quality with moderated grades and curvature. They are unlikely to be widely approved in New Zealand and Tasmania, where the majority of highways are not sufficiently well-developed for both these and regular traffic. Whether other road users would tolerate these road trains on the highways is a political question still to be addressed.

Part F

Appendices

1. Case study – the privatisation and renationalisation of New Zealand's railways

2. The history of efficiency as applied to New Zealand's North Island Main Trunk Line

3. A chronology – significant events in the last 50 years of Australasian commercial freight railways

4. Differences Between Railways in Australasia and North America

5. Managing Access to Rail Networks

   Endnotes

   Acknowledgements

   Image Credits

   Glossary

   References

   Contents in Detail

   Index

Appendix 1

Case Study – The Privatisation and Renationalisation of New Zealand's Railways

Downsizing prior to privatisation

There were four major impacts on New Zealand's railways in the 1980s that led to many changes before privatisation in 1993. These were:
- corporatisation in 1982, requiring NZR to be more profit-focussed,
- the deregulation of land transport in 1983, which led to the loss of some rail traffic to road,
- the reviews and recommendations from American consultants Booz Allen and Hamilton, from 1983 onward,
- electrification of the central part of the North Island Main Trunk line (NIMT), resulting from a government 'think big' initiative designed to reduce usage of imported diesel fuel. Designed in the late 1970s, it was not completed until June 1988.

During this decade between corporatisation and privatisation:
- staff numbers dropped from about 21,600[705] to about 5,000
- wagon numbers were reduced[706] from 25,750 to about 10,000.

Appendix 1

The ways by which this down-sizing was done were various:
- removal of guards and guards' vans from freight trains, reducing train crew size from 3 to 2,
- 'single manning' of freight trains, reducing train crew size from 2 to 1,
- implementing a policy of running 'fewer bigger trains' from 1986 onward, with increased use of multiple locomotives on trains, enabled by increasing the strength of wagon drawgear,
- increasing the proportion of express freight trains (at speeds up to 80km/h) comprising only bogie wagons – these made better use of line capacity by reducing track occupancy times, and improved the service with more overnight connections between cities,
- introduction of radio-control for shunting locos in major marshalling yards, reducing each shunting gang from normally 5 (2 in the loco & 3 on the ground) to just 1 on the ground,
- closure of the Otago Central Branch in 1990 and four other short branch lines, (most other rural branch lines had already been closed by 1982)
- progressive closure of rural stations, with the consequent simplification of train marshalling in major yards, enabling a reduced need for shunters
- disposal of 3,800 staff houses,[707] which had been maintained by railway tradesmen,
- introduction of new high-capacity bottom-dumping wagons for coal and other bulk granular traffics, replacing thousands of four-wheeled highside wagons
- increasing the use of containers and curtain-sided wagons, thus reducing the use of highside and flat wagons which required labour for covering their loads with tarpaulins
- progressive reduction of the numbers of the slower four-wheeled wagons in the fleet, reducing

- maintenance requirements, the need for sidings in yards and hence the need for urban land
- consolidation of signal boxes, train control centres, and train crew depots
- consolidation and mechanisation of track maintenance activities,
- closure of major workshops in Auckland, Wanganui and Christchurch,

To summarise, the great productivity improvements that NZRC achieved were made by reducing the inputs, not by increasing the outputs, i.e., net-tonne-kilometres (NTKs) moved. The latter was impossible due to the greater competition arising from the deregulation of land transport in 1983. Despite these productivity improvements, the NZRC had accumulated a total debt of $NZ1.2 billion by 1989.[708] This debt was mainly from operating losses, due to loss of traffic to road, reductions in freight rates to keep the railway competitive with road, and the cost of the NIMT electrification. At this time, the New Zealand Treasury was considering the complete closure of the railway system, or at least the closure of a substantial part of it. As an alternative, privatisation was seen as

> "the only way of avoiding a situation where in future, railways turned once again into a 'money pit', although this was never explicitly admitted to." [709]

How NZ Rail was privatised

The sale of New Zealand's railway, as a vertically-integrated on-going business, was first considered a possibility in 1988.[710] The Government commissioned a scoping study in 1990 which recommended immediate sale. As a result, New Zealand Rail Ltd was created in October 1990 to operate the trains and ferries, and manage the rail network. This was the core business that could be sold, consisting only of transport activities. Land ownership, property management, and the accumulated debt were left with the New Zealand Railways Corporation (NZRC).[711]

Appendix 1

The Government had had a concern that buyers might be attracted by the possibility of making a quick dollar by selling off land, possibly to the detriment of the rail business. If there was land that could be sold off, then the Government wanted to keep the proceeds. In 1992, all railway land holdings were classified into 'core' (required for current and future rail operations) and 'non-core' (surplus to operational requirements). In the latter category, there were many parcels of land associated with closed stations or suburban freight yards that were being used to park old wagons or were just growing weeds. Thus, when New Zealand Rail Ltd was sold, it had been made clear what land it would rent from the NZRC (at a 'peppercorn' rental) and what land was left to the Corporation to dispose of. NZRC remained as a land-holding government entity, charged with leasing or selling land, or transferring it to other government entities or to local governments for commuter parking and street improvements. All unsold surplus land was transferred to the management of what is now Land Information New Zealand on 1 January 1994.[712]

After the creation of New Zealand Rail Ltd the Government deferred its sale for two years while these land holdings were sorted, and until NZ Rail's profitability had been demonstrated. In late 1992 the government decided to proceed with the sale and appointed Bankers' Trust as government advisors for the sale. Six groups were shortlisted as potential bidders in 1993:[713]

- A consortium led by Wisconsin Central Transportation (an award-winning regional railroad in USA), with investment funders Berkshire Partners (USA) and Fay Richwhite (NZ)
- Sea Containers, with Anschutz Corporation (owner of two large American rail companies: Southern Pacific, and Denver & Rio Grande)
- Mainfreight, a New Zealand based Australasian logistics and transport company, with Railroad Development Corporation (USA)

- Freightways, a New Zealand freight forwarder, with Noel Group, an American investment company
- An all New Zealand consortium of Port of Tauranga, Port of Lyttelton, and Pacifica Shipping, with National Mutual and AMP
- Ports of Auckland, Port of Wellington, Stagecoach, and French shipping company Sofrana-Unilines

On 20 July 1993, the government announced it had sold NZ Rail Ltd to the Wisconsin-led consortium for $NZ400 million. This sum has been estimated to be about one tenth of its replacement value.[714] The bid was described by the Minister of Finance as the "cleanest bid", that is, not necessarily the highest, but it was unconditional.[715] The consortium would take over the company's current debt of $NZ71.7 million, and the balance of $NZ328.3 million would be used by the government to pay off some of its own debt. The sale included all tracks, track structures and buildings, rolling-stock, business contracts, and the transfer of all existing staff. The land of the rail corridors would be leased to the business by the NZ Railways Corporation for $1 per year.

The consortium, known as Tranz Rail, took over NZ Rail Ltd on 1 October 1993.

The Tranz Rail years

What follows are brief descriptions of the then publicly-known[716] events relevant to the ownership and control of the rail system in New Zealand. Not included here are the significant changes to marketing, operations and services, which created an increase of over 50% in NTKs hauled, but without an equivalent gain in revenues. (See in chapter 11, under *New Zealand*)

1994

One of the first things Tranz Rail did was to sell its 15% stake in Clear Communications for $NZ72.6 million.[717] Clear was a telecommunications business in which Railways had acquired shares in the 1980s by granting it the excess capacity of fibre-optic cables buried alongside rail tracks, particularly along the North Island Main Trunk. This sale terminated the income from Clear dividends, and enabled a $NZ100 million capital repayment to the private shareholders in July 1995. (See below)

As a private company until the 1996 IPO, Tranz Rail did not publish annual reports. However, its increasing profitability was published in 1996:[718]

> "Since privatisation operating profits have risen substantially from $54M in 1993 to $105M in 1995 (adjusting for redundancy payments in the 1992-3 year)."

It is likely that some of this increase in profits was due to increased traffic and greater efficiency. However, it is known that part of the reason for a stated increase in operating profits was due to a change in 1994 to the accounting treatment of track renewals,[719] which include long-term maintenance projects such as rerailing, resleepering and ballast cleaning. When the railway was government-owned, the cost of this work was expensed against income. Under Tranz Rail ownership, this cost was recorded as a capital, not an operating expense. The net effect was to boost operating profits higher than they would have been. Tranz Rail also changed the economic lifespans of its assets, creating a similar financial advantage. As reported by a financial analyst:[720]

> "The depreciation life of wagons was extended from 25 to 30 years, ships from 18 to 20 years, tunnels and bridges from 45 to 80 years and locomotives from 13 to 23 years. The longer economic life of these assets led to a dramatic drop in the annual depreciation charge as a percentage of total assets. In the June 1993 year, the last under Crown ownership, the depreciation charge represented 9.1 per cent of average fixed assets. In the June 2001 year, the charge was down to 6.4 per cent."

1995

In July, Tranz Rail made a $NZ100 million capital repayment to its private shareholders.[721] This was done via a buyback of 27 million shares from existing shareholders at $NZ3.70 per share.[722] At this price, the original shareholders were able to retain a majority of their shares while retrieving a majority of their original capital contribution. One of these shareholders, the Wisconsin Central Transportation Corporation had contributed approximately $US22.2 million to the consortium's purchase of NZ Rail and it received back $US21 million from this repayment, which it used to pay off debt in the USA.[723] The New Zealand investment company, Fay Richwhite & Co, had contributed $NZ33.4 million to the consortium's purchase, and received back $NZ28.2 million.[724]

Tranz Rail bought fifteen second-hand locomotives cheaply from Queensland in 1995 to cater for planned increased traffic. These were then rebuilt at its Hutt workshops. However, they were not popular with crews, and after a short period in service in New Zealand, they were sold in 1998 to ATN for use in Tasmania, which has the same track gauge as New Zealand.

Net profit for the 1994/95 financial year was $NZ73.6 million, which was later reported[725] to be a peak, not matched since.

1996

The major event this year for Tranz Rail was the IPO. Before the sale agreement was signed in 1993, the government had sought and received assurances from the consortium as to their intention for a future public share offering.[726] The government's wish was that small investors in New Zealand should be given the chance to share in the prosperity. Hence, Tranz Rail was floated on the New Zealand stock market, at an initial price of $NZ6.19, on 14 June 1996.[727] However, it was also simultaneously listed on the NASDAQ Stock Exchange in New York, and the majority of shares were allocated there. Nearly 20 million shares were traded in New York on the opening day, at over $NZ7.00 per share, making quick profits for speculators. Tranz Rail's intention had been to offer 27 million shares, but the issue was over-subscribed by 15%. Consequently 31 million shares were issued, raising $NZ191.9 million for Tranz Rail to use to pay debt.[728]

In the year that followed the IPO, the Tranz Rail share price rose to a peak of $NZ9, due in part to the publicised growth in freight task of 28% over four years. Berkshire Partners sold most of its shares at more than $8 each between November 1996 and March 1997.[729] Fay Richwhite and Wisconsin Central (which saw itself as a long-term investor) retained most of their shares at this time.

In December 1996, Tranz Rail sold its DFT locomotives and some recently-purchased wagons for $NZ131.5 million to Chicago Freight Car Leasing (CFCL), and as part of the deal it leased them back for 12 years.[730] Hence, in 1996 Tranz Rail raised a total $323 million from this source and the share float, that could be used for debt repayments.

1997–1998

Tranz Rail formed a company in Australia, with Wisconsin Central owning 33%, called Australian Transport Network (ATN) to pursue business opportunities arising from the coming privatisation of various rail systems there. In November, ATN bought TasRail for $A22 million (about $NZ24 million). Early gains in TasRail profitability were achieved by gaining new business and reducing labour costs. Using technologies already proven in New Zealand, remote-control of shunting in yards and driver-only train operations were quickly implemented. ATN announced a profit of $A1.2m for the first seven months of operation,[731] but after that, the financial results were not published. Because TasRail was only about one sixth the size of Tranz Rail, the impact on Tranz Rail's profits was only ever a small one, if at all. (ATN also made a bid for V/Line Freight at the end of 1998, including a lease on the Victorian broad-gauge network, but Rail America won with the highest bid. After that, ATN did not pursue any other purchases of existing Australian railways.)

Between November 1996 and March 1997, major shareholder Berkshire Partners sold most of its shares at more than $NZ8 each.[732] Tranz Rail shares reached their peak price of $NZ9 in July 1997.

1999

In 1999 Wisconsin Central was being pursued by the privatised Canadian National Railway, which was not interested in holding investments in Australasia. Ed Burkhardt, the Wisconsin Central chairman, was replaced in that role in July 1999, and consequently he had to step down as the chairman of Tranz Rail in August 1999. He was replaced by Bob Wheeler. Also, the Tranz Rail CEO since 1990, Dr Francis Small, announced his retirement around this time and was eventually replaced by Michael Beard in May 2000.

Major shareholder Fay Richwhite sold 6.2 million shares at an average $NZ3.67 per share.[733]

Also in 1999, Tranz Rail sold and leased back the newly-built rail-ferry *Aratere*, for $US55 million,[734] about $NZ104 million at that time. This, and the previous sale-and-lease-back of rolling-stock in 1996, added liabilities and reduced Tranz Rail's profitability. They were, in effect, creating cash by borrowing from future revenue. The money from the sale of the *Aratere* was not treated as income, but the operating lease payments were expensed in the following years, until a change in accounting treatment was made in 2002.[735]

2000

The appointment of a new CEO brought with it a change in company strategy. Chairman Bob Wheeler described the issues to shareholders at the October 2000 Annual Meeting:[736]

> "Our current way of operating does not give an adequate return to meet long-term capital requirements. We have

poor asset utilisation. Even our trucks do not work as hard as those of our competitors. Our high fixed costs don't give us flexibility to quickly adjust to changing business circumstances, and we don't have the ability to increase, and in some cases maintain, our freight rates to recover costs."

Tranz Rail announced that it would it sell, close, or otherwise dispose of all its operations except its core rail freight, its door-to-door distribution services, and its Cook Strait ferries. The Distribution Services group would be multi-modal, and rail would only be used for this traffic if it were the most cost-effective transport solution.[737] This signalled an intention to use door-to-door trucking more often, eliminating the linehaul on rail. Non-core operations included commuter services and long-distance passenger trains. Tranz Rail also planned to out-source many of its in-house services, including track maintenance, rolling-stock and locomotive maintenance, and terminal operations. The number of staff expected to transfer to other employers was about 3400, leaving a core of about 600 employed by Tranz Rail. In Bob Wheeler's words:[738]

> "The Tranz Rail of the future will be a transport services management company. It will be smaller, more focused, safer, less capital intensive, driven by service excellence and more profitable."

A 'transport services management company' was how Michael Beard had structured the ANZDL shipping line prior to joining Tranz Rail. The intention was to turn the fixed costs of owning assets into variable costs of their use. The CFO since 1999, Mark Bloomer, was reported to have said about the proposal that[739]

> "Large-scale restructuring [is] sorely needed to bring back a healthy share price and bigger profit after more than a decade of poor performance."

Tranz Rail's share price at around this time was $NZ3.80.

Also included in the announcement at the AGM was an intention to close lines with "dubious returns".[740] These lines included the Napier to Gisborne and the Putaruru to Rotorua lines.

Also at this time, Tranz Rail announced a looming loss for the first quarter of the 2000/01 financial year due to sharply rising fuel costs, nearly double that of the same quarter of the previous year. This was in spite of three tranches of freight price rises totalling 16-17% since March.[741] The former Tranz Rail chairman, Ed Burkhardt, was quoted that Tranz Rail should have foreseen this situation by having fuel-price pass-through provisions written into its contracts with customers.[742]

> "If Tranz Rail is absorbing the price rises itself because they've written contracts that don't provide for it, I don't see it as a fuel price problem – it's a management problem."

It was probably not a coincidence that Tranz Rail introduced, in December, a Fuel Adjustment Factor as a surcharge on its invoices, instead of another rate increase.

2001

In February, Tranz Rail reported a $6.7 million loss for the six months to the end of year 2000, due mainly to the cost of diesel fuel being 91% higher for the December quarter compared with the same period in 1999. This half-year loss also included "an abnormal provision for organisation change"[743] of $16.5 million, the bulk of which was for moving the company's head office from Wellington to Auckland. The cost of this 'reorganisation', including staff redundancy payouts, was later revealed in the full-year financial result to be $21.3 million.[744] The justification for moving the head office to Takapuna was always flimsy. However, the move did enable the new CEO to live and work on Auckland's affluent North Shore.

In June 2001 Tranz Rail sold 50% of its Tranz Scenic business to two directors of the Victorian rail operator West Coast

Railway for $33 million.[745] This sale included long-distance passenger rolling-stock and ten diesel locomotives of the DC class, reclassified as the DCP class, and two EF class electric locomotives. As a result of this sale, some long-distance passenger trains were kept operating while services on other provincial routes were deemed not viable and ceased to run.[746] (In 2004 this 50% share was repurchased from West Coast Railway by Toll NZ.)

After making an operating surplus before tax of less than $1 million from a total revenue of $628.4 million in the 2000/01 financial year,[747] the Board decided to suspend dividend payouts.[748] Up until April 2001, 8.5 cents per share had been paid out every six months,[749] amounting to about $NZ23 million per year, or $115 million in total. Dividends were never paid again after 2001. In mid-2001, Tranz Rail's debt was $NZ450 million.[750]

The other major event in 2001 was the sale of the Auckland rail network and urban passenger trains. In February it was reported[751] that Tranz Rail had reached agreement with the Auckland Regional Council to sell its lease of the rail network in the Auckland area for $112 million. The purpose was to provide a foundation for Auckland's suburban passenger services under a different operator, because Tranz Rail was unwilling to invest in new commuter rolling-stock. During the year, the NZ Government took over the negotiations on behalf of the Auckland Councils, and on 24 Dec 2001 it announced it had bought the network for $81 million.[752] The following year there were calls from Wellington area mayors for government to take over their metropolitan network in a similar way because of dissatisfaction about Tranz Rail's maintenance and performance.[753]

2002

Late in year 2000, the last of the original Tranz Rail shareholders, Wisconsin Central (24%, by then owned by Canadian National

Railway) and NZ merchant bankers Fay Richwhite (15%), announced their wish to sell their remaining holdings, as off-market one-off sales to institutions. In February 2002, they both achieved this, selling their stakes at $3.70 and $3.60 a share respectively, to a range of institutions and pension funds.[754] Tranz Rail stock rose to $3.85 shortly after news of these sales, and by April had risen to over $4.00.

In February, Tranz Rail announced a $43.3 million profit for the six months to the end of 2001.[755] However, this profit was made possible only by the sales of the Auckland metropolitan network to the government and 50% of the Tranz Scenic business. These sales covered a loss on operations for the half-year of $10 million,[756] as well as the interest on debts.

By April 2002 Tranz Rail had completed the out-sourcing of its maintenance needs (part of the restructuring plan announced in October 2000) to international groups — infrastructure to Transfield, and locomotive and wagon maintenance to Alstom. These contracts committed Tranz Rail to regular payments for coming years, but its CEO expected that there would be total annual savings of about 10% as a result.[757]

By mid-2002, both the major ratings agencies (Moody's and Standard & Poor's) had downgraded Tranz Rail's credit ratings, their concern being its planned asset write-downs of up to $170 million.[758] But around the same time, Tranz Rail changed its accounting practice for its leases of rolling-stock and the ferry Aratere. Up till then they had been considered as 'operating leases', meaning the payments were expensed in the year in which they were incurred. With the change, they became 'finance leases', meaning the payments were capitalised (increasing the value of assets) and depreciated. This change had a net effect of increasing the 'ebitda' profit for the 2001/02 financial year by $4.8 million to $78.4 million. [759]

In mid-July, shares had reached a new low of $2.30.[760] Around this time the Rail Freight Action Group (RFAG) was formed. A loose grouping of Tranz Rail's major industrial customers, it comprised: [761]

- Fonterra, New Zealand's major dairy products manufacturer and exporter
- Carter Holt Harvey and Fletcher Challenge Forests, both manufacturers and exporters of timber, pulp and paper
- Solid Energy, the state-owned coal mining company, and
- BHP New Zealand Steel Ltd.

These companies shared concerns that Tranz Rail was in a shaky financial position, and appeared not to be viable for longer-term contracts. Tranz Rail had asked some of these customers to make a contribution to new wagons or track upgrades, which were unwelcome requests at a time when international log and pulp prices were at a low level. RFAG hired a public relations consultant and conducted its campaign through the media. If there was going to be any government intervention to rescue Tranz Rail, as was being advocated by then by two minor parties in parliament, RFAG wanted an input, because it saw that New Zealand's export competitiveness was at stake. Its view was that the government should take over ownership and responsibility for the rail network, but it wanted also that Tranz Rail lose its monopoly right to use the network. An "open access model" would make it easier for the government to make objective decisions about where to spend infrastructure dollars – whether on road or rail.

By September, rumours of 'rights issue' saw the share price drop to $1.30,[762] as institutional investors sold down to avoid this. The rights issue raised $66 million [763] before the end of the year, but in the meantime, Tranz Rail had a public dispute with Citibank over the refinancing of a $250 million "multi-option credit facility" that it had with a group of banks.[764] This dispute was resolved about five weeks after the 15 October expiry date of the credit facility,[765] but it brought to public notice just how much Tranz Rail was struggling financially.

2003

April 2003 was a dramatic month for Tranz Rail. It advised the stock market that its sales and profits would be less than previously forecast, due to a drought affecting agricultural commodities and a strike at a major pulp and paper mill.[766] The share price dropped to 77 cents. Then both the rating agencies again downgraded Tranz Rail, but only after it failed at the High Court to gag Standard & Poor's announcement. It was disclosed at the Court that Tranz Rail was fully drawn on its bank facilities and was depending on "unconcluded future asset sales" to be liquid at the end of June.[767] This was a reference to a $10.7 million sale of rolling-stock proposed by Tranz Rail to Carter Holt Harvey, which the latter later declined. By mid-April, the share price had sunk to its lowest-ever level at 30 cents, giving it a market worth of just $63 million. Within days, the CFO for just on a year, Wayne Collins, was replaced by Tranz Rail director John Loughlin. It was reported that "the company teeters on the brink of insolvency".[768] Although it was trading profitably, it did not have the funds available for a bank loan payment of $14 million, and the next payment of $21 million for the lease of the ferry *Aratere*, due by the end of June.[769]

Two companies had been keeping an eye on Tranz Rail from afar, and on 15 May one of them pounced. Rail America was then a holding company of several regional railroads in the USA and Canada, and one in Australia – Freight Australia, which leased and operated the Victorian broad-gauge network. Rail America made a takeover bid, offering 75 cents per share from 30 May, conditional upon gaining 90% shareholder acceptance. It also offered to take over Tranz Rail's debts at that time of $236 million, making the total offer worth $394 million.[770] On news of the takeover offer, Tranz Rail shares jumped to 76 cents. The other company with an interest in Tranz Rail was Toll, the Australian transport logistics company that owned half of Pacific National. It had been interested in Tranz Rail for two years with a view to acquisition, and was taken by surprise by Rail America's offer.[771] Straight away it began buying up Tranz Rail shares, and by 21 May, it had obtained a 6% stake, at below 80 cents per share.[772] Meanwhile, Rail America had held meetings with the Minister of Transport, unions, and some of Tranz Rail's key customers. Then on 23 May it withdrew its offer without having entered into any formal due diligence process. No reasons were given, but clearly Tranz Rail was not going to be the bargain it was hoping for after Toll started buying up shares. By 23 May, Toll had gained a 10% stake in Tranz Rail.[773] On 29 May, Toll announced it would launch a takeover bid in early June, offering 75 cents per share, as Rail America had done, and similarly would take on Tranz Rail's debt and lease obligations.[774] The purchase was conditional on Tranz Rail not selling any businesses or assets, and that it would be fully funded by debt.[775] However, Tranz Rail needing to meet a debt repayment obligation in June, said it would "press on with sales". This statement was disingenuous because, as we shall see below, Tranz Rail had already secretly agreed to a Heads of Agreement with the government on a package that would see its immediate financial difficulty removed. The government would inject $44 million as part of a broader package to take control of the rail network, subject to the agreement being approved by shareholders in July.

It had been known publicly since February that the NZ Government was pondering how best to prevent even a temporary closure of rail services, a situation that would present the government with what the Finance Minister, Dr Cullen, described as "a horrendous roading problem". One option included subsidising Tranz Rail's freight operations, but not favoured by Dr Cullen because it [776]

> "risked putting too much power into the hands of the subsidised party, which could threaten to stop providing services unless it was given more money"

Another option was for the government to buy back some or all of the rail system. After Tranz Rail approached the government on 21 May because receivership would result if it could not meet lease payments for wagons and locomotives due on 19 June, the Government and Tranz Rail signed a Heads of Agreement (HoA) on 7 June, comprising four key elements:[777]

- the government would buy back the network for $1, and invest $100 million for its upgrading & renewal
- the government would take a controlling 35% stake in Tranz Rail, injecting equity of $75.8 million through the issue of 113 million new shares at 67 cents per share
- Tranz Rail would surrender its lease of the land and be compensated $50 million for loss of property and income from sub-leases; $44 million of this sum to be paid immediately as a down payment, enabling Tranz Rail to stay solvent, and
- Tranz Rail would pay for the use of the network at agreed annual rates that would approximate track maintenance costs, but not cover the capital investment to upgrade the network. It was estimated this would 'subsidise' Tranz Rail by up to $20 million per year.

The government's reasons for the HoA were explained in at the time:

> "We are entering this transaction for important public policy reasons: to ensure that the trains keep running and to secure rail as a vital piece of infrastructure in the national interest ... if the rail system were to cease operating — even temporarily — the disruption to the economy would be significant."

However, Toll did not want the government to be a shareholder in Tranz Rail, and initially it also wanted control of the rail network. In response to the government's proposal, it increased its share price offer to 95 cents in mid-June, hoping to gain at least 51% of shares.

A few days later, Tranz Rail cut its operating profit (ebit) forecast for the year to 30 June from $55.8 million to $40 million. It also reduced its ebit forecast for the 2003/04 financial year from $78 million to $48 million.[778] For some investors, the decreasing credibility of Tranz Rail's management increased the attractiveness of Toll's offer. By 27 June, Toll had bought just under 20% of Tranz Rail shares.

On 7 July the government announced it had reached a draft Heads of Agreement with Toll,[779] which would be activated if Toll Holdings bought Tranz Rail by acquiring at least 90% of the shares. The HoA was similar to the one previously agreed with Tranz Rail, but with substantive differences:

- the government would still buy back the network for $1, but would invest $200 million for its upgrading over five years, and Toll would invest $100 million in new rolling-stock
- the government would not take a stake in Tranz Rail
- Tranz Rail / Toll would surrender its lease of the land and be compensated $50 million for loss of property and income from sub-leases; $44 million of this sum had already been paid as a down payment to enable Tranz Rail to stay solvent
- Tranz Rail / Toll would pay for the use of the network at agreed annual rates that would cover the full cost of the network, except for the initial upgrading investment of $200 million. Therefore, there would be no ongoing subsidy to Tranz Rail / Toll. This was a key point of difference to the previous HoA. It appears that that the government was happy to subsidise a struggling New Zealand company, but not a prosperous overseas-owned one.

The institutional investors in Tranz Rail, which at that time held about 46% of the shares,[780] saw this agreement as benefiting Toll and not themselves. Also, the Tranz Rail Board recommended to shareholders not to accept Toll's takeover offer. On 28 July Tranz Rail shares traded at a high of $1.07.[781]

There was a market expectation of a revised offer from Toll, higher than 95 cents a share, but Toll said it had no intention of increasing its bid. Consequently, a stalemate ensued, with Toll twice extending the closing date for its takeover offer. Then on 6 September Toll announced an increase to $1.10 a share,[782] which convinced some institutional investors to sell. However, Toll still had to win over some 3000 small shareholders. By 10 October, Toll had 82.7% of the shares, appointed its own directors to the Board, and moved in its own top managers, replacing Michael Beard and his team.[783] It had taken Toll nearly five months to gain control of Tranz Rail. In December, Toll renamed Tranz Rail as Toll NZ Ltd.[784]

How the Government regained the rail network

Protracted negotiations on the details of the draft Heads of Agreement between Toll and the government took place from late 2003 through to just before the deadline at midnight on 30 June 2004. Thus, the government took back ownership of the rail network from 1 July 2004.

This event concluded a Labour Government[785] ambition which had been in gestation for somewhat longer than was generally known.[786] Two events had probably alerted the government that all was not well at Tranz Rail. On 24 December 2001, the government announced it had bought the Auckland rail network from Tranz Rail for $81 million, after months of negotiations on behalf of the Auckland Councils. In February 2002, the significance of this sale to Tranz Rail was clear when it reported a profitable half-year to 31 December, but only because this sale made up for an operating loss. Also in February, the last of the shares held by any of the original consortium that bought Tranz Rail were sold. The consortium had left New Zealand, and it had left Tranz Rail owned by an assortment of trusting institutional and small shareholders.

Appendix 1

Meanwhile the government had begun working on land transport funding and policy issues. On 28 Feb 2002, the Cabinet Legislation Committee agreed on a raft of decisions, including these:
- "papers on rail policy are still under consideration, but that **it is a priority within that policy to maintain the integrity and viability of the national rail network**" (My emphasis)
- "transport policy will ensure that, wherever appropriate, incentives work to encourage more heavy freight to be carried by rail"

In March 2002, Tranz Rail put a draft proposal to Government "further to discussions between Dr Cullen and Mr Beard ... that we believe will be acceptable to both Tranz Rail Ltd and the Crown." It purported to address the government's priorities of network preservation and maintenance, and rail viability. It had four parts:
- The sale of Tranz Rail's infrastructure assets to the Crown
- A services agreement whereby Tranz Rail would provide track maintenance, train control and train services, and would be paid sufficiently to enable it to earn its Weighted Average Cost of Capital (WACC) "plus a reasonable profit margin"
- A road & rail pricing equalisation where a government agency would "level the playing field" by subsidising Tranz Rail instead of funding road upgrades
- Tranz Rail would provide track extensions, upgrades and new services if it were subsidised to do so.

Not surprisingly, Dr Cullen (the Minister of Finance) sought more time, and sought advice from Treasury on the government's options for gaining control of the rail network.

On 24 April 2002, Michael Beard wrote[787] directly to Michael Cullen seeking a meeting, but including these paragraphs:

> "Tranz Rail would like nothing more than to be the operator of a wide range of rail freight services over a wide-spread network that is generously maintained. However, the reality is that land transport policies of successive governments have eroded Tranz Rail's ability to compete despite significant improvements to Tranz Rail's efficiency.
>
> As discussed with your officials, we accept the difficulties of increasing road user charges as a means of addressing this. Unfortunately and inescapably, in the absence of some material adjustment to the relative costs of road versus rail, there will be further reduction of rail services. We have a rail business that is increasingly focused on a smaller number of key freight routes, and major restructuring has been required and will continue to be required to achieve satisfactory returns. Outside of these key routes, due to the current policy and market environment, rail services are simply not viable."
>
> "In the absence of an agreement with the Government on key aspects of the Government/Tranz Rail relationship and regulatory environment, we will have no choice but to disinvest in rail services and lines in order to meet the legitimate expectations of our now predominantly New Zealand and Australian shareholders."

There is no record of a reply, but the Finance Minister was taking advice on ways to acquire Tranz Rail as a whole, in order to separate out the network. The consultants' early conclusion was

> "The Crown's position would be much stronger if Tranz Rail were in financial distress. In that event, it is unlikely that there would be other buyer interest, so any offer from the Crown may be the only option to shareholders."

In the next few months, Dr Cullen took advice also on how a government-owned rail network could be operated. One key issue was whether to allow 'open access' to any freight train operator which might want to enter the New Zealand market, or to preserve Tranz Rail's exclusive right to operate freight trains. From July the Rail Freight Action Group (RFAG) was advocating open access because of dissatisfaction with Tranz Rail's service quality, and there being no other rail operator to turn to. However, Treasury had by then received a report from an Australian-based rail consultant which suggested that intramodal competition (which open access can enable) was not feasible for a light-density rail network (which was and still is the case in New Zealand). Open access is an attractive concept in theory, but if there were more than one train operator, each would cherry-pick the main freight flows. As a result, there would be a reduction, not growth, of freight on the railway, as was happening at that time on the NSW network after privatisation of its above-rail operations. Alternatively, with Tranz Rail left as the incumbent operator, it could be too difficult or unattractive for a new operator to start up, as was the situation on the Victorian country network at that time after the State government declared open access while Freight Australia was the incumbent.

Dr Cullen also took advice from Treasury on the government's options for acquiring the rail network. There were three options, none with a certain outcome. One was to make a takeover offer for Tranz Rail, which was risky because no matter what price was offered, some shareholders would hold out for more, on the basis that the government had deep pockets. The second option was to negotiate directly with Tranz Rail. The third option was to wait for a third party to emerge, wanting to acquire Tranz Rail, and agree to acquire the rail infrastructure for a specified amount after the third party's takeover. Hence the government would need to agree the price to be offered by the acquirer. The expectation was that any third party would first approach the government to understand its objectives for the network.

In November 2002, after the Labour government had been re-elected, Tranz Rail asked to resume discussions with the government on Tranz Rail's "requirement for a 'level playing field' between road and rail". Dr Cullen agreed to a resumption of discussions, not directly but with Treasury officials. Discussions were to include "our previously expressed concern about network integrity and service coverage", meaning that there should be negotiation on the government's wish to acquire the rail network.

In December, the government announced its New Zealand Transport Strategy, a document intended to guide future government decision-making on transport policy and legislation. Its main objectives were:[788]

- "To assist economic development;
- To assist safety and personal security;
- To improve access and mobility;
- To protect and promote public health, and
- To ensure environmental sustainability."

Obviously, if the government could control the mainly-for-freight rail network, it would assist in meeting particularly the first and last of these objectives. Within this general strategic framework, the government described its national rail objectives as:

- "network integrity – the ability to maintain (and extend) the integrity of the network in terms of coverage and maintenance levels;
- service coverage – the ability to either increase service levels or alter the type of services provided on the network; and
- alternative operators – the ability for alternative operators to access the network. Options range from open access to the rail infrastructure to, alternative rail operators being able to access the infrastructure at the margins."

By March 2003, the government had been approached by two different parties with an interest in buying Tranz Rail, but not at the then current share prices (over $1). Both were happy to enter into a Heads of Agreement in the future, for the government to acquire the rail network after their purchase of Tranz Rail. Both understood that the network had a negative market value by then, and would allow the Government to acquire it at no charge, given its commitment to a significant amount of refurbishment. In contrast, it was thought that Tranz Rail would want to sell the network only for a figure near to its book value of around $400 million. Such a sale would require the approval of a majority of Tranz Rail's shareholders, and Treasury's advice was that they would refuse a deal at a negligible or modest price.

So the government could not make progress at this time because Tranz Rail was not yet distressed enough for its shareholders to agree to sell the network, and the potential buyers of Tranz Rail were waiting for a fall in share prices before making a takeover bid. Events from April 2003 onward (described above) removed the government's predicament.

The draft Heads of Agreement that it signed with Toll on 7 July 2003 took, for various reasons, nearly a year to be signed. From 1 July 2004 the National Rail Access Agreement came into effect. The government now owned the rail network, managed by its agency called ONTRACK, and Toll had to pay a Track Access Charge for the right to use the network, with an exclusive right to operate freight trains. There would be no Open Access.

The Toll Rail years

The price Toll paid for Tranz Rail on the sharemarket was something over $200 million, but this acquisition actually cost a lot more. In October 2003, Tranz Rail announced it had bought out the lease on the railferry *Aratere* for an undisclosed sum, but likely to have been over $50 million. The deal was financed by Toll Finance (NZ) Limited.[789] In addition, when Toll took control of Tranz Rail, the latter's debt to banks was likely to have been still over $200 million. So, all up, its total financing requirement to take over Tranz Rail would have been approximately $450 to $500 million.

During the five years that Toll controlled the freight rail business, the total traffic task changed little. It remained between 13.15 and 13.75 million net tonnes per year,[790] while total land freight transport grew by 11%, measured in million NTKs. By this measure, rail's market share declined from 22% to 17% in this time. This happened despite a government policy to encourage a shift of freight from road to rail, and an incentive in the access charge agreement for Toll to increase traffic on rail.

Significantly, the Government still had an expectation that Toll would pay access fees, increasing annually so that ONTRACK, the new guardian of the rail network, would not be subsidised forever. The Finance Minister was reported to have said when the deal was announced in August 2003:[791]

> "We recognise [Toll has] the managerial and financial capacity to restore Tranz Rail to viability. Toll's strong balance sheets also mean that it will be able to put in the capital required to rebuild the rail fleet, and to pay full access costs for the rail network in the long term rather than rely on a subsidy from the taxpayer."

The details for the setting of access fees quickly became a matter of dispute, because the two parties to the National Rail Access Agreement (NRAA) had different objectives. ONTRACK wanted to maintain the network to a standard suitable to last for future years, but Toll, as its current user, wanted to avoid any track expense that was more than absolutely necessary. Toll was required to pay the Track Access Charge (TAC) monthly, and for the first Annual Period (1 July 2004 to 30 June 2005) the annual total was $38.379 million, plus GST. This sum became known as the Base TAC.[792] Because ONTRACK had no maintenance cost information at its start-up, this sum was based on budget and supporting information provided by Toll, which had been paying Transfield for network maintenance up till then.

Appendix 1

For subsequent years, the NRAA provided for ONTRACK to put forward a forecast of its expenditure for each of the next three years, which Toll was permitted to dispute. Not surprisingly, the two parties to the agreement did not reach agreement on the TAC to be charged for each of the 2005-06, 2006-07 and 2007-08 years. As provided for in the NRAA, an Independent Auditor reviewed both parties' budgets for the 2005-06 year, with both appearing at a week-long hearing in November 2006. The difference between the two budgets (ONTRACK at $57.96 million and Toll at $42.48 million) was made up of 22 different items; mainly questions of what items should be included or excluded from the TAC, and of how much maintenance was really required. The Independent Auditor's comments on this reveal the underlying philosophical differences of the dispute:

> "To listen to the evidence and submissions for the two parties, one may well have thought that two different Rail Networks were being described. ONTRACK painted a picture of a rundown network, close to collapse, which required substantially more maintenance than should have been necessary, at least until the capital works which were necessary to bring the network up to standard had been incurred. In contrast, Toll described a network which, while requiring a certain amount of additional capital expenditure, was operating reasonably well and did not require substantial additional maintenance to be carried out pending the completion of the required capital works.
>
> Allied to this gulf between the parties, was a wide divergence between them as to what fell into the category of maintenance and what capital work. ...
>
> I accept Toll's point that it should not be required to pay more for maintenance than it would as part of a vertically-integrated business, and that consequently the maintenance charge should not be increased through ONTRACK adopting a role as *guardian* of the network. Commerciality should prevail."

This viewpoint is saying in effect that it is not the train operator's responsibility to sustain and develop the rail network – analogous, perhaps, to truck operators who have no responsibility to sustain and develop the highway network.

The outcome of the Independent Audit process was that Toll was required to pay $53.86 million for the 2005-06 year, and the parties agreed that this sum, adjusted for inflation, would apply also to the 2006-07 and 2007-08 years. However, this did not mean that they had reached a lasting agreement. By the time the Independent Auditor's report was produced, in March 2007, Toll NZ and the government had been in discussions for nearly two years trying to find an alternative to the NRAA as a basis for their on-going relationship.

Rethinking the relationship between government and rail

By June 2005, when "good faith negotiations" on setting the TAC had ended without agreement, Toll, ONTRACK and The Treasury had all come to the view that the NRAA was not a good enough basis for the on-going relationship. Additionally, Toll was resisting implementing its commitment to invest in new rolling-stock, which it agreed in the NRAA to do. Confidential discussions about other broad options had started. The agenda appears to have been at Toll's initiative.

A 'do nothing' option

The impasse on the negotiations for setting the TAC had meant that there was no 'do nothing' option, and it was never contemplated. Both Toll and ONTRACK wanted to find a better basis for their necessary working relationship, and the government wanted to maintain the integrity of the rail network without providing subsidies in the longer term. Something different was needed.

Appendix 1

The franchise option

The first option considered was for the government to own all or some of the rolling-stock and other assets, such as rail-related buildings, freight terminals, and the rail network lease. It would offer Toll NZ the franchise to operate rail services at minimum frequencies for a to-be-defined term, after which the franchise would be opened to other applicants. A Treasury official noted:[793]

> "The working assumption driving this prospective transaction is that because it is not commercially viable, the Crown will need to fund and own all new and substantively refurbished rail rolling stock, and in the long run any new rail ferries."

Another Treasury document noted:

> "The original trigger for this prospective transaction was the desire to ensure that new investment in rail rolling stock in fact takes place. Toll currently has around 200 locomotives. Their intention is that as a result of this transaction, 70 of those locomotives would be replaced by 30 new locomotives, and there would be a corresponding purchase of new wagons. The total capital cost would be around $200 million."

Toll NZ had thus revealed itself to be even more reluctant to invest in the renewal of its aging rail assets than was Tranz Rail previously. Treasury assessed the situation at that time:

> "As Toll is currently earning a comfortable cash flow from its New Zealand operations, its present strategy appears to be to retain the customers and the cash flows while avoiding having to invest capital into the business. This would explain its suggestion that the Crown buy its rolling stock and some of its other physical assets and lease them back to Toll NZ as rail operator. The risk of the capital intensive nature of the business would effectively

be transferred to the Crown, while Toll could continue to have the benefit of the customer contracts."

Toll seems to have been keen on this option because it was a way for the government to tacitly agree that Toll need not fulfil its commitment in the NRAA to invest $100 million in new rolling-stock. It was also seeking government funding for its existing rolling-stock, either in terms of a purchase, or a guaranteed return on assets under the access charge regime. Treasury was wary:

> "Toll is attempting to use the transaction with the Crown as part of a process of selling the substance of its New Zealand assets while retaining the cash flows. ... The danger is that the Crown will facilitate such a transaction on commercially generous terms."

It was Treasury's view that Toll had already decided to renege on its NRAA commitment to buy rolling-stock; therefore, if any renewal of the fleets were to happen, the government would have to be the purchaser. This then raised questions about

- which party would specify the numbers and types of locomotives and wagons, and
- the basis on which Toll would lease the rolling-stock from the government, with negotiations and decisions to be made on rate of return, depreciation, provisions for maintenance, length of the lease term and end-of-lease provisions.

In Treasury's words:

> "The logic of such a transaction is that it would offer Toll NZ concessional finance, thus making operation of new locomotives and rolling stock commercially viable."

Toll also wanted to sell the existing rolling-stock to the government, but Treasury saw no advantage in that for the government, especially as the value of this rolling-stock was disputed. When Toll had bought Tranz Rail, it revalued the rolling-stock from around $200 million to $400 million to reflect the price it paid for the business. While this was an appropriate accounting change, Treasury did not agree that this changed the market value, and therefore it counselled against Toll's insistence that the price would be the book value of $400 million. This difference was predicted to be unresolvable. However, if Toll retained ownership of the existing fleet, complications would arise from the split responsibility for asset management – the future decisions on maintain/scrap/refurbish/renew. The risk that Treasury foresaw was that decisions would be gamed around ownership rather than engineering or financial efficiency.

Another foreseeable problem with the Franchise Option was the continued ownership and operation by Toll of the rail ferries. They were seen as (and are) a key part of the Auckland to Christchurch container services, which was the line-of-business where the government hoped for traffic growth. The ferries would not need to be replaced until after the first franchise term, but substantial growth of this traffic would require additional ferry capacity. Continued ownership by Toll could frustrate the tendering of the franchise after the first term; should the government attempt to buy them from an unwilling seller?

In March 2006, Toll had made a presentation to the Minister of Finance. In the absence of an "acceptable variation to the pricing principle" Toll would "restructure" so that it would cease to operate on about 40% of the current rail network. By June, Toll and ONTRACK had agreed to instigate the provision in the NRAA for use of an Independent Auditor, which produced the Determination in March 2007, described in the section above. From late March to June 2007, there was a series of eight meetings between Toll and ONTRACK exploring the concepts of sale-and-lease-back of rail assets, together with Toll having a long-term franchise as the exclusive freight rail operator. By this time, it was becoming clear to the government that the franchising option was fraught with difficulties, both for implementation and later when the term of the franchise agreement would finish. The other option was by then getting serious consideration.

The purchase option

If the government bought the whole Toll NZ business, it would avoid all the problems envisaged above, which would result from a shared responsibility for owning and operating the rail system. A government-owned rail business could ensure continuation of the existing nation-wide network, which was a part of the current government's Transport Strategy, thus ensuring a transport network complementary to the highway network. In a country prone to earthquakes and floods, some duplication of transport infrastructure has value. Government ownership would enable investment to replace old rolling-stock, which could better meet customers' needs. The future replacement of the life-expired rail ferries, so vital for inter-island trade, could be planned and funded reliably, providing certainty for the business community.

To the Treasury none of this was relevant. In its advice to the government its concern was that a change of ownership would not remove rail's problems. It saw rail as in a long-term decline, due to competition with road and shipping.

> "Government ownership will provide greater control over rail decisions without the need to negotiate with Toll and rely on it to deliver. But it would also bring the Government closer to rail's problems and make it more accountable for them. ... Acquisition risks paying too much for the rail business as the current subsidies will be capitalised into the share price demanded by Toll."

The tone of Treasury's advice was clearly unsupportive, perhaps due an underlying belief in the virtues of 'small government', not shared by the Labour government at that time.

How the Government and Toll reached a sale agreement

Treasury assessed that, if the government needed to provide on-going financial support for a freight railway, its economic rationale was
- "A view that in the long run some of the (particularly) environmental externalities will become much more significant than they are at present, and thus that (the option value of) an operating rail freight system is high.
- The prospect that (especially for specific heavily trafficked routes) the costs of road enhancement to cope with current rail traffic if it were diverted onto the roads would be higher than the costs of long-term support to the rail system."

The NRAA was still the only agreement between Toll NZ and the Government, despite protracted discussions to find an alternative agreement. Given all the foreseeable difficulties of a possible franchise agreement, and that Toll
- was continuing not to pay the full costs of on-going track provision, as agreed in the NRAA,
- was stalling on its investment of $100 million in new rolling-stock, as agreed in the NRAA,
- had warned the government it would withdraw services from about 40% of the network if it could not get the subsidies it wanted (as Tranz Rail had similarly warned in 2002),

Cabinet decided on 23 October 2007 to purchase the whole of the Toll NZ business. The Finance Minister met with Toll's CEO on 29 October to convey the decision. ONTRACK would be the arm of government to make the purchase, with a binding agreement to be reached before Christmas. This last wish would be 'more easily said than done'.

(This situation that had developed of threats to withdraw services, and requests for capital funding, is an example of the duress that a government could expose itself to, when it had by its actions confirmed its belief that the rail system could not be allowed to fail. This possibility is discussed in chapter 10, under *Hopes for Continuation with Improvements*.)

Toll NZ was a shrewd seller. The CEO wrote to the CEO of ONTRACK on 13 November 2007:

> "In our meeting of November 9th, we expressed our concerns about the detail that ONTRACK was proposing to understand about the Toll NZ business before an indicative offer was to be made. Our view is that the process needed to commence with ONTRACK making an indicative offer for the entire NZ business so it could be determined whether Toll Holdings expectation of value could be met. Only at that point would it be appropriate to move into further detailed discussions.
>
> Your proposed timelines and process does not have an indicative offer being made by ONTRACK until December 18th, and requires Toll in the interim to provide substantial commercially sensitive detail around customer contracts, strategic plans and future forecast [sic] financial performance. As a publicly listed company we are not comfortable with this and potentially see unnecessary work being done if a meeting of the minds is not met on value."

Determining the value of Toll NZ, and hence the sale price, was the major area of disagreement over the next six months of negotiations. Each party proposed its own basis and set of assumptions for determining a value for the company, resulting in divergent ranges with the extremes being nil cash value (after allowing for picking up Toll's debts of $NZ204 million) and $1.15 billion. The dominant factor affecting the valuation was the different assumptions about future charges payable by Toll under the NRAA. The bar graph on the next page illustrates a range of valuation considerations for Toll NZ, as provided to ONTRACK by a consultant at the time.

Appendix 1

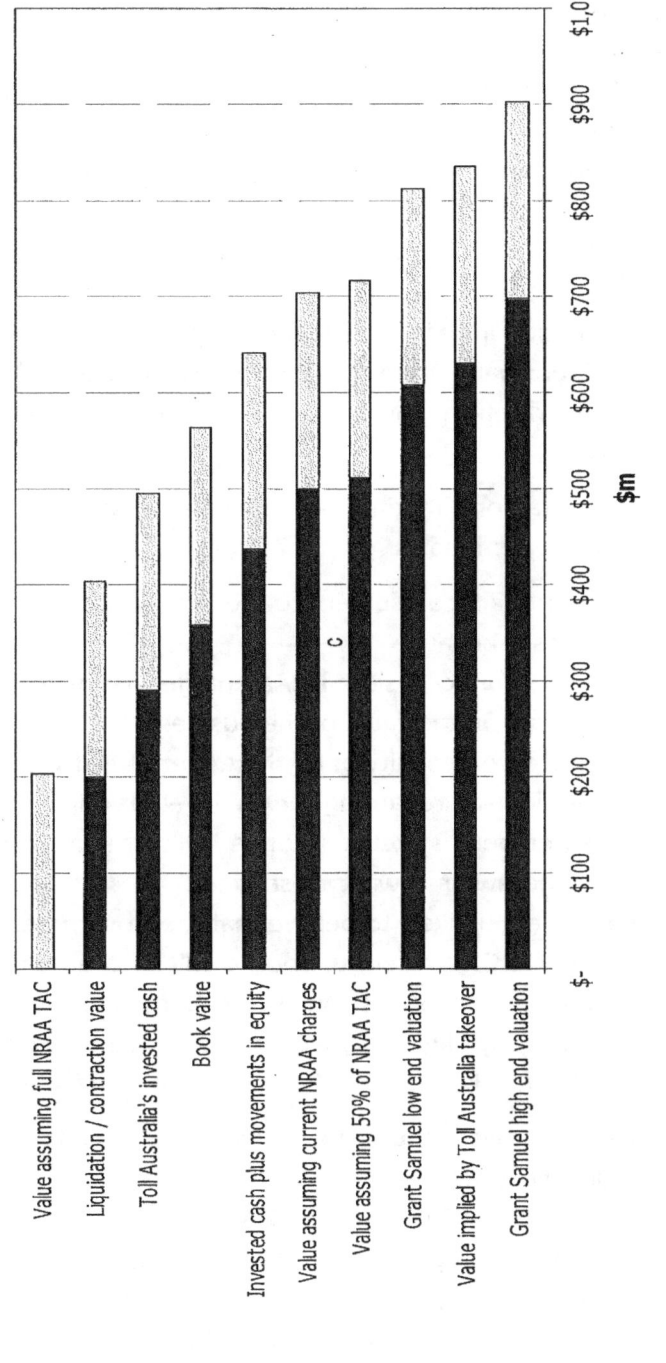

The range of valuations of Toll NZ in 2008.

With reference to the future charges payable by Toll under the NRAA,

- Toll's assumption was that there would be an extension of the then current interim arrangement, whereby annual network access charges would rise from $56 million in 2008 to $75 million by 2018.
- ONTRACK's assumption was that under the NRAA, full Track Access Charges would apply plus payments for depreciation of its capital spending on improvements and renewals, whereby annual network access charges would rise from $56 million in 2008 to $162 million by 2018.

The other factor affecting valuation was what a consultant to ONTRACK described as

> "a strong tactical element to the indicative offer to Toll. This arises because
> - The future course of NRAA charges has major impact on the value of the business.
> - The enforceability of key NRAA terms is disputed, particularly regarding service levels as any agreement is likely to reduce Toll's freedom to withdraw or downscale services.
> - Toll are unlikely to believe that the Government / ONTRACK are serious about a full recovery of NRAA charges, unless a strong signal to the contrary is sent by Ministers followed up by actions from ONTRACK.
>
> Factors that should be considered in pitching an indicative offer are:
> - The extent to which the Government / ONTRACK is willing to pursue full NRAA charges, including a hostile response from Toll in terms of network / service contraction. Toll can be expected to test the Government's resolve in this respect.

- Concerns about 'overpayment' relative to the value of Toll NZ when facing full NRAA charges.
- The desire to reach an agreed transaction quickly.
- The value to the Government of a rapid transition to rail ownership and the ability to pursue more integrated transport sector policies.
- Any concerns regarding negative perceptions by offshore investors if Toll is seen as having lost heavily in its dealings with the Government.

Choosing where to pitch an indicative offer to Toll is heavily dependent on the weighting of these factors."

On 22 November 2007 Toll and the Government signed a confidentiality deed to govern the disclosure of information. In December, ONTRACK made a non-binding indicative offer for the equity (but not the debts) of Toll NZ of between $300 and $350 million. Toll rejected this offer citing multiple reasons, but mainly around the use of discounted cash flow (DCF) methodology which it saw as inappropriate because the future Track Access Charges remained unresolved. It also raised for the first time the

> "need to consider what additional allowance should be made for a control premium given that 100% of the company is being sought by the Crown"

For the next two months both parties exchanged views, sometimes acrimoniously, on the process being followed and on the valuation of the business, without coming close to agreement. These negotiations included a revised offer from ONTRACK of $575 million, and a counter-offer from Toll of $930 million. Up till then the Government's intention to acquire Toll NZ was not known to the public, including the investment community and equity analysts. Because these latter groups did not know about the unresolved issues of the NRAA, particularly that the Government saw itself providing a subsidy to Toll while negotiations continued, the Government believed that they were valuing Toll NZ too highly. Full disclosure would change that. In March 2008, the Minister of Finance prepared a public statement announcing that Toll would henceforth be required to meet the full provisions of the NRAA, and that negotiations on the Government's intended purchase of Toll NZ had ended without agreement. His statement also included background information on the NRAA and the three years of discussions about it, and a series of anticipative questions and answers about the purchase and possible outcomes. However, this statement was not issued pending a final attempt to reach agreement with Toll, and it appears to have shown Toll the seriousness of the Government's position. Toll prepared to raise its commercial rates by 10% to cover the TAC increase.

During the course of the negotiations the two parties agreed that Toll could retain the Tranz Link business, known as TTL, which was essentially consolidation and deconsolidation of less-than-container loads, together with warehousing and logistical services. Consequently, agreement was eventually reached on how to separate out the TTL assets and customers from those for full container lots (FCL), and also on the future relationship between Toll and (what would become) KiwiRail.

In mid-April the Minister of Finance met with the Toll CEO and agreed that the price for the equity in the Toll NZ business would be $NZ665 million. This did not include TTL and its fleet of some hundreds of trucks. The deal was signed and announced to the public[794] on 5 May 2008. It appears that Toll did get some 'premium' for 100% control, but on the other hand, it retained some $200 million of the rail company's debt.

KiwiRail

Government expectation of profitability

The new 'state-owned enterprise', which came into existence in July 2008, was named KiwiRail. In October, at the government's request, it merged with ONTRACK, making the railway vertically-integrated again. In its first year, it had a new board, a new CEO, and changes in the senior management team. Locomotive and wagon maintenance and repair was brought back in-house after being outsourced by TranzRail in 2002. New private sidings at Tangiwai and Rolleston were connected to enable new freight flows on rail. Major customers, including Fonterra, were enthusiastic to increase railed freight after the removal of uncertainty about ownership of the railway.[795]

But the most significant change for KiwiRail's future was the election, at the end of 2008, of a new government in New Zealand led by the same political party that had sold NZ Rail in 1993. It had an unchanged strong belief in the virtue of private enterprise, and consequently, it had little interest in owning, let alone restoring, a run-down railway system. (However, it did agree to fund the purchase of 20 new diesel-electric locomotives, the first such investment since 1980.[796]) Despite the financial failures of Tranz Rail and Toll NZ, this government's official expectation of KiwiRail remained as required by the State-Owned Enterprises Act of 1986:[797]

> "KiwiRail is required to be as profitable and efficient as comparable businesses that are not owned by the Crown."

This expectation was unrealistic, given all that had happened in the previous two decades. The previous Labour government had decided to provide KiwiRail some $90 million per year as 'operating support', plus it had established a five-year program for the upgrade and renewal of rail assets.[798] The new government was obliged to continue this support while it took advice on KiwiRail's future prospects. The Treasury, which had had negative views for some years of the financial viability of railways, and therefore it saw no benefit from the railway system, proffered this advice:[799]

> "Funding decisions should be influenced by their long term objectives for the future of rail. ... Government

spending [should] be restricted to where the greatest public benefits (externalities) can be obtained ... This approach will then govern choices around:

- closing and/or mothballing the least commercial and economic lines
- slowing down the rehabilitation of the track (or at least restricting it to the most commercial lines)
- scaling back the modernisation of the locomotive fleet
- deferring – or at least scaling back – recommended upgrades, service and track extensions, and other improvements to the rail system (and restricting these to where the greatest gains in public benefits can be made)
- revising the Government Policy Statement for transport to modify the medium-term target for freight volumes to be shifted off trucks and onto rail, including its contribution to the goal of reduced emissions."

Other Treasury papers indicated its expectation that continuing the operating support would be necessary for some years, so that KiwiRail could continue to maintain the track network. It would be for the government to decide how much support to provide through its annual budget, and whether mothballing some lines would be an acceptable outcome of reduced support.

The Stratford to Okahukura Line (SOL) was mothballed in November 2009 after a damaging wagon derailment, and an assessment of $400k repair costs.[800] This line connecting the Taranaki region to the NIMT was KiwiRail's most high-maintenance line at the time, with 24 tunnels and 91 bridges on its 144 km length. It traversed very rugged terrain and generated no traffic itself. By 2009, only one inter-regional train each way per day was operating. Since the derailment, this traffic was rerouted to the south, via Marton.

Appendix 1

The plan for eventual profitability

KiwiRail management developed the 'KiwiRail Turnaround Plan' in 2010, a strategic plan for the business, operating on an integrated national network. Its goal was to enable growth of the business to become financially self-sustaining within ten years. The plan won the support of the government, which committed to invest in rolling-stock and infrastructure projects, at $250 million annually for three years. This gave KiwiRail certainty for future planning, which was something that had not been possible for a number of years previously.

During the 2010/11 financial year, KiwiRail's revenues were affected by two large earthquakes in Christchurch, and the Pike River coal mine disaster on the West Coast. Nevertheless, net tonnes hauled increased by 6%[801] and EBITDA operating surplus of the freight business increased by 17% on the previous year.[802] Similar increases were achieved in the following year.

In March 2012, the rail line between Wairoa and Gisborne suffered storm damage that was estimated to cost $4 million to repair. In October, KiwiRail announced [803] mothballing the whole 191-km line from Napier to Gisborne, because it was expensive to maintain and lacked sufficient traffic, making it uneconomic to operate. The volume of freight had dropped markedly by then for reasons beyond KiwiRail's control: sheep farming in the district had become uneconomic, hill farms had been taken over for commercial forestry, so there was reduced demand for fertiliser from Napier, and the export abattoir had closed in 1994 reducing the freight out of Gisborne.

Following the introduction of the first batch of DL locomotives from China (which the government had agreed in 2009 to fund), a second batch of 20 was commissioned in 2013. Improvements in rail infrastructure helped increase tonnages of logs and import-export containers, while export coal had a downturn due to external factors.

FY 2014 was a more challenging year. The rail-ferry *Aratere* suffered a broken propellor shaft and loss of the propellor at sea. As a result, the Interislander service lost 45% of its capacity over the busy summer season. Then the *Aratere* was overseas for 5 months for repairs and routine dry-dock maintenance. Although a replacement roll-on roll-off ferry was hired, the loss of capacity to carry rail wagons affected the railed freight business. The overall cost, including hireage of the replacement ferry and the loss of freight and passenger revenue, was approximately $27 million.[804] There were also issues with the new locomotives, that resulted in them being taken out of service for some months. The 2010 Turnaround Plan was effectively abandoned, the Chairman commenting:[805]

> "The FY 2014 result brings us to the view that the sustainability plan as it was originally conceived, did not make sufficient provision for unexpected events. This should not come as a surprise. No plan could have made provision for the combination of events that have undermined the original revenue premises. As a result of this realisation the Board has instituted a commercial review of the business with the aim of developing a new 30-year plan. The review provides us with an opportunity to re-examine rail's role in the New Zealand economy."

The Commercial Review

The Commercial Review[806] was done in the latter half of 2014 and presented to the shareholding Ministers in December. The Government announced, in the 2015 Budget, its decision not to pursue any of the Review's four scenarios, but to continue to fund KiwiRail as is, as a national rail freight network.[807] KiwiRail chose to release the Review in a heavily redacted form to the public in April 2016.

The Review had developed four different future scenarios for the rail freight business, with assessments of the network capital requirements for each, using a 30-year planning horizon. This was needed to capture the long investment cycles inherent in maintaining and renewing the existing rail network, including

Appendix 1

the sometimes-lumpy capital requirements. This would enable the government to make informed decisions on the future of rail in New Zealand. The four scenarios were all a change from the network that was open at that time, with each one a reduction from the previous one:

- a "trimmed network"; close to the then current network with only small changes made.[808] However, it did assume a phasing out of the rail capacity of the interisland ferries in order to make the acquisition and operation of the interisland services more flexible.
- "separate island networks"; the rationale being it removes all domestic intercity traffic which is the most strongly contested and requires KiwiRail to operate time-sensitive schedules. The interisland ferries would convey only road freight (and passengers), and the Picton to Christchurch line would be closed. Analysis of this scenario showed that the reduction in revenue exceeded the reduction in costs, making it an unattractive option.[809]
- An "Upper North Island network" was defined as concentrating on the Auckland – Hamilton – Tauranga triangle, with extremities at Te Kuiti, Kinleith and Murupara. It is the area of heaviest traffic density and retains the forestry, bulk coal, and IMEX traffic flows. Business scope and complexity would be reduced, being reliant on a small number of customers, but this would make the business more vulnerable to external events compared with a larger network. Transition costs to this network would be high:[810] staff redundancies, removal of 3,200 kms of track, securing or demolishing structures for safety, remediation of level crossings, and unknowable penalty costs of withdrawal from existing customer contracts.
- "Exit"; because the Board could not offer the government any business planning scenario where

the business would become self-sustaining within ten years,[811] complete closure of the freight business had to be an option for consideration, if the government was unwilling to continue investing in the renewal of the freight rail network.[812] The transition costs would be obviously larger than for the previous scenario, and the complete disposal of rolling-stock, specialised track maintenance machinery, and track materials could take years to complete.

In its summary of results, the Review included these two statements:[813]

"Overall, the Board has not been able to develop an option that reaches financial sustainability in the near to medium term."

"On a purely commercial basis (i.e. ranking by the present value of the Crown investment required), Exit appears the highest value option for the Shareholder."

The Government had asked the Board to nominate its preferred scenario, but the Board declined to do this because the analyses included only the financials relevant to the support needed for the continuation of KiwiRail. It was for the Government to consider KiwiRail's future in the broader context of its transport policies, and the impacts on the New Zealand roading networks and the economy. For example, the latter two scenarios would likely have ended the export of metallurgical coal from the West Coast of the South Island via the port of Lyttelton on the east coast.[814] The Exit scenario would probably have led also to the closure of New Zealand's only steel works, because the higher costs of roading its coal supplies and its exported products would have changed its viability. Another consequence would have been additional congestion at ports and on arterial roads, and an increase in the costs to producers wherever currently railed exports changed to road transport. Clearly, the Board had laid down a challenge to the Government: choose between orthodox economic rationality or some other course of action that recognised the wider value of the rail system to New Zealand.

The Treasury was involved in the whole process of the Commercial Review, assisting with the specification of the economic analysis of options.[815] In its paper to Cabinet it showed its preference for network closure, emphasising the net social cost for the government to continue to support KiwiRail as

> "estimated at between $55 million and $170 million per annum based on a national cost benefit analysis."[816]

For this reason, it proposed restricting funding to one year, and that

> "a more comprehensive study be undertaken to better understand the implications of closure to enable the Government to make the most informed choice possible."

The Government decided to commit another $400 million over two years for the network, but it came with a warning from the Minister of Transport:[817]

> "KiwiRail must continue to drive significant efficiency and productivity improvements to reduce an ongoing level of Crown funding required."

The Government's decision was significant because[818]

- The Government at last understood that KiwiRail's network would need to be funded by it forever, and that as a vertically-integrated railway, KiwiRail would never be a profitable entity
- The on-going funding needed was about $200 million per year (which was a fraction of government's annual spend on the highway network)
- This funding had to be committed more than one year in advance, so that KiwiRail had the certainty needed to undertake major projects
- The Government chose to override the advice from the Treasury, which was supporting the closure option

because the size of the on-going subsidy needed was much more than the safety and environmental benefits that it could quantify.

The Labour opposition's comment on the Treasury recommendation for closure revealed a developing transformation in the perception of railways, something of a paradigm shift that was to guide its support for KiwiRail when the new coalition government took over in 2017. The Labour spokesman was reported to have said:[819]

> "KiwiRail was effectively two business – freight and lines – and these should be treated differently. ... While the freight business should be expected to run profitably in its own right, the lines are as much part of our national infrastructure as the roads or the water supply."

KiwiRail took the Minister's warning seriously. Under a new CEO, the strategy for FYs 2015 and 2016 was to "simplify the operating model" and "standardise the assets", in order to meet the government's request to reduce its reliance on subsidies. This simplification included ceasing to haul bulk fertiliser and motor vehicles, both of which required specialised wagons with higher maintenance costs. Also, bulk fertiliser stores are always located out-of-town, so small numbers of wagons (part train-loads) had to be specially shunted to and from private sidings at rural locations. This would have incurred identifiable operating costs additional to the basic line-haul. Shunting wagons at rural locations used to be common up till the mid-1980s, then the need declined quickly with the closure of most rural stations. By 2015, trains shunting sometimes at rural locations, to deliver or pick up fertiliser wagons, no longer fitted with the simplified model of running whole trains directly between terminals.

The Government's 2015 decision to fund the rail network was fortunate, because in November 2016 a magnitude 7.8 earthquake struck the Kaikoura coast of the South Island, causing massive landslides. Both the Main North Line (MNL) and

State Highway One were severely damaged in multiple locations along the coast, closing both eventually for nearly a year. The Government undertook, within days of the earthquake, to fund the restoration of both, covering the uninsured elements. The rail line was re-opened first with temporary structures, after ten months, so that freight could be moved at night, and materials could be delivered by rail for the reconstruction of the highway during daylight hours.

Managed Decline

During the years from 2015 onward, the government was funding the restoration of KiwiRail by about $200 million per year, in addition to KiwiRail's investment of its retained operating surpluses. These funds were being spent on new locomotives, wagons, and improving the busiest part of the network between Auckland, Hamilton and Tauranga: new crossing loops, additional tracks in freight hubs, replacement of century-old wooden bridges with concrete structures. Yet at the same time, KiwiRail was using a cost-saving line maintenance practice called 'managed decline'. This was disclosed by the RMTU in January 2016,[820] reporting that several secondary lines

> "are only being maintained to a standard that KiwiRail acknowledges will result in deterioration".

It is not publicly known when this practice was formalised, but quite possibly soon after the merger in 2008 of the above-rail KiwiRail with the below-rail ONTRACK. Clearly, it was a partial response to the on-going pressure from the government to prioritise profitability over network sustainability. Had this practice continued, it is quite possible that some lines would have been abandoned, in addition to those that were not repaired after derailment (the Stratford-Okahukura Line in 2009) or storm damage (Napier to Gisborne in 2012).

The North Auckland Line (NAL) was certainly a candidate for abandonment. Completed in 1925, its legacy included small tunnels that would not permit hi-cube (9'6") containers on standard flat wagons, and as a result, KiwiRail was steadily losing business as these containers were increasingly replacing standard (8'0") containers for exports. Also, the line had been limited for decades to a maximum train speed of 50 kph, and so it was very uncompetitive with road transport for most freight services. In March 2016, KiwiRail announced it would cease to haul logs from Otiria, at the northern extremity of this line, for its last-remaining customer. The stated reason was "poor commercial returns and life-expired wagons".[821] These 44-year-old wagons, the last four-wheeled wagons in the fleet, would be scrapped. The Otiria line would remain open but not operated or maintained. The rest of the North Auckland line was reduced to one train each way per weekday, with minimal maintenance; a clear case of managed decline, that became a local political issue at the 2017 national election.

The valued railway creates value for New Zealand

In October 2017, a new government was elected, with policies of promoting regional development and expanding the role of railways in the national economy. The following month a report was released, which had been completed about a year before but suppressed by the previous National government. Commissioned by the New Zealand Transport Agency, and done by the consultancy firm Ernst & Young (EY),[822] it showed the value of rail to the New Zealand economy was about $1.5 billion per year.[823] These wider economic benefits came mainly from reduced road congestion, but also from reductions in road accident costs, road maintenance, and emissions. While the greatest benefit came from the urban passenger operations in Auckland and Wellington, the value conservatively estimated for rail freight was approximately $350 million per year of benefits normally unaccounted for.[824]

The new government announced projects to be funded by the Provincial Growth Fund (PGF), including the restoration of the rail line from Napier to Wairoa, which had been mothballed in 2012. The push for reopening this line specifically for export log traffic had come from Napier Port (the destination) and the Hawke's Bay Regional Council, which had wanted to lease the line from KiwiRail as early as 2015.[825] That was not to happen, but the line was reopened in January 2020, with a $6 million grant from the PGF. Logs arriving from the forests at the Wairoa road-rail log assembly yard are scaled and marshalled, instead of this work being done at the port, so that the receival of logs by train at the port is a quicker and more efficient process than receiving logs on trucks. Napier Port is KiwiRail's customer for these trains.

In the 2018 Budget, the new government contributed $230 million[826] for network renewal, plus money for the on-going reinstatement of the MNL. The following year saw a radical change in perception and a major increase in government support. As reported by KiwiRail:[827]

> "In the 2019 Budget, the Government allocated $741 million through Vote Transport over the next two years and made a further $300 million available for regional rail projects through the Provincial Growth Fund (PGF). The money is being used to address legacy issues to improve reliability and resilience for tracks, signals, bridges and tunnels, for new freight handling equipment and a new freight reservation and tracking system. We will also be replacing aging locomotives and wagons and improve our major maintenance depots at Hutt and Waltham. It will also be used to progress the procurement of two new, rail-enabled ferries that will replace Interislander's aging *Aratere*, *Kaitaki*, and *Kaiarahi* ferries."

In September 2019 the Government announced a $95 million funding of maintenance work on the North Auckland line, to repair the effects of the 'managed decline' regime. A few months later it announced a further $109 million from the PGF, primarily to modernise and increase the capability of the line to take hi-cube containers.[828] This work required five old wooden bridges to be replaced by concrete ones, and the floors to be lowered in thirteen tunnels. All this work was done during a six-month closure of the line, which was reopened in January 2021.

The new government also commissioned the Ministry of Transport (MoT) to lead a multi-agency project called "Future of Rail", its purpose being to integrate rail into the transport system, so rail is planned and funded alongside other transport modes. As the MoT explained:[829]

> "Previous investment in New Zealand's rail network has centred on looking at 'how much' needs to be invested in rail to get the existing network functioning. The Future of Rail looks at what purpose rail serves, and what outcomes rail can deliver for New Zealand as part of the transport system."

The main problems for the government identified by the project were[830]

> "The Government is committed to rail and the wide-ranging benefits it can deliver to New Zealand. However, realisation of these benefits have been hampered by:
> - the current state of the rail network, owned and operated by KiwiRail, which is [still] facing a state of managed decline due to long-term underinvestment
> - short-term funding arrangements for the rail network through the annual Budget process, which are inadequate for a long-term network asset."

An outcome from the Future of Rail project was the acceptance that increasing the amount of railed freight will be a long journey. Government committed to at least a decade of future investment to make that possible, as expressed in The New Zealand Rail Plan:[831]

> "The Government is committed to seeing rail play its

part in a multi-modal transport system. Our first priority for rail is to achieve a resilient and reliable rail network that also improves safety. Over the next decade, this investment will take the network out of a state of managed decline and provide a stable platform for future investments for growth."

It has now passed legislation to establish a new long-term planning and funding framework under the Land Transport Management Act 2003:[832]

"This will result in the national rail network being planned and funded on a sustainable long-term basis, alongside the rest of the land transport system, including the road and public transport networks."

While KiwiRail will oversee the work to maintain and upgrade the network, it will be funded by the Government through the National Land Transport Fund (NLTF), as it does for highway maintenance and upgrading. For this, KiwiRail will pay a Track User Charge, conceptually similar to the Road User Charges that truck operators pay.[833] It remains to be seen whether the rail and the road modes will be treated equally in terms of future increases.

In 2021, KiwiRail was still legally a State-Owned Enterprise (SOE), with its obligation to profitable. By this time, Government saw KiwiRail as an integrated rail network operator, with "predominantly commercial" above-rail operations, and below-rail operations "predominantly a public benefit" [834] funded largely from the NLTF. Consequently, KiwiRail was asked to maintain separate above-rail and below-rail financial accounts, to support transparent decision-making.

Government also asked for a review of KiwiRail's status as an SOE, because clearly it no longer fitted well with Government's current expectations, but neither did any other existing Crown entity form. At the time of writing, this project has yet to deliver, but it worth quoting from its Terms of Reference:[835]

"When considered from a combined above- and below-rail perspective, KiwiRail is not a viable commercial business as it generates only a portion of the cash required to fund its investment in above- and below-rail assets. The Crown's willingness to meet the funding gap is due, in large part, to the Crown's desire to purchase wider public benefits associated with rail, such as reduced road congestion and lower emissions."

Also in the Terms of Reference is a statement of what is Out of Scope:[836]

The review will not consider:

- a change of ownership of KiwiRail and/or NZRC, including, for example, the privatisation of assets or functions
- structural separation of KiwiRail away from its current vertical-integration model of an "above-rail" business and a "below-rail" operator of rail track asset management.

To conclude, the New Zealand rail network will be retained, rehabilitated and in due course extended (with a new branch line to Northport). What has changed is how it is viewed by the government, which is both the maker of transport policy and the owner of both the railway and highway networks. Both these networks are now seen equally as national assets to be used for national economic benefit. Neither is measured for its profitability, and that is what counts.

Appendix 2:

The History of Efficiency as Applied to New Zealand's North Island Main Trunk Line

In a railway organisation, the concept of efficiency changes over time, depending on perceptions of what resources need to be better managed. A classic example is in the history of train operations on the central section of New Zealand's North Island Main Trunk line (NIMT), between Hamilton and Palmerston North.[837] Each of these cities has a sizable marshalling yard because they are both effectively junctions in the network, as well as sources and destinations for freight.

Between these cities is 408 kilometres of single track with passing loops. Until the 1960s, relatively small volumes of freight[838] originated or terminated at the stations along the line. However, these rural commodities have now disappeared, and there is no reason to shunt trains anywhere along this line. Since its completion in 1908, the primary function of the NIMT has always been to link the cities and rail networks of the northern half of the North Island with those of the southern half. The line goes up and over the North Island's central volcanic plateau, from both directions. Along the line there are five stations (Te Kuiti, Taumarunui, National Park, Waiouru and Taihape) with yards that are much bigger than were ever required for local traffic. The reason these five yards were built has to do with a former notion of operational efficiency.

In the days of steam, Te Kuiti, Taumarunui, and Taihape

each had a locomotive and crew depot, where locomotives were refuelled and stabled between runs. (These depots were all closed by the 1990s.) Steam locos were individually made, mostly in New Zealand, and not mass-produced. Individual steam locomotives were allocated to each depot, and each was driven by only a small number of crews who got to know each individual locomotive's routine maintenance needs, behavioural characteristics and quirks. Because of the close matching of crews and locomotives, and the rostering practice that saw all crews get back to their home depots at the end of each shift, each locomotive did not usually travel past its neighbouring depot stations.

Probably influenced by the shortage of coal[839] experienced during the years of the Second World War, efficient operational practice meant maximising the tonnage hauled by each steam locomotive. The trailing tonnage leaving Hamilton was the maximum that could be hauled by one loco as far as Te Kuiti. There, some wagons were uncoupled (the tonnage was 'reduced') and the train continued, possibly hauled by another locomotive up steeper grades to Taumarunui, where more tonnage was reduced. The train then tackled the steepest grade including the famous Raurimu Spiral, finishing at National Park. Each locomotive and crew would work a train back to its home depot, or travel 'light engine' if there was no tonnage available. The original tonnage of each train from Hamilton was now located in three different places. Several trains per day would operate like this, so that there were many rakes of wagons temporarily parked each day in the intermediate yards. Extra trains would run from Te Kuiti and from Taumarunui to 'lift' these distributed wagons, with each train built to a maximum trailing weight for the locomotive. In this process the rakes of wagons got remixed as they progressed southward. Consequently, some wagons could do the whole journey in a couple of days, while other took longer, up to a week. This process was mirrored for wagons going northward, with staging being done at Taihape,

Waiouru and National Park. So, although the hauling capacity of the locomotive fleet was efficiently used, the utilisation of wagon time was definitely inefficient, and wagon transit times were very unreliable. Transit times were not a concern for the railway managers then, because land transport regulations made most freight captive to rail. Operating efficiently was considered important and service reliability was not.

When steam locomotives were being replaced by diesel-electric locos during the 1950s and 1960s, the priorities and notions of efficiency changed. Many steam locomotives had been built in New Zealand, but diesels had to be imported, using precious overseas funds.[840] Also, these locomotives were mass-produced, so there was no longer a need for crews to be allocated to specific locomotives. Consequently, these locomotives could be worked right through from Auckland to Wellington if necessary, and this could be done without refuelling en route as well. The notion of efficiency now embraced this possibility, with stops and shunting no longer necessary at the intermediate stations. Furthermore, two locomotives of the same class could be operated together by one crew, so through trains were built to the maximum trailing tonnage for the locomotives on the 'ruling grade' of the whole route. By this means, freight trains could traverse the line in predictable and consistent times, less than about 20 hours. The number of new diesel-electric locomotives was somewhat less than the number of steam locomotives that they replaced, and the operating plan had been changed[841]. Operational efficiency now meant good use of available locomotive time (as a surrogate for the efficient use of investment funds for a new locomotive fleet) as well as of the locomotive hauling capability over the steepest section of the route.

With the advent of deregulation and the loss of traffic from the late 1970s onward, followed by the drive in the 1980s to downsize New Zealand Railways (NZR) and reduce its operating costs, the thrust of operations policy was changed again. In the mid-1980s, the policy changed to operate 'fewer bigger trains'. Restrictions on the numbers and types of locomotive combinations that could be used were removed by negotiation with the drivers' union. As a consequence, trains with more locomotive power on the front on the ruling grades could now be increased to the maximum trailing weight dictated by the strength of rolling-stock drawgear, if sufficient daily tonnage was available. The operational efficiency of the network came to be measured by the average gross trailing weight of trains. However, because NZR was competing from the 1980s onward with road carriers, on service as well as price, having competitive train transit times[842] built into the operating plan was also important. Thus, there could be no return to the policy of maximising train weights over distances shorter than those between the major marshalling yards.

However, a competing notion of efficient operation arose for the NIMT. During 1980s the NIMT was electrified at the government's initiative as part of its national policy for energy self-sufficiency. However, electrification was financially justifiable only for the central section between Hamilton and Palmerston North, where the potential benefits of using electric locomotives were the greatest – hauling heavier trains faster uphill, and saving power by using regenerative braking downhill. Prior to the installation of electrification infrastructure, there had also been investments in curve easements to create longer constant-speed zones, and fewer but longer crossing loops. The outcome of the combination of these investments and the electrically-hauled trains was that a significant shortening of transit times became possible for Auckland to Wellington trains and vice versa, despite the 15-minute dwell times needed at Te Rapa (Hamilton) and Palmerston North yards to change locomotives.

Consequently, more trains could be run overnight between the main centres, making rail services more effective for freight forwarders' traffic, and for moving time-sensitive import/export containers for the shipping lines. But this service improvement affected operational efficiency negatively. Firstly, with the concentration of overnight trains and the correspondingly fewer numbers of trains running on the NIMT during the day, it was not possible for the majority of electric locomotives to be rostered to complete a round trip within 24 hours, as had been assumed during the electrification planning phase in the late 1970s. Secondly, diesel-electric locomotives were still needed to haul NIMT trains between yards in South Auckland and Te Rapa, and between Palmerton North and Wellington. The utilisation of their available locomotive time had been quite efficient when they were used on the Auckland to Wellington trips, but now due to electrification and the consequent bunching of trains, these locomotives were each required to haul trains for only about four hours per 24-hour day.[843] Thus, for all the locomotives used on the NIMT, the utilisation of available locomotive time became much less efficient than formerly, as a result of the operating plan becoming more commercially effective, enabled by electrification. The impact on locomotive fleet size was that acquiring 22 new electric locomotives could release only 12 DX class diesel-electric locomotives for use elsewhere. This came as a surprise to all concerned at the time.

Another effect was that if NIMT trains were built to a maximum trailing weight based on the drawgear limit of 1400 tonnes on the steepest grade (between Kakahi and National Park stations), as was required by the 'fewer bigger trains' policy, two electric locomotives would be needed for each train. But there were not enough electric locomotives in the fleet to achieve this. The pragmatic solution was to operate the commercially sensitive overnight express trains with one electric locomotive and a maximum trailing weight of 900 gross tonnes. This meant acknowledging that the supposed efficiency of the 'fewer bigger trains' policy was not always achievable or desirable. It was pragmatic to accept some inefficiency in terms of train size, in order to achieve the most efficient use of available locomotive power, and to provide commercially effective services.

After thirty-plus years of use, the electric locomotive fleet had reached the end of its economic life, and these locomotives were failing in service more frequently than KiwiRail's overall fleet target. In December 2016, after two years of considering the options, including major overhauls to extend the life of these locomotives, KiwiRail announced it would replace the electric locomotives with new Chinese diesel-electric locomotives.[844] (This would be an additional order of the DL class that KiwiRail had been buying since 2010.) The announcement stated that only eight extra diesel locomotives would be needed to replace the remaining fifteen electrics, because existing locomotives would be used more efficiently. (This is the reverse of the situation that applied when electrified operation started on the NIMT in the mid-1980s.) The CEO was reported as saying at the time of the announcement:

> "KiwiRail is currently running 'a railway within a railway', and that's not efficient, it's more costly and ultimately delivers a less reliable service".

In the context of KiwiRail's policy of standardising its rolling-stock fleet, retiring the electric locomotives would have been more efficient. However, in 2018 KiwiRail agreed to a government request,[845] coming from a wider environmental perspective about national fuel use, to keep the electric locomotives in service, and the government has funded a $35million electric locomotive refurbishment program for this purpose.

The conclusion from all of the above is that railway efficiency is not a uniform concept. Because there are many resources used in railway operations, there are inevitably trade-offs to be made in the use of these resources. Sometimes these trade-offs are made explicitly, sometimes not. Perceptions of efficiency at any given time will depend on which of the resources is seen as the most costly, or the most constrained in its availability. This means that measures of efficiency adopted today may well become obsolete tomorrow.

Appendix 3 – A Chronology:

Significant Events in the Last 50 years of Australasian Commercial Freight Railways

Date	Event	QLD	NSW	VIC	SA	WA	NT	TAS	NZ
July 1975	Australian National Railways Commission formed from Commonwealth Railways as the start of a national vertically integrated system; known as AN				Y	Y	Y		
Mar 1978	State governments transferred TGR & SAR to AN				Y		Y	Y	
1980	Standard gauge line opened from Tarcoola to Alice Springs, replacing an old narrow-gauge line on a route further east from Port Augusta				Y		Y		
1982	Gauge conversion completed: Adelaide connected to standard gauge network at Crystal Brook (SA)				Y				
Oct 1990	NZ Rail Ltd created to operate rail & ferry services, leaving non-core activities (buses & coaches, land) with the New Zealand Railways Corporation								Y
Feb 1992	National Rail Corporation (NRC) established	Y	Y	Y					
Feb 1993	NRC started managing interstate freight revenue	Y	Y	Y	Y				
Sept 1993	Lachlan Valley Rail Freight (LVRF) started hauling grain trains on rural branch lines		Y						
Oct 1993	NZ Rail Ltd sold to a consortium led by Wisconsin Central Railroad; later rebranded Tranz Rail Ltd								Y
Nov 1993	NRC's first train operations Melbourne to Adelaide			Y	Y				
1994	AN's interstate rail business and rolling-stock transferred to NRC				Y	Y	Y		
June 1995	Gauge conversion completed: Melbourne-Adelaide interstate and Portland branch in Victoria, but leaving South Australian branch lines isolated			Y	Y				

Date	Event	QLD	NSW	VIC	SA	WA	NT	TAS	NZ
July 1995	SCT started competing with NRC, using its own box wagons, Melbourne-Adelaide-Perth			Y	Y	Y			
July 1995	Competition Policy Reform Act passed	Y	Y	Y	Y	Y	Y	Y	
May 1996	Tranz Rail IPO, oversubscribed								Y
June 1996	TNT (later Toll) began Melbourne – Perth services			Y	Y	Y			
July 1996	NSW vertical separation: FreightCorp created as a distinct government-owned rail freight business, and Rail Access Corp (RAC) to manage track access		Y						
Jan 1997	South Spur Rail Services founded by Wilson family, specialised initially in hauling infrastructure trains					Y			
1997	Dual gauge line to Port of Brisbane opened	Y							
1997	AustralAsia Railway Corporation established				Y		Y		
1997	ATN (Australian Transport Networks) established	Y	Y						
May 1997	Patrick Corp started container train land-bridge service between Port Adelaide & Port Melbourne			Y	Y				
July 1997	VicTrack established to hold & manage Victorian railway land and infrastructures			Y					
Sept 1997	Northern Rivers Railroad (NRR) started freight services under sub-contract to FreightCorp		Y						
Oct 1997	Privatisation: AN's SA freight ops and branch lines sold to Australia Southern Railroad (ASR) which was owned by Genesee & Wyoming Australia				Y				
Nov 1997	Privatisation: AN sold TasRail operations and network to ATN (67% owned by Tranz Rail Ltd)							Y	Y
Dec 1997	Great Northern Rail Services was the first private freight train operator on the Victorian network			Y					
May 1998	ATN TasRail bought Emu Bay Railway							Y	
1998	Pinnaroo & Loxton branches converted from broad to standard gauge, reconnecting at Tailem Bend				Y				
July 1998	Australian Rail Track Corporation (ARTC) was established, with the network transferred from AN, and the interstate standard gauge lines between NSW and SA via Melbourne leased		Y	Y	Y	Y			
Jan 1999	P&O Trans Australia (POTA) incorporated as an integrated port logistics service company	Y	Y						
May 1999	V/Line Freight Corp sold to Rail America (trading as Freight Australia) with broad gauge network leased			Y					
Aug 1999	Silverton Rail started hook & pull service between Cobar & Narromine, contracted to NRC, later to PN		Y						
Aug 1999	Silverton Rail started trip trains to Port Botany		Y						
Date	Event	QLD	NSW	VIC	SA	WA	NT	TAS	NZ

Appendix 3

Date	Event	1	2	3	4	5	6	7	8
June 2000	ATN Access started hauling grain for Australian Wheat Board from Riverina (NSW) and Dimboola (Vic) areas, on standard-gauge lines	Y	Y						
Oct 2000	Privatisation: Australian Railroad Group (ARG) bought WestRail as a vertically integrated business, including a 49-year lease of the network.			Y					
May 2001	FreightCorp ran first trip trains, Minto-Port Botany	Y							
July 2001	Alice Springs – Darwin railway construction began, under a BOOT contract from AustralAsia Railway				Y				
Feb 2002	Privatisation: Pacific National Pty Ltd (PN) formed from the joint sale of NRC and FreightCorp	Y	Y	Y	Y				
2002	QR bought NRR, rebranded it Interail to compete in NSW on standard gauge	Y							
Nov 2002	Great Northern Rail Services ceased operations due to cost of public liability insurance		Y						
2003	Bowmans Rail started services to Port Adelaide			Y					
May 2003	Freight Australia started Melbourne-Sydney trains for CRT Ltd, using CRT depots at Altona & Yennora	Y	Y						
May 2003	Interail (QR) started container trains from Casino (NSW) to Port of Queensland	Y	Y						
May 2003	Rail America made, then aborted, a takeover offer for Tranz Rail								Y
July 2003	Agreement for Tranz Rail to be vertically separate: Toll to takeover company, then to sell the network to NZ Govt for $1, both to invest to restore railway								Y
Nov 2003	ARG entered NSW, Manildra work taken from PN	Y							
Nov 2003	Rail America put Freight Australia up for sale	Y	Y						
Sept 2003	CRT Group started shuttle service between Altona and Port of Melbourne; ceased in Feb 2007		Y						
Dec 2003	Southern Shorthaul Railroad (SSR) established, using locos previously owned by Great Northern	Y	Y						
Jan 2004	RailCorp formed by NSW Govt as a vertically integrated passenger railway network, permitting freight trains to run only outside of curfew hours	Y							
Jan 2004	First trains between Adelaide & Darwin on new standard gauge line, managed by FreightLink, and operated by GWI under hook-&-pull contract				Y	Y			
Feb 2004	ATN, including TasRail, sold to Pacific National	Y	Y				Y		
Apr 2004	Interail (QR) started Brisbane-Melbourne services	Y		Y					
Aug 2004	Freight Australia business and its Victorian country network lease sold to Pacific National	Y	Y						

495

Date	Event	QLD	NSW	VIC	SA	WA	NT	TAS	NZ
Sept 2004	ARTC leased NSW interstate & Hunter Valley lines		Y						
Sept 2004	ARTC contracted by NSW RIC to manage and maintain NSW country branch line network (CRN)		Y						
Mar 2005	PN started container trains for Toll within Qld	Y							
May 2005	ARG started daily intermodal service between Melbourne (Swanson Dock) and Port Adelaide			Y	Y				
June 2005	QR bought CRT Ltd (food and plastics transporter) giving it rail access to terminals at Yennora (in western Sydney) and Altona (Melbourne)	Y	Y	Y					
July 2005	Interail (owned by QR) started operating in the Hunter Valley hauling export coal for BHP Billiton		Y						
2005	PN started hauling compacted waste from Sydney to Tarago on Canberra line; new traffic for rail		Y						
Feb 2006	Silverton Rail sold to South Spur Rail of WA		Y						
Feb 2006	Wesfarmers sold ARG's above-rail business to QR for $446 million, and WestNet Rail (below-rail business) to Babcock & Brown for $835 million.		Y			Y			
Feb 2006	Genesee & Wyoming acquired control of ASR				Y				
Oct 2006	LVRF sold to Macarthur Intermodal Shipping Terminal (MIST), rebranded as Independent Rail		Y						
Oct 2006	SCT started trains between Parkes (NSW) and Perth, operated by South Spur Rail Services		Y			Y			
Nov 2006	Victorian Government agreed to buy back the track lease from PN for $133.8 million, from May 2007.			Y					
Dec 2006	El Zorro started container train operations			Y					
Feb 2007	SCT Logistics bought locomotives from PN			Y	Y	Y			
Mar 2007	South Spur Rail Services sold to Coote Industrial		Y			Y			
May 2007	Tasmanian Govt renationalised TasRail network							Y	
Oct 2007	NZ Government announced intention to buy Toll NZ's rail operations, after 3 years of dispute over network access fees and extent of subsidies								Y
Nov 2007	Lance Hockridge, from BHP, appointed as QR CEO	Y							
Nov 2007	QR started Melbourne-Adelaide-Perth services			Y	Y	Y			
Nov 2007	Asciano (PN) announced end to grain haulage and intrastate services in Vic and NSW in March 2008		Y	Y					
Dec 2007	El Zorro started grain haulage on both gauges			Y					

Appendix 3

Date	Event	QLD	NSW	VIC	SA	WA	NT	TAS	NZ
Mar 2008	El Zorro announced takeover of PN's Warrnambool – Melbourne container train contract			Y					
Mar 2008	PN ceased operations in Victorian country network			Y					
May 2008	NZ Govt bought back the above-rail business for $690m from Toll after 6 months of negotiations								Y
May 2008	ARTC and Victorian government agreed to extend lease of interstate lines by another 45 years, with 200km of broad-gauge North-East line to be converted to standard-gauge			Y					
June 2008	PN announced end to Tasmanian operations							Y	
July 2008	ARTC enabled start of double-stacked container trains between Parkes (NSW) and Perth		Y		Y	Y			
July 2008	QR started Horsham-Melbourne service on the ARTC line, entering the Victorian intrastate market			Y					
Aug 2008	El Zorro started grain haulage for Australian Wheat Board (AWB) in new wagons supplied by AWB		Y	Y					
Aug 2008	Competition on CQCN: PN wins first coal contracts	Y							
Sept 2008	El Zorro started hauling containerised mineral sands Portland to Melbourne, new traffic to rail			Y					
Oct 2008	El Zorro lost Warrnambool–Melbourne container train contract to Patrick Corp, providing direct access to Melbourne docks			Y					
Nov 2008	NSW Govt announce closure of 5 grain-only lines		Y						
Nov 2008	ARG lost Manildra contract to Patrick Portlink		Y						
Nov 2008	FreightLink placed in voluntary administration				Y		Y		
Feb 2009	P&O Trans Australia (POTA) took over running the Yennora to Port Botany shuttle from Interail		Y						
Mar 2009	VicTrack leased Portland-Maroona line to ARTC			Y					
June 2009	GrainCorp started own grain train operations, taking over wagons and 48-class (branch line) locos from NSW Govt, trains run by PN		Y						
June 2009	Freightliner Australia (UK subsidiary) started operations hauling export containerised cotton		Y						
Sep 2009	Freightliner contracted with Xtrata to operate export coal trains in Hunter Valley using locos and wagons owned by Xtrata (now Glencore)		Y						
Sep 2009	Renationalisation: Tasmanian Govt bought TasRail above-rail business from PN, taking over in Dec							Y	
Oct 2009	ARTC leased Benalla-Oaklands branch line from VicTrack after its conversion to standard gauge			Y					
Jan 2010	ARTC leased Queensland section of standard gauge interstate line, from the border to Acacia Ridge	Y							

Date	Event	QLD	NSW	VIC	SA	WA	NT	TAS	NZ
Mar 2010	Shell Australia ceased dispatching petrol tanker trains from Sydney to Tamworth, Dubbo & Canberra, sending all state-wide distribution by road. Patrick Portlink's loss.		Y						
April 2010	Southern Shorthaul Railroad (SSR) replaced PN hauling coal to Port Kembla for Centennial Coal		Y						
June 2010	Genesee & Wyoming Inc bought FreightLink				Y		Y		
June 2010	PN ceased services between Dubbo & Port Botany		Y						
June 2010	Asciano closed its container park at Sandown		Y						
June 2010	South Spur & Silverton Rail sold to P&O Trans Aust		Y			Y			
July 2010	QRN (freight business and CQCN) split off from QR	Y							
Nov 2010	QRN's IPO, with Qld Govt as minority shareholder	Y							
Dec 2010	WestNet Rail sold to Brookfield Infrastructure, renamed Brookfield Rail in August 2011					Y			
Apr 2011	Qube Logistics became a train operator through its acquisition of P&O Trans Australia (POTA)		Y	Y		Y			
June 2011	Albury-Seymour broad gauge track converted to standard gauge, creating interstate double line			Y					
June 2011	ARG and Interail ceased trading as separate brands, became part of QR National		Y	Y		Y			
Jan 2012	The management contract for the NSW country branch-line network (CRN) was transferred by the NSW government to the John Holland Rail Group, creating a third track provider in the State.		Y						
Jan 2012	QR National started hauling iron ore to Geraldton					Y			
Mar 2012	CBH invested $175 million in new locomotives and grain wagons, contracted Watco to operate grain trains, replacing services provided by ARG/QRN					Y			
Jun 2012	Qube Logistics bought MIST and Independent Rail, thus expanding its rolling-stock fleet		Y						
Aug 2012	Sydney's Metropolitan Freight Network (including Port Botany line) leased by TfNSW to ARTC		Y						
Dec 2012	QR National changed its name to Aurizon	Y	Y			Y			
Jan 2013	ARTC's Southern Sydney Freight Line opened		Y						
Jun 2013	El Zorro ceased trading, went into liquidation		Y	Y					
Feb 2014	Sydney Rail Services (SRS) started operations between Sandgate (Newcastle) & Port Botany		Y						
June 2014	Brookfield Rail effectively closed 'tier 3' grain lines, against the wishes of its customer CBH, and the WA government which is the rail network owner.					Y			

Appendix 3

Date	Event	QLD	NSW	VIC	SA	WA	NT	TAS	NZ
Aug 2014	Aurizon sold its stake in CRT to Qube Logistics		Y	Y					
2014	KiwiRail started 4-year period of 'managed decline'								Y
Mar 2015	Genesee & Wyoming acquired Freightliner Group		Y						
July 2015	Fletcher Industrial Exports (FIE) started trains from Dubbo to Port Botany to transport own products		Y						
Aug 2015	Pinnaroo & Loxton branches, owned by Genesee & Wyoming Australia, ceased to be used because the one customer transferred all grain haulage to road				Y				
Aug 2015	Govt announced plan to convert 3 Murray Basin lines from broad to standard gauge, with heavier axle-loads, serving growing minerals & grain flows			Y					
May 2016	Aurizon started operations at the Enfield Intermodal Logistics Centre, western Sydney		Y						
May 2016	SSR bought Greentrains fleet of locomotives formerly owned by Silverton, then Allco, then Cootes		Y	Y					
Aug 2016	Asciano broken up; Pacific National now owned by a group of pension funds and investment banks	Y	Y	Y	Y	Y			
Sep 2016	Bowmans Rail takes Broken Hill to Port Adelaide mineral sands traffic from Pacific National		Y		Y				
Nov 2016	Major earthquake closed South Island's Main North Line for a year; KiwiRail moved Auckland to Christchurch services to coastal shipping								Y
Dec 2016	GWA acquired Glencore's fleet of 30 locomotives and 894 coal wagons for $A1.14 billion, with a 20-year contract to haul 40 million tonnes p.a.		Y						
Jan? 2017	Qube hauled grain on the Victorian broad-gauge country network for first time			Y					
Jan 2017	SCT started its own Melbourne-Wodonga-Brisbane trains, after using Aurizon's interstate trains for four years to move its own SCT wagons	Y		Y					
Aug 2017	Aurizon announced it would quit its unprofitable intermodal business, selling Qld services to a consortium by mid-2018 (since blocked by the ACCC), and closing its intermodal (but not other) freight business in other states by Dec 2017	Y	Y	Y	Y	Y			
Sept 2017	South Island's Main North Line reopened for limited service after Kaikoura earthquake								Y
Dec 2017	Aurizon did not renew contract with Wilmar Sugar; Wilmar freight contract signed with PN	Y							
Feb 2018	Aurizon ceased operations at Enfield Intermodal Logistics Centre; contracted by NSW Ports to Linx Cargo Care Group which runs own trains to port		Y						
Oct 2018	Aurizon announced sale of its Qld intermodal business to Linfox, and a 10-year take-or-pay deal to linehaul Linfox trains within Qld	Y							

Date	Event	QLD	NSW	VIC	SA	WA	NT	TAS	NZ
Feb 2019	Mt Isa line closed for 3 months by flood damage	Y							
June 2019	Viterra ceased to send grain by rail on Eyre Peninsula network, leaving it open but unused					Y			
Nov 2019	Qube started IMEX trains between Port Botany and Moorebank Logistics Park, western Sydney		Y						
Dec 2019	Watco started operations for GrainCorp, becoming only the third train operator on Queensland's narrow-gauge network	Y							
Dec 2019	NSW's Blue Mountains line closed for 3 months due to bush fires between Lithgow and Mount Victoria, and landslip at Leura due to heavy rain		Y						
Dec 2019	NZ Government: rail network investment to come from National Land Transport Fund, via a long-term strategy, treating road and rail equally								Y
Jan 2020	NZ Government announced $70m to rebuild the Northland line, previously under 'managed decline', to take new business from road-haul.								Y
Feb 2020	Genesee & Wyoming world-wide sold; GWA now owned by Macquarie Infrastructure & others, and renamed One Rail Australia (ORA)	Y	Y	Y	Y	Y			
May 2020	Northland Line closed for 7 months for a $70m major upgrade, from managed decline to full use; 13 tunnel floors lowered, 5 bridges replaced								Y
Sept 2020	Bowen Rail Co launched; owned by Adani, it hauls Adani coal from Galilee Basin to Abbott Point	Y							
Oct 2020	Linx Cargo Care Group started train service between Sydney and Bathurst		Y						
Aug 2021	CBH announced 6+2+2 year contract with Aurizon for full operational services, using CBH's fleet, with Aurizon to provide 3 more grain trains. Contract with Watco terminated 6 months early.					Y			
Oct 2021	Aurizon announced proposed acquisition of ORA for $2.35B, subject to divestment of ORA's east coast business	Y	Y	Y	Y	Y			
Jan 2022	The management contract for the NSW country branch-line network (CRN) awarded to UGL by NSW government, in competitive tender		Y						
Mar 2022	Moss Vale to Unanderra line closed for 6 months by flood damage		Y						
Feb 2023	Aurizon captured major customer TGE from PN, with a contract for train capacity nationwide	Y	Y	Y	Y	Y	Y		
Feb 2023	Storms causing landslips and washouts caused the North Auckland and Hawkes Bay lines to be closed for many months for repairs								Y
April 2023	Aurizon re-entered interstate intermodal market, based on a nation-wide contract with TGE	Y	Y	Y	Y	Y			
May 2023	PN secured contract extension to haul GrainCorp products through to 2029		Y	Y					

Appendix 4:
Differences between railways in Australasia & North America

Rail industry cultures

In Chapter 3 (Overview), the issue of railway culture was briefly raised, and in particular, the significant differences between the Australasian railway culture and that of the North American railroads. Culture affects everything but is often invisible to those inside an industry or organisation until something or someone tries to change it. One explanation of business culture is

> "one of the most vague yet prevalent words you hear when people explain the success (or failure) of any business initiative. It is hard to explain, to quantify... It's like background music – sometimes you hear it, sometimes you don't – but it's always there." [846]

I had personal experience of becoming aware of the cultures in the rail industry, and realising that they are inherent and "always there", and are usually invisible. I experienced a clash of railway cultures when, as a Senior Research Officer with New Zealand Railways (NZR) in the 1980s, I was asked to work closely with a group of railroad consultants from the USA, to find ways to bring about improvements, efficiencies and cost savings in NZR's freight train operations. At the time, neither the consultants nor I had any understanding that there could be significant cultural differences in the operational norms for rail systems that we each understood deeply. Crucially, NZR management also had no understanding that differences in operational norms could lead to inappropriate advice being given by the consultants. These differences quickly became obvious, but it took a while to appreciate how fundamental these were. (Hence, trying to concur on productive changes to the Operations Plan was frustrating for both parties.) An explanation follows of my understanding of some of the ways in which the two cultures vary in their norms.[847]

Train timetabling & scheduling, versus on-demand train operations

Most commercial railways have many customers, many different traffic flows and a variety of commodities hauled. Some types of wagons are specialised to a particular type of commodity while others are more generally useful. This all makes for complexity in the management of operations. How a railway deals with the complexity of its operations is essentially cultural.

Australasia

One fundamental of Australasian (and European) railway operations is that the whole network and every train on it should operate to a planned timetable or schedule. Each train has a planned 'path' that takes account of both the train's expected attributes (the assigned loco power, gross trailing weight and length) and its planned route (route topography, signalling system, planned stops, etc.) It does not matter whether the planning of the path has been done hours or months ahead of the train's actual trip on the day – a path must exist before each train departs.

The compilation of schedules planned for individual trains creates the timetable planned for each railway line. This enables the sharing among many trains of the line's capacity, which is necessarily finite in the medium term.[848] Consistency from day to day for line and network timetables is a highly valued feature. It enables certainty of transit times for freight moving across the network, which is valuable for marketing. Consistency is also the basis for crew scheduling, so that when crews are assigned by their roster to a schedule for each day, they can know the timing of each day's work weeks in advance, and they can plan their non-work activities accordingly.

Train timetable planning is an iterative process that starts with the creation of a master timetable, sometimes years ahead of a given operational date. The master timetable is the basis for operational consistency from day to day. Copies of this master are modified for specific dates to include planned temporary changes, such as train cancellations, additional trains, and partial network closures planned to enable track maintenance activities.

The master timetable (and all its derivatives) takes account of the different priorities and running speeds of trains. For a single-track railway line with passing loops, it includes also the places and times where trains should meet to pass one another, if they are all running on time.

Iterative planning continues even as the trains are operating on the line. It is the job of the Train Controller in charge of the line to monitor the progress of every train against its planned path, and if necessary to plan an alternative path when any train runs into trouble. This is done day by day and hour by hour. The planning of the detail of train operations is fundamental to Australasian railway operations.

North America

Traditionally in North America, freight trains did not run to predictable timetables (although since year 2000 some trains conveying non-bulk traffic have been operated on a scheduled basis). Freight trains were run when enough 'cars' had accumulated in the starting yard to justify the direct costs of running the train. Railroads assumed that maximising train size or weight would reduce the costs for fuel, crews and locomotives per car hauled. However, it is now acknowledged that this method of train operation has hidden costs. Rolling-stock stands stationary for much more time than when it is rolling and generating revenue. Locomotives and crews get bunched up, and often not located where they are needed. Yards are either too congested or empty. Worst of all, the unreliability of freight transport times generates negative feedback from customers.

This type of operation is sometimes described as a 'push' operation, whereas a timetabled network has a 'pull' operation. In a 'push' operation, the crew is called to duty only when it is known when its freight train will depart. The crew will work a certain time and or distance, then go to barracks for a rest period and wait to be called for their next assignment. Train crews can be away from their home depot for many days without knowing when they will return home.

It says something about the cultural isolation of North American railroads, with regard to the rest of the world, that the major American management consultancy Oliver Wyman could publish this in 2006: [849]

> "Scheduled railroading is a fairly recent phenomenon, as tight schedules would have been almost impossible to create with pencil and paper or even with early computers, given the complexity of freight railroads."

In Australasian railway systems, as in Europe, scheduling trains with pencil and paper has been done since the 1930s, if not earlier. Specialised computer systems started to replace pen and paper in Australasia in the 1980s! [850]

The differences resulting from unscheduled vs scheduled rail operations

In the absence of statistics, it is still possible to make some comparisons. Trains are likely to be heavier and longer in the USA compared to Australia. Average speeds per car per day in the USA appear to be ridiculously slow by Australasian norms. The reason for the slowness is that cars spend much more time stationary, waiting to connect with trains.

Freight transport elapsed times are much more predictable in Australia compared with the USA. A consequence of dispatching trains when ready is that the management of the progress of trains across complex networks can only be done in a reactive fashion. Hence conflicts are unavoidable, creating both less-than-optimal use of line capacities, and irregular transit times for trains and the freight they carry. The combination of irregular train times and variable waiting times for cars at exchange yards makes for very unpredictable delivery times for customers' consignments. In more recent years, some US railroads have begun to address this unreliability by operating some timetabled point-to-point freight trains. For example, it was reported[851] in 2016 that the Class 1 railroad BNSF launched a daily direct intermodal service from Portland (Oregon) and Seattle (Washington) to Dallas / Fort Worth (Texas) to improve its competitiveness against road for the distribution of the Pacific Northwest fruit harvest. The trains arrive in Dallas /Fort Worth on the morning of the fifth day after departure, which is two days earlier than the minimum transit time achievable using a sequence of yard-to-yard trains.

In North America, the practice of scheduled operations now goes by the tag 'Precision Railroading', and a 2018 article indicates that it was still considered revolutionary.[852] CSX has recently implemented this, following the example of Canadian National and Canadian Pacific, replacing its previous 'hub-and-spoke' operating method. Freight shippers are now required

> "to load smaller batches of cars more days per week".

CSX was reported[7] to have harvested

> "the huge advantages of precision railroading: Transporting the same or more freight with far less capital in the form of railcars, locomotives and expensive-to-run switching facilities."

By contrast, continuous loading is the norm in New Zealand. For example, pulp and paper plants have been loading directly from the end of their production lines directly into railway wagons for daily trains direct to the products' destination, albeit on much shorter hauls, since the 1950s.

How railed freight is moved across the country

In Australia, where the railway networks are managed separately[853] from the trains, freight is moved always on one train owner's wagons and services, moving across one or more separate 'open access' rail networks. The train operator manages its access to the networks by buying 'train paths' in the network operator's timetables, some time in advance (hours to months) of the train being operated. The train operator thus provides an 'all or nothing' offering to the freight shipper. The train operator will move the shipper's traffic from its origin to its destination, or there is no contract possible. Because of the competition between train operators, there is no wish and no attempt to co-operate, in the sense that shippers could have their consignments moved by a sequence of different train operators. There is no organisational or physical scope for the interchange of wagons, and thus no possibility of independent 'short-line railroads' such as are common in North America. Consequently, some intra-state freight shippers find that there may be no rail service available, particularly for occasional and less-than-trainload consignments, and using a road carrier is the usually the only option.

In North America (USA, Canada and Mexico) freight rail companies own (or at least lease) their own lines and they operate their trains only on their own lines, except where 'trackage rights' have been negotiated with another railroad. When Canadian National (CN), which owns railroad lines in the USA, decided to avoid the congestion of Chicago (a major hub in the American railroad network), its solution was to buy a small railroad company, the Elgin, Joliet & Eastern, which had a line that circles the outer parts of Chicago from north to south.[854] With this purchase, CN was able to route its freight trains from Canada to connect directly to other railroads heading south to New Orleans.

The practice of permitting another rail company trackage rights on your own network is at the discretion of the track owner, except where it is mandated by law to enable the intercity passenger train companies to operate (the major operators being Amtrak in USA and Via in Canada). The broader concept of 'open access' on a shared network is alien to most North American freight rail companies.

In North America, railcars are passed between railroad companies at pre-agreed exchange yards. If a railroad company is hauling cars that it does not own, it has to rent them at agreed daily ('per diem') rates. This practice requires a serious amount of accounting to keep track of which cars are under the control of which railroad companies, day by day, and to authorise the per diem transfers among the companies. The Association of American Railroads started a service to do just this. It has since become an independent company called RailInc which provides this service to all American railroad companies. This method of operation enables railroads to accept and haul car-load consignments, whether the loads are in their own or some other company's cars.

Such a system as this is not needed in Australia. Most Australian freight train operators don't have and don't need good wagon location tracking systems, because wagons always remain under their control, at least while they are loaded.[855] When there were only state-based government-owned rail systems in Australia, there was exchange of each other's wagons at the borders, but this practice ceased with the advent of the National Rail Corporation and the start of vertical separation. Another reason for not needing systems for tracking individual wagons is that most train operators have specialised to move only train-load traffic, moving between limited numbers of locations. Typically, wagons are removed from these fixed-consist trains only for maintenance purposes.

One exception with regard to wagon tracking is a company named Qube. Although its rail business and fleet were acquired by absorbing a number of small operators, it portrays itself as a freight logistics company, not a railway company. It operates both road and railway services to and from the container ports in New South Wales and Victoria. It has chosen to specialise in managing and hauling containerised import and export traffics, and for this it needs maximum flexibility. It has a modern information system to keep track of containers and wagons, and perhaps because of this it has a majority share in this segment of the freight transport market in these states. It has the added complexity of ensuring that export containers arrive at particular stevedores' sites within the container ports, within specified delivery windows a few days wide, so that containers can be marshalled for loading onto specific ships going to different export markets. Export shipping has a complexity of its own. Qube has the modal flexibility and the information management systems to be successful in this particular freight market.

In New Zealand, KiwiRail still accepts wagon-load traffic because that is the nature of its business in a small economy. It still has a legacy system from 1990s called Amicus (meaning 'friend' in Latin) which is used to keep track of containers and wagons as they are added to and taken off scheduled trains and inter-island ferry sailings.

Appendix 4

Network rationalisation

In Australasia, railway network development and operations were managed and funded largely[856] by colonial, then state governments, for want of any other organisation or business capable of such undertakings. In the USA, companies were granted land by governments to fund the construction and operation of railway lines, which resulted in many duplicated lines where railroad companies competed with one another.

Hence the rationalisation of the North American railroad industry that took place mainly between the 1950s and the 1990s was triggered by bankruptcies, company mergers and acquisitions, leading to rationalisation of assets – lines, yards and depots – to remove the duplications. Some mergers created traffic disruptions that took years to resolve.[857] (US Railroad mergers also created clashes between long-established company operational norms and traditions, which robbed the newly merged companies of some of the benefits of merging.[858])

In Australasia, governments built railway lines into every region where there was actual or potential economic activity, if topography permitted. Their purpose was to open up the country for settlers, who would extract natural resources or create farms. The network rationalisation that happened between the 1950s and the 1980s was typically much less organisationally disruptive than in North America. Networks were trimmed at the edges by closing or abandoning[859] branch lines in rural areas where little traffic remained after loss of business to road haulage. The exceptions to that rural trimming were lines that served the networks of grain storage silos, and those that served mines. Also, the complexity of yards and sidings in the cities was reduced.

Appendix 5:
Managing Access to Rail Networks

Why did this become an issue?

Implicit in the National Competition Policy of the early 1990s (see in chapter 5), was a statement of faith that competition among train operators for access to rail networks would be possible. How this would be achieved was not a concern at that time. However, the first step was understood – organisational separation of track provision (including both infrastructure maintenance and control and allocation of line capacity) from the operation and marketing of trains. This separation then enabled negotiation and contractual arrangements between network providers and train operators. Such separation was achieved on the Australian National network in 1995, then in NSW and Victoria in 1996. It did not happen in WA and Queensland till some years later, because these States were not interested in fostering competition on their rail networks at that time.

The Productivity Commission's bizarre recommendation

By the time the Productivity Commission (PC) produced its *Progress in Rail Reform* report in 1999, competition among freight train operators existed only on the interstate intermodal sectors (see in chapter 12). Because the PC placed much value on competition between train operators on the same tracks, it included a recommendation on how to manage access to rail networks. In its report of 1999, it wrote:[860]

"Recommendation 8.1: The pricing and allocation of train schedules should reflect the value that users place on the track. [There should be] a market approach for allocating schedules or transferring capacity on the interstate network."

This indicates that the Productivity Commission believed that the theory of price-based competition should be applicable to the allocation of train schedules. It was therefore advocating some kind of periodic auction, after which the winning bidders would have the right to use the most valuable train schedules or paths. Such a method of path allocation has never been implemented, so it is useful to explore why not. The following sections discuss how train schedules can be priced, various reasons why auctioning train paths was an unworkable notion, the nature of line capacity, and what is the most important feature for allocating train paths in the Australian context.

Putting prices on train schedules or paths

Progress in Rail Reform identified three possible approaches to pricing train paths:[861]

- **Posted Prices** are not negotiable, are openly published to all train operators, with details that define exactly the terms and conditions under which operators can gain access to the tracks. Conditions include specifications for maximum train lengths, maximum axle-loads and maximum train speeds, reflecting the costs of track maintenance for routine usage. Typically, for any specified section of track, trains with maximum axle-loadings (e.g. hauling minerals or grains) will be limited in their maximum speed compared with trains with axle-loadings substantially less than the maximum, for example trains carrying empty containers. The ARTC uses and argued for Posted Prices because it creates a 'level playing-field' and "gave the operators confidence in their competitive position". The PC did not support Posted Prices because it enables 'first come first served' arrangements and 'grandfathering' of existing paths, and it would be "unlikely that such systems will allocate train schedules efficiently, since they do not reflect the value that new or different operators place on the schedules." [862]

- **Negotiated Prices** can result from commercial negotiations between a track provider and a train operator, sometimes with constraints set by an arbitrator of upper and lower bounds on the price. This method is used on some state-based regimes. Perhaps the most notable example is the Western Australian situation where negotiations, arbitrated by the State's Economic Regulation Authority, continued from 2013 until 2019 between the private sector track provider Brookfield Rail and its customer CBH (Co-operative Bulk Handling). CBH stores grains in a network of 200 silos across the wheatbelt, located mostly where there are (or were) rail sidings for load-out, and it transports grains for export mainly on rail using its own rolling-stock and a contracted train operator. (There is more on this unique situation in chapter 15.)
- **Prices Set by Auctioning Mechanisms**: The PC described what it meant by these as:[863]

    "Potential operators bid for segments of track, train schedules or packages of train schedules and the access provider optimises the allocation of these subject to the size of the bids, their feasibility and the cost of service."

Despite feedback on this notion from rail industry participants, the PC failed to understand that train schedules/paths are not 'economic goods'. They are like permits, which are unable to be sold or traded. Therefore, they are not suitable to be allocated using a competitive 'market approach' where price is the determinant of value. Train operators assess the value of train schedules by their serviceability factors, and pricing is subservient to these other factors. Prices are based largely on maximum permitted axle weights and maximum train speeds, which together are related to track maintenance costs over the medium term.

Is auctioning of train schedules viable?

From my reading of *Progress in Rail Reform*, particularly chapter 8 *Access to Rail Infrastructure Services*, I think the PC based its recommendation for auctioning mechanisms on several unstated and questionable assumptions:

1. that a railtrack provider starts as a new business with a new operation on day one,
2. that it is primarily motivated to make a profit, and is therefore concerned to make the most efficient use of its line capacity,
3. that it offers train schedules which are tradeable, such that buyers will pay more for some than others, and
4. that train operators have to arrange track access with only one track provider in the region in which they operate.

All these assumptions are faulty. Why?

1. A new railtrack provider inherits operations from its predecessor

In relation to the first assumption, the PC wrote[864]

> "Auctioning provides a market mechanism for the initial allocation of schedules to train operators. Although auctioning is not currently used in Australian rail markets, it has been proposed as a future option — especially in networks which are or become more congested as a result of new entry and increased activity. As the market for schedules develops, the pricing and allocation of

schedules is likely to evolve from posted and negotiated prices to more market-based mechanisms."

The first problem with this statement is that there can never be an "initial allocation of schedules". When a railtrack provider is created out of a formerly vertically-integrated railway, as has always been the case in Australia, it takes over an existing operation. It starts business with train schedules already planned and contracted. These represent existing commitments made to the train operators who have taken over the above-rail business of the formerly vertically-integrated railway. Ultimately these are incorporated as contractual commitments made to the train operators' customers.

The second problem in the paragraph quoted above is that with increased activity on a rail network, "the pricing and allocation of schedules is likely to evolve from posted and negotiated prices to more market-based mechanisms." This might happen if the rail network was the only effective means of land transport available, as it is for bulk commodities moved in millions of tonnes per year, such as coal and minerals. But for non-bulk freight on the interstate network, and most intrastate freight (other than coal and minerals), there is a very efficient means of limiting the value of schedules for freight trains – the existence of freely available and very under-priced highways. Auctioning of train paths to the highest bidders cannot be viable where highways are an alternative means of moving freight. The reality is that highways and road transport operators set an upper limit at a low level for the value of train paths, so that the ARTC and other track providers are forced to be price-takers rather than price-makers. Therefore, getting efficient use of line capacity can never be a higher priority than meeting customers' requirements. Hence an efficient allocation of train schedules, in relation to the great majority of the total route kilometres of Australasian rail networks, is an unobtainable and illusory ideal, based on a misunderstanding of the nature of scarcity in land transport capacity.

2. Should track providers be profit-oriented?

The second assumption listed above is that track providers should be and even can be primarily motivated to make a profit. The reality is in Australasia that providers of railtrack to train-operating customers have (with one important exception) always been created as government-owned entities. Their primary reason for being is to provide services that can enable multiple train operators to get reasonable access to the rail networks previously built by governments. The most important thing in these circumstances is that the train operators can trade profitably in competition with road haulage; otherwise, why go to the bother of vertical separation, and indeed, privatisation? These track providers are instruments of government, benign monopoly providers, there to give effect to government policy for land transport. Therefore, while it is desirable that such entities break even on their operating costs, profits should not be their primary objective.

The important exception mentioned above is Brookfield Rail, the American-owned rail network lessee and manager in Western Australia. The WA network is unusual because the Western Australian Government Railways (WAGR) had withdrawn from hauling all but bulk commodities before its privatisation and subsequent vertical separation. The intrastate traffic which uses rail (grains, chemicals and minerals) is shipped in train-load quantities daily, and therefore switching it to the rural road network it is not realistic. Brookfield has a long-term lease of the network, has spent millions of dollars on track upgrading, and can charge for rail access at levels which enable it to operate profitably. This is discussed more in chapter 15, under *The Western Australian Experience*.

As has been explained in chapter 4, the Commonwealth Government does not have a considered and comprehensive policy for land transport. It does not understand that railtrack providers cannot be primarily profit-oriented, and therefore are not suitable for privatisation. Consequently, it took seriously a recommendation in 2014 from the National Commission of Audit to sell the ARTC. (There is more on this topic in chapter 15, under *Should the Commonwealth have sold the ARTC?*) It authorised a scoping study from consultants,[865] but the outcome is unknown. However, the government quietly announced its decision in the 2016 Budget that privatisation would be incompatible with its investment in the Inland Rail project, via increasing its equity in the ARTC.[866]

3. Are freight train schedules transferable?

In relation to the third assumption on page 513, train schedules are just lines on a diagram and data in a train timetable. They do not exist as equivalent entities in a tradeable form, as for example, shares and bonds do. A train schedule or path is the expression of a contract in which the train operator is granted a right to run trains in the future between nominated places on the network, only on specified days of the week, and to an agreed schedule. Possibly that right may be sold, but the train path is just a segment of line capacity that can only be rented. (See below, under *Railway Line Capacity is a Unique Offering*.)

The contract requires trust and a willingness to share information and cooperate for everyone's benefit. Certainty of tenure of the contract is fundamental for the train operator; this means that trains with similar attributes can be permitted to run time and time again, and the contract will continue until such time as the train operator indicates that it is no longer needed. Thus, for the train operator, the price is subservient to security of tenure. It is also understood that the track provider guarantees not to allocate the path to a higher bidder without the train company's consent. Hence, the usual 'market forces' do not apply in the management of line capacity. Price is not the main factor in the daily transactions of train running.

Train schedules for passenger trains, and for bulk loads of coal and minerals, are similar to one another to the extent that the train weights and the allocation of locomotive power are normally consistent from day to day. Hence their schedules are derived from known and predictable factors, and so they usually run in close accordance with their schedules.

In contrast, train schedules for freight trains operating in the general and intermodal freight markets are not so similar one to another. (There are differences in the trailing weights and the allocation of locomotive power, comparing one train operator with another, and often due to daily load variations that each operator experiences.) Therefore, these train schedules have to be based on **estimates** of future train weight and locomotive power allocation. In operation, the differences in these planned factors can be compounded by crew idiosyncrasies in train driving techniques, and/or reduced adhesion of locomotive driving wheels when the rails are wet. All these factors combine in daily operations to make the adherence of each freight train to its planned schedule somewhat approximate, and variable from day to day. In addition, the progress of each train along its planned path is contingent upon the progress of all other trains sharing the track at the same time, and how the train controller manages these. This is especially so on single-track lines, which comprise the majority of trackage in all freight rail networks in Australasia. Consequently, for the operating plan of a freight railway line to be viable, there must be some contingency time built into all the train schedules to allow for daily variation.

There is little scope for an effective operation of what the PC called 'capacity transfer mechanisms' between different train operators. The only possible exception is where there is a commercial rail network carrying only trains of fixed size and of bulk commodities, and there is only one instance of this[867] – the Central Queensland Coal Network.

4. Obtaining train paths across multiple access regimes

In relation to the fourth assumption on page 513, management of the networks in both Victoria and NSW is split between the ARTC and state-based providers. In NSW, there are two State-based providers, and therefore three access regimes in total. RailCorp manages tracks in the major metropolitan areas, and the John Holland Group is contracted by the NSW Government to manage the State's other branch lines. Therefore, the process of planning train paths for freight trains is more difficult than it was when there were only the State networks. Each current track provider has its own priorities, and wants to control when trains may cross its boundaries. Setting up new train paths is therefore an iterative process between the train operator and all the track providers involved. Altogether, this would be the most unsuitable situation in which to auction train schedules! [There is more on this topic of multiple access regimes in chapter 16 under the heading *The Legacy of the Reform Process in NSW.*]

Railway line capacity is a unique offering

Train operators are intermediaries, like airlines, shipping companies and road carriers. All provide services for paying customers. Freight train operators can sell space on their trains to their customers. All modes face constraints in their access to terminals. However, unlike aircraft and ship operators who ply free and clear airspace and seas, and road carriers who have unrestricted use of relatively free and clear interstate highways, train operators are constrained over every kilometre of the routes of their trains.

These constraints are due to the nature and specifics of the railway lines, and by the presence of other trains on the lines. Train paths are therefore a necessary input to the running of trains, and all train operators need certainty of pathing both for marketing and operational planning reasons.[868] It is up to the network manager to adjust the train paths, both in timetable planning and in daily operation, to achieve some equitable sharing of line capacity among various train operators. To allow price-based competition for train paths (as the PC recommended) would see the most sought-after paths going to the highest bidders, and other bidders would be left with paths that could be unsatisfactory for meeting their clients' needs. While the PC would be delighted with this outcome, it would be a case of 'the tail wagging the dog'. As a result, some railable freight would likely be moved instead by road at a higher cost to the shipper, just because the highways have almost infinite capacity. Also, because Australasian freight railway networks can usually get economies of scale, the loss of traffic on rail would be counter-productive.

Part of the problem for a network provider in renting its line capacity is that quantifying its available line capacity is very difficult. Line capacity is determined by a combination of mostly variable factors:

- **Infrastructure characteristics** such as
    — the topography of the route (which can dictate maximum train weight),
    — designed maximum train speeds and axle loadings (determined from rail weight and strength),
    — current actual track condition, (which, if less-than-good, can result in semi-permanent speed restrictions for trains, which travel more slowly, increasing line occupancy and thus reducing line capacity)
    — the type of safe-working system provided,
    — distances between signals,
    — signal clearance times,
    — whether the line is single or double track or a mix of both, and,
    — for single tracks the distances between passing loops and the lengths of shortest passing loops (which normally dictate maximum train length).
- Operational parameters such as
    — temporary speed restrictions due to awaiting and in-progress track maintenance,
    — diversity of use – the mix of train types with

different performance characteristics,
- the regularity or not of train timetables – repeating or irregular train pathing,
- the concentration of traffic flows causing peakiness in demand,
- whether some classes of train have to be prioritised over others,
- the expected reliability of trains in adhering to their schedules, which affects the amount of slack time built into train schedules to improve timetable robustness.

Analysts can define line capacity in four ways:[869]

- **Theoretical capacity** is the number of trains that could run over a route, during a specific time interval, in a strictly perfect mathematically-generated environment, with the trains running permanently and ideally at minimum headway. It is the upper limit for line capacity. It assumes that traffic is homogeneous, that all trains are identical, and that trains are evenly spaced throughout the day with no disruptions. It ignores the variations in traffic and operations that occur in reality. Hence, it is never possible to run reliably as many trains as can be calculated mathematically.
- **Practical capacity** is an upper limit of representative traffic volume that can be moved along a line with reasonable reliability. It reflects the actual train mix, train priorities and peakiness in demand, under normal operating conditions. It may reach as much as 75% of theoretical capacity, but is often less. The difficulty for freight railways to be operated consistently at their practical capacity is the lack of uniformity, and of resilience – the ability to recover when operating conditions are not normal, creating unreliability.
- **Used capacity** measures the existing traffic and

operations on a line, as expressed in its master operating plan. It is what the ARTC had to manage, because of pre-existing contracts, when it took control of each of its lines. Used capacity will change when there are changes to the operating plan for each line.
- **Available capacity** is the difference between practical capacity and used capacity. This is what Australian network providers can offer to train operators seeking new train paths.

In practice, as the used capacity increases, resilience decreases, and operational unreliability increases. This trade-off means that it is rare for the used capacity of a freight railway to be consistently as much as its practical capacity. It also means that renting available line capacity is best done incrementally, so that operational experience can guide the track provider towards its level of practical capacity without causing excessive disruption.

Thus, renting railway line capacity is not like booking seats on aircraft flights, or container slots on ship sailings, where in both cases there is a known fixed capacity, port to port, available to be booked in advance. In these cases, the method of booking may be on a first-come first-served basis, or the airline or shipping company may practise yield management. In this situation, the purchase of seats or slots by buyers may be at different prices, but this still does not restrain other buyers' ability to buy, until the carrying capacity of the aircraft or ship is fully booked. Thus, each purchaser has their own allocated space that does not constrain any other user from purchasing other space.

Public railway lines are different because they are necessarily a shared resource. The planned use by one train operator may well constrain the planned use by other operators, especially on single tracks with passing loops, which comprise the majority of the Australian and New Zealand freight networks. The greater the density of trains planned to be run on a single track on any given day, the more potential interference there is among the train schedules. In operation, increasing the number of trains on a track increases exponentially the total train delays.[870] Hence there is complexity in both planning and in operation. Increasing the complexity increases the likelihood of uncertainty.

The need for certainty

The Productivity Commission (PC) was told a number of times in submissions to its inquiry into *Progress in Rail Reform* of the importance of certainty, and therefore the unsuitability of auctioning train schedules. The NSW Rail Access Corporation argued that one of its concerns with auctioning was:[871]

> "... that it may have a negative impact on the market. If a rail operator needs to invest time and resources in developing a market, it will only do so if it has reasonable certainty over its train path. Under an auctioning system there is a risk that operators will be discouraged from market development. (sub. DR102, p. 23)"

Similarly, the interstate train operator SCT argued:[12]

> "The provision of spot pricing, like auctioning, would give rise to a great deal of uncertainty in the market which in turn would not allow investment to take place in the rail industry ... The use of spot pricing and auctioning techniques could ... give rise to uncertainty insofar as the investment plans of another operator are concerned. (sub. DR100, p. 4)"

This is what National Rail (the first interstate train operator) told the PC about gaining track access: [872]

> "Contracts for track access should give sufficient security of tenure of train time-paths to enable train operators and their customers to enter into binding transport contracts, with terms commensurate with

commitments to capital investment and commodity sale contracts. This means a minimum of 15 years, with options for renewal."

Another interstate train operator submitted:[873]

> "To our knowledge, no country in the world has devised a working method for selling train paths by competitive bidding. (sub. DR95, p. 4)"

The PC's report then noted the difficulty of auctioning a continuous path across a corridor, quoting the National Rail Corporation's submission:[874]

> "There are strong inter-actions between time-paths on the network, both 'vertically' (between time-paths on the same track), and 'horizontally' (between time-paths on adjacent sections of track, which are administered by different access providers). The practical difficulties of coordinating auction of a continuous path across a whole corridor (eg, Sydney-Perth) would make an auction impossible. (sub. DR117, p. 16)"

Despite the quote above, and the general and specific opposition from the rail industry to the auctioning of train paths, the PC's report then stated:[875]

> "The practical issues raised by participants present challenges to the development of a path auctioning system. However, they are not sufficient to rule out the concept. Appropriate design and implementation of an auctioning system can overcome many of these issues. An effective auctioning system will provide information on individual users valuation of train paths and facilitate the efficient development of the rail industry."

What the PC chose to ignore in making its recommendation for auctioning train schedules was the primary need of all train operators for certainty of their train paths. This enables them to plan crew rosters and locomotive allocations to trains, including allowing times for locomotive refuelling and routine maintenance. Certainty is also a prerequisite for train operators to know that they can meet their clients' own requirements for certainty about freight loading and unloading times, so that the clients in turn can plan their dispositions of staff and equipment. The PC clearly underestimated the fundamental importance of certainty in the timing of events in every Australian railway system and throughout the freight logistics chain. Planning for certainty has been a part of the railway culture for generations, because it is an essential element for service reliability and operational efficiency. This need for planning was reinforced by the vertical separation of the industry in the 1990s, which then required formal agreements between its various participants on a range of issues, including operational arrangements. The reality is that in this trading environment, and even in a vertically-integrated railway, the efficient use of line capacity *per se* must take the lowest priority.

The need for certainty means that the rail industry cannot compete with road on the basis of short-term flexibility. The rail industry's competitive strengths are its service reliability, lower unit costs and prices, and reduced environmental externalities compared to trucking.

Conclusion

Notwithstanding that train operators had written, in effect, that without security of tenure of train paths, having access to track was of very little value, the Productivity Commission (PC) concluded its section on Pricing and Allocating Train Schedules in *Progress in Rail Reform* with this:[876]

> "It is not apparent that existing access regimes include market-based mechanisms for allocating and transferring schedules. The introduction of such mechanisms would be particularly relevant to the interstate network"

There are two likely reasons why the PC made this recommendation, despite industry opposition.
- It could not recognise any situation in which prices are not the ultimate arbiter of value, because this was beyond its worldview in which market reasoning is pre-eminent. (See in chapter 16, under *The discussion in economics and policy commentaries* for an explanation of the influence of worldview on thinking.)
- It assumed that line capacity is a scarce resource, which it can be, and therefore the economic theory dealing with scarcity was applicable on the interstate network. However, how freight railway line capacity users should respond to such scarcity cannot be assumed in a country over-supplied with highway capacity (outside of the cities) as the alternative to sending freight by rail. The PC ignored that strong competition for railable freight already existed. The reality is that any auctioning of train paths would create uncertainty of tenure, and an inability for train operators to provide longer term service reliability at any cost. This would quickly drive potential railway customers to the alternative mode, because the highway system has vastly more capacity to move freight than does the interstate rail network.

The PC's promotion of "market-based mechanisms" was unsuitable for managing access to the interstate rail network. Any commercial track provider wants to attract as much traffic as possible to its rail network, to spread its substantial fixed costs over the broadest base. It would not then want to use a line capacity allocation method that discouraged line use.

The PC's lack of understanding of the true nature of train schedules and line capacity, its assumption of the supremacy of prices, and its insistence on recommending a market approach in the face of rail industry opposition, has been noted in chapter 5. It was therefore arrogant of the PC to ignore the practical experience and wider awareness of the railway industry, which had evolved methods for sharing line capacity that recognised that a high degree of certainty in train pathing is a fundamental for train operators and their clients. Suffice to say that auctioning of train paths still does not take place in the Australian railway industry.

Endnotes

1. Source: Industry Commission (1991), p.119
2. The only jurisdictions where a government-owned railway has been closed due to lack of viability are Malta (1931), Sierra Leone (1974), Nicaragua (1993) and Paraguay (2006).
3. Source: Rapley (2017), p.297
4. Source: Industry Commission (1991), p.3
5. The Australasian Railway Association, in its 2010 *Submission to Infrastructure Australia's National Freight Network Plan* wrote on page 7: "Rail freight is up to 9 times safer than road freight. Rail freight is 10 times more fuel efficient and causes up to 10 times less emissions than road freight." Source: ARA (2010a)
6. Source: Laird (2004), p.3

Chapter 2

7. Some of these include:
John Gunn *'Along Parallel Lines: A history of the railways of New South Wales 1850-1986'* published 1989
Eric Harding *'Uniform Railway Gauge'* published 1958
Geoffrey B. Churchman & Tony Hurst *'The Railways of New Zealand: A journey through history'* pubd. 1990
Tim Fischer *'Transcontinental Train Odyssey: the Ghan, the Khyber, the globe'* published 2004
John Kain's research paper *'A Spirit of Progress? Assessing Australian Rail Transport Policy'* includes a good summary of the multiple gauges and standardisation initiatives; it can be downloaded from the Parliamentary Library website *https://www.aph.gov.au/binaries/library/pubs/rp/1994-95/95rp31.pdf*
8. Source: Productivity Commission (2006), p.41
9. Source: Bromby (2014) chapter 3
10. Source: Kain (1995), p.9
11. Wallangarra is north of Armidale and is not on the rail line that now crosses the border.
12. Kain (1995), p.9
13. Source: Laird et al (2001), p.187
14. Sir Harold Clapp was Commonwealth Director-General of Land Transport (1942-1951) and formerly Commissioner for Victorian Railways (1920-1939), and before that the Vice-President of the Southern Pacific Railroad in Columbus, Ohio.
15. Quoted by Laird et al (2001), p.189
16. Source: Victorian Government (1998), p.15

17 In Victoria, the fuel widely used for industrial and domestic purposes was briquettes made from brown coal. These were distributed across the state in highside wagons, in bagged or bulk form, and often unloaded manually.
18 In New Zealand, these industries included dairy factories, abattoirs, wool-scourers, and urban gasworks. In Australia, coal was also a major commodity, used for fuelling electric power stations.
19 Except in mechanical engineering
20 Even today, in New South Wales, the development priorities for RailCorp (Sydney's commuter rail system) change when the state government changes at elections. Furthermore, the electorate and the press hold the state government responsible for the performance of RailCorp. In 2011, a new Coalition state government was elected partly on the promise of "fixing the trains".
21 Source: Gunn (1989), p.490
22 Source: McQueen (2005), p.39
23 Some New Zealand examples include the Kaihu branch (inland from Dargaville) and the Moutuhora branch (inland from Gisborne), both closed in 1959, and the isolated Nelson to Glenhope line closed in 1954.
24 As described under the heading 'Advent of Trucking ...', an outcome of competition from road was that traffic **from** the rural branch lines declined faster than traffic **to** the rural areas.
25 There are extensions of the Victorian network across the border, to Deniliquin since 1923 and to Oaklands since 1938, because these locations in south-west NSW are much closer to Melbourne than any other port.
26 The official unemployment rate from the 1950s to 1980 was always under 2%. Source: *http://www.dol.govt.nz/publications/discussion-papers/current-recession/fig1-img.asp*
27 After the closure of the Cable Price Downer foundry in Thames (early 1980s?)
28 Source: WestRail 1977 Annual Report, quoted by Wills-Johnson (2006), p.2
29 Source: Reserve Bank of New Zealand *http://www.rbnz.govt.nz/statistics/key_graphs/inflation/*
30 Source: King (1996), p.3
31 What follows is my personal recollection; I had been asked at the time to investigate the yard congestion.
32 Source: *http://www.kiwirail.co.nz/about-us/history-of-kiwirail/150yearsofrail/stories/road-transport-regulation.html*

Endnotes

33 Transporting livestock by rail rather than road was known to improve the quality of the meat, and as New Zealand was exporting frozen meat to Europe to compete with locally grown fresh meat, maintaining a reputation for top quality was important.
34 Source: Toleman (1990), p.35
35 I led this program from 1986 to 1989.
36 Freight consignments in individual or small groups of wagons were the norm, thus most trains were multi-customer and multi-functional, conveying wagons for several destinations. Trains conveying one product for one customer were then few in number.
37 'Daylighting' means removing the top and sides of a tunnel, creating a cutting instead.
38 Although containers used by freight forwarders within New Zealand had a height of 8 feet, import/export containers of 8 foot 6 inches were becoming common.
39 The exception was between Victoria and South Australia, where both systems had broad-gauge lines.
40 Source: NSW State Transport (Co-ordination) Act 1931, section 18. Available on the internet at *http://www5.austlii.edu.au/au/legis/nsw/num_act/sta1931n32365.pdf*
41 BTE (1979), pp 9-10
42 Source: Lee (2003), chapter 10.
43 From a report written by Philip Shirley, Chief Commissioner of the NSW Public Transport Commission, quoted in Gunn (1989), p. 487.
44 BTCE (1993), p.7
45 Reported in Hawker (1989)
46 Industry Commission (1991), table 10.4, p.251
48 Industry Commission (1991), p.252
49 Source: Toleman (1990), p.26
50 There were no female freight train drivers in those days.
51 Source: ISCR (1999a), p.54
52 Source: Laird (1994), p.18
53 Source: Webb (2000)
54 Source: Laird (2001), p.515
55 Industry Commission (1991), table 6.1, p.120 © Commonwealth of Australia.
56 In 1989-90, Queensland Rail operated with a small surplus, and the Western Australian Government Railways recorded only a small deficit.
57 Source: Industry Commission (1991), p.119
58 Source: Industry Commission (1991), p.120
59 See *http://www.ara.net.au/history*
60 So described in Affleck (2002)

61	Bullock et al (1990), p.426
62	Source: Laird (1994), p.7
63	Source: Bullock et al (1990)

Chapter 3

64	The original reason for the break-up of British Rail was ostensibly to promote competition among train operators to reduce fares, but due to lack of line capacity on the principal routes, what resulted was a set of private regional monopolies. (Source: *Broken Rails* by Christian Wolmar, 2001)
65	Although some lines were built by private companies in the mid nineteenth century, typically they failed as businesses, and their assets and operations were taken over by colonial governments in the interests of economic development and network expansion.
66	The rail networks and operations in New Zealand and Tasmania have both reverted to government ownership after periods of ownership and operation by a succession of companies. They have also been re-formed as vertically integrated organisations.
67	Examples of railway customers owning their own rolling stock include In NSW: Centennial Coal, Fletcher International Exports, GrainCorp In WA: Mineral Resources, Cooperative Bulk Handling (CBH).
68	Source: *http://www.aurizon.com.au/sustainability* 24 Nov 2014
69	These former GWA lines are now owned/leased by Aurizon.
70	Source: these data have been derived from tables in BTRE (2006)
71	Source: Hearsch (2007) page 4
72	Source: Probert (2015b)
73	Source: extracted from Table 14, BITRE (2022) Trainline 9 Statistical Report, page 50. Licensed use under a Creative Commons Attribution 3.0, © **Commonwealth of Australia**
74	Reported in Carter (March 2014)
75	Reported in Saulwick (2014)
76	Source: Webb (2000)
77	BITRE (2010), chapter 6

Chapter 4

78	Source: Kain (1995), p.2
79	Source: Laird (1992), p.16
80	An opinion expressed in Bullock et al (1990), p.427
81	Source: Laird (1999), p.42 The electrification project had flow-on effects – NZ Rail (with the same narrow-gauge as Queensland) was able to purchase a number of surplus diesel-electric locos at a good price, and later some of these were on-sold to ATN to work in Tasmania.

82	In November 2015, the Commonwealth Government granted ARTC $15 million for extensions to five crossing loops on this line, to enable more trains to run at up to 1800 metres in length, thereby increasing line capacity.
83	Source: Laird (1999), p.28
84	Source: Laird (1999), p.30
85	Source: HRSCCTMR (1997), p.23
86	Australia's per capita greenhouse gas emissions due to transport are the fourth highest of any OECD country and the seventh highest in the world. Source: http://www.garnautreview.org.au/chp7.htm accessed 20 Oct 2015
87	Source: HRSCCTMR (1997), p.8
88	Source: Laird (1999), p.34
89	The Hume Highway connects Sydney and Melbourne.
90	Source: Mitchell (2010), p.10
91	Source: Laird (1994), p.9
92	The Pacific Highway is the busiest route between Sydney and Brisbane, but the section north of the Hunter Valley was not included in the 1974 definition of the National Highway system, due to the parallel New England Highway, west of the Great Divide, being seen as more suitable for upgrading.
93	Source: quoted in Webb (2000a), p.6
94	Source: Webb (2000a), p.7
95	Source: HRSCCTMR (1997), pp 15 – 18
96	HRSCCTMR (1998), paragraph 2.46
97	Quoted in Webb (2000a), p.7
98	Productivity Commission (1999), p.xxxiii
99	Anderson (2000), p.1
100	Quoted in HRSCCTA (2001) p.7, from a speech given by the Minister to the Ausrail Conference in 1999.
101	The ATC comprised the Transport Ministers from the Commonwealth and all the States and Territories. Its decisions were often subject to ratification by the Council of Australian Governments (COAG).
102	Source: from an article published in Australian Transport, quoted in Gunn (1989) p. 492
103	Industry Commission (1991) p.23
104	Quoted in Laird (1994), p.6
105	Source: SSCRRAT (1997) section 2.6, quoting the Brew Report recommendation 3(c)
106	Source: DOTARS (1998), p.7
107	Source: ANAO (1998), p.23
108	ASR later became part of Genesee and Wyoming Australia (GWA)
109	Source: ANAO (1998), p.23

Off the Rails

110 Source: DoTaRS Annual Report 2003-04, p.96
111 House of Representatives Standing Committee on Transport, Communications and Infrastructure (1989) report titled Rail: Five Systems – One Solution
112 Source: Painter (1998), p.133
113 Source: Barber (1994), p. 560
114 Source: Affleck (2002), p.7
115 Source: Painter (1998), p.134
116 Painter (1998), p.135
117 Source: Painter (1998), p.134
118 Following the transfer of AN's mainland interstate rail freight to NRC in 1993, the Commonwealth converted approximately $160 million of AN's debt (mostly for the Tarcoola to Alice Springs railway line) to equity. Source: Laird (1994), p.7
119 Source: Affleck (2002), p.1
120 Source: Affleck (2002), p.4
121 as revealed in the NRC Statement of Corporate Intent in July 1992
122 Source: Affleck (2002), p.6 – the estimate included both the direct loss of traffic and the reduction in average freight rates due to the competition.
123 Affleck (2002), p.6
124 Quoted in Commonwealth Competitive Neutrality Complaints Office (2000), p.2
125 Source RTBU website *http://www.rtbu-nat.asn.au/52.html* accessed 27 October 2015
126 Source: Barber (1994), p. 565

Chapter 5

127 Industry Commission (1991), p.1
128 Industry Commission (1991) p.xiv
129 Industry Commission (1991) p.16
130 Industry Commission (1991) p.xv
131 Industry Commission (1991), p.xvii
132 Industry Commission (1991) pp.91 & 93
133 Industry Commission (1991), p.94
134 Including in North America – see Appendix 4 for an explanation.
135 Source: Laird (1994) in the Executive Summary
136 By 2005 the Rail modal share of the Sydney-Melbourne sector was reported to be about 11%. Source: ARTC website, reported in Laird et al (2005), p.4
137 Keating (1992), p.15
138 Kain (1995), p.ii
139 Boothe & Petchey (1996), p.158

140	After the agreement to create the ARTC, the Commonwealth committed $250 million over four years to upgrade the interstate network. This was equivalent to 4% of its road funding over the same period. About half of these investment funds were to be spent on the Southern Sydney Freight-only Line. Source: Webb (2000a), p.5
141	BTCE (1995), p.1
142	BTCE (1995), p.63
143	BTCE (1995), p.xiv
144	Carter (2003) page 1, and ….
145	From the National Competition Policy Website *http://ncp.ncc.gov.au/pages/reform*
146	Source: Webb (2009), p.5, sourced in turn from the ATC Communiqué 10 September 1997
147	BTCE (1997), p.3
148	BTCE (1997), p.xii
149	Source: DoTaRS (1998), p.14
150	The National Party is the minor party in the (right-wing) Coalition federal government, representing rural and regional interests, whereas the major party is stronger in the cities and is funded by and beholden to the interests of big business.
151	Quoted in Laird et al (2001), p.91
152	Source: HRSCCTMR (1998), Executive Summary, under the heading – Investment and Ownership
153	Source: Owens (2004), p.285
154	Source: DoTaRS (1998), p.17
155	Source: Webb (2000a), pp20-26
156	Source: Productivity Commission (1999), p.4
157	Productivity Commission (1999), p.xxix
158	Productivity Commission (1999), p.xxxi
159	The quote from W.C.Fields came to my mind on reading this: "If you can't dazzle them with brilliance, baffle them with bullshit."

Chapter 6

160	Source: Anderson (2000), pp 1-6
161	Source: Anderson (2000), pp 2-3
162	Source: Anderson (2000), p.10
163	Source: Anderson (2000), p.27
164	Source: Anderson (2000), p.28
165	Source: Anderson (2000), p.21
166	Source: Productivity Commission (1999), p.260
167	Source: Anderson (2000), p.22
168	DoTaRS (1998), p.14
169	DoTaRS (1998), p.15

170	DoTaRS (2000). The section on Land Transport is now available only online and has no page numbers.
171	Source: Laird (2006a), p.4
172	Source: HRSCCTA (2001), p.1
173	Source: HRSCCTA (2001), p.8
174	Source: HRSCCTA (2001), p.10
175	Source: HRSCCTA (2001), p.10
176	Source: HRSCCTA (2001), p.12
177	Source: Webb (2009), p.16
178	DoTaRS (2004), p.2
179	Webb (2004), p.2
180	DoTaRS (2004), p.21
181	Source: Webb (2004), p.3
182	DoTaRS (2004), p.32
183	DoTaRS (2004), p.33
184	DoTaRS (2004), p.97
185	Reported in Keane (2009)
186	Source: Webb (2009), p.11
187	Source: Banks (2006), p.1
188	Source: from the Terms of Reference reproduced in Productivity Commission (2006), p.v
189	Source: HRSCCTMR (1997), p.23
190	Productivity Commission (2006), p.314
191	Productivity Commission (2006), p.315
192	Productivity Commission (2006), p.xxx
193	$10.4 billion was the annual average for the three years to F.Y 2004/05 for the total spending on roads Australia-wide – source: Productivity Commission (2006), p.xxx
194	Source: Productivity Commission (2006), p.116
195	Source: Productivity Commission (2006), p.117
196	Source: Productivity Commission (2006), sec 5.4 "Do road user charges achieve cost recovery?", pp 116-127
197	Productivity Commission (2006), finding 8.2, p.LIII
198	Source: Productivity Commission (2006), chapter 9
199	DoTaRS (2004), p.21
200	COAG (2007), p.16
201	Infrastructure Australia (2011), p.2

Chapter 7

202	COAG was replaced in 2020 by the National Cabinet – a grouping similar to COAG, but which meets monthly by electronic means.
203	Source: Moore & Starrs (1993), p.426
204	Source: NTC (2008)
205	John Hearsch Consulting Pty Ltd (2008), p.32
206	John Hearsch Consulting Pty Ltd (2008), p.15

207	NTC (2009), p.1 of the Summary
208	NTC (2009), p.3 of the Summary
209	Source: NTC (2009), pp. 21-26
210	Source: NTC (2009), pp. 26-29
211	NTC (2009), p.30
212	NTC (2010), p.4
213	Source: NTC (2010), pp 7-8
214	TISOC (2013), p.15, recommendation 13
215	Source: ATA (2015)
216	Source: TAIC (2015), p.3
217	TAIC (2015), p.5
218	TAIC (2015), p.6
219	TAIC (2016?)
220	NTC (2022), pp.2-5
221	NTC (2022), p.3
222	ARA, BIS Oxford Economics, and Hadron Group (2023)
223	ITMM (2022), p.1
224	Source: Burton (2023)
225	Source: Webb (2009), p.11
226	Infrastructure Australia (2011)
227	SCOTI (2012)
228	SCOTI (2012), p.1
229	Infrastructure Australia (2016)
230	Infrastructure Australia (2016), p.9
231	DIRD (2017)
232	TAIC (2019a)
233	Source: Transport and Infrastructure website, *https://www.transportinfrastructurecouncil.gov.au* Accessed on 14 January 2021
234	Source: the Transport and Infrastructure Council website, accessed 19 January 2021 at *https://www.transportinfrastructurecouncil.gov.au/council-members*. This website stated that it would cease on 31 January 2021.
235	TAIC (2019b), p.1
236	TAIC (2016?)
237	DIRDC (2018), p.5
238	DIRDC (2018), p.19
239	Source: DIRDC (2018), p.6
240	Sydney, Melbourne, Brisbane and Perth
241	Source: Australian Government (2020), pp 12-13

Chapter 8

242	Source: BTE (1979), p.15
243	Source: BTE (1979), p.16
244	Source: BTE (1979), p.18

245 Reported in The Canberra Times, 12 and 13 July 1988
246 Source: Dodd (2018)
247 Juturna Consulting (2012), p.5
248 Source: ARA (2010b) chapter 3
249 Source: ARA (2010b), p.31
250 Source: Laird (1990), p.43
251 Source: Laird (1987), p.140
252 Industry Commission (1991), p.96
253 Industry Commission (1992), pp.197-198
254 Productivity Commission (1999), p.249
255 Productivity Commission (2006), p.253
256 Australian Treasury (2011), p.29
257 Source: COAG Road Reform Plan (2011), undated newsletter, p.2
258 Source: Moore & Starrs (1993), p.426
259 Moore & Starrs (1993), p.432
260 Source: Moore & Starrs (1993), pp.437-438
261 Source: Productivity Commission (1999), p.D7
262 Source: CRRP (undated), page 3 of a 4-page pamphlet announcing the start of a feasibility study.
263 Source: ALC (2012), p.1
264 Source: Swier (2014), p.17
265 Productivity Commission (2006), finding 8.2, p.LIII
266 Source: SCOTI (2013), p.3
267 Source: Farrier Swier Consulting (2013), pp 3-6
268 Source: NCOA (2014b), pp.22-24
269 Source: Gardner (2014)
270 TAIC (2014), p.2
271 Juturna Consulting (2014)
272 For example, Juturna Consulting (2012)
273 Juturna Consulting (2014), excerpts are from the Executive Summary, p.4
274 Source: Gordon (2014)
275 Juturna Consulting (2014), p.23
276 TAIC (2016), pp.3&4
277 TAIC (2016), p.5
278 TAIC (2016), p.6
279 Infrastructure and Transport Ministers (2021)
280 Infrastructure Australia (2016), p.117

Chapter 9

281 Source: NZ Treasury website, *http://www.treasury.govt.nz/government/assets/saleshistory*, accessed on 13 March 2014
282 Source: Williams et al (2005), p.20
283 Source: Williams et al (2005), p.27
284 Source: Williams et al (2005), p.28

Endnotes

285 Source: Williams et al (2005), p.23
286 Source ARTC Annual Report 2005, p.13
287 Source: Victorian Auditor-General (2009), page 25. The audited estimate of final cost to the Victorian Government after the sale was $A214.5 million.
288 The term used in Gray et al (2015), p.4
289 FROG (2007), p.15
290 Transport for NSW (2012), p.5
291 Source: Pearce (2020f)
292 Quoted in DoTaRS (1998), p.10
293 Quoted in DoTaRS (1998), p.8
294 Source: DoTaRS (1998), p.14
295 Source: ARTC (1999c)
296 Source: ARTC Annual Report 1999, p.2
297 Improving the yield included increasing axle load specifications, enabling longer trains, reducing transit times (improving fuel efficiency and above rail costs), lifting train weight restrictions (Adelaide Hills from 3800 gross tonnes to 5000 tonnes) and the facilitation of driver only operations over large signalling segments of the network.
298 Source: ARTC annual reports
299 Source: Anderson (2000), p.3
300 Source: ARTC (2001)
301 Source: ARTC Annual Report 2013, p.7
302 Source: ARTC (2004a)
303 Source: ARTC (2004b)
304 Source: ARTC Annual Report 2005, p.17
305 Source: ARTC Annual Report 2005, p.4
306 ARTC Annual Report 2005, p.11
307 ARTC (2007), p.2
308 Sourced from ARTC (2007), pp.10,11
309 Source: ARTC Annual Report 2006, p.4
310 Source: ARTC Annual Report 2010, p.4
311 Source: ARTC Annual Report 2008, p.5
312 ARTC Annual Report 2009, p.1
313 The Silverton Tramway Company was established in 1886 to operate across the border between New South Wales and South Australia. After this link was standardised and taken over by AN in 1970, Silverton became a short-haul operator serving mining companies on their extensive sidings at Broken Hill.
314 Productivity Commission (1999), p.118
315 *Rail Freight System Bill gets second reading in the Legislative Assembly*, Media Statement, Government of Western Australia, Perth, 3 June 1999; quoted in EISC (2014), p.23

316 Source: West Australian railscene e-Mag, issue #176, 13th February 2012, page 1. Accessed 9/8/18 from *http://jimbisdee.com/wp-content/uploads/2013/08/West_Aust_Railscene_e-Mag_issue_number_176.pdf*
317 Source: Chambers (2017)
318 Source: Keating (1992), p.15
319 Wills-Johnson (1996), p.3
320 Source: Williams et al (2005), p.27
321 Source: Kopicki & Thompson (1995), p.117
322 Source: Prebble (1996) p.87
323 Quoted in KiwiRail (2017a)
324 Williams et al (2005), p.x
325 Victorian Government (1998?), p.2
326 Source: Williams et al (2005), p.23
327 Deputy Premier, Western Australia, Legislative Assembly, *Parliamentary Debates* (Hansard), 3 June 1999, p 8772; quoted in EISC (2014), p.42
328 Source: EISC (2014), p.42, information attributed to the Auditor-General
329 Source: Baines (2014), p.167
330 Source: Toleman (1990), p.22
331 Source: Productivity Commission (1999), p.53
332 Wills-Johnson (2006), p4
333 King (1996), p.6
334 Williams et al (2005), p.ix

Chapter 10

335 Baines (2014), p.51
336 Privatisation of railways in Britain, Japan and Chile did not occur till the mid-1990s. Freight railways in North America have always been privately owned.
337 Attributed to Richard Dawkins
338 Source: NZISCR (1999a), p.68
339 King (1996), p.4
340 Source: from a copy of the Hansard reproduced on the Member's website *https://robkatter.com.au/641-2/* accessed on 1 November 2019
341 Heatley (2009a), p.46
342 Heatley (2009a), p.49
343 Kain (1995), p.25
344 Toleman (1990), p.27
345 EISC (2014), p.i
346 Source: Victorian Government (1998?), p.18

347	Source: EISC (2014), p.41, quoting from the Deputy Premier, Western Australia, Legislative Assembly, Parliamentary Debates (Hansard), 3 June 1999, p 8771.
348	Source: an unidentified news report republished on the Railpage website on 21 April 2005, accessed 14 November 2019 from *http://www.railpage.com.au/news/s/sa-minister-looks-at-eyre-peninsula-rail-plan*
349	SMEC (2018) Eyre Peninsula Freight Study
350	Source: SMEC (2018), p.22
351	Source: SMEC (2018), p.9
352	Productivity Commission (1999), p.117
353	See in Chapter 4, *The Response from the Commonwealth Government*
354	Anderson (2000), p.3
355	ARTC (1999b), p.10
356	Sources: Williams et al (2005), Chapter 3
357	See in Chapter 4, *Creation and Funding of the National Highway System*
358	*KiwiRail's Evolution: Annual Integrated Report 2019*, p.20
359	See *https://teara.govt.nz/en/kaitiakitanga-guardianship-and-conservation/page-1*
360	Source: EISC (2014), p.147
361	Source: ARTC Annual Report 2013, p.8
362	Source: *https://www.transport.nsw.gov.au/projects/current-projects/maldon-to-dombarton-railway-line*
363	DolaT (2011)
364	Reported in Rail Express, 1 October 2014: *Maldon to Dombarton Rols Open Soon*
365	e.g. 97% of the costs of the CRN grain lines are paid by the NSW Government. Source: Transport for NSW (2012), p.11
366	Source: Victorian Auditor-General (2009), page 25. The audited estimate of final cost to the Victorian Government after the sale was $A214.5 million.
367	Source: ABC News, 12 Dec 2007
368	Sources: Pearce (2020d) and Sexton (2021)
369	Source: Probert (2016e)
370	Source: VRFNR (2007), p.20

Chapter 11

371	Source: part of Table 1.2, in Richard Paling Consulting (2008), p.4
372	King (1996), p.5
373	Source: Cullen (2003b)
374	Source: NZ Ministry of Transport website *https://www.transport.govt.nz/rail/recent-rail-history/* Accessed 9 January 2020

375 Someone in the business, but I cannot remember who. I thought it was an insightful remark.
376 King (1996), p.7
377 Strategic ignorance is described in The Intelligence Trap by David Robson (published by Hodder & Stoughton, 2019) as the short-term benefit of not questioning the longer-term consequences of one's decisions.
378 The concept of CEO Michael Beard, quoted in Ruth (2000), p.1
379 Source: Gaynor (2002)
380 Gaynor (2002)
381 Source: Beard (2002)
382 Source: Shoeshine (2002)
383 Source: Fox (2002)
384 Source: an unattributed news item published by Stuff, 10 July 2002, headed: *Tranz Rail says operating profit up to $26 million for 2002*
385 Source: Beard (2002)
386 Source: Gaynor (2004)
387 Source: King (1998), p.8
388 Source: Fox (2002)
389 Source: Wilson (2010), p.16
390 Source: an unattributed news item published by The Independent Weekly Business Tabloid, 7 June 1998, headed: *Tranz Rail, other newish issues and a wealth warning*
391 Source: NZPA (2009)
392 Source: Gaynor (2002)
393 Source: The New Zealand Maritime Record website, accessed 23 June 2019 from *http://www.nzmaritime.co.nz/aratere.htm*
394 Source: TranzRail media release, reported by Scoop. Accessed 10 October 2019 from *http://www.scoop.co.nz/stories/BU0310/S00002/tranz-rail-completes-aratere-buy-out.htm*
395 Source: NZPA (2004)
396 Source: Cullen (2001)
397 Victoria University of Wellington Professor Don Trow was quoted in Weir (2002).
398 Source: Laird (2013), p.4
399 Source: Toll NZ (2005), p.3
400 Source: Laird (2013), p.3
401 From an unattributed newspaper report "Tranz Rail posts 43.3 million profit" published by Stuff 7 February 2002. Accessed 18 Dec 2019 from *https://www.massey.ac.nz/~cprichar/303cm/transrailnews.html#woes*

Endnotes

402 A prototype well wagon was built and tested in 1996, with gull-wing doors operated by compressed air, but it was unreliable in use, and abandoned after a few months.
403 Source: Fox (2003a)
404 Source: Shoeshine (2003)
405 Source: NZ Treasury (2008a)
406 Williams, Greig & Wallis (2005), from the Preface, p.v
407 Williams, Greig & Wallis (2005), table 3.2, p.16, © 2005 The International Bank for Reconstruction and Development/The World Bank
408 Source: Macalister (2003)
409 Source: a working paper included in the *Crown Purchase of Toll New Zealand Rail and Ferry Business Information Release*. Issued by the NZ Treasury on 19 December 2008, it is an online archive of government working documents, not written for publication, covering the lead up to the government resuming control of the railway business. Copyright: Creative Commons Attribution 4.0 International.
410 Source: Victorian Government (1998?), p.2
411 Source: Williams et al (2005), p.26
412 Part of the quote from chapter 10, endnote 345
413 Hearsch (2007), p.9
414 Source: VRFNR (2007), p.25
415 Source: VRFNR (2007), p.25
416 Hearsch (2007), p.7
417 Source: VRFNR (2007), p.26
418 VRFNR (2007), p.27
419 Hearsch (2007), p.10
420 Source: Productivity Commission (2006), p.144
421 Source: Victorian Auditor-General (2009), page 21
422 Source: Victorian Auditor-General (2009), page 15
423 Source: Victorian Auditor-General (2009), page 25
424 VRFNR (2007), p.12
425 VRFNR (2007), p.5
426 VRFNR (2007), p.4
427 Source: VRFNR (2007), pp4 - 6
428 VRFNR (2007), p.31
429 Source: Victorian Department of Transport (2011), p.19
430 Source: Quoted from a PN spokesperson in Hopkins (2008)
431 Source: Harvey & Tsolakis (1991)
432 Source: Williams et al (2005), p.20
433 Source: Williams et al (2005), p.19
434 Source: Productivity Commission (1999), p.147

435 Source: EISC (2014), p.42, quoting from the Deputy Premier, Western Australia, Legislative Assembly, *Parliamentary Debates* (Hansard), 3 June 1999, p 8771
436 Source: Arc Infrastructure (2017), p.15
437 Source: Brookfield Rail (2014), p.1
438 Source: Arc Infrastructure (2017), p.13
439 Source: EISC (2014), p.147
440 WA Department of Transport (2014), p.2
441 WA Department of Transport (2013), p.9
442 WA Department of Transport (2013), p.11
443 Source: Garnett (2014)
444 Source: Thompson (2014)
445 WA Department of Transport (2020), p.1
446 WA Department of Transport (2020), p.3
447 Source: Pearce (2020b)
448 Source: Chan (2022b)
449 Source: CBH (2017), p.10
450 In 2016-17 CBH received a record 16.6 million tonnes. Source: The West Australian, 3 February 2017, accessed on 18 Jan 2018 at https://thewest.com.au/business/agriculture/wa-farmers-deliver-record-grain-harvest-ng-b88358122z

Chapter 12

451 Keating (1992), p.15
452 Source: Smith (2020)
453 Source: Trackside blog https://trackside.wordpress.com/qrnational/
454 Source: Chambers (2017)
455 Source: Carter (2017)
456 Source: Pacific National (2019)
457 In 2021, PN has reported a 15% increase in interstate intermodal business, from this low base, due to a shift from road to rail brought about by Covid-related State border crossing challenges. Source: Chan (2021a)
458 The curfews are described in Chapter 2, under *Infrastructure Constraints in New South Wales*.
459 Source: Aurizon (2015)
460 Source: Probert (2016c)
461 Source: *SRRATRC* (2021), p.29
462 Source: DITRDC (2021)
463 Source: Transport for NSW (2012), p.15
464 Source: ARTC (2019), p.12
465 Source: Fullerton (2019)
466 Source: ARTC (2020), p.9
467 Source: ARTC (2020), p.59

468	Source: Chan & May (2022a)
469	For example, the Logan City Council objected to noise from increased rail traffic on the ARTC's existing interstate line to Acacia Ridge intermodal terminal. Source: Skatssoon (2021)
470	Source: Chan et al (2022)
471	Source: Chan & May (2022b)
472	Source: AustralAsia Railway Corporation website, *http://www.aarail.com.au/railway/the-project/australasia-railway-corporation*, accessed on 6 December 2017
473	Source: a news item published on the Adelaide Now website, *http://www.adelaidenow.com.au/business/* on 9 June 2010, accessed on 13 December 2017.
474	GWA has since been bought by One Rail Australia, which in turn has been bought by Aurizon.
475	Source: Chan (2023)
476	Source: Aurizon (2023)
477	At the time of creation of Pacific National, there were two stevedoring companies at Port Botany; now there are three.
478	Source: Rosendorff (2009)
479	Source: Hopkins (2003)
480	Source: Hearsch (2007), p.9
481	Source: Victorian Department of Economic Development, Jobs Transport and Resources: *Grain Industry Profile, December 2014*
482	Source: Quoted from a PN spokesperson in Hopkins (2008)
483	Source: ABC News (2008)
484	Source: Johnson (2008)
485	Source: Victorian Department of Transport (2011), p.10
486	Source: Victorian Department of Transport (2011), p.19
487	Source: Victorian Department of Economic Development, Jobs Transport and Resources: *Grain Industry Profile, December 2014*
488	Source: VRFNR (2007), p.20
489	Source: Farm Weekly (2021)
490	Source: WA Department of Transport (undated)
491	Source: Productivity Commission (2006), p.148
492	Source: Perry (2009)
493	Source: ACCC (2018)
494	Source: Probert (2019b)
495	Source: Aurizon (2019)
496	Source: ACCC (2019)
497	Source: Stevens (2019)
498	Source: Carter (2018)
499	Source: O'Sullivan (2002)
500	Hudson (2011), p.8

Chapter 13

501 Productivity Commission (1999), p.37
502 The full extent of the NIMT is from Auckland to Wellington.
503 Productivity Commission (1999), p.126
504 See Appendix 4 for a discussion of the cultural differences between Australasian railways and North American railroads.
505 Productivity Commission (1999), pp.59-60
506 Source: NSW Coal Association submission to Industry Commission Rail Transport inquiry, sub31, p.4, quoted in Productivity Commission (1999), p.36
507 Productivity Commission (1999), p.xv
508 Productivity Commission (1999), p.33
509 The NCP was described in chapter 4, under *Commonwealth Influences on Rail Development in the 1990s*
510 Keating (1992), p.15
511 Hilmer (1993), p.16
512 Kain (1995), p.iv
513 Productivity Commission (1999), p.103
514 Maddock (1999), p.2
515 NCC (2001), p. 10.5
516 Productivity Commission (1999), p.104
517 I have experienced this in the operations management of a regional freight rail company in NSW.
518 Source: NCC (2001), p.10.2
519 Productivity Commission (1999), p.131
520 Productivity Commission (1999), p.232
521 ARTC (1999?), p.9
522 This information was sourced from Webb (2000b), p.3
523 DoTaRS (1999), p.7
524 Quoted in Productivity Commission (1999), p.235
525 Productivity Commission (1999), p.236
526 Productivity Commission (2006), p.206
527 Productivity Commission (2006), p.xxxvi
528 Source: Productivity Commission (2006), p.xxxvi
529 NTC (2006), 3rd page of the Executive Summary, (pages not numbered)
530 Source: NTC (2008)
531 Productivity Commission (2006), finding 8.2, p.LIII
532 NTC (2009), p.26
533 For example, see in chapter 4 under *Creation and funding of the National Highway System*
534 ARTC (1999?), p.9
535 The BTE also uses the term Benefit-Cost Analysis (BCA). It has the same meaning as CBA.
536 BTE (1999), p.2

537 DoTaRS (1999), p.8
538 BITRE (2014), p.2
539 Odgers & Low (2010), p.16
540 Martin (2017)
541 Source: ARA (2020)
542 A research group in the USA (On-Track North America) has now been able to quantify the benefit of using rail instead of road in terms of land requirements, which is relevant for cities everywhere: "Consider space, an increasingly critical resource. The same amount of goods moving on a one-mile [moving] train requires a 27-mile convoy of trucks." (Source: OTNA 2019, p.1) Thus a single line of freight railway equates to 27 times as much of two-lane highway, given that trucks have to share the highway with faster private vehicles travelling in the same direction.
543 This explanation in this paragraph is based on BTE (1999), p.3
544 BITRE (2014), p.9
545 Terrill & Batrouney (2018), p.3
546 Source: Ben Mason – an extract from the transcript of his speech to AusRail in November 2016, quoted with his permission.
547 Terrill & Batrouney (2018), p.9
548 Quoted in Productivity Commission (1999), p.132, from the FreightCorp submission of 27 October 1998.
549 FreightCorp (1999), p.5
550 ARTC (2007), p.2
551 Source: Transport for NSW (2016)
552 Source: NSW Government (2018), pp 3-4
553 Source: Pavey (2018b), Ministerial Media Release
554 Source: Pavey (2018a), Ministerial Media Release
555 ARTC (1999a), p.7
556 GHD Advisory (2022), p.30
557 Source: Railway Gazette 'Intelligence' 1 July 2000
558 NTC (2009), p.v
559 Silverton (1999)
560 Source: Carter (2018)
561 Source: Aurizon Annual Report 2012-13, p.6
562 Source: Bisdee (2015), p.1
563 Source: *https://www.locomotivesforafrica.com/* accessed 8 August 2018
564 BTCE (1993), p.7
565 Source: Thornthwaite (2016)
566 Source: Karp (2016)
567 Source: Yun (2023)

Chapter 14

568 There were a few exceptions where a foundry was established near a goldfield to supply cast iron machinery for mining and crushing rock.
569 Source: Sexton (2016)
570 Quoted in Productivity Commission (1999), p.119
571 Freightliner was a subsidiary of the UK Freightliner group, then Genesee & Wyoming Australia (GWA). Following the buyout of GWA, it has been absorbed by Aurizon.
572 These are the Regional Freight Transport Services and the Livestock Transport Services Contracts. Source: Probert (2016a)
573 Quoted by Productivity Commission (1999), p. 105, from 'Competition and Railroads' published in *Journal of Competition Law and Policy* vol. 1, no. 1, pp 149-228
574 Pittman (2005), p.185
575 Pittman (2005), p.186
576 Source: Quoted by BTRE (2003), p.19, from Railway Gazette International 2003, p.427
577 Quoted by BTRE (2003), p.140, from a British report on the incidence of rail defects.
578 Source: BTRE (2003), p.xxv
579 Source: Carey & Gray (2016)
580 Later publications of the ATSB reports showed the reasons for these derailments were the combination of rail creep and heat stress, together with inadequate management of the cumulative real creep. See ATSB (2017a) and (2017b).
581 Source: Rail Express 15 Nov 2017.
582 ARTC (2007), p.8
583 ARTC (2007), p.2

Chapter 15

584 Source: SSCRRAT (1997) section 2.6, quoting the Brew Report recommendation 3(c)
585 Source: EISC (2014), p.44, with quotes from clauses in the lease agreement
586 Source: EISC (2014), p.61
587 Source: EISC (2014), p.63
588 Source: Arc Infrastructure (2017), p.12
589 Arc Infrastructure (2017), p.14
590 Source: Queensland Rail website *https://www.queenslandrail.com.au/forbusiness/the-regional-network/mount-isa-line-system* Accessed 30 October 2019
591 Source: Rail Express news item, 25 January 2012, unnamed writer
592 Queensland Rail (2012), p.11

593	Source: from a copy of the Hansard reproduced on the Member's website *https://robkatter.com.au/641-2/* accessed on 1 November 2019
594	Source: Railway Gazette news item, 9 November 2014
595	Source: ATSB (2016), p.44
596	Source: Probert (2016b)
597	Source: Probert (2017d)
598	Source: Bailey (2018)
599	Queensland Rail (2019), p.32
600	Source: Probert (2019a)
601	Source: Bailey (2019)
602	Chan (2021b)
603	Source: ARTC (2008), p.17
604	Source: BITRE & ARA (2019), p.11
605	Transport for NSW (2012), p.5
606	Source: VRFNR (2007), p.29
607	Victorian Department of Transport (2020)
608	Shown in its Annual Reports.
609	World Bank (2011), p.100
610	OECD (2005), p.138
611	ARTC (2006), p.22
612	Productivity Commission (2006), p.152
613	Source: ARTC (2006), p.15
614	Source: Probert (2019d)
615	Source: TAIC (2017), p.3
616	There is a description of what 'line capacity' is, in chapter 13, under the heading *Railway Line Capacity is a Unique Offering*.
617	Source: Probert (2017c)
618	Source: Chan & May (2022a)
619	Source: Probert (2019c)
620	The National Commission of Audit was established in October 2013 and given a wide-ranging brief to review and report on the current performance, functions and roles of the Commonwealth government, and make recommendations for where those things should change in order to achieve a long-term sustainable government. It disbanded after submitting its reports in March 2014.
621	Source: NCOA (2014a)
622	Source: NCOA (2014b), p.185
623	Source: Cormann (2015)
624	Murden (2016)

625 The State-owned vertically-separated rail networks in Queensland, NSW and Victoria do not have this requirement placed on them, because of their long history of being provided as a public service.
626 Source: DoTaRS (1998), p.14
627 Source: National Commission of Audit, Phase 2 report, p.9
628 Ten years later, it is clear that there will be traffic growth on this line, from 2027 when the Inland Rail route is opened. Traffic from Brisbane to Adelaide and Perth will use this route instead of going via Melbourne.
629 Source: Probert (2017a)
630 The Whyalla steel mill is the last steel mill still operating in Australia and its owner, Arrium, was then financially troubled. The Commonwealth therefore had strategic interest in keeping it going. Not coincidentally, it also wanted to be seen supporting jobs in South Australia, a State with chronic unemployment. As is discussed in chapter 16, big rail projects can get funded by governments if job numbers can be announced.
631 Source: based on an estimate in Laird et al (2005), p.7
632 Source: Laird (2005), p.1
633 Source: Laird et al (2005), p.1
634 Strategic ignorance is described in *The Intelligence Trap* by David Robson (published by Hodder & Stoughton, 2019) as the short-term benefit of not questioning the longer-term consequences of one's decisions.
635 Source: see Appendix 1, end-note 84
636 Reported by Smellie (2015)
637 Source: Burr (2017)
638 Source: The Dominion Post (2016)
639 EY (2016) *The Value of Rail in New Zealand*
640 KiwiRail (2017b)
641 Source: Kirk (2017)
642 Robertson (2019)
643 RNZ News (2019)
644 Source: Rowe (2020)

Chapter 16

645 Source: Rowe (2021)
646 Source: I remember these numbers as inputs to network simulation modelling that I did in 1984, of options for infrastructure and rolling stock investments, with corresponding operating plans for the national rail freight network.
647 Source: KiwiRail Annual Integrated Report 2023, p.10

648 Source: Meldrum (2004)
649 In New Zealand, "interconnected trains" includes individual scheduled sailings of the rail-ferries that operate 24/7 between the North and South Islands. For freight movement planning purposes, a shipload of wagons is just like a train, with a maximum length, a known weight, and scheduled departure and arrival times. However, for the mariners, there are other considerations, such as planning the positioning of the wagons on the rail-deck for each sailing, to ensure a balanced load for the ship.
650 From January 2022, the UGL group replaced JHG as the contracted manager of the CRN.
651 The term used in Gray et al (2015), p.4
652 Between Maldon and Dombarton in the Illawarra area.
653 With the exception of shunting its interstate coil steel trains at sidings at Villawood.
654 Source: reported in Rail Express, 12 April 2017
655 BIS Oxford Economics (2018), p.1
656 BIS Oxford Economics (2018), p.2
657 BIS Oxford Economics (2018), p.3
658 Source: Pearce (2020a)
659 *Rail Freight System Bill gets second reading in the Legislative Assembly*, Media Statement, Government of Western Australia, Perth, 3 June 1999; quoted in EISC (2014), p.23
660 Source: WA Department of Transport (2020), p.3
661 Source: WA Government (2020)
662 This description of wicked problems comes from "The problem with wicked problems" by Matt Palmen, published 17 December 2015 in Linked In Pulse.
663 Source: Sexton (2016a)
664 A classic example of a misunderstanding arising from a partial view comes from the days before mechanised track maintenance; the train passenger who concluded that track workers were a lazy lot because every time her train passed a track gang, they were always seen standing on the side of the track resting on their shovels.
665 A recent example (in July 2018) is the Federal Coalition and Victorian Labor governments each promising $5 billion to build a rail line to Melbourne Airport, well before any cost-benefit study has been done.
666 Source: a news report in Rail Express quoting from a report released by the Grattan Institute – Probert (2016d)
667 Odgers & Low (2010), p.16

668 Pearce (2020e)
669 The influence of your worldview on your thinking applies in many fields, including the sciences and medicine. There is a more in-depth explanation of this reality in Raworth (2017), p.22
670 'Externalities' is the economists' name for the consequences of economic decisions that ripple through the economy and society, that are tangible yet often hard to measure.
671 Source: "Rail Business Intelligence" on the Think Railways website, accessed on 20 October 2016 http://www.think-railways.com/austria-invest-eur-15bn-rail-infrastructure-projects/
672 Nestor (2007)
673 Keane (2015)
674 Source: ARTC (2015), p.5
675 Source: ARTC (2015), p.12
676 Source: Transport for NSW website, accessed 5 February 2022 from https://roads-waterways.transport.nsw.gov.au/projects/newell-highway/improvement-program.html
677 *SRRATRC (2021), p.1*
678 Source: *SRRATRC (2021), p.vii*
679 Source: *SRRATRC (2021), p.27*
680 Source: ARTC (2020), p.3
681 For example, in ARTC (2020), pp 13 and 21-23
682 *SRRATRC (2021), p.38*
683 Source: Australian Government (2021), p.4
684 Source: Morton (2023)
685 Source: Evans (2023)

Chapter 17

686 Source: KiwiRail (2014), p.121
687 Michael J Sandel: *What Money Can't Buy: the Moral Limits of Markets*. Farrar, Straus & Giroux, New York, 2012
688 Source: Rutherford (2015)
689 These terms are from KiwiRail (2016?), p.9
690 Source: MoT (2021c), p.3
691 MoT (2022), p.18
692 Martin (2013), p.47
693 Source: Probert (2019d)
694 Smith (2020)
695 Source: ARTC Annual Report 2020, p.7
696 ARA (2021)
697 Productivity Commission (1999), p.249
698 Source: Chan (2022a)
699 NTC (2009), p.30
700 John Hearsch Consulting Pty Ltd (2008), p.15

701	TAIC (2016?)
702	Source: ARTC Annual Report 2020, p.4
703	The New Zealand, Victorian, Tasmanian and Western Australian Governments
704	The New Zealand, Victorian, Tasmanian and Western Australian Governments

Appendix 1

705	Source: King (1996), p.2
706	Source: NZISCR (1999a), p.64
707	Source: King (1996), p.2
708	Source: NZISCR (1999a), p.5
709	Reported by Clark (2010), p.2
710	Source: NZISCR (1999a), p.68
711	Source: NZISCR (1999a), p.61
712	Source: Archived Directory of Official Information. Accessed 8 December 2019 from *https://web.archive.org/web/20130223054227/http://justice.govt.nz/publications/global-publications/d/directory-of-official-information-archive/directory-of-official-information-december-1997/alphabetical-list-of-entries-1/r/railways-corporation-new-zealand*
713	Source: Jaspers (1993)
714	Source: Clark (2010), p.3
715	Source: Edwards (1993). The Minister of Finance at the time was Ruth Richardson.
716	In 2008, the NZ Government released an archive of confidential documents that revealed the development of its thinking in 2002 and 2003 on how to get ownership of the rail network.
717	Source: Gaynor (2004)
718	King (1996), p.5
719	Source: Gaynor (2002)
720	Gaynor (2002)
721	Source: Wilson (2010), p.16
722	Source: an unattributed news item published by The Independent Weekly Business Tabloid, 7 June 1998, headed: *Tranz Rail, other newish issues and a wealth warning*
723	Source: webpage of Securities Information (1996) 'Investment in Tranz Rail Holdings Limited.' Accessed 23 June 2019 from *http://www.secinfo.com/durh4.8d.htm*
724	Source: Gaynor (1996)
725	Source: Yoke Har Lee (2000)
726	Source: NZ Treasury website *http://www.treasury.govt.nz/government/assets/saleshistory* accessed on 13 March 2014
727	Source: NZISCR (1999a), p.70
728	Source: Booker (1996)

729 Source: Gaynor (2004)
730 Source: NZPA (2009)
731 Source: Productivity Commission (1999), p.147
732 Source: Gaynor (2004)
733 Source: Gaynor (2004)
734 Source: Gaynor (2002)
735 Source: Shoeshine (2002b)
736 Source: Wheeler (2002)
737 Source: Boeyen (2000)
738 Quoted in Ruth (2000), p.1
739 Source: Williams (2001)
740 Wheeler (2002)
741 Source: Lilley (2000)
742 Quoted in Bryant (2000)
743 Source: Bouyen (2001a)
744 Source: Bouyen (2001b)
745 Source: NZPA (2004)
746 Passenger services that kept running were between Auckland and Wellington, Picton and Christchurch, and Christchurch and Greymouth; also the commuter service between Palmerston North and Wellington. Services that ceased were between Auckland and Hamilton, Rotorua, and Tauranga; between Wellington and Napier; and between Christchurch, Dunedin and Invercargill.
747 Source: Bouyen (2001b)
748 Source: Bouyen (2001c)
749 Source: Laird (2013), p.4
750 Source: O'Brien (2001)
751 Source: Bouyen (2001a)
752 Source: Cullen (2001)
753 Source: a TVNZ report, 5 September 2002, accessed 9 January 2020 from *http://tvnz.co.nz/content/129519/4202557.xhtml*
754 Source: Love (2002)
755 From an unattributed newspaper report "Tranz Rail posts 43.3 million profit" published by Stuff, 7 February 2002. Accessed 18 Dec 2019 from *https://www.massey.ac.nz/~cprichar/303cm/transrailnews.html#woes*
756 Source: Shoeshine (2002a)
757 Source: Claridge (2002)
758 Source: van den Bergh (2002)
759 Source: Shoeshine (2002b)
760 Source: Stride (2002)
761 Source: Daniels (2002)
762 Source: Steeman (2002)

763 Source: O'Brien (2002)
764 Source: Shoeshine (2002b)
765 Source: Howie (2002)
766 Source: Fox (2003a)
767 Source: Fox (2003b)
768 Source: Shoeshine (2003)
769 Source: Kay (2003)
770 Source: Fox (2003c)
771 Source: Fox (2003d)
772 Source: Howie (2003)
773 Source: Fox (2003e)
774 Source: Rochfort (2003)
775 Source: Fox (2003f)
776 Source: du Fresne (2003)
777 Source: Cullen (2003a)
778 Source: Fox (2003g)
779 Source: Cullen (2003b)
780 Source: Fox (2003h)
781 Source: NZPA (2003a)
782 Source: Steeman (2003)
783 Source: NZPA (2003b)
784 Source: Heatley (2009a), p.16
785 The Fifth Labour Government was the government of New Zealand from December 1999 to November 2008. It replaced the right-wing government which had privatised New Zealand Rail Ltd in 1993.
786 The source of most of the information in this section comes from the *New Zealand Rail Transaction Information Release*. Issued by the NZ Treasury on 21 February 2008, it is an online archive of government working documents, not written for publication, covering the lead up to the government resuming control of the railway network. Copyright: Creative Commons Attribution 4.0 International.
787 This letter illustrates (unintentionally) the clash of expectations between government, as the former railway owner, and the company now in control. This issue is discussed in chapter 10, under *Unfulfilled hopes from privatisation – Hopes for continuation with improvements*.
788 Source: Swain (2002)
789 Source: Tranz Rail (2003)
790 Source: Richard Paling Consulting (2008), p.4

791 Source: Macalister (2003)
792 Source: from an unpublished report, *New Zealand Railways Corporation – Toll NZ Ltd: Determination of Track Access Charge*, dated 9 February 2007, written by Bill Wilson QC, who was an Independent Auditor. This, and many other documents relating to the NZ Government's reacquisition of the above-rail operations, are the source of most of the information in this section. It was included in the *Crown Purchase of Toll New Zealand Rail and Ferry Business Information Release*. Issued by the NZ Treasury on 19 December 2008, it is an online archive of government working documents, not written for publication, covering the lead-up to the government resuming control of the railway business. Copyright: Creative Commons Attribution 4.0 International.
793 Source: a working paper included in the *Crown Purchase of Toll New Zealand Rail and Ferry Business Information Release*, described above.
794 Source: Kitchen (2008)
795 Source: *KiwiRail Annual Report 2008-09*, p.13
796 Source: *KiwiRail Annual Report 2008-09*, p.5
797 Source: *KiwiRail Annual Report 2008-09*, p.43
798 Source: NZ Treasury (2008c), p.4
799 Source: NZ Treasury (2008c), p.8
800 Source: Dearnaley (2009)
801 Source: *KiwiRail Annual Report 2010-11*, p.13
802 Source: *KiwiRail Annual Report 2010-11*, p.11
803 KiwiRail (2012)
804 Source: *KiwiRail Annual Report 2013-14*, p.34
805 *KiwiRail Annual Report 2013-14*, p.9
806 KiwiRail (2014)
807 Source: KiwiRail (2016)
808 Because of the redactions in the published Review, no details were visible of what railway lines would be "trimmed", but it is a reasonable assumption that they would include the neglected North Auckland line, which had been listed for future mothballing in 2010 – see Dearnaley (2010).
809 Source: KiwiRail (2014), p.104
810 Sources: KiwiRail (2014), p.27 & 107
811 Source: KiwiRail (2014), p.115
812 For all scenarios, the Auckland and Wellington metro services were assumed to continue, but under this scenario they would have to bear the full costs of maintenance of their networks.
813 Source: KiwiRail (2014), p.121

814   Two million tonnes a year are railed through the Southern Alps via the 8-km Otira tunnel. The alternative road route goes over the Southern Alps. Coal mining on the West Coast is a major industry in an economically depressed area.
815   Source: KiwiRail (2014), p.4
816   NZ Treasury (2015), p.10
817   Reported by Smellie (2015)
818   Source: The New Zealand Herald (2015)
819   Rutherford (2015)
820   Source: RMTU (2016)
821   Source: de Graaf (2016)
822   EY (2016) *The Value of Rail in New Zealand*
823   Source: Kirk (2017)
824   Source: EY (2016), p.4
825   Source: Hendery (2015)
826   Source: *KiwiRail Annual Integrated Report 2018*, p.28
827   Source: *KiwiRail's Evolution: Annual Integrated Report 2019*, p.2
828   Source: Dinsdale (2020)
829   MoT (2019b), p.1
830   MoT (2019a), p.7
831   MoT (2021a), p.19
832   MoT (2021a), p.20
833   Source: KiwiRail (2021b), p.21
834   Source: MoT (2021c), p.2
835   MoT (2021c), p.3
836   MoT (2021c), p.4

Appendix 2

837   The full extent of the NIMT is from Auckland to Wellington.
838   For example, wool, livestock, coal for domestic use, bulk fertiliser and lime for farmers.
839   Actually, there was adequate coal in the ground, just a shortage of coal-miners.
840   In those days, the national 'balance of payments' was a serious matter for the New Zealand government. Nowadays governments appear not to be too concerned if the balance of payments is negative.
841   All railways work to an operating plan, but sometimes it is more implicit than explicit, as would have been the case with NZR at this time.
842   Competitive train transit times came to mean overnight service between main cities within each island.

843 Diesel engines are intended to operate continuously at a constant temperature, but these locos' engines were subjected to twice daily heating and cooling, which created a new set of maintenance issues.

844 Reported in *Railway Gazette* 21 December 2016.

845 Source: KiwiRail (2018)

Appendix 4

846 Hoang et al (2012)

847 The English language used for Australasian railways and North American railroads differs for historical reasons. In writing about these two cultures, I have used the terms appropriate to each. Terms are defined in the glossary.

848 Line capacity is a function of many factors. Fixed factors include the number of tracks and/or passing loops, the type of signalling system in use, maximum train speeds calculated to take account of the degree of curvature and loading gauge tolerance limits. Variable factors include the mix of train types running at any given time period and whether their average speeds are compatible or different.

849 Carl Van Dyke and Kevin Foy (2006)

850 I managed the introduction of computerised train timetable planning in New Zealand in 1986, using software originally created for the WestRail network.

851 Source: Railway Gazette International, 6 September 2016

852 Source: Tully (2018)

853 With the exception of Tasmania, where there is only one vertically integrated railway in the state.

854 Source: Comment by Phillip Fine in a LinkedIn online discussion group in 2015.

855 Empty wagons can be hired to augment a train operator's fleet, and subsequently dehired. Typically, the hireage is for weeks or months, thus their control changes at these times.

856 There were some instances of private railway building and operation, but typically when railway companies failed financially, colonial governments assumed ownership and responsibility for their assets and operations.

857 Drew and Ludewig (2011)

858 A detailed account of the merger of two large railroads, and the clash of company cultures, is given in "No Way to Run a Railroad: the Untold Story of the Penn Central Crisis" by Stephen Salsbury, published in 1981.

859 In NSW, formally closing a railway line requires an act of parliament, which has rarely happened, so there remain some 3000 kilometres of "unused lines", technically still open, but not used and probably not usable.

Appendix 5

860 Productivity Commission (1999), p.186
861 This discussion is drawn from Productivity Commission (1999), pp.177-185
862 It is true that there is grandfathering of existing paths, and this is not ideal. The solution lies in looking at a bigger picture. There is also inefficient allocation of train schedules from the point of view of maximising the use of line capacity. However, this is a concern only if the track provider will not invest to increase line capacity when the need is foreseen, because it is required to be profitable, and is thus risk-averse. The solution lies in funding railway lines as though they were highways, with an element of "build it and they will come". This concept is developed in chapter 15.
863 Productivity Commission (1999), p.177
864 Productivity Commission (1999), p.180
865 Cormann (2015)
866 Source: Carter (2016)
867 The Hunter Valley coal chain is not an example because its railtracks are shared with intrastate and interstate general freight trains, together with regional and local passenger trains, which all have different schedule characteristics.
868 See in Appendix 4 for why North American railroads are the exception in this respect.
869 Source: Abril et al (2008), pp.4-5
870 Source: Wardrop (2009), p.140
871 Quoted in Productivity Commission (1999), p.182
872 National Rail Corporation Ltd (1999), p.14
873 Quoted in Productivity Commission (1999), p.181
874 Quoted in Productivity Commission (1999), p.183
875 Productivity Commission (1999), p.183
876 Productivity Commission (1999), p.185

Acknowledgements

I have been fortunate to have lived in a time when researching and writing a book such as this has been possible to do entirely at home, due to the availability of the internet and the vast number of publications and other documents it contains. I am therefore thankful to the hundreds of writers, politicians and other commentators whose work I have used as sources of information and points of view, and whose words I have often quoted to help tell the story. They are listed in the References section at the end of the book.

I am also thankful to the late Sir Michael Cullen (the NZ Minister of Finance, 1999-2008) for his decisions to make available online the collections of confidential government documents relating to firstly, the NZ Government's nationalisation of the railway network (2002-2003) and secondly, the Government's acquisition of the Toll NZ above-rail business (2006-2008). These documents provided information and perspectives not otherwise available to me, nor to journalists and other commentators writing at the time of these events. It follows from the above that all my sources and quotations are in the public domain. I have also added my own interpretations and recollections, for which I alone am responsible.

I am grateful to the late Euan McQueen, who as a mentor to me in the 1970s gave me his insight that a railway network, once built, becomes a unique national asset worth preserving for future generations. That was the foundation from which I observed the events of the last forty years as a railway manager and business analyst, and that led me to research and write this book.

I also thank
- Ben Mason for permission to quote at length from his speech to the AusRail conference in 2016, on the

effects of using different BCA discount rates;
- Merv Harvey for his advice on the reasons for track buckling;
- my beta-readers Warren Bell, Philip Laird and Robert Vale for their thoughtful feedback on my drafts.

No artificial intelligence (AI) has been used in writing this book.

Last but not least, I want to thank my wife Linda for her forbearance while I researched and wrote, and also for her frequent help when I was refining my text to find exactly the right words for each situation.

Spencer Naith
October 2023

Image Credits

Best endeavours have been made to find the sources of photos and other images.

Cover photo	reproduced with permission of the licensor through PLSclear. © Road Transport Media Ltd, Britain. Photographer not identified.
P 51	Photo by John Masson. Source: website "Johnnyspages.com", accessed 19 August 2016, now unavailable
P 53	Photographer not known; usage licensed under Creative Commons 3.0
Pps 60–63	Source: BITRE (2010) Interstate Freight in Australia, report 120, chapter 6
P 129	Photo used with permission from Qube Holdings
P 140	Photo by Scott Davis; usage licensed under Creative Commons 3.0
P 176	"Pathway Ahead" Source: from the website of the federal Department of Infrastructure, Transport, Regional Development, Communications and the Arts; available up till early 2024
Pps 196, 197	Source: ARTC (2007), North-South Corridor Strategic Investment Outline, pp.10 & 11. Reproduced with permission of the ARTC
P 241	Source: *www.nzrailwaysrollingstocklists.weebly.com/nz*
P 318	Source: Terrill M & Batrouney H (2018), p.9. Usage licensed under Creative Commons Attribution-NonCommercial-ShareAlike 3.0 Unported License
P 340	Source: Finn R (2020); photographer not found
P 344	Reproduced with the permission of Australian Transport Safety Bureau. From ATSB report, Rail Occurrence Investigation, RO-2015-022
P 357	Reproduced with the permission of Queensland Police © **State of Queensland (Queensland Police Service) 2016 is licenced under CC BY 3.0**
P 358	Reproduced with the permission of Queensland Rail
P 384	Photographer not found
P 388,	Source: Transport for NSW	Review of NSW Rail Access Regime-Issues Paper, p.24
P 404	Source: 'Makatote Viaduct's massive $13m refurbishment' Contractor magazine, p.34, 13 March 2017. Photo by TBS Group.
P 469	Graph reproduced with the permission of its creator.

Glossary

Term	Explanation
above-rail	A generic term including all of the railway activities that have to do with operating and maintaining trains and rolling-stock, plus all aspects of dealing with freight shippers. Cf 'below-rail'.
ACCC	Australian Competition and Consumer Commission, an independent Commonwealth statutory authority that promotes competition and fair trading.
accreditation	The regulated process of ensuring that a rail transport operator has the competence and capacity to manage safety risks associated with railway and train operations.
AN, ANR	Australian National Railway Commission, 1975 to 1998, owned by the Australian federal government
ARA	Australasian Railway Association, the peak body for the industry.
Arc Infrastructure	The company in WA that manages the rail network; it was previously known as Brookfield Rail
ARG	Australian Railroad Group, operated in WA, SA, NSW; bought by QR National in 2006
ARRDO	The Australian Railway Research and Development Organisation, 1978 to 1985
ASR	Australian Southern Railroad, operated in SA, partly owned by Genesee & Wyoming
ATC	Australian Transport Council, 1993 to 2011, a COAG body to coordinate transport matters, comprising the Transport Ministers of the Commonwealth, States, Territories and New Zealand. Succeeded by SCOTI.
ATN	Australian Transport Network, jointly owned by TranzRail (67%) and Wisconsin Central Railroad (33%); ATN owned TasRail from Nov 1997 to Feb 2004
Australasia	Used in this context as the region comprising Australia & New Zealand.
AustralAsia Railway Corporation	Created in 1995 by the South Australian and Northern Territory Governments to oversee the building and lease of a new railway from Alice Springs to Darwin (NT).

AWR	Australian Western Railroad Pty Ltd, a joint venture between Genesee & Wyoming and Wesfarmers, created to buy WestRail in 2000; became part of ARG in 2002
axle load, axle loading	The gross weight in tonnes on any one axle of a rail vehicle; 'maximum axle-load' is a measure of track strength
B-double	A truck and trailer combination, consisting of a prime mover and two semi-trailers, up to 26 metres long, totalling nine axles, used for line-hauling 3 TEU of containerised freight in all Australian states. Known as a B-train in New Zealand.
ballast	Crushed hard rock of irregular shapes and approximately uniform size, laid along the railway track so that its weight holds the sleepers and rails firmly in place, while its porous nature enables rainwater to drain away quickly from the rail track.
banker loco, banking	The practice of helping a train climb a bank or grade, by providing extra locos on the front or the rear, just in the section where required. A banking loco usually needs its own crew. Fragmentation of train operations, and more focus on labour efficiency in place of locomotive efficiency, has reduced the perceived benefits of banking trains since privatisation, so it is rarely done now.
below-rail	A generic term including all of the railway activities that have to do with management and maintenance of track, bridges, tunnels, signalling, lighting, and overhead wiring.
BOOT	Build Own Operate and Transfer, a type of contract for asset development, in which ownership is transferred to the sponsoring government after a stated period.
break-of-gauge	A location where two rail networks of different gauges meet, needing the transfer of passengers, transhipment of freight, or wagon bogie exchange for continued journeys.
Brookfield Rail	The North American company that bought the lease to the WA rail network in 2010, which in Western Australia now goes by the name Arc Infrastructure
bgtk	Billion gross tonne-kilometres – a measure of annual railway operating activity

Glossary

bulk granular products	Examples: coal, mineral ores, shingle for use in concrete, grains (wheat, barley, oats, etc.). The common feature for railways is that these materials can be loaded into, and discharged from, rail wagons with the aid of gravity.
cabotage	The transport of goods between two places in the same country by a transport operator from another country; in Australia & NZ it refers to shipping companies.
car, railcar	In North American usage, a railway vehicle for carrying freight.
car, railcar	In Australasia and the UK, a railway vehicle for carrying passengers.
CBH	Cooperative Bulk Handling, WA's major grain storage and marketing organisation.
COAG	Council of Australian Governments (1992 to 2020): a bi-annual forum attended by the Commonwealth Prime Minister and Premiers of the State and Territory governments; replaced by the National Cabinet.
commercial railway	A term used in this book to include all aspects of the rail industry where the use of railway assets (track and/or rolling-stock) is the means by which a railway organisation trades in the freight market; hence, mining and other special purpose railways, that are operated solely as a part of a larger one-company logistics chain, are not commercial, and not included in this book.
common carrier	A freight-moving organisation which is obliged by law to accept all consignments offered; typically, government railways had common carrier obligations.
Commonwealth	The federal government of Australia, including its government departments. Also known as the Australian Government.
Commonwealth Railways	The first federally-owned railway organisation, created in 1917 to operate the Trans-Australia Railway; absorbed into Australian National Railway in 1975
contestable freight	Freight consignments that can be managed equally well and economically by both road and rail freight companies; anything that can be palletised and/or loaded into a wagon or container.
CQCN	Central Queensland Coal Network, now operated by Aurizon

CRN	The NSW Country Rail Network – lines not managed by RailCorp or the ARTC.
crossing loop	The NZ term for a passing loop on a single-track railway; the name is based on locations on the train controllers' train graph where drawn train paths may cross each other.
derailment	Any event which results in any wheels of rolling-stock coming off the rails.
drawgear	The equipment located at each end of a piece of rolling-stock that simultaneously couples it to the next piece while it acts as a buffer to keep the rolling-stock separated. The drawgear takes the weight of the whole train that trails behind. It incorporates a buffer box which absorbs the shock forces that are inherent in the movement of a train. For safety, drawgear must be the weakest part of any train.
dual gauge	A railway track formed to permit trains of two different gauges to run on the same route: in Western Australia and Queensland it combines narrow and standard gauges; in Victoria it combines broad and standard gauges.
Ebit, (or ebitda)	Terms in financial accounting to describe profit: Earnings Before Interest, and Tax, (or ebit plus Depreciation and Amortisation)
externalities	The consequences, usually negative, of economic activity which are experienced by unrelated third parties. The costs of externalities are usually not included in pricing, thus distorting market decisions. When freight shippers select road transport over rail, the externalities include additional accident costs, greater air pollution and GHGs. These are all hidden, but they are the aggregate costs borne by society and governments.
first-mover advantage	The advantage gained in a market situation by the initial significant occupant of a segment of the market, especially where what is on offer is finite, such as line capacity.
flange	The straight projection around the inner edge of rail vehicle wheels, which function to keep the vehicle on the rails during motion.

Glossary

FreightCorp	The rail freight organisation owned by NSW government, created in July 1996 by vertical separation of the State Rail Authority of NSW. FreightCorp was privatised by sale in February 2002 with National Rail Corporation to form Pacific National
Freightliner	British-based rail operator with a subsidiary operating in NSW. The international Freightliner Group was bought by Genesee & Wyoming in 2015.
FreightLink	The rail operator created to operate the AustralAsia Railway from Tarcoola to Darwin, after the opening of the Alice Springs to Darwin line in 2004. Saddled with repaying the construction costs, it went into receivership in 2010, and was bought by GWA.
frog	Part of the structure of a turnout or diamond crossing where the left and right rails intersect. Designs vary, but they all guide the wheels of passing trains over or through this intersection safely.
furphy	An Australian word for something improbable but claimed to be absolutely factual.
gauge, track gauge	The distance between the rail centres of a railtrack. Rail networks in Australasia are mostly one of three gauges, known as narrow, standard and broad.
GHGs	Greenhouse gases, produced by animal farming, energy production, cars, and transport operators in the sea, rail, road, and air sectors (in order of increasing impact).
GTKs, gtkm	Gross tonne-kilometres, a measure of total haulage work done, combining the net weight of freight and the tare weights of rolling-stock moved.
GWA	Genesee & Wyoming Australia, rail operator from 1997 to 2020; sold to a consortium trading as One Rail Australia.
horizontal separation	Applies to railways separated by product (freight and passenger services) and/or by geographic scope of services (interstate, regional and urban).
Interail	A small standard-gauge company bought and rebranded by QR in 2002, to enable QR to participate in due course in both the interstate intermodal and the Hunter Valley coal markets. It ceased to exist in 2011, being absorbed into QR National.

interface agreement	An agreement between two legally defined rail operators, which should include all safety and operational matters relating to their interactions; it is required by law as a consequence of the fragmentation of the rail industry.
intermodal freight	Containerised freight, which can be easily transferred between road, rail &/or ship; it may include refrigerated foods, manufactured goods, bulk granular (e.g. grains or mineral ores), or bulk liquids and compressed gases.
IPO	Initial Public Offering – a means of sale of a business entity, or a fund-raising exercise, where shares are sold to the public and the company becomes listed on a stock exchange. The seller retains a share of the equity usually for later sale, and with the hope of a better share price.
kaitiakitanga	A Maori word used in NZ English, its meaning being similar to guardianship, but it is broader than a legal obligation; it incorporates protection and preservation, thus requiring a proactive approach. KiwiRail used this word in its 2019 annual report to acknowledge its responsibility for the network; a significant change from its previous 'managed decline' strategy.
level crossing	Where a roadway crosses a railway line (without bridging) within the rail corridor.
line, railway line	Normally used to identify a railway track across a landscape and on maps, where the sense is that it provides a route to connect places using trains.
line capacity	A concept of the finite carrying capacity of a railway line, determined by a complex mix of infrastructural and operational elements, which make it difficult to quantify. Theoretical line capacity is always greater than practical line capacity, the difference being the amount needed to manage exigencies and thus avoid disabling congestion.
livery	The organisational colour scheme usually applied to locomotives and carriages.
loading gauge, or outline gauge	The defined extent of clearance above and on each side of a railway track, sufficient to allow trains swaying normally in motion to pass without touching any structure.

Glossary

loco, locomotive	A rail vehicle with an engine, that part of a freight train which pulls (or pushes) the remainder of the train. Locos are often operated together, 'in multiple', to increase the tractive effort, enabling larger (heavier &/or longer) trains to be operated.
LWL/LCL	Less than Wagon Load, or Less than Container Load, re consignment size.
market distortion	Any interference in a market, usually government-sourced, that significantly affects prices and/or the allocation of assets.
market failure	"Market failure occurs where the operation of market forces does not produce satisfactory outcomes for the community." Ross Gittins (2015)
market reasoning	A term introduced by philosopher Michael Sandel; if all transactions are viewed as though they were happening in a market, other considerations get ignored. Market reasoning thus crowds out moral and environmental reasoning.
Major Periodic Maintenance (MPM)	Track renewal projects such as rerailing, resleepering and ballast cleaning, that require line closure for days at a time, are planned years ahead, and are done at 25 to 40-year intervals for any given section of track. MPM has often been deferred or reduced on rail networks under private sector management in order to increase annual profits.
managed decline	The term used by KiwiRail for the strategy it had to adopt when owned by an indifferent government; operating with minimal funding so that assets were not renewed when due, and service performance and reliability gradually declined, leading to customers' withdrawal of their freight from rail.
MNL	New Zealand's Main North Line, from Christchurch to Picton, in the South Island.
mtpa	Million tonnes per annum, a pragmatic measure of practical line capacity.
National Rail Corporation (NRC)	Established in 1992, owned by Commonwealth, New South Wales and Victorian governments; privatised by sale in February 2002 with FreightCorp to form the train operator Pacific National (PN).

neoliberalism	Describes the 20th century resurgence of 19th century ideas associated with free-market capitalism. It includes governmental policies of privatisation of government assets and services, and reductions in government spending in order to reduce taxes and to increase the role of the private sector in the economy.
network, railway network	A complex system of railway lines, with one primary track gauge and with something in common e.g. state/region &/or ownership &/or management.
NIMT	New Zealand's North Island Main Trunk line, Auckland to Wellington.
NRAA	National Rail Access Agreement (between NZ Government and Toll NZ)
NRTC	the (Australian) National Road Transport Commission
NTC	the (Australian) National Transport Commission
NTKs, ntkm	Net tonne-kilometres, a measure of a railway's annual freight traffic task. Cf GTKs
NZR	New Zealand Railways, a former government department, then a government corporation
NZTA	New Zealand Transport Agency, the regulator for all transport modes in NZ
off the rails	"If someone has gone off the rails, they have lost track of reality." From the Urban Dictionary http://www.urbandictionary.com "In an *abnormal* manner, especially in a manner that causes *damage* or *malfunctioning*" from Wiktionary http://en.wiktionary.org/wiki
One Rail Australia (ORA)	Previously GWA, an independent rail company owned by a consortium, started in Feb 2020. It owned/leased and operated on the Adelaide to Darwin line, and operated trains in the Hunter Valley and CQCN. Sold to Aurizon Oct 2021.
open access	Where a government, as transport policy-maker, mandates Open Access for a vertically-integrated railway, the incumbent operator's obligation to other operators is to grant access to railway lines, for agreed times, with agreed conditions and with payment of agreed fees. The incumbent, as track provider, has to manage the running of all trains to ensure that they run as agreed and without interference from one another.

Glossary

passing loop	A track parallel to the main line, connected to it at both ends, built to enable a train to be standing aside while another train passes or overtakes the standing train.
path, train path, train schedule	An entitlement granted to a train operator by a track provider to access its network by reference to the day of the week and to the departure, transit and arrival times between the entry and exit points on its network.
permanent way	An old term for a railway track, so called because it appears not to degrade in use as does a roadway. The term 'perway' remains in use to mean machinery, staff, activities and sidings dedicated to track maintenance.
PIRR	Progress in Rail Reform, an inquiry with a report published in 1999 in Australia.
points	A track structure: With reference to a train's direction of travel – 'facing points' make one track become two tracks, 'trailing points' join two tracks into one.
PN	Pacific National, the most extensive Australian train operating company.
private siding	A length of track connected to a commercial rail network, but which is owned and maintained by a non-rail business, to enable rail wagons to be positioned within or next to industrial buildings or other structures for freight loading or unloading.
privatisation	The act of transferring ownership of a government organisation to a private sector company or consortium.
Queensland Rail, QR	The State government railway. Before 2010 it was fully vertically-integrated. After the creation of QR National as a freight operator, and the separation of the Central Queensland Coal Network, QR became the provider of the remaining network, and the operator of suburban and long-distance passenger trains.
Qube	An integrated logistics company, focused on containerised exports & imports, that includes port, trucking and train operations in Australia. Its train operations stem from acquisitions of P&O Trans Australia (POTA) and Independent Transport Group (ITG).
rails	The lengths of rolled steel which initially support the weight of a train; their smooth upper surfaces are where contact with rolling-stock wheels occurs.

rail corridor	The strip of land (defined on cadastral maps) that accommodates the railway track(s) and ancillary structures such as poles, signals, stations and yards.
rail industry	A category of land transport, defined by the rail transport mode; it includes all aspects of production, operations and maintenance of railway services and assets.
railable	In the context of this book, it describes freight that, by virtue of its physical characteristics and proximity to rail networks, has the possibility of being transported by rail.
railroad	A North American word, with the same meaning as 'railway'.
Railway Express	An Australian rail industry news website, found at https://www.railexpress.com.au/
Rail Reform	A generic term used in Australia for all aspects of government-initiated change in the ownership and regulation of the freight rail industry.
railway line	Normally used to identify a railway track across a landscape and on maps, where the sense is that it provides a route to connect places using trains.
railway track, railtrack, track	The structure that combines all the materials that trains operate on: steel rails, supported by and fixed to sleepers with special fastenings, which are surrounded by ballast for stability, laid along a prepared base within the rail corridor.
resleepering	A type of MPM or cyclic asset renewal program, of wholly or partially replacing degraded wooden sleepers to restore track strength, so that temporary line-speed restrictions can be lifted, enabling trains to operate at normal line speeds.
rights issue	An issue of shares offered at a special price by a company to its existing shareholders in proportion to their holding of older shares.
Road Reform	A generic term used in Australia for any aspects of change in the regulation of the road freight industry in safety, vehicle registration and licensing, and road user charges.
RoI	Return on Investment, one measure of a project's financial viability
rolling-stock	A generic term spanning all mobile railway assets: locomotives, wagons and carriages

Glossary

rort (verb)	"to engage in sharp practice; to work to obtain the greatest benefit whilst remaining within the letter of the law" from the Australian Concise Oxford Dictionary, 4th ed.
ruling grade	The steepest section of track between two significant locations on a railway line, that determines (a) the loco power required to get a train of a known gross trailing weight up that grade, and (b) the maximum gross trailing weight of any train, given the design strength of the drawgear on its rolling-stock.
SCOTI	The (COAG) Standing Committee on Transport Infrastructure, 2011 to 2013
siding	A section of railway track, either parallel to a main line or in a railway yard, usually used for temporary parking of a train or a rake of wagons or perway machinery.
single track	A railway route with only one track, which requires that trains can travel in only one direction at a time between passing loops. The majority of railway routes in Australia and New Zealand used by freight trains are single track.
sleepers	The beams (made of wood, concrete or steel) used to support the rails in railway track; the term is used in NZ and Australia, but not in North America (see ties).
SRA NSW	State Rail Authority of NSW, which existed from July 1980 until December 2003.
TAC	Track Access Charge, the main issue of dispute in the NRAA in New Zealand
TAIC	In Australia: the Transport and Infrastructure Council, which reports to COAG.
TAIC	In New Zealand: the Transport Accident Investigation Commission.
tanker, tank wagon	A specialised wagon for carrying bulk liquids such as petroleum products, LPG, milk or water.
ties	A term used in Western Australian and American English, with the same meaning as 'sleepers'.
Toll Rail	NZ's above-rail business with Toll Holdings as majority owner; shares were bought from TranzRail, it was delisted & existed 2003–2008 until sold to the NZ Government.
track	See 'railway track' above

track alignment	Refers really to the alignment of the rail corridor and/or the prepared way for the track to be laid on: good alignment is level and straight, poor alignment is steep and/or curvy.
track possession	A planned downtime when commercial trains are banned from a stretch of track while maintenance or reconstruction is done; hence, the track is possessed by the engineers for a specified duration and location.
track renewal	See Major Periodic Maintenance
trackage rights	A North American term meaning an agreement between railroad companies granting one railroad company limited use of another railroad company's network. This is a more restricted concept than open access.
trade sale	Sale of a business entity that involves giving full control of it to the buyer. (The seller has an alternative but more costly means of disposal – an IPO.)
train	The physical combination of loco(s) and wagon(s) or carriages that are operated as one unit on a railway line. A train is also an entity in timetabling with a unique identity – the planned and actual movement of any combination of rolling-stock between locations A and B.
train control	The office and function of directing all rail operations on the railtrack in real time, including train movements and maintenance activities within the rail corridor; the purposes of train control are to ensure safety, while managing the implementation of the operating plan, and optimising the use of line capacity taking into account any deviations from the daily train plan that may occur.
train controller	The person rostered to perform the functions of train control, usually in a central office that gives him/her oversight of the whole network or large sections of it.
train operator	A company that manages trains; it may own all or some or none of its rolling-stock, and it may use its own or temporarily hired train crew. Its fundamental purpose is to be accredited to contract with the track provider(s) for train paths, pay for train paths, then each day to ensure that the trains operate to their schedules, by allocating sufficient locomotive power and having crews available and rostered to work the trains.

Glossary

train schedule	See 'path'
TranzRail Ltd	NZ's vertically-integrated private railway company, 1993 to 2003; Bought by a consortium as NZ Rail Ltd, floated on the stock market in 1996, taken over by Toll in 2003 after vertically separating to sell the network back to the NZ Government for $1.
trip train/service	A term used for a short, loosely scheduled, container train within the Sydney urban rail network
turnout	A track structure; a set of points where normally one divergent track is straight and is the main line, and the other is curved so that a train turns out from the main line.
vertically-integrated	A business organisation that owns its supply chain is vertically-integrated. For railway organisations this typically means the ownership, maintenance and control of their railway lines, freight transfer yards, rolling-stock, operations, marketing, customer service and support. Vertical integration is still the most usual structure for railways worldwide.
vertical separation	The purposeful but often flawed process of restructuring a vertically-integrated organisation into separately controlled and owned segments which may then be bought and sold separately, and which need to negotiate contracts with one another to continue operations.
wagon	An unpowered railway vehicle for carrying freight, normally moved by a loco.
WAGR	Western Australian Government Railways, which existed 1890 to 2000.
waybill	A multi-copy document that records all details about a freight consignment; it is the evidence of a contract between the shipper and the carrier; it acts as a receipt that the carrier has accepted the shipment; it is the data source for both operational and accounting information systems. Equivalent to the North American Bill of Lading.
WestRail	From 1975 the trading name of Western Australian Government Railways.
WestNet Rail	The business unit of ARG managing the leased WA network, 2002 – 2009, sold to Babcock & Brown in 2006, sold again to Brookfield Rail in 2009.
wheelset	Two wagon wheels fixed to their axle, movable as one unit for maintenance purposes.

References

ABC News (2007) 'Pacific National to sell or close rail freight business' 11 Dec 2007

ABC News (2008) 'Vic Govt unveils $20m rail funding package' 27 February 2008

Abril M, Barber F, Ingolotti L, Salido M, Tormos P & Lova A (2008) 'An assessment of railway capacity' Transportation Research Part E: Logistics and Transportation Review, 2008

ACCC [Australian Competition and Consumer Commission] (2018) 'ACCC takes action against Pacific National and Aurizon' ACCC Media Release, 19 July 2018

ACCC [Australian Competition and Consumer Commission] (2019) 'Court dismisses ACCC proceedings opposing rail freight consolidation' ACCC Media Release, 15 May 2019

ACIL Tasman Pty Ltd (2011) 'Maldon-Dombarton Rail Link Feasibility Study: Final Report' Published September 2011 by Department of Infrastructure and Transport, Canberra

Ackerman F (2008) Critique of Cost-Benefit Analysis, and Alternative Approaches to Decision-Making Global Development and Environmental Institute, Tufts University, Medford MA, USA

Affleck Consulting Pty Ltd (2003) The Australian Rail Industry: Overview and Issues. National Road Transport Commission

Affleck F (2002) 'National Rail, 1991-2002: investing in policy reform' 25th Australasian Transport Research Forum, Proceedings

ALC [Australian Logistics Council] (2012) 'ALC Initial Response to the Heavy Vehicle Charging and Investment Reform – Overview' December 2012

Allen Consulting Group (2010) National Freight Network Strategy: Background Paper.

ANAO [Australian National Audit Office] (1998) Sale of SA Rail, TasRail and Pax Rail. Performance Audit Report no.28

Anderson J (2000) 'Response of the Federal Government to Reports of the House of Representatives Standing Committee on Communications, Transport and Microeconomic Reform 'Planning not Patching' and 'Tracking Australia'; Report of the Rail Projects Taskforce 'Revitalising Rail'; Report of the Productivity Commission 'Progress in Rail Reform'. Department of Transport and Regional Services, April 2000

ARA [Australasian Railway Association] (2010a) Submission to Infrastructure Australia's National Freight Network Plan.

ARA [Australasian Railway Association] (2010b) Road Pricing Reforms in Australia: Why Road Pricing is Vital to Australia's Prosperity'

ARA [Australasian Railway Association] (2020) 'New rail freight line to drive growth, bust congestion in SE Melbourne' Media release, 25 August 2020

ARA [Australasian Railway Association] (2021) *Rail Freight Action Plan to lead focus on reform, investment and modal shift* Media release, 17 September 2021

ARA [Australasian Railway Association], BIS Oxford Economics & Hadron Group (2023) *Benefits of a national local content policy* March 2023

Arc Infrastructure (2017) Issues Paper Submission 17 November 2017.

ARTC [Australian Rail Track Corporation] (1999a) 'Submission to the Productivity Commission's Inquiry into Progress in Rail Reform' Undated document

ARTC [Australian Rail Track Corporation] (1999b) Submission to the Productivity Commission in response to the draft report on Rail Reform. Untitled and undated document

ARTC [Australian Rail Track Corporation] (1999c) 'Melbourne – Adelaide Rail Corridor More Efficient' ARTC media release 14 September 1999

ARTC [Australian Rail Track Corporation] (2001) 'Rail Audit Shows $500m Investment Needed' Media Release, 1 May 2001

ARTC [Australian Rail Track Corporation] (2004a) 'The Agreement in Summary' Fact Sheet, undated. Accessed 29 January 2015

ARTC [Australian Rail Track Corporation] (2004b) 'Faster Transit Times Between Sydney and Melbourne' Fact Sheet, undated

ARTC [Australian Rail Track Corporation] (2006) 'Submission to Productivity Commission Inquiry into Road and Rail Freight Infrastructure Pricing' May 2006

ARTC [Australian Rail Track Corporation] (2007) 'North-South Corridor Strategic Investment Outline'

ARTC [Australian Rail Track Corporation] (2008) '2008-2024 Interstate and Hunter Valley Rail Infrastructure Strategy'

ARTC [Australian Rail Track Corporation] (2015) 'Inland Rail Programme Business Case'

ARTC [Australian Rail Track Corporation] (2020) 'Inland Rail, Melbourne to Brisbane: Inland Rail Route History 2006 – 2019' A PowerPoint presentation submitted as Additional Information #5 to the Senate's Rural and Regional Affairs and Transport References Committee review of the progress of Inland Rail. 30 January 2020

ATA [Australian Trucking Association] (2013) 'Submission to Heavy Vehicle Charging and Investment Reform – Options Development Discussion Paper 25 July 2013'

ATA [Australian Trucking Association] (2015) 'Peak body urges heavy vehicle charges freeze' Media Release, 10 April 2015

ATSB [Australian Transport Safety Bureau] (2017a) 'Derailment of grain train 9150: Nunga, near Ouyen, Victoria, 9 November 2015' ATSB Transport Safety Report Rail Occurrence Investigation RO-2015-022 Final – 15 May 2017

ATSB [Australian Transport Safety Bureau] (2017b) 'Derailment of grain train 9156: Ouyen, Victoria, 29 December 2015' ATSB Transport Safety Report Rail Occurrence Investigation RO-2015-029 Final – 12 July 2017

Aurizon (2015) 'Aurizon welcomes SIMTA and MIC Moorebank agreement' Media Release, 4 June 2015

Aurizon (2019) *'Aurizon completes sale of Queensland Intermodal business to Linfox'* Media Release, 1 February 2019

Aurizon (2023) *'Aurizon grows containerised freight business with major new national contract'* Media Release, 20 February 2023

Australian Government (2020) *'Australian Government response to the House of Representatives Standing Committee on Infrastructure, Transport and Cities report: Building Up & Moving Out'* May 2020

Australian Government (2021) *'Australian Government response to the Senate Rural and Regional Affairs and Transport References Committee report: The Management of the Inland Rail project by the Australian Rail Track Corporation and the Commonwealth Government.'* December 2021

Australian Treasury (2011) *'Tax Reform: Next Steps for Australia'* Tax Forum Discussion Paper, 28 July 2011

Bailey M (2018) *'Budget delivers more record road and transport spending for Northern Queensland'* Media Statement by the Minister for Transport and Main Roads, 22 June 2018

Bailey M (2019) *'Palaszczuk Government to boost outback connectivity and jobs'* Media Statement by the Minister for Transport and Main Roads, 28 June 2019

Baines S (2014) *Steel on Steel: Inside the battle for the future of Australia's biggest railroad.* Custom Publishing, University of Queensland Press

Banks G (2006) *'Road and rail pricing: some early observations ... and more questions'* Productivity Commission, undated document

Barber E (1994) *'Impact Analysis of the Structural Reforms to the Australian Rail Networks'* 19th Australasian Transport Research Forum, Proceedings pp 557-581

Beard M (2002) *'Sustainable future for rail is the goal'* The Dominion, 11 March 2002. Letter to the Editor from the Managing Director of Tranz Rail

BIS Oxford Economics (2018) *'Australasian Railway Association Skills Capability Study – Skills Crisis: A Call to Action'* November 2018

BITRE [Bureau of Infrastructure, Transport and Regional Economics] (2010) *'Interstate Freight in Australia: Report 120'*

BITRE [Bureau of Infrastructure, Transport and Regional Economics] (2014) *'Overview of Project Appraisal in Land Transport'*

BITRE [Bureau of Infrastructure, Transport and Regional Economics] & ARA [Australasian Railway Association] (2019) *'Trainline 7 Statistical Report'*

BITRE [Bureau of Infrastructure, Transport and Regional Economics] (2022) *Trainline 9 Statistical Report*

Boeyen P (2000) *'Profit Warning from Tranz Rail Amid Structure Shake-up'* ShareChat, 10 October 2000

Boeyen P (2001a) *'Tranz Rail Q2 Revenue Up but Fuel Costs Bite'* ShareChat, 1 February 2001

Boeyen P (2001b) *'Reorganisation Derails Tranz Rail Result'* ShareChat, 2 August 2001

Boeyen P (2001c) *'Tranz Rail Tosses Dividends'* ShareChat, 23 August 2001

Booker M (1996) *'Gloom descends on sharemarket as foreigners snatch up Tranz Rail'* The Independent (weekly business tabloid), 14 June 1996

Boothe P & Petchey J (1996) *'Assigning Responsibility for Regional Stabilisation: Evidence from Canada and Australia'* Chapter 7 of Paul Boothe (ed.), "Reforming Fiscal Federalism for Global Competition: A Canada-Australia Comparison"; no.4 in the Series 'Western Studies in Economic Policy', University of Alberta Press

Briginshaw D (2007) *'New Zealand comes full circle.'* International Railway Journal – editorial, June 2007

Bryant N (2000) *'Former Tranz Rail Boss Fires Broadside at Fay Richwhite'* The National Business Review, 27 October 2000

Bromby R (2014) *New Zealand Railways: Their Life and Times*. Highgate Publishing

BTCE [Bureau of Transport and Communications Economics] (1991) *'The Future of the Tasmanian Railway System: A Cost–Benefit Assessment of Options, Report 69*

BTCE [Bureau of Transport and Communications Economics] (1993) *'The Road Freight Transport Industry; Information Paper 38'*

BTCE [Bureau of Transport and Communications Economics] (1995a) *'Adequacy of Transport Infrastructure – Rail; Working Paper 14.2'*

BTCE [Bureau of Transport and Communications Economics] (1995b) *'Analysis of the Rail Deficit: Information Paper 40'*

BTCE [Bureau of Transport and Communications Economics] (1997) *'Quality of Rail Freight Service: The Customer's Perspective'*

BTE [Bureau of Transport Economics] (1979) *'The Long Distance Road Haulage Industry: report 041'*

BTE [Bureau of Transport Economics] (1999) *'Facts and Furphies in Benefit-Cost Analysis: Transport: Report 100'*

BTRE [Bureau of Transport and Regional Economics] (2003) *'Rail Infrastructure Pricing: Principles and Practice: Report 109'*

BTRE [Bureau of Transport and Regional Economics] (2006) *'Freight Measurement and Modelling in Australia: Report 112'*

BTRE [Bureau of Transport and Regional Economics] (2009) *'Road and rail freight: competitors or complements?'* Information Sheet 34

Bullock R, Galbraith R, Williams R & Hill T (1990) *'Modelling the National Rail System: RIO and NFI'* 15th Australasian Transport Research Forum, Proceedings pp 425-453

Burr L (2017) *'Government hints at KiwiRail overhaul as company under review'* Newshub, 30 May 2017

Burton T (2023) *'National cabinet seeks to end scourge of multiple rail systems'* Australian Financial Review, 16 January 2023

Carey A & Gray D (2016) *'Bumper grain harvest threatened as V/Line bans freight trains on 33 degree days'* Sydney Morning Herald, 14 December 2016

Carter M (2003) *'Open access brings mixed results'* Railway Gazette, 01 March 2003

Carter M (2014a) *'Inland Rail – Going Around in Circles'* Rail Express, 19 March 2014

Carter M (2014b) *'Competition – you can't have it both ways'* Rail Express, 30 April 2014

Carter M (2014c) *'Rail Market Share – Need for More than Words'* Rail Express, 1 October 2014

Carter M (2015) *'No more train to the Mallee'* Rail Express, 30 June 2015

Carter M (2016) *'ARTC news slips spotlight as election takes hold'* Rail Express, 7 June 2016

Carter M (2017) *'Aurizon runs final interstate intermodal trains'* International Rail Journal, 21 December 2017

Carter M (2018) *'Watco expands Australian rail freight operations'* International Rail Journal, 3 July 2018

CBH [Cooperative Bulk Handling Ltd] (2017) *'Inquiry into National Freight and Supply Chain Priorities: Submission from the CBH Group'*

Chambers M (2017) *'Aurizon to shut intermodal business as it swings to loss, plans buyback'* The Australian, 14 August 2017

Chan G (2014) *'Australia 'addicted to roads' says leaked infrastructure report'* The Guardian Australia, 23 July 2014

Chan G & May N (2022a) *'Australia's inland rail: a long-held dream, but for whom and at what cost?'* The Guardian Australia, 25 January 2022

Chan G & May N (2022b) *'Tony Windsor backs five independent candidates in inland rail electorates'* The Guardian Australia, 8 April 2022

Chan G, Bowers M, Ball A & May N (2022) 'Trouble on the tracks: is Australia's $14bn inland rail project going off the rails?' The Guardian Australia, 25 January 2022

Chan R (2021a) 'Full capacity for Pacific National' Rail Express, 16 September 2021

Chan R (2021b) 'Logistics trial to reduce freight costs in NW Queensland' Rail Express, 9 December 2021

Chan R (2022a) 'Unlocking policy gridlock for Australia' Rail Express, 28 February 2022

Chan R (2022b) '$200 million boost for WA regional rail freight' Rail Express, 4 May 2022

Chan R (2023) 'TGE lifts capacity with Aurizon partnership' Rail Express, 20 February 2023

Claridge A (2002) 'Tranz Rail deal to let services' The Press, 14 December 2001

Clark R (2010) 'Full Circle: Rail Industry Privatisation in New Zealand, and a New Theory of Its Fundamental Conceptual Weaknesses'. Association for European Transport, 2010

COAG [Council of Australian Governments] (2007) 'COAG National Reform Agenda: Competition Reform April 2007.'

CRRP [COAG Road Reform Plan] (undated) 'A Feasibility Study'

Commonwealth Competitive Neutrality Complaints Office (2000) 'National Rail Corporation Limited, Investigation no. 3'

Cormann M (2015) 'Appointment of Advisors for the Scoping Study into the Australian Rail Track Corporation Ltd' Minister of Finance Media Release, 14 December 2015

Crispin D (1998) '[ATN] Submission on Progress in Rail Reform.' 2 October 1998

Cullen M (2001) 'Auckland rail deal clinched' NZ Finance Ministerial Media release, 24 December 2001

Cullen M (2003a) 'Govt moves to protect rail network' NZ Finance Ministerial Media release, 7 June 2003

Cullen M (2003b) 'Govt Toll reach accommodation on Tranz Rail' NZ Finance Ministerial Media release, 7 July 2003

Daniels C (2002) 'Trouble at Tranz Rail' The New Zealand Herald, 12 September 2002

De Graaf P (2016) North's rail line to be mothballed' The Northern Advocate, 3 March 2016

Dearnaley M (2009) 'Line's mothballing sets off alarm bells' The New Zealand Herald, 9 November 2009

Dearnaley M (2010) 'Fears for Northland rail link' The New Zealand Herald, 19 May 2010

Dinsdale M (2020) *'$109m for Northland rail network in latest Govt announcement'* The New Zealand Herald, 30 January 2020

DIRD [Department of Infrastructure and Regional Development] (2016) *'Heavy Vehicle Road Reform – What we are doing and why we are doing it'* 16 August 2016

DIRD [Department of Infrastructure and Regional Development] (2017) *'Inquiry into National Freight and Supply Chain Priorities, Discussion Paper – May 2017'*

DIRDC [Department of Infrastructure, Regional Development and Cities] (2018) *'Inquiry into National Freight and Supply Chain Priorities, Report, March 2018'*

DITRDC [Department of Infrastructure, Transport, Regional Development and Communications] (2021) 'Why Inland Rail' website page

Dodd K (2018) *'Poll shows 90% have considered a blockade'* Big Rigs, 19 February 2018

DoTaRS [Department of Transport and Regional Services] (1998) *'Submission to the Productivity Commission Inquiry into Progress in Rail Reform'*

DoTaRS [Department of Transport and Regional Services] (1999) *'Comments on Productivity Commission's Draft Report on Progress in Rail Reform'*

DoTaRS [Department of Transport and Regional Services] (2000) *'Annual Report 1999-2000'*

DoTaRS [Department of Transport and Regional Services] (2004) *'AusLink White Paper'*

Drew J (2006) 'Rail Freight: *The Benefits and Costs of Vertical Separation and Open Access'*. Association for European Transport 2006

Drew J & Ludwig J (2011) *'Reforming Europe's Railways – Learning from Experience'* 2nd edition, 2011. DVV Media Group GmbH | Eurailpress

Du Fresne K (2003) *'Cullen considers giving rail freight a helping hand'* ShareChat, 14 February 2003

Edwards B (1993) 'R*ail buyer in for the long haul'* The Evening Post, 21 July 1993

EISC [Economics and Industry Standing Committee] (2014) *'The Management of Western Australia's Freight Rail Network'*, Report #3 October 2014, Legislative Assembly, Parliament of Western Australia

Evans S (2023) *'Labor's carbon plan means more trucks: rail bosses'* Australian Financial Review, 30 March 2023.

EY [Ernst & Young] (2016) *'The Value of Rail in New Zealand'* For the New Zealand Transport Agency, 2 September 2016

Farm Weekly (2021) *'CBH gets new rail service provider'* no author, 6 August 2021

Farrier Swier Consulting (2013) *'Economic regulatory input to HVCI reform project: Collated working papers (January to March 2013)* October 2013

Ferreira L & Kozan E (1992) *'Road/rail container transfer facilities: operational efficiency and customer service'* 17th Australasian Transport Research Forum, Proceedings pp 605-617

Finn R (2020) *'cargo-partner Expands Weekly LCL Rail Transports from Europe to China'* Logistics Manager, 3 May 2020

FreightCorp (1999) *'Submission to the Productivity Commission in Response to Progress in Rail Reform Draft Report'* 30 June 1999

FROG [Freight Rail Operators' Group] (2007) *'ARTC Interstate Access Undertaking: Freight Rail Operators' Group Submission to ACCC'* July 2007

Fox A (2002) *'Tranz Rail clears air'* The Dominion Post, 24 July 2002

Fox A (2003a) *'Tranz Rail's credit rating on the line'* The Dominion Post, 8 April 2003

Fox A (2003b) *'Troubled Tranz Rail needs 'magic' touch'* INL Newspapers, 17 April 2003

Fox A (2003c) *'Banks crucial in Tranz Rail bid'* The Dominion Post, 17 May 2003

Fox A (2003d) *'Tranz Link may be Toll's ace card'* The Dominion Post, 22 May 2003

Fox A (2003e) *'Rail America bows out'* The Dominion Post, 24 May 2003

Fox A (2003f) *'Aussies to make full bid for Tranz Rail'* The Dominion Post, 30 May 2003

Fox A (2003g) *'Toll still market choice in rail bid'* The Dominion Post, 26 June 2003

Fox A (2003h) *'Tranz Rail directors say don't sell to Toll'* The Dominion Post, 1 August 2003

Fullerton J (2019) *'Business Case based on inter-capital freight'* Letter to the editor of Australian Financial Review by the CEO of ARTC, published 1 April 2019.

Gardner B (2014) *'No Appetite for Changes to Heavy Vehicle Changes: HVCI Member'* Australian Transport News, 15 December 2014

Garnett O (2014) *'Historical rail lines in WA's Wheatbelt close as CBH and Brookfield continue negotiations'* ABC Radio, WA Country Hour, 1 July 2014

Gaynor B (1996) *'Tranz Rail deals leave trail of unanswered questions'* The National Business Review, 21 June 1996, p.53

Gaynor B (2002) *'Shares in a down-hill train-ride'* New Zealand Herald, 15 July 2002

Gaynor B (2004) *'A tough case ... and a long one'* New Zealand Herald, 15 October 2004.

GHD Advisory (2022) *'Freight Modal Shift: Mode Shift Impediments and Opportunities'* March 2022. A report prepared for and published by the ARA, available on the ARA website

Gittins R (2015) *'Time to get the economics of environment right'* Sydney Morning Herald, 17 July 2015

Goldsmith B (2017) *'V/Line has $534m maintenance backlog'* Australian Associated Press, 9 August 2017.

Gordon J (2014) *'Billions spent on roads in "hideously inefficient" way'* The Age, 22 July 2014

Gray I, Laird P & Montague N (2015) *'Rail freight for regional development.'* A paper presented at the SEGRA Conference, Bathurst NSW, 21 October 2015

Gunn J (1989) *Along Parallel Lines: A history of the railways of New South Wales 1850 – 1986*. Melbourne University Press

Harper I, Anderson P, McCluskey S & O'Bryan M (2015) *Competition Policy Review: Final Report* The Treasury, Canberra

Harvey M & Tsolakis D (1991) *'TASRAIL – A Cost-Benefit Assessment of Options'* 16th Australasian Transport Research Forum, Proceedings pp 137-156

Hawker D (1989) *'No Ticket, No Start – No More!: Who Reaps the Benefits – A Chronicle of the Wheat Debate'* Conference Papers of the H.R. Nicholls Society Inc.

Hearsch J (2007) *'Victoria's Regional Railway: Past, Present and Potential'.* RTSA Regional Rail Symposium, Wagga Wagga, 1 February 2007

Heatley D (2009a) *'The history and future of rail in New Zealand'* ISCR [New Zealand Institute for the Study of Competition and Regulation] June 2009.

Heatley D (2009b) *'KiwiRail: strategic asset or strategic blunder?'* ISCR Competition and Regulation Times, July 2009, issue 29, pp 1-3.

Heatley D & Schwass S (2011) *'Rail Transport in New Zealand'* Chapter 10 of C Findlay (ed.) "The impacts and benefits of structural reforms in transport, energy and telecommunications sectors." Asia-Pacific Economic Cooperation Support Unit, Asia-Pacific Economic Cooperation Secretariat, Singapore

Hendery S (2015) *'KiwiRail rejects line venture'* Hawkes Bay Today, 13 March 2015

Hilmer F, Rayner M & Taperell G (1993) *National Competition Policy.* AGPS

Hoang J, Collins D, Rafinejad D & Latimer L (2012) *'A Tale of Three Bins, A Waste Reduction Case Story through a Systems Thinking Lens'* - a case study produced for Sabre Holdings by Presidio Graduate School.

Hopkins P (2003) *'Alarm on bid for Victorian rail freight'* The Age, 8 December 2003

Hopkins P (2008) *'Off the Rails'* The Australian, 21 March 2008

Howie C (2002) *'Finance row over, but fears over rail remain'* The Dominion Post, 23 November 2002

Howie C (2003) *'Rail America plays down rival bid talk'* The Dominion Post, 21 May 2003

Hudson S (2011) *'NZ Rail Corporation (KiwiRail) Performance Evaluation'* Macquarie Equities Research, 1 November 2011. Bespoke research provided for the NZ Treasury.

HRSCCTMR [House of Representatives Standing Committee on Communications, Transport and Microeconomic Reform] (1997) *'Planning Not Patching'*

HRSCCTMR [House of Representatives Standing Committee on Communications, Transport and Microeconomic Reform] (1998) *'Tracking Australia – Executive Summary'*

HRSCCTA [House of Representatives Standing Committee on Communications, Transport and the Arts] (2001) *'Back on Track: Progress in rail reform'* The Parliament of the Commonwealth of Australia, April 2001

Industry Commission (1991) *Rail Transport*. Report no. 13, AGPS

Industry Commission (1992) *Annual Report 1991-92*.

Infrastructure and Transport Ministers (2021) *'Pathway Ahead: Heavy Vehicle Road Reform'*

Infrastructure Australia (2011) *'National Land Freight Strategy: Discussion Paper'* February 2011

Infrastructure Australia (2016) *'Australian Infrastructure Plan: Priorities and Reforms for Our Nation's Future'* February 2016

ITMM [Infrastructure and Transport Ministers Meeting] (2022) *'ITMM Communiqué: 9 December 2022* Canberra

Jaspers M (1993) *'Lining up for a slice of transport history: Mixture of foreign and local firms in consortiums bidding for NZ Rail'* The Dominion, 23 June 1993

John Hearsch Consulting Pty Ltd (2008) *'Rail Productivity Information Paper'* Commissioned and published by the National Transport Commission. March 2008

Johnson A (2008) *'The end of the line: Operator dumps rail freight company'* The Standard, 12 October 2008

Juturna Consulting (2012) *'Economic Reform of Australia's road sector: Precedents, principles, case studies and structures'* Prepared for Infrastructure Australia, February 2012

Juturna Consulting (2014) *'Spend more, waste more. Australia's roads in 2014: moving beyond gambling'* Prepared for, but withdrawn by, Infrastructure Australia, July 2014

Kain J (1995) *'A Spirit of Progress? Assessing Australian Rail Transport Policy'* Parliamentary Research Service, Research Paper no. 31, 19 June 1995

Karp P (2016) *'Union anger over delay of minimum pay rates for truck owner-drivers'* published by The Guardian, Australian edition, 5 April 2016

Kay M (2003) *'On the brink of disaster'* The Dominion Post, 2 May 2003, p.B5

Keane B (2009) *'Budget countdown: Auslink infrastructure planning fail'* Crikey, 24 April 2009

Keane B (2015) *'Inland fail: the $10 billion rail line to nowhere'* Crikey, 23 September 2015

Keating P (1992) *One Nation: Statement by the Prime Minister The Honourable P.J.Keating, MP; 26 February 1992.* Australian Government Publishing Service.

King M (1996) *'Rail Reform'* 20th Australasian Transport Research Forum, Proceedings pp 1-13

King M (1998) *'Benefiting from Worldwide Associations'* The NZ Railway Observer, Autumn 1998

Kirk J (2020) *'Unlocking rail access to Australia's largest port'* Railway Gazette International, September 2020

Kirk S (2017) *'Rail has saved New Zealand $1.5 billion a year, study shows'* The Dominion Post, 27 November 2017.

Kitchen R (2008) *'Govt buys back rail, ferries for $665m'* The Dominion Post, 5 May 2008

KiwiRail (2012) *'KiwiRail to mothball Napier-Gisborne line'* Media Release, 2 October 2012

KiwiRail (2014) *'KiwiRail Commercial Review'* Provided confidentially to shareholding Ministers; released to the public in a heavily redacted form by KiwiRail, 27 April 2016.

KiwiRail (2015) *'Road transport regulation a controversial measure to protect railways'* From http://www.kiwirail.co.nz/about-us/history-of-kiwirail/150yearsofrail/stories/road-transport-regulation

KiwiRail (2016) *'KiwiRail focuses on future as Commercial Review is released'* KiwiRail Media Release, 27 April 2016.

KiwiRail (2016?) *'Statement of Corporate Intent 2016-2018: Reshaping and Delivering'*

KiwiRail (2017a) *'The rail privatisation experiment divided opinion and generated strong emotions'* From http://www.kiwirail.co.nz/about-us/history-of-kiwirail/150yearsofrail/stories/rail-privatisation.html

KiwiRail (2017b) *'$1.5billion annual hidden benefits from rail network are "real ... huge"'* KiwiRail Media Statement, 27 November 2017

References

KiwiRail (2018) *'Electric locomotives to continue with Government investment'* Media Release, 30 October 2018.

KiwiRail (2021a) *'KiwiRail joins Infrastructure Sustainability Council of Australia'* Media Statement, 5 July 2021.

KiwiRail (2021b) *'Track User Charge comes into effect'* The Express, Issue 367, December 2021.

Kopicki R & Thompson L (1995) *'Best Methods of Railway Restructuring and Privatization'* World Bank, CFS Discussion Paper Series, Number 111

Laird P (1987) *'Freight Transport Subsidies in New South Wales'* 12th Australasian Transport Research Forum, Proceedings pp 125-146

Laird P (1990) *'Improving land freight transport efficiency in Australia'* 15th Australasian Transport Research Forum, Proceedings pp 39-54

Laird P (1992) *'Australian Intercity Rail Upgrading Options'* Parliamentary Research Service, Research Paper no. 20, 8 September 1992

Laird P (1994) *'Rail and Urban Public Transport: Commonwealth Funding and Policy Issues'* Parliamentary Research Service, Research Paper no.12, 30 August 1994

Laird P (1999) *'Interstate Road and Rail Investment and Access Pricing'* 23rd Australasian Transport Research Forum, Proceedings pp 27-42

Laird PG, Newman PWG, Bachels MA & Kenworthy JR (2001) *Back on Track: Rethinking Transport Policy in Australia and New Zealand.* UNSW Press

Laird P (2001) *'Rail freight competition and efficiency gains in Australia.'* Proceedings of the 36th Canadian Transport Research Forum, Vancouver May 2001, pp 512-528

Laird P (2004) *Submission to the Productivity Commission re Energy Efficiency.* http://www.pc.gov.au/__data/assets/file/0006/44745/sub001.rtf

Laird P (2005) *The Sydney to Melbourne Railway: Yesterday, today and tomorrow.* Second International and Thirteenth National Engineering Heritage Conference 2005, Sydney

Laird P, Michell M, Stoney A & Adorni-Braccesi G (2005) *Australian freight railways for a new century.* AusRail Plus LLDCN.

Laird P (2006a) *Supplementary Submission to the House of Representatives Standing Committee on Transport and Regional Services Inquiry into the Integration of regional rail and road freight transport and their interface with ports. August 2006*, Submission 181.

Laird P (2006b) *Rail Research Industry Report, Project 24, Rail Transport Energy Efficiency and Sustainability.* Rail CRC

Laird P (2006c) *'Freight transport cost recovery in Australia'* 29th Australasian Transport Research Forum, Proceedings pp 1-13

Laird P (2009a) *'Australian Freight Railways and Commodity Exports'* Canadian Transportation Research Forum Proceedings of 44th Annual Conference, p 641

Laird P (2009b) *'Supplementary Submission to the House of Representatives Standing Committee on Economics: Inquiry into raising the level of productivity growth in the Australian Economy.'*

Laird P (2013) *Government Rail Asset Sales, and Return to the Public Sector, in New Zealand and Tasmania.* Research in Transportation Business & Management, vol 6 – "Railroad Privatization and Deregulation: Lessons from Three Decades of Experience Worldwide", pp 116-122.

Laird P (2014) *A Competitive Interstate Rail Freight and Passenger Network.* Conference on Railway Excellence, Proceedings (pp. 121-130). Australia: Railway Technical Society of Australasia (RTSA).

Laird P (2017a) *'Time to Rebalance the Transport Mix'* Track and Signal, vol 21 no.2, pp 6-7

Laird P (2017b) *'Trucks Are Destroying Our Roads and Not Picking Up the Repair Cost'* The Conversation, 23 June 2017

Lee R (2003) *Linking a Nation: Australia's Transport and Communications 1788 – 1970.* Australian Heritage Commission.

Lilley R (2000) *'Tranz Rail under fire for fourth price hike'* ShareChat, 24 November 2000

Loneragan D (2018) *'ARA demands action to avert skills crisis'* Rail Express, 27 November 2018

Love P (2002) *'Tranz Rail cornerstone stake sells'* The Evening Post, 21 Feb 2002

Macalister P (2003) *'Toll's Deal with Govt Exclusive'* ShareChat, 7 August 2003

Maddock R (1999) *'Rail and Rail Policy'* Submission to the Productivity Commission Review of Rail.

Martin P (2017) *'The fake economics cookbook: how to make bad transport projects look good'* Sydney Morning Herald, 22 November 2017.

Martin S (2013) *'Rail Privatisation: A Success or A Failure?'* Track and Signal, Winter 2013, p.47

McQueen AE (2005) *Rails in the Hinterland: New Zealand's Vanishing Railway Landscape.* Grantham House Publishing

McKinnon A (1998) *'The abolition of quantitative controls on road freight transport: the end of an era?'* Transport Logistics vol 1, no.3, pp211-223.

Mason B (2019) *'Transport Economics: A New Paradigm'* AITPM (Australian Institute of Transport Planning and Management) 2019 Conference

Meldrum B (2004) *'Freight off the rails: Pacific National suspends rail services to Portland'* Portland Observer, 17 December 2004.

Michael E (1992) *'Reforming Australia's Railways: The Privatisation Option'* Policy, vol.8, no.2, Winter 1992, pp 17-21

Mitchell D (2010) *'Heavy Vehicle Productivity Trends and Road Freight Regulation in Australia'* 33rd Australasian Transport Research Forum, Proceedings pp 1-18

Moore B & Starrs M (1993) *'Road Transport Reform in a Federal System'* 18th Australasian Transport Research Forum, Proceedings pp 425-442

Morton A (2023) *'Safeguard Mechanism: what is it, will it cut emissions and what role do carbon offsets play?"* The Guardian, Australian edition, 16 February 2023.

MoT [NZ Ministry of Transport] (2019a) *'The Future of Rail and Investment to Support a Resilient and Reliable Rail System'* Cabinet Paper (redacted) 16 May 2019.

MoT [NZ Ministry of Transport] (2019b) *'Future of Rail'* published 23 October 2019.

MoT [NZ Ministry of Transport] (2021a) *'The New Zealand Rail Plan'* April 2021.

MoT [NZ Ministry of Transport] (2021b) *'Joint report: Approving Terms of Reference for entity form review of KiwiRail and New Zealand Railways Corporation'* Report no. OC210738, 15 September 2021. Memo to Ministers, released under the Official Information Act.

MoT [NZ Ministry of Transport] (2021c) *'Terms of Reference: a review of the entity form of KiwiRail Holdings Limited and the New Zealand Railways Corporation'* 10 November 2021.

MoT [NZ Ministry of Transport] (2022) *'New Zealand freight and supply chain issues paper'* undated document – released on MoT website 20 April 2022.

Murden S (2016) *'Australian Rail Track Corporation kept under Government ownership'* Australian Mining, 4 May 2016.

National Rail Corporation Ltd (1999) *Comments from National Rail Corporation Ltd [re] Draft Report on Progress in Rail Reform.* 24 May 1999

NCC [National Competition Council] (1998) *'Submission to Productivity Commission's Inquiry into Progress in Rail Reform'* 10 November 1998

NCC [National Competition Council] (2001) *'Assessment of Governments' Progress in Implementing the National Competition Policy and Related Reforms: June 2001'.* Chapter 10, Rail

NCOA [National Commission of Audit] (2014a) *'Towards Responsible Government: Phase One'* February 2014.

NCOA [National Commission of Audit] (2014b) *'Towards Responsible Government: Appendix, volume 2'* February 2014.

Nestor J (2007) *'Cargo Cult Railway Proposals'* Policy, vol.23, no.3, Spring 2007, pp 30-33

Norley K & Ferreira L (1993) *'Long-Distance Rail Freight in Australia: Towards 2000 – The Role of Capital Investment'* 18th Australasian Transport Research Forum, Proceedings pp 683-692

NSW Government (2018) *'Fixing Country Rail Round 1 – Expression of Interest Form'* Version 1.1, as of 24 September 2018.

NTC [National Transport Commission] (2006) *'Productivity Commission Inquiry into Freight Infrastructure Pricing: Submission'* 12 May 2006

NTC [National Transport Commission] (2008) *'Rail Industry Productivity Review: An NTC Initiative'* June 2008

NTC [National Transport Commission] (2009) *'Freight Rail Productivity Review – Final Position Paper'* August 2009

NTC [National Transport Commission] (2010) *'The Role of Government in Rail Freight Investment: Discussion Paper'* 18 October 2010

NTC [National Transport Commission] (2022) *'National Rail Action Plan'* 1 August 2022

NZ Ministry of Transport (2005) *'Surface Transport Costs and Charges Study: Summary of main findings and issues'*

NZ Treasury (2008a) *New Zealand Rail Transaction Information Release*. Issued 21 February 2008. An archive of government working documents, not written for publication, covering the lead up to the government resuming control of the railway network.

NZ Treasury (2008b) *Crown Purchase of Toll New Zealand Rail and Ferry Business Information Release*. Issued 19 December 2008. An archive of government working documents, not written for publication, covering the lead up to the government resuming control of above-rail operations.

NZ Treasury (2008c) *'NZ Railways Corporation (KiwiRail): Background Advice.'* Unpublished report for the Minister of Finance, 8 December 2008; released under the Official Information Act.

NZ Treasury (2015) *'Budget 2015 Information Release'* July 2015

NZISCR [New Zealand Institute for the Study of Competition and Regulation] (1999a) *'The Privatization of New Zealand Rail Part 1: Assessment of History, Markets and Data.'* Report to the Treasury, 10 July 1999

NZISCR [New Zealand Institute for the Study of Competition and Regulation] (1999b) *'The Privatization of New Zealand Rail Part 2: Quantitative Cost Benefit Analysis'*

NZPA [New Zealand Press Association] (2003a) *'Toll's 95c offer to buy Tranz Rail too low – Samuel'* INL Newspapers, 28 July 2003

NZPA [New Zealand Press Association] (2003b) *'Toll picks up Tranz Rail reins'* Fairfax New Zealand Ltd, 14 October 2003

NZPA [New Zealand Press Association] (2004) *'Toll NZ buys back Tranz Scenic passenger services'* NZ Herald 20 May 2004.

NZPA [New Zealand Press Association] (2009) *'Rolling stock decision looms for Toll NZ'* The Dominion Post, 31 January 2009.

O'Brien P (2001) *'Tranz Rail move one of burst of takeover actions before deadline'* ShareChat, 29 June 2001.

O'Brien P (2002) *'Cash issue puts heat on Tranz Rail'* ShareChat, 22 November 2002.

Odgers J & Low N (2010) *'Travel time savings, transport infrastructure and path dependence, the case of Melbourne, Australia'* 12th World Congress on Transport Research.

OECD [Organisation for Economic Co-operation and Development] (2005) *'Structural Reform of the Rail Industry'*

OTNA [On Track North America] (2019) *'OTNA's Rail vs Road Data Comparison Project: North America's Most Important Infrastructure Project'*

O'Sullivan F (2002) *'Man at top has bold plans to get Tranz Rail back on track'* New Zealand Herald, 11 September 2002

Owens H (2004) *'Rail Reform Strategies: The Australian Experience'* in "Governance, Regulation, and Privatization in the Asia-Pacific Region, NBER East Asia Seminar on Economics, Volume 12" National Bureau of Economic Research, University of Chicago

Pacific National (2019) *'Australia's major highway now a conveyor belt for big trucks'* PN Media Release, 28 July 2019.

Painter M, (1998) *Collaborative Federalism: Economic Reform in Australia in the 1990s.* Cambridge University Press [digital version 2009]

Panelli A (1994) *'Operations Management System to be Implemented by Third Australian Railway'* Australian Transport and Freight Magazine, vol 37, no.1-2, pp 24-25

Pavey (2018a) *'$60 million to boost rail freight for the NSW food bowl'* Media Release from the Minister for Roads, Maritime and Freight – Melinda Pavey; 28 May 2018

Pavey (2018b) *'$40 million funding boost for rail upgrade'* Media Release from the Minister for Roads, Maritime and Freight – Melinda Pavey; 29 May 2018

Pearce C (2020a) *'The NRAP: Putting reform into action'* Rail Express, 3 September 2020

Pearce C (2020b) *'WA to progress business cases for reopening three Tier 3 grain lines'* Rail Express, 25 September 2020

Pearce C (2020c) *'EOI for Victorian section of Inland Rail released'* Rail Express, 9 June 2020

Pearce C (2020d) *'Rail freight competitiveness scheme gets a $4m extension'* Rail Express, 2 June 2020

Pearce C (2020e) *'Where are rail's "shovel-ready" projects?'* Rail Express, 3 July 2020

Pearce C (2020f) *'Government-industry group formed for rail freight in Victoria'* Rail Express, 24 February 2020

Peck D & Hollingworth K (2017) 'Second stage of $440 million Murray Basin Rail Project good news for farmers and industry' ABC Rural, 2 August 2017

Perry J (2009) *'PN commences QLD coal haulage operations'* Rail Express, 20 May 2009

Pittman R (2005) *'Structural Separation to Create Competition? The Case of Freight Railways'* Review of Network Economics, vol 4 issue 3, September 2005

Potterton P (2012) *'30 Years of Australian Transport Policy: What Makes for Success?'* a paper presented to a University of Wollongong workshop, 23-24 Feb 2012, on "Infrastructure Economics and Policy: New Tools for Old Problems"

Prebble R (1996) *I've Been Thinking* Seaview Publishing, NZ

Preston J (2002) *The Transaction Cost Economics of Railways.* Quarterly Journal of Transport Law, Economics and Engineering, special issue August 2002 "Deregulation and Vertical Separation in the Railway Sector"

Probert O (2015a) *'Two rail sidings named for upgrade'* Rail Express, 21 May 2015

Probert O (2015b) *'Andrews backs Murray Basin project'* Rail Express, 17 August 2015

Probert O (2016a) *'Two key Aurizon contracts renewed to 2017'* Rail Express, 4 January 2016

Probert O (2016b) *'Construction begins at Julia Creek derailment'* Rail Express, 11 January 2016

Probert O (2016c) *'Qube buys Aurizon out of Moorebank for $99m'* Rail Express, 2 August 2016

Probert O (2016d) *'Politics key cause in $28 billion in transport overspending: Report'* Rail Express, 24 October 2016

Probert O (2016e) *'NSW funds ten regional rail projects'* Rail Express, 8 August 2016

Probert O (2017a) *'10,000 tonnes of Adelaide-Tarcoola rail delivered'* Rail Express, 10 March 2017

Probert O (2017b) *'Aurizon to sell Queensland Intermodal to PN/Linfox, will close interstate terminals'* Rail Express, 14 August 2017

Probert O (2017c) *'Adelaide-Melbourne Upgrade Complete for 1800m Trains'* Rail Express, 25 September 2017

Probert O (2017d) *'Palaszczuk promises $50m to Mount Isa line'* Rail Express, 13 November 2017

Probert O (2019a) *'40km of major washouts on Mt Isa Line'* Rail Express, 21 February 2019

Probert O (2019b) *'Acacia Ridge sale approved by Federal Court'* Rail Express, 16 May 2019

Probert O (2019c) *'Election fallout: 6 key takeaways for rail'* Rail Express, 21 May 2019

Probert O (2019d) *'Dalla Valle renews push for road-rail access equality'* Rail Express, 22 Nov 2019

Productivity Commission (1999) *Progress in Rail Reform.* Report no.6

Productivity Commission (2005) *Review of National Competition Policy Reforms.* Report no.33

Productivity Commission (2006) *Road and Rail Freight Infrastructure Pricing.* Report no.41

Productivity Commission (2014) *Public Infrastructure.* Inquiry Report no.71, vol 1

Pullar-Strecker T (2020) *'KiwiRail's future as state-owned enterprise in question after Covid'* Stuff, 15 December 2020

Qube Logistics (2013) *'Submission to the Review of NSW Rail Access Regime'* Letter of 28 February 2013.

Queensland Rail (2012) *Mt Isa Line Rail Infrastructure Master Plan*

Queensland Rail (2019) *Annual and Financial Report 2018-19*

Rail Futures Institute (2017) *Submission to inquiry into National Freight and Supply Chain Priorities* July 2017, ref A0059839B

Rapley J (2017) *Twilight of the Money Gods: Economics as a Religion and How it all Went Wrong.* Simon & Schuster

Raworth K (2017) *Doughnut Economics: Seven Ways to Think Like a 21st-Century Economist.* Penguin Random House Business Books

Richard Paling Consulting (2008) *'National Freight Demands Study: September 2008'*

RMTU [Rail and Maritime Transport Union] (2016) *'Rail union condemns managed decline of rail network'* RMTU Press Release, 27 January 2016

Robertson G (2019) *'Minister of Finance Wellbeing Budget speech'* 30 May 2019.

Rochfort S (2003) *'Toll fills the breach with $139m bid for Tranz Rail'* Sydney Morning Herald, 30 May 2003

Rosendorff D (2009) *'Concerns about oil company's switch from rail to road'* ABC News, 8 August 2009

Rowe D (2020) *'KiwiRail to consider closing Wairio track if it can't secure funding'* Stuff, 24 July 2020

Rowe D (2021) *'$5m deal reached to maintain Ohai to Invercargill railway line'* Stuff, 18 January 2021

Ruth J (2000) *'Tranz Rail quits the train business'* The Independent, 11 October 2000

Rutherford H (2015) *'Treasury urged government to consider closing most of Kiwirail'* Stuff, 9 July 2015

RNZ News (2019) *'KiwiRail investment through Land Transport fund: government proposal 'historic'.'* 14 December 2019.

Sandel M (2012) *What Money Can't Buy: the Moral Limits of Markets.* Farrar, Straus and Giroux, New York

Saulwick J (2014) *'More trucks on Sydney roads as government fails to hit rail share targets'*, Sydney Morning Herald, 21 September 2014

SCOTI [Standing Council on Transport and Infrastructure] (2012) *'National Land Freight Strategy – A place for freight'* Published by the Department for Infrastructure and Transport, Canberra

SCOTI [Standing Council on Transport and Infrastructure] (2013) *'Communiqué: Brisbane, Friday 15 November 2013'*

SCT Logistics (2020) *'Port Rail Strategy Driving New Investment For Victoria'* Press Release 22 July 2020.

Securities Information (1996) *'Wisconsin Central Transportation Corp – '10-K' for 12/31/96'* Website accessed 23 June 2019 from http://www.secinfo.com/durh4.8d.htm

SSCRRAT [Senate Standing Committee on Rural and Regional Affairs and Transport] (1997) *'Report on the Brew Report and on the Continuing Role of the Commonwealth in the Australian Rail Industry'*

Sexton D (2016a) *'Infrastructure Boss Questions Inland Rail'* Rail Express, 21 June 2016

Sexton D (2016b) *'Murray Basin project well Underway'* Rail Express, 28 July 2016

Sexton D (2016c) *'TasRail finds strength in troubled times'* Rail Express, 26 July 2016

Sexton D (2021) *'Rail freight highlighted in Victorian budget'* Rail Express, 21 May 2021

Silverton Rail (1999?) *'Submission by the Silverton Tramway Company Limited to the Productivity Commission.'* Undated document.

Shoeshine[1] (2002a) *'Tranz Rail takes the market on a rollercoaster ride'* ShareChat, 5 April 2002.

Shoeshine[1] (2002b) *'Bubble, bubble as market grasps at Tranz Rail's trouble'* The National Business Review, 16 August 2002, p.47

Shoeshine[1] (2003) *'Tranz Rail a case for Public Private Partnership'* The National Business Review, 24 April 2003, p.39

Skatssoon J (2021) *'Council cries foul over nation's biggest freight rail project'* Government News, 28 January 2021

---

1 "Shoeshine" is an anonymous financial analyst who writes regularly for New Zealand's National Business Review newspaper.

SMEC (2018) *Eyre Peninsula Freight Study,* reference #3005591, prepared for the [South Australian] Department of Planning Transport and Infrastructure and Genesee and Wyoming Australia

Smellie P (2015) *'Govt warns KiwiRail annual support won't last'* Published by Scoop, 21 May 2015

Smith G (2020) *'Australia: The hard truth about interstate freight'* Railway Gazette, 9 July 2020

SRRATRC [The Senate Rural and Regional Affairs and Transport References Committee] (2021) *'Inland Rail: derailed from the start'* August 2021

Steeman M (2002) *'Tranz Rail hits record low'* The Dominion Post, 5 September 2002

Steeman M (2003) *'Toll lifts Tranz Rail offer'* The Dominion Post, 6 September 2003

Stevens M (2019) *'Qube rules out an intermodal future after ACCC defeat'* Australian Financial Review, 17 May 2019

Stride N (2002) *'Fund managers fume as Tranz Rail sinks.'* ShareChat, 12 July 2002

Swain P (2002) *'New Zealand Transport Strategy Released'* NZ Transport Ministerial Media release, 4 December 2002

Swier G (2014) *'Heavy vehicle road charging and investment reform in Australia.'* A presentation to the ACCC / AER Regulatory Conference, Brisbane, 8 August 2014

TAIC [Transport and Infrastructure Council] (2014) *'Communiqué: Alice Springs, Friday 23 May 2014'*

TAIC [Transport and Infrastructure Council] (2015) *'2015 Review of the National Transport Commission: Report to the Transport and Infrastructure Council by the National Transport Commission Review Expert Panel'* August 2015. Accessed 19 April 2017

TAIC [Transport and Infrastructure Council] (2016) *'Heavy Vehicle Road Reform – What we are doing and why we are doing it.'* 29 April 2016. Accessed 20 April 2017

TAIC [Transport and Infrastructure Council] (2016?) *'National Rail Vision and Work Program'* undated document

TAIC [Transport and Infrastructure Council] (2017) *'Communiqué: Hobart, 10 November 2017'*

TAIC [Transport and Infrastructure Council] (2019a) 'National Freight and Supply Chain Strategy: August 2019' published by the Department of Infrastructure, Transport, Cities and Regional Development, Canberra

TAIC [Transport and Infrastructure Council] (2019b) *'Terms of Reference: August 2019'*

Terrill M, Emslie O & Coates B (2016) *'Roads to Riches: Better Transport Investment.'* Grattan Institute Report no. 2016-5, April 2016

Terrill M & Batrouney H (2018) *'Unfreezing Discount Rates: Transport Infrastructure for Tomorrow'* Grattan Institute Report no. 2018-03, March 2018

The Dominion Post (2016) *'Editorial: Govt made the right call by keeping Kiwirail'* 29 April 2016

The New Zealand Herald (2015) *'Closure of most of KiwiRail was an option if company didn't get more public funding'* no author, 9 July 2015

Thompson B (2014) *'Brookfield secrets outed'* The West Australian, 17 October 2014

Thornthwaite L *'Controversial history of Road Safety Tribunal shows minimum pay was doomed from the start'* The Conversation, 15 April 2016

TISOC [Transport and Infrastructure Senior Officials Committee] (2013) *'2012 Review of the National Transport Commission and Other Relevant Transport Bodies'* March 2013, Department of Infrastructure and Transport, Canberra

Toleman R (1990) *'Structural Reform of New Zealand's transport system'* 15th Australasian Transport Research Forum, Proceedings pp 21-37

Toll NZ (2005) *'Toll NZ Presentation to New Zealand Union Conference, Wellington, 14 June 2005'*

Transport for NSW (2012) *'Review of NSW Rail Access Regime: Issues Paper'* Pub M.202, November 2012

Transport for NSW (2016) *'Fixing Country Rail: Pilot Round Overview'* April 2016

Tranz Rail (2003) *'Tranz Rail completes Aratere buy out'* Press Release, 1 October 2003.

Tully S *'Why Hunter Harrison's Railroad Revolution Will Outlive Him at CSX'* Fortune, 20 January 2018

Van den Bergh R (2002) *'Tranz Rail's credit rating downgraded'* The Dominion Post, 25 July 2002

Van Dyke C & Foy K (2006) *'The Scheduled Railroad: A New Paradigm?'* from the Oliver Wyman website of Surface Transportation Insights

Victorian Auditor-General (2009) *'Buy-back of the Regional Intrastate Rail Network'* VAGO

Victorian Department of Transport (2011) *'Grain Logistics Taskforce Report'*

Victorian Department of Transport (2020) *'Rail Freight Working Group to establish industry priorities'* Media Release, 29 February 2020

Victorian Government (1998?) *'Victorian Government Submission to the Productivity Commission's Inquiry into Progress In Rail Reform.'* Undated document

VRFNR (Victorian Rail Freight Network Review) (2007) *'Switchpoint: The template for rail freight to revive and thrive'* Victorian Department of Infrastructure

Wallis I & Chandler (?) (2005) *'The New Zealand Surface Transport Costs and Charges Study'* 28th Australasian Transport Research Forum, Proceedings pp 1-22

WA Department of Transport (2013) *'Western Australian Regional Freight Transport Network Plan – Executive Summary'* undated document

WA Department of Transport (2014) *'Western Australian Regional Freight Transport Network Plan – 2014 Report Card'*

WA Department of Transport (2020) *'Revitalising Agricultural Region Freight Strategy – FAQs'*

WA Department of Transport (undated) *'Fact Sheet: Fremantle Container Rail Subsidy'*

WA Government (2020) *'Business case to be prepared for Tier 3 grain lines'* from Media Statements webpage, 24 September 2020

Wardrop A (2009) *'Use of Railway Analysis Tools from an Australian Perspective'* Networks and Spatial Economics, vol 9, pp 123-143

Webb R (2000a) *'Issues in Rail Reform.'* Parliamentary Research Service, Research Paper no. 14, 7 March 2000

Webb R (2000b) *'Cost Recovery in Road and Rail Transport.'* Parliamentary Research Service, Research Paper no. 28, 27 June 2000

Webb R (2004) *'The AusLink White Paper: an overview'* Parliamentary Library Information and Research Services, Current Issues Brief no. 5, 2004-05, 9 August 2004

Webb R (2009) *'Commonwealth Involvement in Reform of the Rail Freight Industry.'* Parliamentary Research Service, Research Paper no. 19, 7 January 2009

Weir J (2002) *'Tranz Rail in the line of fire'* The Dominion Post, 18 July 2002

Wheeler R (2002) *'Speech by Bob Wheeler, Chairman, Tranz Rail, to AGM: 11 October 2000'* Scoop Media

Willett E (2000) *'Assessing the State of National Competition Policy for Rail'* Rail Competition and Access Conference, Sydney, 18 February 2000

Williams P (2001) *'Off the Rails: Buffeted by diminishing returns, customer complaints and shareholders selling out, what's the future for Tranz Rail?'* The Evening Post, 3 February 2001

Williams R, Greig D & Wallis I (2005) *'Results of Railway Privatization in Australia and New Zealand'* Transport Paper TP-7, September 2005. Transport Sector Board, The World Bank Group

Wills-Johnson N (2006) *'Competition in Rail: A likely proposition?'* Planning and Transport Research Centre (PATREC) Working Paper no. 5, September 2006

Wills-Johnson N (2007) *'Competition Policy and Railway Investment – Project Summary.'* Planning and Transport Research Centre (PARTEC) Working Paper no. 12, February 2007

Wilson J (2010), *'Short History of Post-Privatisation in New Zealand'* New Zealand Treasury, document #1982752v1.

Wolmar C (2001) *Broken Rails: How Privatisation Wrecked Britain's Railways.* Aurum Press

World Bank (2011) *Railway Reform: Toolkit for Improving Rail Sector Performance.* The International Bank for Reconstruction and Development / The World Bank.

Yoke Har Lee (2000) *'Boss who took Tranz Rail up a gear'* New Zealand Herald, 30 June 2000

Yun J (2023) *'Knife edge: Trucking operator pushed to the brink, transport leaders warn'* Sydney Morning Herald, 2 March 2023

Contents in Detail

Part A: Prologue   1

1. **Introduction**   2
   - a. Railways and high ways – different expectations   2
   - b. The background to the transformation of freight railways   3
   - c. Government bias   5
   - d. Commercial and other freight railways   6
   - e. Outline of this book   7

2. **A brief history of Australian and New Zealand railways up to 1990**   11
   - a. The development of railways in the colonies   11
   - b. Australia: a nation-wide standard gauge network?   13
     - i. Decisions at Federation   13
     - ii. Studies and reports   14
     - ii. Progress at last   15
   - c. The advent of trucking: regulation of railways' competition   18
   - d. New Zealand: the place of railways in society   19
   - e. Railways in decline   20
   - f. Shrinking networks   22
   - g. Railways as government departments   24
     - i. Maintaining full employment   24
     - ii. Resisting inflation   25
   - h. Deregulation in New Zealand   27
     - i. Livestock traffic   27
     - ii. The increasing competition with NZR   28
   - i. Deregulation of Australian road & rail competition – the effects on railways   30
   - j. Staff reductions, but accumulating deficits   35
     - i. New Zealand   35
     - ii. Australia   37
   - k. Australia: joint industry initiatives – ARA, ARRDO, RIC, NFI   39
     - i. The Australasian Railway Association   39
     - ii. The Australian Railway Research and Development Organisation   40
     - iii. The Railway Industry Council   41
     - iv. The National Freight Initiative   42

3.	**An overview of the rail freight industry today**		**43**
	a.	Timetables are fundamental to Australasian railway culture	43
	b.	Integration and separation	44
	c.	Open access and competition	45
	d.	From vertical integration and unified ownership to separation and fragmentation	46
		i. Increasing complexity	47
		ii. Resistance to change	47
		iii. Australasian railways today	48
	e.	A multitude of track providers	49
	f.	The track gauge issue	51
	g.	A legacy of physical constraints	54
		i. Infrastructure constraints in New South Wales	54
		ii. Other impediments to freight trains	57
	h	A who's who of freight train operators in Australasia	57
	i	The competitive position - rail vs road	58

Contents in Detail

Part B: The Commonwealth and Australian Rail Reform   64

4. The roles of the Commonwealth Government in Australian land transport   65
    a. The Commonwealth government's historic position on railways   65
    b. Creation and funding of the National Highway System   68
    c. No comprehensive strategic planning for land transport   70
    d. The creation of the Australian National Railways Commission (AN)   74
    e. The demise of Australian National Railways (AN)   75
    f. The establishment of the National Rail Corporation (NRC)   77
    g. The performance of National Rail   79
    h. Perceptions of the railways problem in the early 1990s   82

5. Commonwealth initiatives on rail development in the 1990s   86
    a. The Industry Commission's 1991 report – *Rail Transport*   86
    b. The *One Nation* program   94
    c. The adequacy of the interstate rail network   96
    d. The National Competition Policy (NCP)   98
    e. The National Rail Summit of 1997   100
    f. Research into the quality of rail freight service   101
    g. The Neville Report – *Tracking Australia*   103
    h. The Smorgon Report – *Revitalising Rail: The Private Sector Solution*   106
    i. The Productivity Commission's 1999 Report – *Progress in Rail Reform*   112
        i. The terms of reference   113
        ii. The main topics   114
        iii. The recommendations   116

6. Procrastination and evasion   119
    a. The response from the Commonwealth Government   120
    b. The Parliamentary Report – *Back on Track: Progress in Rail Reform*   127
    c. AusLink   131
    d. The Productivity Commission's 2006 Report – *Road and Rail Freight Infrastructure Pricing*   135
        i. The terms of reference   135
        ii. What the Productivity Commission found   136
        iii. The outcome   142

7. **Transport sector reform by commissions and councils** **144**
   a. Overview 144
   b. The National Transport Commission (NTC) 145
      i. Establishment 145
      ii. A proposal for coordination in planning and policy 146
      iii. Another proposal 149
      iv. Review of the NTC's operational effectiveness ... 151
      v. The National Rail Action Plan 152
   c. Infrastructure Australia and The National Land
      Freight Strategy 155
   d. The Transport and Infrastructure Council (TAIC) 157
   e. Changes in the focus of transport sector reform 159

8. **Australian Road Reform** **163**
   a. The truckies' blockades 163
   b. The need for Road Reform 165
   c. Slow progress in Road Reform 170
      i. National Road Transport Commission 170
      ii. Heavy Vehicle Charging and Investment Reform 171
      iii. An inconvenient truth 173
      iv. Heavy Vehicle Road Reform 174

Part C: Outcomes — 178

9. How and why the rail freight industry changed — 179
- a. Changes in railway ownership and organisation structures — 179
  - i. Some railways changed control in their existing vertically-integrated form — 180
  - ii. Some railways were vertically separated years ahead of privatisation of train operations — 182
  - iii. Some railways were vertically separated after privatisation — 183
  - iv. Division of the rail networks of south-east Australia — 184
  - v. An overview of the key events in the history of vertical separation, privatisation, and renationalisation — 186
- b. The Australian Rail Track Corporation (ARTC) — 189
  - i. In the beginning … — 189
  - ii. The interstate track audit — 191
  - iii. Expansion into NSW — 192
  - iv. Extended lease in Victoria — 199
  - v. Shifting priorities — 200
- c. The principal reasons for ownership changes — 202
  - i. Faith in the benefits of competition — 202
  - ii. Faith in the private sector and privatisation — 206
  - iii. Other ideological and pragmatic reasons — 208
- d. Benefits postulated as reasons for privatisation — 210

10. Privatisation – hopes and outcomes — 212
- a. Privatisation as the solution to deficits — 212
  - i. Privatisation was better than closure — 212
  - ii. The issue of land ownership in New Zealand — 214
  - iii. The method of privatisation — 216
- b. Unfulfilled hopes from privatisation — 217
  - i. Hopes for continuation with improvements — 217
  - ii. Evidence for hopes unfulfilled — 219
- c. A hope for private sector financing — 222
  - i. Mobile assets financed but generally not network assets — 222
  - ii. Little recognition of the government role of stewardship — 224
  - iii. Assessment of the Maldon to Dombarton link line — 227
  - iv. Unrealistic expectations exposed — 228

Off the Rails

11. The privatisation of four vertically-integrated railways — **231**
- a. New Zealand — 231
  - i. Tranz Rail, in brief — 231
  - ii. An analysis of Tranz Rail's difficulties — 233
  - iii. Why and how the government took back the rail network — 242
  - iv. Why and how the government took back the above-rail business — 245
- b. Victoria — 246
  - i. Privatisation and its outcome — 246
  - ii. Control of the country network retrieved — 249
- c. Tasmania — 252
- d. Governments to the rescue — 253
- e. Western Australia — 255

12. Competition outcomes — **260**
- a. The significance of competition — 260
- b. The interstate intermodal sectors — 262
  - i. The east to west corridor — 262
  - ii. The south to north corridor of the eastern States — 264
  - iii. Inland Rail – the alternative south to north corridor — 268
  - iv. The Adelaide to Darwin corridor — 269
  - v. Continued competition — 271
- c. New South Wales — 272
  - i. The advent of Pacific National created opportunities for others — 272
  - ii. A success for competition policy — 274
- d. Victoria — 277
  - i. Competition discouraged — 277
  - ii. The effects of droughts — 278
  - iii. Government incentives for rail use — 279
- e. Western Australia — 281
- f. Queensland — 282
- g. Rail competition with road in New Zealand — 287

Part D: Analyses — 291

13. The application of economic concepts to rail reform — 292
- a. 'Efficiency', 'Effectiveness', 'Performance', 'Best Practice' — 292
    - i. What these terms mean — 292
    - ii. Best practice – the pot of gold at the end of the rainbow — 294
- b. Railways as a monopoly? — 295
- c. The concept of competition in the Australian rail industry — 298
    - i. More competition between rail and road was not intended — 298
    - ii. The perceived need for competition — 299
    - iii. Open Access was insufficient to enable competition — 300
    - iv. Market segmentation evolved instead — 302
- d. Competitive neutrality — 304
    - i. Neutrality between government and private sector — 304
    - ii. Neutrality between road and rail modes — 305
    - iii. Government investment in highways versus railway infrastructure — 307
- e. The economic appraisal of rail network projects — 311
    - i. Inconsistent project cost-benefit analysis between the modes — 311
    - ii. The application of benefit-cost analyses — 313
    - iii. The significance of the BCA discount rate — 315
    - iv. The NSW experience — 319
- f. Barriers to entry — 321
    - i. Too many unknowns created too much risk — 322
    - ii. The ineffectiveness of the open access policy for vertically-integrated networks — 323
    - iii. Contracts for regular train-load consignments — 324
    - iv. Control of rolling-stock and facilities by the incumbent operator — 325
    - v. The road freight industry — 329

14. Vertical integration versus vertical separation — 332
- a. The current situation — 332
- b. Organisational benefits from vertical integration — 333
- c. Vertical separation led to market fragmentation — 335
- d. Vertical separation for network recovery — 337
- e. The locus of vertical separation — 338
- f. Different approaches to managing care of the track — 340
- g. Managing railway lines in summer — 342
- h. Differences in sharing line capacity — 345
- i. Investing for capability improvements to the vertically-separated interstate rail network — 346

15. The profitability of rail networks — 349

a. Profitability of lines in former government-owned vertically-integrated railways — 349
b. The Western Australian experience — 350
c. The Mt Isa Line experience — 353
   i. The phantom privatisation — 353
   ii. The benefit of State ownership — 356
d. Most vertically-separated rail networks are inherently unprofitable — 360
   i. The current reality — 360
   ii. Most State networks are subsidised — 361
   iii. The ARTC's impossible mission — 363
e. Should the Commonwealth have sold the ARTC? — 367
   i. The proposition and response
   ii. Would a sale of the ARTC to the private sector have been realistic? — 368
f. Government investment in rail network infrastructure — 370
   i. Why invest? — 370
   ii. Investment purposes — 371
   iii. Combined purpose investments — 373
g. New Zealand: ways used to fund the railway network — 375
   i. User pays: one access agreement with two interpretations — 375
   ii. Drip-feed, with reluctance — 377
   iii. Change the perception of railways in the economy — 378

Part E: Epilogue 382

16. Some observations 383
- a. Simplification of the traffic task 383
- b. The legacy of the reform process in NSW 386
    - i. The consequences of the division of the State's rail network 386
    - ii. The disposal of FreightCorp, and RailCorp's dominance 390
- c. Passive resistance to growth within the rail freight industry 392
    - i. A focus on cost reductions and compliance with industry regulations 392
    - ii. Fragmentation of the rail industry created a more inward focus 393
    - iii. The lack of skills training
- d. The consequences for State governments of ceding control 396
- e. Bearing the risks of year-to-year changes in grain harvests 398
- f. The national discussion on freight transport and infrastructure 399
    - i. Politicians' influence on investment decisions 399
    - ii. The discussion in economics and policy commentaries 402
    - iii. The discussion about Inland Rail 405
    - iv. The Senate inquiry into Inland Rail 407
    - v. Discussions in relation to environmental aspects 409

17. Summing-up 411
- a. New Zealand: privatisation and renationalisation 411
    - i. The influence of politics 411
    - ii. The outcome of privatisation was both success and failure 412
    - iii. Keeping the rail network open was a key decision for the future 415
    - iv. Years of grudging support and 'Managed Decline' 416
    - v. The evolution of a new perspective on rail network value and funding 418
- b. Outcomes in Australia 419
    - i. Competition and Privatisation 419
    - ii. Intermodal competition and the outlook for interstate rail 422
    - iii. Network issues 426
- c. Conclusions 430
    - i. Short-sighted governmental decisions 430
    - ii. Government funding of freight rail networks is now an accepted necessity 431
    - iii. Industry Outlook 433

Part F: Appendices — 435

Appendix 1: Case study – the privatisation and renationalisation of New Zealand's railways — 436

   a. Downsizing prior to privatisation — 436
   b. How NZ Rail was privatised — 438
   c. The Tranz Rail years — 440
   d. How the Government regained the rail network — 454
   e. The Toll Rail years — 459
   f. Rethinking the relationship between government and rail — 462
      i. A 'do-nothing' option — 462
      ii. The franchise option — 463
      iii. The purchase option — 466
   g. How the Government and Toll reached a sale agreement — 467
   h. KiwiRail — 472
      i. Government expectation of profitability — 472
      ii. The plan for eventual profitability — 475
      iii. The Commercial Review — 476
      iv. Managed Decline — 481
      v. The valued railway creates value for New Zealand — 482

Appendix 2: The history of efficiency as applied to New Zealand's North Island Main Trunk Line — 487

Appendix 3: A chronology – significant events in the last 50 years of Australasian commercial freight railways — 493

Appendix 4: Major differences between railways in Australasia and North America — 501

   a. Rail industry cultures — 501
   b. Train timetabling & scheduling, versus on-demand train operations — 502
      i. Australasia — 502
      ii. North America — 503
      iii. The differences resulting from unscheduled vs scheduled rail operations — 505
   c. How railed freight is moved across the country — 506
   d. Network rationalisation — 509

Appendix 5: Managing access to rail networks in Australia — 510
    a. Why did this become an issue? — 510
        i. The Productivity Commission's bizarre recommendation — 510
        ii. Putting prices on train schedules or paths — 511
    b. Is auctioning of train schedules viable? — 513
        i. A new rail track provider inherits operations from its predecessor — 513
        ii. Should track providers be profit-oriented? — 515
        iii. Are freight train schedules transferable? — 516
        iv. Obtaining train paths across multiple access regimes — 517
    c. Railway line capacity is a unique offering — 518
    d. The need for certainty — 522
    e. Conclusion — 524

Endnotes — 527
Acknowledgements — 558
Image Credits — 560
Glossary — 561
References — 574
Contents in Detail — 597
Index — 608

Index

A

abandonment of traffic
  by Pacific National 303, 385
  for more profit 218, 257, 421, 432
  in New Zealand 289, 377, 418
Acacia Ridge
  rail terminal 53, 195
Anderson, John 120, 131, 134
ARA 39, 153, 394, 395, 422, 426
Aratere
  out of service 475
  repurchase of 459
  sale-and-lease-back 239, 444, 448, 450
Arc Infrastructure 258, 352, 360, 427
ARTC
  access fees 361, 364, 422, 514
  as track provider 51, 388, 521
  business strategy 201, 348, 367
  & cost benefit analysis 306, 311
  formation & growth 77, 97, 101, 116, 123, 127, 183, 200, 246, 320
  & Inland Rail 55, 366, 409
  possible sale of 370
  profitability 428
  & track possession planning 389
Aurizon
  & CQCN 49, 222
  & Darwin line 332, 427
  in Queensland 337, 354, 360
  in South Australia 427
  intermodal operations 264
  operations in NSW 420
  operations in WA 204
  overseas disposal of locos 328
AusLink 134, 142, 148, 221, 309
Australian National Railways
  as integrated railway 262
  as track provider 100
  creation & demise 77, 119, 180, 183, 187, 209, 221, 349
  gauge conversion 17, 66
  ownership of TasRail 252
  vertical separation of 510
Australian Railroad Group (ARG)
  company structure 183, 351
  operations in NSW 326
  operations in WA 204
  purchase by QR 205, 263, 265, 328
  purchase of WestRail 181, 255
Australian Transport Council (ATC) 73, 97, 145, 148, 157
Australian Transport Network (ATN)
  as Tranz Rail in Australia 443
  grain haulage 203, 278, 324
  purchase by Pacific National 181
  purchase of TasRail 76, 253
Australian Treasury 169

B

Beard, Michael 444, 445, 454, 455
Berkshire Partners 412, 413, 443
bogie exchange centres 16
border hopping 31
break-of-gauge 17, 71, 95, 386
Brookfield Rail 50, 138, 184, 222, 226, 255, 352, 397, 512, 515.
  See Arc Infrastructure
BTCE
  adequacy of interstate rail network 98, 129
  quality of rail service 101
  TasRail viability study 252
Burkhardt, Ed 444, 446

C

CBH 204, 259, 336, 353, 398
Centennial Coal 304
Chullora 192, 326, 390
Clapp Report, 1945 16

closing down a public railway 3, 418
Commonwealth Railways 14, 66, 75, 180, 262
competitive neutrality
  between rail and road 115, 122, 124, 130, 136, 140, 151, 166, 171, 174, 177, 306, 308, 311, 423
  government & private sector 99, 107, 189, 305
Costello, Peter 105, 135
CQCN 49, 117, 182, 222, 427
cross-subsidies
  in railway charges 83, 117, 296
  in road vehicle charges 139, 141, 174
Cullen, Michael, Dr 451, 458

D
Darwin line 50, 119, 228, 332, 427

E
earthquakes 242, 363, 466, 475, 480
electric locomotives
  abandonment in NSW 391
  in New Zealand 492
  in Queensland 67
El Zorro 301, 325
Emu Bay Railway 181
Eyre Peninsula 77, 134, 148, 219, 221, 309, 337, 427, 428

F
Fay Richwhite 412, 443, 444
flood risks & damage
  in New Zealand 242, 466
  in South Australia 75
  in Tasmania 334
  on Mt Isa line, Queenland 359
Freight Australia
  creation of 181
  operations 264, 277
  sale to PN 278
  Victorian network lease 220, 247

G
Genesee & Wyoming Australia (GWA)
  Darwin line 50
  Eyre Peninsula 221, 399
government-owned railways
  improved productivity of 105
GrainCorp 304, 328, 336, 398

H
Hilmer Report 98, 299

I
Independent Rail 326
Interstate Rail Network
  adequacy of 98
  & economic development 406
  improving capability of 348
  lack of investment in 93, 95, 123, 309
  length 68
  management of 189, 200, 425, 525

K
Keating, Paul 94, 98, 202, 260, 299, 419
Keynesian economics 3, 18, 165

L
Laird, Philip, Dr
  on rail's market share 93
  on road freight subsidies 166
  on transport energy use 6
line capacity
  & auctioning train paths 511, 516, 526
  competition needs more of 346
  components of 519
  definitions of 521
  efficient use of 513, 514, 524
  finite in the short term 118
  & managing track access 425, 521
  & Open Access 46, 302
  sharing it in Sydney 55, 56, 149
  & track maintenance 355
  & train transit reliability 348

ways to increase it 67, 195, 437
livestock traffic
  in New Zealand 28

M

major periodic maintenance (MPM) 192, 373, 389
managed decline 218, 379, 411, 418, 481, 484
Manildra Group 304
Mode Shift Incentive Scheme (MSIS) 229

N

National Commission of Audit 172, 367, 373, 516
National Competition Policy. *See also* Hilmer Report
  hopes for 202
  influence of 79, 114, 135, 510
  non-observance of 278, 419
  objectives of 300
  requirements of 100
  responses to 246, 260
National Freight and Supply Chain Strategy 157, 162, 407, 409
National Highway System
  for economic development 217, 224
  & Hawke Government 41
  investment in 70, 93, 95, 299, 309
  lack of cost recovery 136, 142
National Land Freight Strategy 73, 143, 157, 159
National Rail Corporation (NRC)
  & competition 99, 305, 419
  establishment 82, 95, 182, 183, 262
  sale of 126, 203, 431
National Transport Commission (NTC) 155, 166, 310, 325, 396, 425
neoliberalism 4, 165, 260
network interface management 185, 323, 387
Neville, Paul, MP 103, 120, 127, 129

Neville Report, 1998 71, 105, 119, 425
North Australia Railway 179
NSW petroleum distribution 277
NZ Treasury 417, 438, 466, 473, 479

O

One Nation program
  as fiscal stimulus 96
  & intercapital rail network 17
  source of competition ethos 202, 260, 299
Open Access
  & competition 46, 300
  & incumbent operator 204, 302, 324, 327
  needs vertical separation 182, 183
  not suitable in NZ 457
  was an untested concept 91, 93, 299

P

Pacific National (PN)
  abandonment of traffic 384
  acquisitions 181, 224, 263
  & competition 203, 205, 265, 420
  creation 82, 117, 326, 431
  in Queensland 354
  Victorian network lease 220, 229, 248
  withdrawal from Victoria 252, 303
preventive maintenance 218
private sector investment 11, 105, 106, 120, 126, 130, 223, 228, 252
Productivity Commission
  1999 report, PIRR 118, 125, 292, 294, 296, 425
  auctioning train paths 10, 525
  report on infrastructure pricing 142, 364, 423
Progress in Rail Reform 118, 292
  auctioning train paths 526
  & competitive neutrality 168, 305, 307, 423

lack of national strategic plan 72, 399, 421
limited benefit from competition 204
& monopoly rents 297
submissions to 126, 211, 322, 327, 334
success of privatisation 222
types of competition 300, 302

Q

QR National
  in other States 183
  reasons for IPO 210
  sale by IPO 117, 188
  separation for IPO 181
Qube
  & Moorebank terminal 56
  operations 266, 336, 354, 508
  & takeovers 393, 420

R

Rail America
  in New Zealand 450
  in Victoria 181, 204, 248
rail network investment 124, 372, 426, 500
  & shovel-ready projects 402

S

sale-and-lease-back 239, 413, 444, 465
SCOTI 144, 151, 156, 157
SCT 81, 99, 265, 304, 522
Silverton Rail 14, 203, 324, 327
Small, Francis, Dr 444
Smorgon Report 72, 119, 425
Southern Shorthaul Railroad 326, 336
SRANSW 182, 296, 391
strategic ignorance 235, 375

T

TAIC 144, 159, 177
Tier 3 grain lines 138, 258, 352, 397

Toll
  in Australia 82, 183, 253, 263, 328
  in New Zealand 184, 208, 239, 244, 289, 376, 454, 472
too big to let fail 219, 232, 430
track possessions 387, 389
track renewals
  accounting for 237, 413, 441
  spending on 222, 247, 354, 373
trip trains 203, 327

U

unforeseen policy outcomes
  policy conflict 10, 353
  policy gridlock 424
  policy neglect 185
  policy vacuum 147

V

Viterra 222, 398

W

Watco 328
Wheeler, Bob 444
wheel-rail interface 338, 342
wicked problems 399, 409, 423
Wisconsin Central Railroad
  as owner of ATN 253, 443
  as owner of Tranz Rail 180, 236, 412, 414, 440, 442, 447

www.ingramcontent.com/pod-product-compliance
Lightning Source LLC
Chambersburg PA
CBHW071950290426
44109CB00018B/1981